RIGHTS IN CRIMINAL LAW

This collection of 17 original essays is the first volume to provide an in-depth exploration of the potential of a rights-based approach to criminal law.

The book presents a comprehensive treatment of the role of rights in criminal law, ranging from a conceptual analysis and questions of justified criminalisation, to specific legal implications for substantive criminal law and criminal procedure.

The collection addresses the academic and practical questions that are related to individual entitlements protected by criminal law, including:

- Who currently holds and who should hold a right not to be wronged by others?
- Is it a violation of individual rights, rather than the infliction of harm, that constitutes a reason for criminalisation?
- Does the idea of criminal law as regulating interpersonal legal relations contradict its public character?

Furthermore, the edited collection provides a theoretical framework for the study of consent and sexual offences, investigates the background of ideas of restorative justice, and explores both the victim's and the offender's rights in prosecution and trial.

Rights in Criminal Law

Studies on a New Paradigm in Criminal Law and Procedure

Edited by
Philipp-Alexander Hirsch
and
Elias Moser

•HART•
OXFORD • LONDON • NEW YORK • NEW DELHI • SYDNEY

HART PUBLISHING

Bloomsbury Publishing Plc

Kemp House, Chawley Park, Cumnor Hill, Oxford, OX2 9PH, UK

1385 Broadway, New York, NY 10018, USA

Bloomsbury Publishing Ireland Limited, 29 Earlsfort Terrace, Dublin 2, D02 AY28, Ireland

First published in Great Britain 2025

We acknowledge financial support by the Max Planck Institute for the Study of Crime, Security and Law and the Karl-Franzens-University Graz.

A catalogue record for this book is available from the British Library.

A catalogue record for this book is available from the Library of Congress.

Library of Congress Control Number: 2024947936

ISBN: HB: 978-1-50997-347-7
ePDF: 978-1-50997-349-1
ePub: 978-1-50997-348-4

Typeset by Compuscript Ltd, Shannon

CONTENTS

PART III
INDIVIDUAL RIGHTS AND PUBLIC SANCTIONS

PART IV
CRIMINAL LAW IN A RIGHTS-BASED LEGAL ORDER

PART V
INDIVIDUAL RIGHTS IN CRIMINAL PROCEDURE

CONTRIBUTORS

Markus Abraham is a Senior Research Fellow at the University of Hamburg. In his dissertation, *Norm, Sanction, Belief. The Significance of Pain and Punishment Today* (2018), he argues for a penal system without hard treatment. His current research focuses on the duty to rescue strangers as a criminal duty. His research interests include criminal law, criminal procedure and, more generally, questions at the boundary between ethics and law.

Gregory Antill is an Academic Fellow and Lecturer in Law at Columbia Law School. He received his PhD in Philosophy at UCLA where he was an Andrew W Mellon Fellow in Humanistic Studies. His research applies recent conceptual advances in philosophy and cognitive science to traditional legal questions about *mens rea*, culpability, competence, and expert testimony.

Michelle Coleman is a Lecturer in law at Swansea University. After practising law as a public defender in the United States, she earned her PhD in 2018. Prior to that she received her LLM in international human rights and criminal justice from Utrecht University. Her research interests include evidence, criminal procedure, and international criminal law.

Ivó Coca-Vila is a tenure-track Professor (Ramón y Cajal) at the Law Faculty of the Pompeu Fabra University (Barcelona) and Senior Researcher at the Max Planck Institute for the Study of Crime, Security and Law (Freiburg). Coca-Vila's main research interests lie in the foundations of criminal law, in particular the theory of crime and criminalisation, recent topics at the intersection of criminal law, philosophy and ethics, as well as theoretical questions concerning property and white-collar crimes.

Michał Derek is a Senior Research Fellow at the Jagiellonian University in Kraków, where he teaches criminal law and medical law. He earned a PhD in 2020 for his doctoral thesis on consent in criminal law. His current research is focused on the theories of criminalisation. Since 2021 he has also practised as a Senior Assistant of the Judge in the Criminal Chamber of the Supreme Court of Poland.

Mark Dsouza is an Associate Professor at the Faculty of Laws, University College London. He specialises in the theory, philosophy, and doctrine of the criminal law, and also has research interests in general jurisprudence. Previously, he practised at the Supreme Court of India and in High Courts and Tribunals across India for almost five years. He took his PhD and LLM from the University of Cambridge.

Antony Duff is Professor Emeritus of Philosophy at the University of Stirling. He works in the philosophy of criminal law: on criminalisation, on the structure of criminal liability, on the aims of the criminal process, and on criminal punishment.

Matthew Dyson is Professor of Civil and Criminal Law at the Faculty of Law, University of Oxford, and Director of the Institute of European and Comparative Law. He is interested in criminal law, tort law, and the relationship between the two, particularly from a comparative legal historical lens.

Philipp-Alexander Hirsch is a legal scholar and philosopher. He has been leader of an independent research group on criminal-law theory at the Max Planck Institute for the Study of Crime, Security and Law in Freiburg since 2022. His research focuses on criminal law and criminal procedure, legal philosophy and legal theory, and the history and philosophy of criminal law in the Age of Enlightenment. His most recent book on the issue of rights in criminal law is *Das Verbrechen als Rechtsverletzung. Subjektive Rechte im Strafrecht* (Berlin 2021).

Robyn L Holder is a Senior Research Fellow with Griffith Criminology Institute, Griffith University, Australia. She is a socio-legal scholar and a specialist in the research-policy nexus, and in the reform of systems and services. She has over 30 years of experience in research, public policy and law reform in Australia and the UK. Holder focuses on the interface between people victimised by violence and institutions of justice, and the mediating effect of rights. More recently, she has turned to examine how these institutions understand their duties to citizen-victims as rights-holders.

Tatjana Hörnle is Director of the Max Planck Institute for Research on Crime, Security and Law and Head of the Department of Criminal Law in Freiburg since 2019. At the same time, she is an Honorary Professor at the Faculty of Law of the Humboldt University in Berlin. Her research focuses on ethical and social issues in the field of criminal law. These include theories of criminalisation, theories of punishment, and evaluations of criminal law. She is also an expert in sexual criminal law and the philosophy of human dignity.

Sören Lichtenthäler is a Senior Research Fellow at the University of Mainz. He studied law at the Johannes Gutenberg-University in Mainz. After passing the first state law examination in 2016, he wrote his doctoral thesis on the protection and restriction of property rights by criminal law (*Eigentumsschutz und Besitzverbot*). Until 2022 he worked as a legal clerk at the Higher Regional Court OLG of Frankfurt am Main and passed the second state law examination 2022.

Elias Moser is a Postdoc Researcher and Lecturer at the Section Practical Philosophy, University of Graz. He accomplished his doctoral degree in philosophy at the University of Berne, Switzerland, in 2017, where he worked as a Praedoc Assistant at the Institute of Criminal Law. Before coming to Graz in 2019, he held positions as Researcher at the University of Vienna and the Austrian Academy of Sciences. From 2021 to early 2022, he was a Fellow at the Centre for Philosophy of Natural and Social Science, London School of Economics LSE.

Joachim Renzikowski is Professor of Criminal Law and Legal Philosophy and Legal Theory at Martin-Luther-Universität Halle-Wittenberg. He earned his doctoral degree in 1993 with a dissertation on emergency and self-defence and his habilitation in 1997 at the University of Tübingen. His main fields of research are the theory of norms and crimes against sexual autonomy.

Galia Schneebaum is a Lecturer at the Harry Radzyner Law School at Reichman University, Israel. She earned her PhD from Tel-Aviv University, was a visiting scholar at the University of Toronto, and a Postdoctoral fellow at the Hebrew University of Jerusalem. Her research is at the intersection of criminal law, sociological, and political theory and she focuses on studying emerging conceptions of wrongdoing in the law. She also works on criminalisation theory, sex offences, workplace bullying, family abuse, and the legal regulation of abuse of power.

Hamish Stewart is a Professor of Law at the University of Toronto Faculty of Law, where he has taught criminal law, evidence, and legal theory since 1993. His work-in-progress includes a treatise on procedural rights, an account of the role of criminal punishment in a liberal legal order, and a series of papers on problems in the meaning and application of the rule of law.

Malcolm Thorburn is a Professor of Law at the University of Toronto where he also holds the Chair for the Legal, Ethical and Cultural Implications of Innovation. He is an Associate Editor of the journals *Law and Philosophy* and *Criminal Law and Philosophy* and he works and writes on theoretical questions concerning all aspects of criminal justice in its constitutional and public law context.

COURT DECISIONS

Constitutional and Human Rights Courts

Common Law Decisions

Introduction: A New Paradigm?

PHILIPP-ALEXANDER HIRSCH AND ELIAS MOSER

1. Whose Rights are at Stake in Criminal Law?

Consider the following scenario: A hits B in the face, causing a painful bruise. This is undoubtedly an assault and, if found guilty, A is criminally liable. It is clear that A has committed a criminal offence. In turn, B, the victim, is directly affected by this criminal act – she alone suffers from having been inflicted a bruise. Yet the question remains: Who has really been wronged by A's actions? In other words: Whose rights are at stake in criminal law?

The answers to these questions are not immediately obvious. In the painted scenario, it seems natural to consider B the wronged party. Here, A had a duty towards B to avoid causing harm, and B had a corresponding right to expect A to act accordingly. It could be argued that it is B's right to physical integrity that is encroached on as a result of A's wrongful act, and that criminal sanctions are designed to protect B's rights. This perspective is supported by the fact that B could have consented to A's actions, thereby relieving A of her obligations and legitimising what would otherwise be considered a criminal act. However, the physical harm inflicted by A may also constitute a transgression against the legal community or the polity. It could be argued that A had a duty directed towards the state to respect the physical integrity of others, and that the state had a right to demand that A refrain from causing physical harm. After all, it is the state that passes and enforces criminal laws. If we were to consider only B's rights, it would be difficult to justify why crime and criminal justice concern the public at large.

Criminal law scholarship predominantly leans towards the latter view. We believe there are essentially two reasons for this: first, traditional interpretations of criminal law often resist viewing it through the lens of protecting individual rights. On the one hand, many theorists in the Anglo-Saxon world see the role of criminal law in the prevention of harm or moral wrongdoing (e.g. Feinberg 1984; Moore 1997; Alexander and Ferzan 2009; Simester and von Hirsch 2011; Tadros 2016). On the other hand, continental legal scholars often conceive of criminal law's purpose as the prevention of violations of legal goods or interests (Roxin and Greco 2020, § 2). Both schools tend to view the claims that criminal law seeks to protect – and the violations of which constitute crimes – as impersonal. The reasons against criminal behaviour are said to be agent-neutral: the obligation not to harm others is based on the notion that the causation of harm is intrinsically bad (on moral or legal grounds), regardless of the perspective or status of those affected by it. Thus, even where individual interests are at stake, criminal law theory often does not regard individuals as holders of normative claims (i.e. rights), but merely as beneficiaries of rules.

This traditional interpretation of criminal law may be reinforced by rights-theoretical considerations, in particular a narrow interpretation of the 'will theory of rights' that is widespread in legal theory and doctrine. The theory holds that only those who have the legal capacity (a) to enforce obligations themselves, (b) to release others from these obligations, and (c) to waive a claim to compensation in case of violation are true rights holders (Hart 1982). As victims of crime typically lack these possibilities, will theorists have argued that they should not be considered rights holders (e.g. Kearns 1975; Steiner 1994; Simmonds 1998; Edmundson 2012; Darwall 2013c). Consequently, if criminal law were to assign rights, then only the state could be considered a right holder, as the state alone decides on the prosecution and punishment of crimes – with the victim usually having no say in these decisions. For example, a prosecutor's decisions are not necessarily guided by what she perceives to be in the victim's will (or interest), but by what is deemed necessary to maintain public order (Steiner 1994).

While these observations may explain why individual rights have traditionally played no prominent role in considerations about the nature of criminal law, this paradigm has, of course, not remained unchallenged. 'Impersonal' approaches in criminal law theory, such as the 'harm principle', have been criticised for theoretical inconsistencies and explanatory deficits (e.g. the problem of harmless wrongdoing) and for disregarding the legal status of victims in the theoretical understanding of crime. By contrast, a rights-based approach has been promoted as an alternative that addresses these shortcomings (e.g. Dan-Cohen 2002; Ripstein 2006; Stewart 2010; Renzikowski 2012; Hörnle 2014b; Moser 2019; Hirsch 2021: 85–132). Indeed, a rights-based approach provides an alternative normative principle for criminalisation that recognises the moral significance of violating individual autonomy. It offers a framework explaining why individuals can nullify another's criminal law obligations through valid consent. Thus, a rights-based approach – especially within a will-theoretical framework – allows to attribute a central explanatory function to one's normative standing as an autonomous person in criminal law theory. Last, but not least, a rights-based perspective on criminal law potentially justifies new prosecutorial elements (e.g. procedural rights for victims, Cavadino and Dignan 1997) and crime rectification strategies (e.g. restorative justice, Zedner 1994; Ashworth et al. 2005), which are difficult to accommodate under an impersonal view of criminal law.

However, the justificatory and explanatory benefits of a rights-based approach may come at a cost. They challenge the 'public wrong' conception of crimes, which holds that criminal law, unlike other legal areas, addresses illegal conduct on behalf of the entire legal community – in contrast to civil law, which deals with private wrongs on behalf of individuals (e.g. Pawlik 2004; Lamond 2007; Husak 2008; Edwards and Simester 2014; Duff 2011; 2013; Stevens 2014; Lee 2015). If criminal law were to be redefined as a domain governed by individual rights, the extent to which crimes and criminal justice should remain a public matter and the state's concern would be unclear. We might risk the 'privatisation' of criminal prosecution and punishment. Moreover, the ability of a rights-based approach to distinguish crime from tort and criminal law from civil law, as well as its treatment of victimless crimes, remains largely unresolved.

A rights-based approach might also be a conceptual challenge to the traditional offender-centric foundation of criminal law. In particular, Anglo-American criminal law theory understands criminal liability and criminal culpability broadly in terms of 'reason-responsiveness' (e.g. Alexander 2000; Brink and Nelkin 2013; Husak 2016; Yaffe 2018; Antill 2022). Crimes tend to be identified based on an assessment of the offender's quality-of-will or her dispositions to respond to moral or legal reasons. In contrast to the offender-centric foundation, a rights-based account of criminal law introduces a fundamentally victim-centric (or at least interpersonal) perspective. It is yet to be investigated how this will affect the understanding of criminal law, which has hitherto focused exclusively on the intentions and attitudes of the offender. Finally, going beyond these questions of criminal law theory, it remains largely unresolved what normative implications a rights-based approach to criminal law might have for substantive criminal law (e.g. for the doctrine of consent, cf. Moser 2019) and criminal procedure (e.g. victim impact statements or victims' procedural rights, cf. Hirsch 2021: 250–66 and 312–19), and how strengthening the normative standing of the victim requires a counterbalancing of the rights of the accused.

Last, but not least, it is an open question whether there is *the* rights-based approach to criminal law, or whether one should rather speak of a plurality of – potentially incompatible – rights-based approaches in criminal law theory. For example, individual rights may 'merely' function as the protected goods of criminal law provisions (e.g. Ripstein 2006; Renzikowski 2007), without implying an individual right of the victim correlating with a duty whose violation is worthy of punishment. At best, this would have implications for the theory of criminalisation because the 'harm' principle would ultimately be replaced by a 'rights' principle. On this account, the state's monopoly on criminal prosecution and sanction would remain unaffected. The state's authority would only be challenged if the duty (whose violation is punishable) is itself understood as the correlate of an individual right (e.g. Moser 2019; Hirsch 2021). Only then does the question arise whether victims of crime should not also be more closely involved in criminal conflict resolution (e.g. prosecution and sanctioning). A rights-based approach to criminal justice is therefore far from being clearly defined and firmly established in theory.

2. Mapping the Field of a Rights-Based Approach to Criminal Law

These questions about the nature of a rights-based approach to criminal law, its explanatory power, and its normative conclusions when held against competing paradigms for assessing criminal wrongdoing and criminal law remain under-discussed. This theoretical disinterest notably bucks a trend, as the issue of rights has increasingly found its way into moral philosophy, legal theory, and doctrinal jurisprudence in recent decades. It is hardly surprising, given that individual rights are crucial for safeguarding personal freedom, upholding democratic governance, protection against authoritarianism, and promoting social progress. Rather than representing mere legal entitlements, rights are intimately tied to ethical principles and political philosophy. By recognising individual rights, legal systems acknowledge the inherent worth and agency of an individual, enabling her to make decisions about her own life within a realm of guaranteed freedoms.

Despite the undeniable significance of individual rights and the resultant scholarly interest, a comprehensive and unified discussion of the role of individual rights in criminal law (beyond procedural rights) remains conspicuously absent.[1] This gap is particularly surprising given the considerable potential that the perspective of individual rights has been demonstrated in other fields. At best, critical discussion of the role of individual rights in criminal law is fragmented. Where it has occurred,[2] it has sometimes been idiosyncratic, failing to engage with other rights-based approaches. At other times, the debate has been confined to academic (sub)disciplines, despite the fact that the issue is prevalent in all legal systems and raises interdisciplinary questions in various branches of legal theory and criminal law, from criminalisation to doctrinal issues of substantive criminal law or procedural law.[3]

The purpose of this book is to fill this research gap and – by cutting through different disciplines and jurisdictions – to examine the merits of the concept of individual rights for assessing criminal wrongdoing and criminal law. It aims to make a compelling case for a rights-based approach to criminal law by exploring the essential questions that emerge from conceptualising normative relations in

[1] It goes without saying that many of these issues have been addressed in the literature on the theory of criminal law and theories of rights; yet there is no single volume that attempts to bring them together in a concise and comprehensive manner. In particular, no comprehensive efforts have been made to link rights theory and criminal law theory and substantive law and criminal procedure.

[2] Some noteworthy examples are Ellis (1994); Steiner (1994); Dan-Cohen (2002); Ripstein (2006); Renzikowski (2007); Bergelson (2009); Stewart (2010); Edmundson (2012); Hörnle (2014b).

[3] On the one hand, whether and how criminal law can take into account the violation of individual rights depends to a large extent on the underlying description of the nature of rights – a concept that is not only controversial but also discussed against different backgrounds in moral philosophy and legal theory. On the other hand, the (ir)relevance of rights in criminal law depends on the historically developed particularities of either Anglo-American or continental European criminal law doctrines, which must be taken into account.

criminal law through the lens of individual rights: How can the theory of rights and the theory of criminal law inform each other? Who does and who should hold a right not to be wronged by others: the victim or the state? Is it the violation of individual rights, rather than harm, that provides a basis for criminalisation? What are the concrete consequences of these questions for substantive criminal law and criminal procedure? We also strive to define the limits of a rights-based approach to criminal law and reveal its weak spots: Can a rights-based approach convincingly depict all forms of criminal wrongdoing? Does the notion of interpersonal legal relations entail a problematic departure from an offender-centric foundation of criminal law, and does it contradict the public character of criminal law? Would it even lead to an undue predominance of the alleged victim in substantive and procedural law at the expense of the possibly innocent defendant?

At any rate, this list of questions is not exhaustive when considering the issue of a new paradigm in criminal law theory. Moreover, many (if not all) of the above questions would justify a separate study that could fill another book. Nevertheless, the lack of a comprehensive and unified discussion of a rights-based approach justifies a broader perspective. In particular, we believe that the debate will gain from a pioneering attempt to draw an explanatory line all the way from the theory of rights to criminal law theory, to the doctrine of substantive law and criminal procedure. The following chapters of this book are dedicated to achieving this goal.

2.1. Conceptualising Rights in Criminal Law

Part I starts off with two chapters that address fundamental methodological concerns in the analysis of rights in criminal law. In Chapter 1, dealing with different theories of rights and their application to criminal law, Elias Moser (University of Graz) outlines different understandings of individual rights with regard to their elements. Based on this analysis, he asks the crucial question of how consenting to otherwise criminal conduct can be best conceptualised in a theory of rights. He defends the thesis that classical rights theories – the interest, the will theory, as well as recent proposals of a hybrid account (Sreenivasan 2005) – are in need of adaptation if the aim is to serve as an explanation of the ability to consent to criminal wrongdoing. Building on this discussion, he then outlines the conditions of a successful theory of rights which is capable of making sense of consent in criminal law.

In Chapter 2, Matthew Dyson (University of Oxford) analyses the concept of rights from a legal perspective and queries whether rights, duties, interests, and related concepts exist independently of being clothed in categories such as 'criminal' or 'tortious'. He criticises the belief that the concepts of rights and duties can be uniquely assigned to one area of law – for example, private law, or criminal law. Neither should deal exclusively with rights and interpersonal duties. Dyson claims that that there is no conceptual advantage in such a distinction. Instead, it would be theoretically productive to conceive of rights as existing separately from any one area of law. Doing so would offer opportunities to show why rights are more easily identified at some points of criminal law, but not at others. It might also allow us to see whether, like in tort law, criminal law in practice includes non-rights-related doctrines, or whether they are merely doctrines that happen not to be formulated in terms of rights.

2.2. Rights and the Assessment of Criminal Wrongdoing

In Part II, the book shifts its perspective from methodological concerns to implications of rights for the assessment of criminal wrongdoing. Starting with the nature of criminal wrongdoing, Ivó Coca-Vila (Pompeu Fabra University Barcelona) observes that standard conceptions of criminalisation are commonly regarded as insufficient for encompassing all types of criminal wrongdoing. In Chapter 3, he argues that too little attention has been paid to an alternative proposal to the mainstream theories of criminalisation, namely the theory of the violation of individual rights. After critically analysing the various existing efforts to limit criminalisation to the violation of rights, Coca-Vila shows that this approach is a good starting point for thinking about criminalisation in liberal states. To this end, he outlines the core features of what he calls a "thin rights-centred theory of criminalisation". This monist theory draws on a supra-positive and far-reaching conception of rights as a *pro tanto* reason for criminalisation.

Following Coca-Vila's reflections on criminalisation, Galia Schneebaum (Reichman University) exemplifies the possible advantages of a rights-based approach by pointing to sexual offences in Chapter 4. According to her, the field of sex offences challenges the standard view of criminal law dealing with public, rather than private wrongs. For, as widely accepted, the main purpose of the prohibition of sex offences is to vindicate individuals' rights to sexual autonomy (rather than to defend some idea of public morals or maintain public order). However, she picks out a host of newly emerging criminal offences she calls 'abuse offences' (e.g. domestic violence or abusive, rather than non-consensual, sex in hierarchical relationships) to scrutinise a binary division of public vs private wrongs (Tadros 2005; Schneebaum 2015). Schneebaum suggests a neo-republican conception of a right to freedom from domination: Domination presupposes structures of power and is hence distinct from a mere offence aimed at autonomy. She concludes that abuse offences can neither be reduced to private wrongs nor be solely considered public wrongs; instead, elements of both are relevant.

In Chapter 5, Tatjana Hörnle (Max Planck Institute for the Study of Crime, Security and Law) broadens the perspective by mapping the landscape of how the concept of victims' rights can be meaningfully applied to other areas of criminal law theory. After anchoring a rights-based approach in the constitutional guarantees of liberal states, which are committed to normative individualism, she identifies possible implications of a rights-based approach for criminal punishment, criminalisation, doctrinal criminal law and criminal procedure. In particular, Hörnle argues that such an approach challenges the adequacy of traditional ways of evaluating criminal wrongdoing that rely on basic categories such as the harm principle (Anglo-American tradition) or non-individualistic perspectives (German tradition). In particular, she criticises the prominent role of referring to an 'evil mind' in standard offender-centric foundations of criminal law and advocates for paying more attention to the impact of criminal behaviour on victims and their rights.

However, Gregory Antill (Columbia University) is critical of such a departure from the offender-centred view. In Chapter 6, he observes that a rights-based account of criminal law with its attendant normative structure of privileges, claims, powers, entitlements and duties would present a far different kind of normative conceptual apparatus than is typically used by philosophers of criminal law to account for criminal culpability and criminal liability. Rather than a rights-centred normative structure, criminal law should typically be understood in terms of reason-responsiveness. Culpability, he states, is an assessment of the offender's quality-of-will or dispositions to respond to reasons. Antill suggests that, at least in the context of criminal law, a rights-based account (which leads to a fundamentally victim-centred understanding of criminal law) is at odds with this 'standard' offender-centred foundation of criminal law. Based on this diagnosis, he criticises the rights-based approach, by outlining the dramatically different outcomes to which it would lead in criminal law doctrine.

In the same vein, Mark Dsouza (University College London) examines, in Chapter 7, the (ir)relevance of victims' rights in justifications in terms of a rights-based understanding of consent. According to Dsouza, victims' rights usually play a crucial role in justifications, since, on most accounts, a justification denies both that the victim was wronged, all things considered, by what the defendant did, and that the defendant was culpable. The former denial usually depends on the claim that the victim somehow waived her relevant rights, and thereby became liable to victimisation. Accordingly, justifications are sensitive to victims' rights in that a justification is only available if the rights were not violated, all things considered. Where that is not the case, a defendant can, at best, be excused. Dsouza, however, tries to show that the predominant theories of justification often fail to convey the necessary information about the all-things-considered wrongness of the deed. Therefore, he argues, a theory of justification should focus solely on providing information about an offender's blameworthiness, which in turn centres on her guilty mind.

2.3. Individual Rights and Public Sanctions

Based on the debate illustrated above, Part III discusses whether a rights-based approach leads to a problematic privatisation of criminal law. The assumption that the violation of individual rights is constitutive of criminal conduct and thus justifies criminalisation seems to be at odds with the common conviction that the power of criminal prosecution and the imposition of criminal sanctions is the exclusive right held by the state and not the right of the injured person. In Chapter 8, Philipp-Alexander Hirsch (Max Planck Institute for the Study of Crime, Security and Law) attempts to demonstrate that there is no contradiction here. He draws on Stephen Darwall's (2006; 2013) conception of second-personal normativity. His argumentative starting point is the power of consent in criminal law, which serves as a piece of evidence for the claim that the normative authority to decide on the (non-)existence of a criminal duty lies with the potential victim. Therefore, crimes are primarily a violation of individual rights, the distinctive feature of criminal liability (as distinguished from civil liability) being that the offender culpably disregards this particular *individual authority*. However, this individual authority to consent is vested in the individual by the legal community. It can exist only if there is also a *shared authority*, which the potential victim possesses together with third parties. This explains why crimes necessarily possess both: a supra-individual and an intersubjective dimension. The former justifies the state's right to public prosecution, the latter justifies victims' participation in criminal proceedings.

The possible consequences of such a view for the rectification of criminal wrongdoing are illustrated by Michał Derek (Jagiellonian University Cracow) in Chapter 9. He considers whether a reconciliation between the victim and the offender can be a sufficient response to a crime. As a piece of evidence, he introduces the example of Article 59a of the Polish Criminal Code, which was introduced in 2015 and repealed ten months later. He portrays a conception of 'reconciliation' between offender and victim as an implication of the victim's right to decide on her interests and argues that the victim's power of consent – which is universally recognised despite the differences between liberal, paternalistic and communitarian models of criminalisation – extends to the post-crime behaviour between victim and offender. According to Derek, the victim has the right to prevent punishment by means of reconciling with the offender in a number of crimes, even if this might contradict public interests.

Sören Lichtenthäler (Johannes Gutenberg University Mainz) however, is highly critical of reconstructions such as those by Hirsch and Derek. In Chapter 10, he asserts that the specific task of criminal law, as distinguished from other parts of the legal order, implies taking a position in the debate on the meaning and purpose of punishment. Lichtenthäler notes that none of the predominant theories associates punishment with the infringement of individual rights. Regarding the preventive or consequentialist theories, this conclusion arises from the fact that the crime committed is not an essential element of the justification of punishment. According to these theories, punishment is imposed to prevent future crimes, so that individual rights are only relevant insofar as the rights of all members of society as potential victims of crime are concerned. Retributive theories, he argues, are not concerned with the individual rights of the victim either. Even retributive theories that include the victim in the justification of punishment do not claim that punishment essentially responds to the infringement of the victim's rights, but rather to the inherent attack on her status as a free and equal legal person.

In Chapter 11, Markus Abraham (Hamburg University) tries to reconcile the two contrary positions. Drawing on a social contract account, he argues that the state's right to criminal sanctions is primarily justified based on the existence of irresolvable private conflicts, i.e. the violation of rights, and thus the victim's claim against the perpetrator who transgressed a norm. The state's assertion of competence to resolve the conflict or to deal with the violation of rights, on the other hand, is, in Abraham's words, an additional 'accessory competence'. By appropriating the right to a criminal sanction, the state at the same time assumes the duty to protect citizens from crime and – in the event that it does not fulfil its duty to protect – a subsidiary duty vis-à-vis the injured person to effectively rectify crimes that have occurred. Based on this argumentation, Abraham identifies two different rights of the individual that underlie the state's right to criminal prosecution and to criminal sanctions: a primary right vis-à-vis the offender and a secondary right vis-à-vis the state.

2.4. Criminal Law in a Rights-Based Legal Order

Part IV of this volume raises the question to what extent criminal law can serve as an instrument for the protection of individual rights. Hamish Stewart (University of Toronto) observes in Chapter 12 that, in the last two decades, rights have increasingly entered the stage of criminal law theory. Several accounts (e.g. Farmer 2016; Duff 2018a; Thorburn 2020a) understand the role of criminal law as part of a rights-based legal order, i.e. an institutional structure that is not instrumentally directed at the achievement of any particular good (e.g. assigning just desserts) but, instead, is designed to enable free and equal persons to interact rightfully. Although he agrees with the latter conception, he pushes back against the idea that a rights-based account provides a justification of criminal sanctions. Stewart holds that such an approach cannot help to identify any characteristic that makes conduct inherently deserving of punishment. Instead, he argues, it is better to understand criminalisation and punishment as instruments for discouraging conduct and thereby as making an instrumental contribution to the legal order's non-instrumental task of constituting and preserving a rights-based civil order.

In Chapter 13, Joachim Renzikowski (Martin Luther University Halle) agrees with the view that criminal law makes an instrumental contribution to constituting a rights-based civil order. He suggests, however, that understanding crimes as rights violations may well be central to criminalising human behaviour. Following an analysis of the logical relations between rights and duties, he states that punishment for unlawful conduct logically presupposes norms from which the unlawfulness results. These norms are defined by prohibitions imposed by the authorities, which entail duties, the violation of which may be punishable. Since duties usually correspond to rights, the question arises: What is ontologically prior – the right or the duty? If it were the duties, it would be (as in Bentham's imperative theory) the state assigning rights to individuals by enacting commands backed up by criminal sanctions. In a liberal legal system, however, fundamental rights are not created by the state, but are assumed to precede it. They are grounds for duties that are given legal form in the civil law system. Such a view, however, sets limits to criminalisation, since the state may criminalise only the violations of individual rights which are already recognised by civil law.

Departing from this, Malcolm Thorburn (University of Toronto) shows in Chapter 14 that in such an instrumental rights-based approach, the justification for state punishment is ultimately grounded in the state's right to rule. The state's central justifying purpose is to provide a single set of shared terms of social cooperation, which stands in contrast to the unilateralism characteristic of the 'state of nature'. According to Thorburn, criminal wrongdoing consists in violating that very authority of the state to establish and preserve that framework. This, in turn, puts the state in the legitimate position to take action against the accused and, ultimately, to impose punishment. For Thorburn, it is an essential feature of any legal order that it threatens and sometimes imposes coercive sanctions on those who undermine the state's rule of law by unilaterally imposing one's own terms on others. Therefore, both criminal wrongdoing and criminal justice are about the state's sole authority to make the legal rules.

2.5. Individual Rights in Criminal Procedure

If public prosecution is understood as a right of the state – as in Thorburn's account – this naturally leads to the question of how to understand the individual rights of participation of the accused and possibly the victims in procedure. In Part V, Antony Duff (University of Stirling) considers in Chapter 15 how the procedural rights and guarantees of the accused could be adequately conceptualised. He opposes the view that offenders enjoy such rights parasitically (i.e. that rights properly belong to the innocent, and are only enjoyed by the guilty because they must be presumed innocent until proven guilty). On his account, procedural rights properly belong to all defendants, by virtue of their role as citizens who are called to answer a charge of criminal wrongdoing. Therefore, according to Duff, the rights to 'effective participation' as stated in Article 6 of the ECHR belong to both innocent and guilty defendants for the same reason: they enable them to discharge their civic duty to take part in their trial.

Complementary, Robyn Holder (Griffith University) emphasises in Chapter 16 that the participation of victims in proceedings can also be understood as civic action. She argues against the idea that people who are victims of crime and violence enter the public space of criminal justice only in pursuit of private ends, without social and political status as members of the public. Instead, Holder shows that victims are better understood, first and foremost, as citizens who have a political relationship with the state and its criminal justice agents. They have interests in criminal justice that emerge as participatory practices of democratic citizenship. In this way, the 'public space' of criminal justice becomes both a place where victims or defendants appear as citizens with rights, and a realm in which state agencies carry out their duties to respect and uphold those rights.

Lastly, in Chapter 17, Michelle Coleman (University of Swansea) addresses the resulting tension between the participation of victims in proceedings and the legal status of the accused. According to her, the increasing interest in a rights-based approach to criminal law has led to an expansion of victims' rights and agency within criminal procedure. She shows that this expansion of rights can come into conflict with the existing rights of accused people. She identifies a particular risk with regard to the presumption of innocence, which is commonly seen as a fundamental right of the accused person and a bedrock to ensuring that individuals are not punished without conviction. The chapter outlines areas where victims' rights and the presumption of innocence might clash.

With this collection of original texts on various aspects of the possibilities and limitations of a rights-based approach, we hope to contribute to the descriptive assessment and normative evaluation of the normative structure of criminal law and procedure. Both the defence and the critique of such an approach should encourage a rational discourse on the nature and characteristics of criminal wrongdoing and criminal law, but also on how the role and powers of the state and the individual in criminal justice might be shaped in the future. It is left to the reader to decide to what extent this new view of criminal law – a rights-based paradigm shift – should be adopted and pursued. We invite you to engage with these ideas, to continue the discussion, and to explore the potential of a rights-based approach in shaping the future of criminal justice.

3. Acknowledgements

In preparation for this volume, we held a three-day conference at the University of Graz from 6 to 8 July 2022. It was made possible through finanical support from the Referat Wissenschaft und Forschung of the County of Styria (Austria) and the Max-Planck Institute for the Study of Crime, Security, and Law (Freiburg i.Br., Germany). The conference was essential for the analysis of the role of rights in criminal law, as it brought together philosophers and legal scholars to explore all the questions that arise from conceptualising normative relations in criminal law through the lens of individual rights. We would therefore like to begin by thanking the speakers at the conference for their presentations and the participants for their lively discussions. We would also like to express our gratitude to all the authors for their contributions to this volume and for their patience with the long production time. We gratefully acknowledge the financial support for the Open Access publication provided by the Max Planck Institute for the Study of Crime, Security and Law and the University of Graz. Last, but not least, we would like to thank the members of the independent research group 'Criminal Law Theory' at the Max Planck Institute for the Study of Crime, Security and Law for their assistance in preparing the manuscript, in particular Patrick Joseph Siegle.

PART I

Conceptualising Rights in Criminal Law

1

Theories of Rights and Making Sense of Consent in Criminal Law

ELIAS MOSER

1. Introduction

Consent is a voluntary and informed agreement between parties, regarding activities that could otherwise be considered wrongful. The presence of valid consent can serve as a defence in criminal cases. But it may also exclude the possibility of an action as being regarded worthy of punishment. The possibility to give valid consent generally emphasises the value of respecting an individual's autonomy and right to self-determination within the bounds of the law (Hurd 1996; Alexander 1996). In a legal system, it assigns the individual with the role of a *norm-setter*. A person can alter and relinquish legal norms, grant permission and discharge people from their duties.

The individual's capability to adjust criminal law norms plays an important role in offences that endanger or impair the individual legal sphere, such as freedom, property, physical integrity, or life. But also, when it comes to the question of reforming the criminal law and criminalising certain types of behaviour, a consenting person's autonomy is recognised as a core value. For example, the Istanbul Convention,[1] emphasises the principles of autonomy and self-determination to ensure that women have the freedom to make their own choices and control over their sexual lives. The convention marks a clear shift from a legal moralism in criminalising sexual practices towards the protection of women's autonomy. The presence or absence of consent becomes the key determinant to decide whether sexual practices are deemed lawful or unlawful.

In order to understand when and to what extent an individual should have the autonomy to act in this norm-setting way, the idea of *rights in criminal law* is crucial. The dominant principle of criminalisation in legal theory – John Stuart Mill's 'harm principle' (Feinberg 1984) – reaches its limits here. It states that the only

[1] Council of Europe (2011), Convention on preventing and combating violence against women and domestic violence. Istanbul, 11.V.2011.

reason for which force can be rightfully exercised against any member of society and for which his or her liberty can be restricted is to prevent harm to others (Mill 2009: 22). The principle is both *too narrow* and *too broad* when it comes to consent. As Hamish Stewart (2010) outlined, on the one hand, there is conduct that is objectively harmful to the affected person, but which can (and should) be permitted by an expression of one's will. On the other hand, there are actions that are not harmful at all, but the denial of permission alone makes them illegitimate.[2]

To understand consent in criminal law, I therefore start from the assumption that rights do provide a ground for criminalising conduct (Moser 2019): Because it is an individual right that establishes others' duties to refrain from acting, the individual has the authority to suspend those duties. Now the question immediately arises as to how we have to understand the concept of 'rights'. On the one hand, a proper conception of rights is able to *comprehend* central characteristics of criminal law with regard to consent (descriptive) and, on the other hand, an understanding of rights provides us with guidance on how positive law *should be* structured (normative).

Since the idea of individual rights as grounds for criminalisation, enforcement, and punishment is not widespread among criminal law scholars, it has not been given much attention by theories of rights.[3] My aim in this chapter is to fill this gap. I intend to explore what the different theories of rights have to offer in response to the question of justification of consent to criminal acts. I will address the classic distinction between interests and will theories and attempt to show where the advantages and limitations of each theory can be located. On this basis, I will derive a proposal as to how a theory of rights should be designed in order to be capable of making sense of consent in criminal law.

The chapter is structured as follows: Section 2 explains the different normative elements that are included in rights and describes the two main theoretical strands – the interest and the will theory. Section 3 provides an understanding of what we mean by the term 'consent'. Section 4 then subjects the theories of rights to a critical appraisal, and Section 5 derives conditions for a successful theory of rights with regard to consent in criminal law. Section 6 concludes.

2. Theories of Rights

The interest theory (or benefit theory) of rights (von Jhering 1865) and the will theory (or choice theory) of rights (von Savigny 1841) have been the two main theoretical strands since legal theory's emergence as a serious academic discipline, and their assumed irreconcilability persists today. Both theories consider themselves descriptive theories, in that they observe and explain what rights *in fact* are,

[2] See also Hörnle 2016; cf. Simester and von Hirsch 2011.
[3] Some noteworthy exceptions are Steiner 1994; Kramer 1998.

to whom they can be attributed, and what one can have rights to (Sumner 2013; van Duffel 2017). But ideally, they also justify normative judgements (Campbell 2006), in that they demonstrate in which cases the law should attribute rights and in which it should not.

One way of identifying the starting point of the more recent discourse on theories of rights in the second half of the 20th century could be the question of the *correlativity of rights and duties* (Feinberg 1966). Does every right necessarily imply a duty? And what makes a right more than merely the 'reflex' of a legal obligation (Lyons 1970)? If we could express all sentences (i.e. in legal texts, parliamentary motions, judgments, or legal commentaries) that contain the expression 'right' with a much simpler term, that of 'duty', while maintaining the same meaning, the concept of a right might be redundant.

Theories of rights come into play here. They start from the vantage point that rights are a non-reducible legal and moral category. The attempt is to show why they are more than just the flip side of a legal obligation. Both the interest theory and the will theory provide their own reply to the challenge. The interest theory assumes that a right exists if the fulfilment of the legal duty is beneficial to the duty addressee (Lyons 1969) or if it is the interest itself that *provides a reason* for the duty to exist (Raz 1984). The will theory, by contrast, assumes that a right exists when the person to whom the duty is owed has *control* over the existence and enforcement of the duty (Hart 1982). He or she must be able to dispose of it.

Later in this section, I will take a closer look at the two major theories. However, first, it is important to see that rights contain different elements that cannot be reduced to obligations. In most cases, rights are a conglomerate of freedoms, obligations, and abilities. Therefore, we must start by analysing these different elements.

2.1. Rights

Common ground in the debate over rights is Wesley Hohfeld's (1913/17) analysis of rights as consisting of 'fundamental legal relations'. He describes four legal 'positions' that individuals can hold in relation to one another: claims, privileges, powers, and immunities.

(1) *Claim*: A person A holds a claim vis-à-vis a person/institution B to perform an action φ, if B is held under a duty to perform φ.
(2) *Liberty*: A person A holds a liberty vis-à-vis a person/institution B *not* to perform an action φ, if she *has no duty not to* perform φ and (consequently) B has no claim to φ against A.
(3) *Power*: A person A holds a power vis-à-vis a person/institution B, if he or she can create, alter, or waive either B's duties or liberties. Hohfeld describes a power as a 'second-order' legal relation, enabling a person or a legal entity to change or discard first-order legal relations, i.e. duties or liberties.

(4) *Immunity*: A person A holds an immunity vis-à-vis a person/institution B if B has no power over A to create, alter, or waive the duties or liberties held by A. Immunities are, for example, included in constitutionally protected fundamental rights specifying which legal norms cannot come into effect.

Rights usually consist of a bundle of these Hohfeldian positions (cf. Honoré 1961). For example, in each property right several of these features are included: All non-owners have a duty to refrain from using the good that is owned. So, a property right always includes claims. The owner also has the freedom to make – i.e. no duty not to make – use of the property (provided this does not infringe upon the rights of others). Furthermore, the property right entails the power to transfer the property – to gift or sell it (Waldron 1988; Munzer 1990). However, with a few exceptions, rights always contain claims. Rights usually oblige other persons or institutions to perform or refrain from performing certain acts.

With regard to rights in criminal law, the main focus lies on these claims. The holder of a property right, for example, is protected by criminal law in that theft, expropriation, and fraud are prohibited and prosecuted; bodily integrity is protected in that serious bodily injury is prohibited and charged; the right to life is protected by the prohibition of homicide. If, however, it were only the claims that protect the individual rights, the question could be raised whether it is necessary to speak of rights at all or whether criminal law could not instead be sufficiently described as a conglomerate of legal duties. A theory of rights in criminal law therefore asks what additional elements must be attached to the duties and the correlating claims in order to meaningfully talk about rights.

2.2. Interest Theory

The interest theory of rights claims that a person possesses a right if the fulfillment of duties of other persons are intended to promote his or her interest – to satisfy needs, to fulfil desires, to increase capabilities, to enable a good life, etc. In Joseph Raz's formulation …

> X has a right if X can have rights, and, other things being equal, an aspect of X's well-being (his interest) is a sufficient reason for holding some other person(s) to be under a duty (Raz 1984: 166).

In the classical debate between adherents of an interest theory and those of a will theory, the former has been criticised for being *too broad*. In particular, the problem of so-called 'third-party beneficiaries' (Hart 1982; cf. MacCormick 1977; Kramer 1998) has attracted much attention. Persons or groups who gain from the existence of a right, but who obviously cannot be regarded as rights holders, are difficult to exclude by means of the theoretical implications of the theory. We would not, for example, consider a domestic firm whose business is protected by a scheme of import taxes a right holder.[4] Although the firm clearly benefits from the duty of foreign firms to pay taxes, it has no entitlement that they do so.

However, the conceptual breadth of the theory can just as well be seen as a virtue, in that the theory allows to encompass a variety of rights a will theory cannot – such as the rights of minors and children (MacCormick 1984), or fundamental inalienable rights (MacCormick 1977; cf. Steiner 2013). Rights in criminal law have also been treated as something that only an interest theory is capable of comprehending (Kramer 1998; Steiner 1994). Rights in criminal law are allegedly excluded by a will theory due to the victim's lack of powers to enforce them, to influence process, and to demand and renounce a claim to compensation.

In order to properly understand the normative implications of the interest theory we need to be precise about what we mean by the term 'interest'. One might draw a parallel to classical distinctions between conceptions of wellbeing here (Scanlon 1996). On the one hand, there are *objective* definitions that recognise certain values as universally valid and independent of an individual's appreciation – for example, basic needs, the good life, or objective lists of goods. On the other hand, there are approaches that determine wellbeing *subjectively*. Welfare is then either linked to a psychological state, a feeling of happiness or pleasure – that is a so-called 'hedonist' account – or it is viewed as dependent on individual desires or preferences (whether they are fulfilled in the best possible way). Usually theories of wellbeing incorporate elements of objective and subjective views – such as the accounts of 'informed desires' or 'rational desires' (Griffin 1986). Hedonist interest theories are almost never found in legal theory.

The differences between an interest and a will theory become potentially greater *the more objectively* the interest of a right holder is determined. To demonstrate this, let us assume that the interest is described as exclusively dependent upon the fulfilment of an individual's *actual desires* – i.e. completely subjective. In this case, the answers of the interest theory to the questions of who should have rights and what they have to protect are largely congruent with those of the will theory as the interest is nothing other than an expression of the individual choice. By contrast, if one assumes that the interest is determined in a purely objective manner, major differences become apparent. The function of rights is then no longer to protect individual freedom of choice, but to promote those values that are recognised as universally valid for all members of society. I will call this distinct feature of the interest theory the 'objective value' assumption.

2.3. Will Theory

The will theory of rights is deeply rooted in the legal philosophy of Immanuel Kant. Rights, from the Kantian perspective, are a sphere of personal freedom,

[4] The classic example by von Savigny 1841, re-used by Hart 1982.

within which a person can exercise his or her capacity for self-determination without undue interference from others ([1797] 1996: 386–90). A right's function is seen in protecting the will – i.e. the free decision – of the individual. Hence, to possess a right is a person's power to dispose of what others owe to him or her and to control it through the exercise and expression of his or her own will.

According to major will theorist HLA Hart, this element of *control* over the actions and omissions of other people is of crucial importance. Every right holder, he claims, is a 'small-scale sovereign' (Hart 1982: 183) who, with respect to the duties directed to him or her, can decide which actions the duty bearers are to perform, and which ones not. Hart states that a right grants the 'fullest measure' of control if a claim (and the included duty of the addressee) is accompanied by three Hohfeldian powers:

(a) The possibility to enforce (or refrain from enforcing) compliance with a duty.
(b) The possibility to discharge the addressees from their duty.
(c) The possibility to waive a claim to compensation in the event of a violation of the duty.

These three powers are indeed the defining feature of rights in a will theory. Right holders possess the legal ability to create, alter, or renounce duties. In contrast to the interest theory, the theory perceives a right to be an active position. A right holder can do things with it and is not a mere passive beneficiary from a duty. The will theory is often criticised for being a conceptually narrow theory that is not able to capture all the relevant uses of the term 'right' in judicial and political contexts (MacCormick 1977). However, will theorists generally make different metatheoretical assumptions about the success of a theory; whereby capturing and explaining of the everyday use of language is not seen as a major a criterion for a theory to fulfil its purpose. Rather, they claim, the aim is to sharpen the legal-technical use of language and thus to revise language and to arrive at more precise judgements about rights (Cruft 2005).

There is, however, another difference between the two theories that is more significant for the purpose of this treatise. Unlike the interest theory, the will theory does not assume a substantive, comparable, and aggregable value that provides the basis for establishing rights. A person's autonomy, which represents the moral ground for each right, is not something that can be increased or realised to a greater extent. Different rights are not commensurable with regard to the weight of the autonomy, and so the theory does not presuppose that two different rights can be traded off with respect to their underlying value (Waldron 1989). This is due to the fact that a right is *formally determined* by its function to protect the individual decision (regardless of content). The answer to the question if and how the decision is protected – i.e. how the right is enforced, whether the duty is owed, and whether compensation is due – depends exclusively on the autonomous decision of the individual. I will call this distinct feature of the will theory the 'formal criterion' of a right's existence.

3. Consent

If an essential function of criminal law is to protect individual rights, it is necessary to examine how these two theories account for the possibility of consent as a justification or suspension of criminal law norms. Before any such examination can be undertaken, however, we need to have a clear understanding of 'consent'. A right holder's consent can significantly *shape the normative landscape* of criminal law by delineating boundaries between permissible and wrongful conduct.

It serves as a cornerstone in distinguishing between legally acceptable behaviour and offences. As legal philosopher Heidi Hurd (1996) illustrated convincingly, consent holds an extraordinary normative power to transform actions that would otherwise be morally impermissible into morally permissible ones. She uses vivid examples, such as the distinctions between rape and consensual sex, or theft and borrowing, to illustrate how the incidence of consent dramatically changes our moral assessment of an action.

> [Consent] turns (...) a kidnapping into a Sunday drive, a battery into a football tackle, a theft into a gift, and a trespass into a dinner party (Hurd 2005: 305).

According to Hurd, this normative transformation occurs because consent involves a waiver of rights: The consenting individual voluntarily relinquishes a claim against the other party, granting him or her permission to act in a way that would have infringed upon those rights without consent. The possibility of consent vests the individual with the status of norm-setter. He or she can change legal facts. Duties and claims can be reversed or abolished, and thus new nominative realities may emerge without being imposed on individuals by the legislator or the legal authorities. To a certain extent, the faculty of consent *individualises the law* and enables legal rules to be adjusted on an interpersonal level. As Vera Bergelson puts it:

> The state justifies employing the harshest and most intrusive powers against an individual by the overarching need to enforce the rights and obligations of all members of society. Consent involves changing the balance of those rights and corresponding obligations (Bergelson 2014: 172).

In criminal law, there are two ways in which consent can play a role. On the one hand, there are certain criminal offences that necessarily involve the non-consent of the person affected. Consent to the act would therefore be a contradiction: the offence cannot be committed in the first place. For example, theft is logically excluded by the consent of the person who is deprived of his or her possession. On the other hand, consent can act as justification. In this case, an offence is reported to the police and brought to trial, but impunity is granted based on proven consent. The difference between these two roles of consent in criminal law is of significance depending on the conception of the wrongfulness of actions. However, a further explanation of the underlying norm-theoretical distinction would go too far for the purpose of this chapter. In both cases, I assume that consent removes an obligation to refrain from acting towards the addressee of the obligation.

The possibility of discharging another person from his or her duty by consent is clearly understood as a Hohfeldian 'power' (Koch 2018). This means that the consenting person can create or annihilate first-order legal relations (Hohfeld 1913/17). This understanding of consent as a legal power entails some limitations that should be mentioned here. To exercise a power requires a *communicative act* (Alexander 1996; Kleinig 2010). Since privileges and obligations are social facts that are, in general, recognised by the holder and by the legal community, there needs to be a socially acknowledged or verifiable act to dissolve them. Consent can therefore not be understood *in foro interno*, as a mere state of mind or, as it is sometimes conceived, as the congruence of the attitudes of the affected person with the intention of the agent (Bergelson 2014). It requires an expression either by action, signal, or gesture: Explicit consent that can be recognised by the duty bearer and could, in principle, be understood by the legal community. Furthermore, it is also difficult to imagine that consent as the execution of a power can be withdrawn *ex post*, as the existence or non-existence of the duty at the specific point in time depends on the norm-setting of the duty addressee.

The transformative power of consent is essentially dependent on the circumstances under which the person grants consent. These circumstances separate what is presumed to be *valid* from *invalid consent*. Let me distinguish four criteria that play a role in determining the validity of consent (see Kleinig 2010): the competence of the consenting agent, the voluntariness of the consent, knowledge of the outcome, and the intention of the consenting agent.

(1) Competence refers to the ability of the individual to reflect upon itself, its attitudes, and intentions. This implies a cognitive threshold that the individual must meet. For example, *minors* and individuals with certain mental incapacities may not be considered competent to grant consent.
(2) Consent must be given freely and without coercion, manipulation, or undue influence. The presence of any form of *pressure* – be it psychological, economic, or physical – can vitiate the voluntariness of the decision, thereby rendering the consent invalid. For consent to reflect an individual's genuine desires, it must emerge from the individual's own initiative, free from overbearing external forces.
(3) Knowledge of the outcome requires a clear understanding of all relevant facts, implications, and potential risks and benefits associated with the decision. The consenting individual must be provided with all the *necessary information* in an accessible and comprehensible manner.
(4) The intention of the consenting agent encompasses the willingness to accept not only the benefits but also the risks and responsibilities associated with the decision. The individual's intention reflects its *purposeful and deliberate*

decision to consent, which should align with the understood parameters of what is being agreed upon.

Obviously, these 'factors' should not be considered as 'conditions' in the strict sense, which are either fulfilled or not (Bullock 2018). They are objectives that can be gradually fulfilled and for which it is difficult to set a universally valid critical threshold: In the case of disabled persons or children (1), it is still possible that they can give valid consent under specific circumstances. Coercive situations (2) can never be completely ruled out in a situation. Complete information about the possible consequences (3) is neither possible nor necessary for valid consent and, therefore, not all consequences can, or need be intentionally (4) taken into account. These objections represent a challenge but not one that is insurmountable (Miller and Wertheimer 2010). However, it is crucial for any conception of consent that it attempts to specify these four requirements.

Lastly, it should be noted that these four factors for the validity of consent are *formal restrictions* on the act of expressing consent. They are conditions for the exercise of a power and the successful discharge of another person from his or her legal duty. None of the factors imposes a *substantive restriction* on the decision-making possibilities of the consenting person – i.e. a restriction of a specific content of the decision.

4. Making Sense of Consent

The question a theory of right seeks to answer is, therefore, to what extent individuals can consent and where the boundaries of consent lie. The challenge is the following: Why is a legal obligation (and the correlative claim protected by it) supplemented by a power to release the bearer from this obligation? So, the main task for a theory of rights is to explain the possibility of consent. But ideally, a theory of rights also provides the tools to enable *normative judgements* on the structure and implementation of criminal law norms.

4.1. Critique of the Interest Theory

The answer provided by the interest theory is that consent – the power to transfer or revoke a right – benefits (or should benefit) the right holder. In many instances, this is the case. Just imagine if a person could not legally allow another to hug him or her without it being considered assault. It would obviously deprive him or her of an ability that is crucial for his or her wellbeing. It clearly promotes the welfare of the individual if he or she can dispose of rights and discharge another person from duties. However, the interest-based explanation of consent also implies a restriction. The power to dispose of the right and the obligation *must* serve the interests of the right holder. Therefore, the power should not exist if it is not in the interest of the right holder to waive the right voluntarily.

Here the interest theory becomes peculiar (Stewart 2010: 23–26). The existence of a power to suspend or transfer the right – i.e. the possibility of justifying criminal acts by consent – is contingent upon it being in the person's interest. Thus, in some cases of self-harming permissions, it could be claimed that the affected person should not possess the power to consent. However, such a conclusion is neither descriptively nor normatively adequate. It is *descriptively inadequate* because criminal law facilitates many forms of consent without examining the interests of the person who consented. For example, a person can get a tattoo or dye his or her hair green, even if this might lead to objective disadvantages. In a legal context, however, the question of whether this lies in his or her interest is not even raised, as the criterion of consent depends solely on the will of the person and its successful expression.

It is *normatively inadequate* because, if we accepted an interest-theoretical justification for the establishment of legal norms, we would have to implement far-reaching restrictions on the liberty of rights holders to dispose of their rights. These restrictions are tantamount to what can be called 'indirect paternalism' (von Hirsch 2009). It is 'paternalist' as a person's freedoms are legally restricted for his or her own good (Dworkin 1983). The restriction of freedom is 'indirect' because it arises from the lack of a power to allow others to transgress and does not directly impose a duty. However, the fact that it is impossible to exercise the power to discharge people from their directed duties clearly restricts the freedom of the agent.

It should be noted that this problem for an interest-theoretical justification of consent in criminal law arises when interests are defined objectively (independently of the individual's attitudes). If, by contrast, the interest was determined subjectively and exclusively on the basis of desires or preferences, it would be hardly possible to derive paternalistic legal norms. The *objective-value property* of the interest theory therefore leads to these descriptively and normatively problematic implications.

Furthermore, a critic of the interest-theoretical conception of rights might ask the following question: Why should consent be respected at all? Imagine the example of a person who does not want to be vaccinated, although this would be highly desirable in view of eliminating health risks. The interest theory has difficulty explaining the limits that are placed on the interference of others by non-consent. In this case, the objective interest of the person does not by itself justify the existence of the duty of the doctor not to vaccinate against the patient's will.

For these reasons, I do not consider the interest theory to be suitable for mapping consent in criminal law. The theory is not able to explain why consent that is harmful to the individual must nevertheless be respected, nor why non-consent to actions that are beneficial for the individual must be respected. The possible normative conclusions from the theory are either potentially paternalistic, or the theory contains a conception of interests as the fulfilment of actual desires, which is problematic for many reasons.

4.2. Critique of the Will Theory

Let us now recall the three Hartian powers that are inherent in each right according to the will theory. Specifically, (a) the power to enforce and (c) the control over compensation are at odds with the idea of individual rights in criminal law. On the one hand (contra a), criminal offences are investigated *ex officio* and brought to court by the public prosecutor, with the state being the plaintiff and the victim serving primarily as a witness. Although the victim can refrain from reporting certain offences (and thus the case is not investigated), as soon as the case is filed, the victim no longer has any control over it. On the other hand (contra c), although in particular cases there is victim compensation from the offending party, it comes merely as a supplement to punishment. There are only limited possibilities for the victim to influence the sentence, to confront, or even to exculpate, the offender.

These two observations have created an unease for will theorists with regard to rights in criminal law, and they have been criticised for that by adherents of an interest theory (e.g. MacCormick 1977; Kramer 1998). The will theory is presumably incapable of comprehending individual rights in criminal law, and will theorists have reacted to this charge in two ways: Either they *bit the bullet* (Hart 1982; Simmonds 1998), upholding the view that criminal law does not confer rights. Or, in order to rescue the claim that criminal law confers rights, they identified the state (or the general public)[5] as the right holder (Kearns 1975; Steiner 1994). Both solutions are somewhat problematic in terms of their descriptive capabilities as well as their normative implications. Elsewhere I have argued why the possible existence of rights in criminal law is not inevitably an objection against the will theory and I attemptet to show why it makes sense (normatively) to understand these rights in a will-theoretical framework (Moser 2019). In this chapter, however, my focus is only on (b), the power to consent.

With regard to this aspect, the will theory seems to have an advantage over the interest theory. By specifying only *formal conditions* for the existence of rights – i.e. that the will of the right holder is reflected – and by not substantively specifying what value ought to be protected by the right, the will theory can make sense of the fact that non-consent must be respected even if an encroachment of the right would realise a presumed value. The will of the individual is either given or not, it cannot be outweighed by a more advantageous outcome. Therefore, the *formal criterion* of the existence of the right avoids the interest-theoretical problem of disregarding the individual refusal to consent. The will theory can appropriately depict *why* consent is needed to legitimately infringe upon a right. It is not possible that the will theory allows for paternalistic restrictions on consent as the individual's decision is considered binding regardless of its content. Any reference to the interest of the consenting person does not provide a reason to disregard his or her will to exercise the power to waive the right.

[5] As many criminal law scholars do. See Duff 2018, for a useful discussion on this view; see also Abraham, Chapter 11 in this volume.

However, the theory exhibits a major problem when it comes to the theoretical underpinning of crimes against the individual that cannot be justified through consent. Hart (1982) identifies what he calls 'absolute duties' in criminal law. In contrast to 'relative duties' these cannot be relinquished. Such absolute duties are present when it comes to killing or severe bodily injuries. A person cannot justify killing on request through his or her consent (Stewart 2011). Nor can he or she, for example, grant a person permission (and thus impunity) for cutting off an arm. The criminal law restrictions remain in force regardless of any interpersonal agreement.

The will theory cannot make sense of these restrictions in a *descriptive* sense as it cannot explain or adequately reflect them. Accordingly, the duty not to kill and the duty not to injure a person cannot be conceived of as implications of individual rights. But arguably, there is no need to overestimate the force of this objection (Moser 2019). In fact, there are very few offences where consent is impossible. Most duties under criminal law that aim to protect the individual sphere can be disposed of by the individuals. For example, the right to *sexual integrity* grants its holder full control to permit almost every sexual action through consent. Right holders are also able to justify most forms of infringements upon a right to bodily integrity – even heavy ones, e.g. a *medical surgery*. The permission for *voluntary euthanasia* and assisted suicide in some European countries also points to the fact that consent to killing, depending on the jurisdiction, is not entirely impossible.

Nevertheless, the prohibition of killing on demand is anchored in all modern criminal law codes, and the impossibility of consent to serious bodily injury is an important restriction to protect individuals from assaults. Here, will theory is either forced to abandon the basic assumption of this treatise and refuse to recognise individual rights as the basis for the criminalisation of conduct or it considers the ability to give up the right to life and physical integrity as a *normative claim* to the reform the existing criminal law (see Vandervordt 1990). The theory then becomes difficult to justify to those who are not willing to support these normative implications; it might lose its robustness as it argues for a radical application of the *volenti non fit injuria* principle in criminal law.

4.3. Hybrid Account?

One attempt that has been undertaken at several stages in the debate over rights is to merge the two theories into one single theory of rights (e.g. Ennecerus and Nipperdey 1959) – a so-called hybrid account. As one of the most prolific examples by Gopal Sreenivasan's (2005) hybrid theory acknowledges the importance of both the autonomy of individuals in exercising their rights and the interests that these rights are meant to protect. The account allows for a more comprehensive understanding that can accommodate some of the strengths of both the will and the interest theories while partly mitigating their weaknesses.

Sreenivasan starts with identifying the main problem of each theory: First, the challenge to the interest theory is that it is too broad, recognising legal duties as rights because they serve the interest of particular persons but are not owed to them and thus do not constitute a right – i.e. the problem of third-party beneficiaries. Second, the problem that the will theory is too narrow, as it cannot encompass rights in which claims are included but the three Hartian powers (a)–(c) are (in part or fully) not present (rights of minors, inalienable rights, etc.). I will focus on Sreenivasan's 'simple hybrid theory', as it deals exclusively with power (b) to waive a claim and discharge the right addressee from his or her duty. He writes:

> Suppose X has a duty φ. Y has a claim-right against X that X φ just in case: *either* Y has the power to waive X's duty to φ *or* Y has duty to waive X's duty to φ, but (that is because) Y's disability advances Y's interest on balance (Sreenivasan 2005: 267).

Legal relations are considered a right if other persons have a duty that is accompanied by power to terminate the right, unless the exercise of power is not in the interests of the duty addressee 'on balance'. On the one hand, this addresses the problem of third-party beneficiaries in that (in order to be considered a right) duties generally have to be accompanied by the power to dispose of them, and there are only specified exceptions. Since third parties usually have no such power they are conceptually excluded from the set of right holders (Kramer and Steiner 2007). On the other hand, Sreenivasan takes account of the problem that right holders sometimes lack the power to waive the right and to consent to an encroachment. Only if it is in the interests of the right holder to waive her claim right, should an encroachment be justifiable by consent. Sreenivasan's approach can thus partially account for the restriction of consent by e.g. minors due to the temporary loss of autonomy, coercion, and lack of information. In these cases, it is likely not in the interest of the individuals to be able to exercise their power and thus to waive their rights.

Let us recall, however, that we can either adopt an *objective* or a *subjective* concept of interest. The former entails the unwelcome feature that control over a right might only be granted in a few cases. To take up the previous example, one could claim that it is in an individual's best interest not to get a tattoo or dye his or her hair. Arguably, the person's absence of interest is weighty enough to limit the possibilities for consent. Such an approach would, however, contradict the fundamental normative idea of a will theory, namely, that a person should have control over his or her own right (Frydrych 2017). A myriad of very *intrusive* legal interferences with the individual sphere of discretion and with private life could be argued for based on such a hybrid theory.

If, however, we employ the latter conception of interest – the subjective definition – the limitation of power to waive a right as introduced by the hybrid theory is insignificant. If the interest is determined exclusively by subjective factors, the *actual desires* of a person are decisive. But such a definition would deprive the hybrid account of its major advantage over the will theory. The actual, unqualified desires of people who are coerced, or poorly informed would have the same legal effect as well-informed decisions. Therefore, subjective interests need to be further specified without reference to objective interests in order not to fall afoul of the same problem that emerged as a result of the assumption of *substantive values*.

5. Conditions for a Theory of Rights

As has been shown, the interest theory is not suitable to depict consent in criminal law. As it does not formally determine consent, the validity (and thus the effective waiver of the criminal law obligation) is a matter of degree. The expression of one's will is not enough. It is only valid if the consent is also in the interest of the individual – a condition that opens the door to paternalistic restrictions on the individual's freedom to dispose over his or her rights. The same problem applies to Sreenivasan's hybrid theory, because it contains the very same condition. The interest theory also exhibits problems in answering the question of why consent needs to be respected at all. If a person's interest is the substantial value that justifies a duty, there can always be cases in which consent can be disregarded for the good of the right holder.

The will theory, on the other end, can make sense of consent in criminal law by establishing a formal criterion for the validity of the waiver of a duty. Irrespective of the content, it only depends on whether or not the individual in fact exercises his or her power to discharge the duty holder. However, the theory cannot descriptively account for certain prohibitions under criminal law that do not allow for justification through consent – killing on request, the absolute prohibition of serious bodily injuries, etc. To understand these implications of the theory as a normative request to change the existing criminal law would clearly be revisionist.

A recourse to the objective values of life or body would lead back to the same problems that interest and hybrid theories have. A central caveat of a theory of rights that can make sense of consent in criminal law is that it sets formal criteria for validity of consent. My suggestion is therefore that a theory of rights needs to further specify the validity of the exercise of the power to waive a claim right based on a will-theoretical framework. The framework needs to specify the conditions of the appropriate exercise of the power to waive a claim and to discharge the other people from their duties. This cannot be done in relation to the *content* of the decision but only with regard to the *form* of the decision – the circumstances under which it is made and expressed.

The four factors for valid consent mentioned above provide an adequate framework for the validity of the exercise of the power to relinquish a right. First, the person giving consent must be a responsible person capable of self-reflection (1). Second, coercion (2) should be sufficiently excluded. The person must be able to form and express his or her will independently of external pressure. More than one alternative needs to be available. Third, there must be a sufficient degree of information (3) about the possible consequences of the permission available to the agent. Fourth, the absence of coercion and misinformation must allow the person to form his or her own intention (4) and act purposefully so that the consent reflects his or her own intention.

But what does this mean for the *absolute obligations* under criminal law and the impossibility of consent to killing? Can such a theory handle this descriptive problem? On the one hand, the answer is no, and the theory is forced to draw the *normative conclusion* that killing on demand should be permitted and serious bodily harm can be consented to. On the other hand, a theory of rights that requires a specification of the quality of the will of a consenting person can argue better than a pure will theory why these restrictions exist in this form. The argument refers to the *absence of autonomy* on the part of the person who, for example, either expresses a wish to be killed or voluntarily wishes to suffer a serious injury. Such an absence is contingent upon the circumstances therefore is not categorically given. However, the rare number of cases in which such consent is valid (and represents the authentic intention of the person) is so significant that a general prohibition might be justified.

6. Conclusion

The starting point of this chapter was the assumption that one of the major purposes of criminal law is the protection of individual rights. An important motivation for taking this assumption is the fact that the consent of an affected person plays a central role in the understanding of criminal law norms, their applicability, and that only the incidence of rights can make sense of this fact. The main question of this treatise, then, was to outline how different theories of rights – interest or will theories – understand and justify consent: Why does a right holder have this legal power at all? When should it be possible to exercise it and when not? Having discussed the two main theoretical strands in the debate over rights, the chapter raised doubts as to whether the existing theories are actually capable of accounting for the scope and limits of consent in criminal law.

Based on that, I have established conditions for the formulation of a successful theory of rights that might be capable of making sense of consent in criminal law. Rights and the associated competence to release persons from their duties should be determined formally, not substantially. The interest theory is therefore not suitable because it makes the possibility of consent dependent on the content of the decision and considers consent to be impossible where it contradicts the interests of the right holder. The will theory is better equipped to make sense of consent. However, further qualifications of the will of persons are required.

Not every exercise of a power can and should be considered legally binding. Such qualifications can be provided by accounts on the distinction between valid and invalid consent. A person must be mature and absent from coercion and equipped with sufficient information to be able to formulate his or her own intention. Any possible justification of absolute prohibitions that cannot be repealed by consent has to address the determinants of the invalidity of consent and show why they apply to particularly serious crimes.

2

Naked Rights

MATTHEW DYSON*

1. Introduction

What could rights-reasoning within substantive criminal law look like, and what could it offer?

Those questions could be answered on many levels and, in particular, by the possible advantages of learning from other areas of law where rights-reasoning is already used, compared to a 'home grown' and intended to be autonomous definition. An autonomous definition might appear easier to create; but it might also be more wasteful. It might be wasteful of past effort given and experience gained in other areas of law, and wasteful of the future effort negotiating between two or more autonomous definitions of rights within the legal system. But the question might better be answered by understanding how much rights-reasoning can be free from particular areas of law. Rights might be seen and celebrated as for their nakedness, rather than perceived only in the clothing of the area of law first showing them off.

This chapter will explore (2) what reasoning about substantive criminal law rights might be within criminal law, (3) what rights-reasoning is used to do in tort law; (4) what rights might be used to do might be used to do in criminal law; (5) the wider reasoning processes within a legal system; before considering (6) 'naked rights', rights free from a particular area of law.

It will be noticed immediately that the chapter's focus is the kinds of things thinking about substantive criminal law in terms of rights might lead to, not a particular area and the possible formulations of rights around those areas, such as a right to bodily integrity, or a right to a reputation.[1]

Additionally, the substantive law focus makes this chapter a complement to other chapters in this volume, particularly those where procedural rights in

* With particular thanks to my research assistant, Margot Calmar, and to the organisers for their patience and support.

[1] A right to a reputation, for example, is protected in some legal systems by use of the criminal law, and even was in England and Wales, until Seditious libel, defamatory libel and obscene libel were all abolished by the Coroners and Justice Act 2009; in practice prosecution was not common for a significant time, much if not most of the twentieth century.

criminal law are considered.[2] There is an interesting distinction here, in that framing questions within criminal procedure around rights is common, both within many legal systems, and for laypeople in those systems. Discussion of the defendant's 'right to silence'[3] and right to give evidence, and even to victims' rights' have made sense to lawyers in that context. Those formulations are not new. For example, while the 1950 European Convention of Human Rights has required adaptation for many legal systems, the application of its procedure protections in terms of rights, such as the right to a fair trial under Article 6, has not normally been the cause of why that can be difficult. As the very project of this volume highlights, such formulations have been rarer in the substantive criminal law of many legal systems. That the ECHR has some expressly substantive *rights*, such as the right to life (art 2), to liberty and security (art 5) and to respect for private and family life (art 8) is also well known. Similarly, there are articles expressly imposing prohibitions, typically understood as imposing restrictions on the state in respect of individuals. Finally, the ECHR declares *freedoms* which have effect in substantive law, such as freedom of thought (art 9), expression (art 10) and assembly (art 11).[4] In practice, for many legal systems, those substantive rights and freedoms were integrated into national law in ways other than generating a new and wide-ranging rights discourse. English law was used as the model for some of the drafters of the Convention, and it was thought that it was formulated to reflect existing English law even if not normally expressed in those terms (Duranti 2017). The ECHR is not the focus of this chapter and further work is merited on it and the other places where substantive rights have been discussed within criminal law.

2. What would *Rights* be in Criminal Law?

The first step in exploring what rights-reasoning within criminal law might be, and what it might do, is to have a working approach to rights within law more generally. The literature is large (Kramer and Steiner 2007; Feinberg 1980) and, for present purposes, one version has been selected: Hohfeld's seminal work on rights. It was selected as a good template for how rights might be conceived and, within the common law world, is the starting point for rights formulation.[5] The deeper philosophical waters, between rights as expressions of will, and rights as related to interests, are not needed for present purposes (Hart 1955; Hart 1973; Sreenivasan 2005; Wenar 2005).

Just over a century ago, Hohfeld sought to clarify the language of rights and offered a power set of conceptual terms for dealing with how the claims within a

[2] See, for example, the chapters by Lichtenthäler and Renzikowski, Chapters 10 and 13 in this volume.

[3] Even though it has now been circumscribed in some legal systems.

[4] See later, in the discussion of Hohfeld, for where this use of 'right' does not actually entail another's duty to support it, though it might prevent others acting against it; similarly, where 'privileges' or later, 'liberties' are one way to capture some of what a 'freedom' might mean.

[5] For a 'thicker' understanding of rights, see Renzikowski, Chapter 13 in this volume.

system can be broken down (Hohfeld 1913:17). Importantly for our purposes, he rejected the idea that everything in a legal system was a right or a duty. He picked up the language of Salmond, writing a little earlier, who dealt with Rights (interests protected by the law by imposing duties on others), Liberties (interests of unrestrained activity) and Powers (when the law actively assists a person in expressing his or her will) (Singer 1982). Hohfeld preferred to think in terms of 'claims', but the sense of a 'claim-right' and thus 'right' is a sufficient alternative for our purposes. Later theorists have tended to prefer 'liberty' over 'privilege'. These terms could be conceived in positive terms, a right that a person has to do; and in negative terms, a right a person has that another does not. Hohfeld completed the set of four, up from Salmond's three, but adding Immunities and their opposites, Disabilities. That is, the right/duty, and liberty or privilege and no-right are first order concerns of human behaviour and interactions. Powers/Liabilities and Immunities/Disabilities are second order relations, dealing primarily with human entitlements.

The distinctions between claim-rights, privileges and powers, are not always easy to grasp. In Hohfeld's scheme, rights must have a duty of another to support the right. By contrast, a privilege shows another has no right, or put another way, it is an exemption to another's claim of a right. A power expresses control over another's jural relation, whereas an immunity expresses someone's independence from another's power.

Hohfeld's important clarification was to conceive of pairs of correlativity. First, that every passive right has a corelative duty on the part of others to perform the act covered by the passive right. Second, that every active right has a correlative absence of a right in others. Both have been subject to criticism, though the first has received less critique (Thomson 1990; Corbin 1920/1921).

A neat summary of these correlatives can be found in the later work of Glanville Williams (1956: 1138), one of the most significant English criminal lawyers (and, separately, tort lawyers) of the twentieth century and a leading legal theorist in his own right.[6]

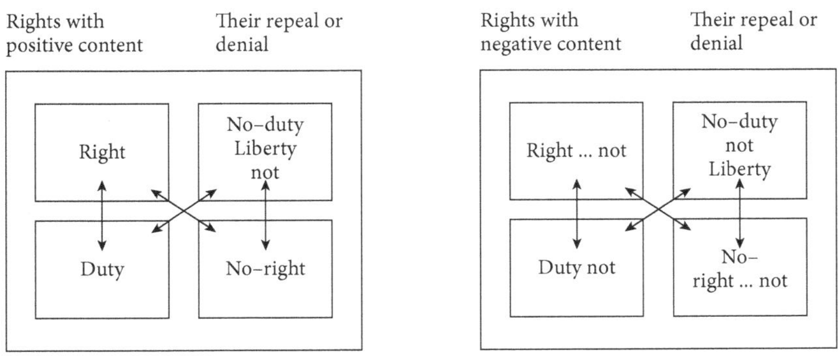

[6] Note 'liberty' over original 'privilege'; Hohfeld's scheme also had Immunity cf. liability and power cf. disability.

For present purposes, the important issue to highlight is whether rights-reasoning in criminal law would hold to the two forms of correlativity Hohfeld espoused. In reality, despite Hohfeld's work being well known, 'rights' language is still used by many, including senior judges, imprecisely. However, the state of the discourse now is that any rights-reasoning attempted should be able to show how it fits into or denies Hohfeld's scheme.

We turn now to consider how tort law uses rights-reasoning, to see what we can learn about its benefits and drawbacks.

3. What do We Use Rights *to do*? The Example of Tort Law

We can now consider some possible formulations of rights-reasoning from within tort law as a prelude to Section 4 considering what they might help us understand about possible uses in criminal law.

3.1. Rights, Duties and Wrongs

The first formulation picks up the first co-relativity Hohfeld described: that rights have co-relative duties. This is the most common way that rights-reasoning is used within private law in the common law tradition, particularly within tort law. For example, Lord Reed, one of the Justices of the UK Supreme Court, recently said that:

> The law of tort is concerned with civil wrongs … breaches of duties imposed by the law, sometimes generally and sometimes on those who are party to particular relationships or have assumed particular responsibilities, which protect the interests of others in respect of such matters as their bodily integrity, their liberty, their property, their privacy and their reputation.[7]

There is a simple process, here, of treating private law claim-rights between persons as the bond which, when interfered with, generates a wrong. As we will see below (at 4.1), that might be more complicated in criminal law, but we can hold on to the simplicity of the position for the moment (Birks 1997: 34–35).

The core value of designating the relevant rights, duties and thus *wrongs* is to justify the imposition of liability as well as delimit it. Only where a person has a right that another behave in a specific way, should there be liability if the other fails to do so. That means there may simply be no right to a given thing, and no corresponding duty that the other support you in having it. Rather, tort lawyers

[7] Per Lord Reed (a Scots-trained, and later President of the UK Supreme Court) in *Morris-Garner v One Step* [2018] UKSC 20, [31].

consider there can be a loss without a wrong, *damnum sine injuria*, in the Roman law sense. The key issue, then, is what rights we have and why. There are different theories about that, and they rise and fall over time. One of the dominant theories now is corrective justice, which derives from Kant a set of rights we must have one against another to live lives without unduly interfering with each other. Those rights are expressed as bilateral relationships between legal persons. That said, there is no single set of agreed rights (Stevens 2007). Even legal systems which appear to have broadly similar civil and criminal architectures for deciding on the grounds of unlawfulness, like the German, do not seem to have fully accepted integrated methods across their 'protected interests' in both civil and criminal law.

3.2. Practical Claims

There is also a useful grammar to the rights formulation. The interference with the right is what is a precondition for there being a wrong. That does not mean that every wrong has a remedy. For example, there can be a wrong which is not actionable without a loss. Thus, the tort of negligence is only actionable when A breaches her duty to take reasonable care of B and thereby causes B a legally recognised form of harm. By contrast, the common law tradition also recognises torts which are actionable without proof of loss, such as assault or battery, and one possible explanation is that the interference with the right actionable per se: the mere infringement with the right is sufficient to generate liability. It is true, compensatory damages will not be paid without the claimant also alleging and proving some kind of loss, but even without that, what common law systems call nominal damages (of £1 for instance) can be awarded, marking out that there was a wrong.[8] A similar statement might be made about injunctions, that they protect against threatened or actual infringements of rights. It also allows for universality across tort law: the classic place a legal system might otherwise struggle to explain the contours of liability and their justification is in liability for omissions. A common position is that the greater the restrictions on an individual's ability to act, the greater the justifications must be, and thus generally liability for omissions should be carefully delineated. That argument tends to be stronger in criminal law, where the consequences of liability are paradigmatically higher. But selecting when to impose omissions liability can at least on its face be eased by framing it in terms of a duty and, most likely, a correlative right in the other party that you act. If the formulation used there is in terms of rights and duties, then there is a certain simplicity in using the same formulation across tort law. Thus, a rights approach can also explain some of the features of tort law.

[8] If a legal system does not recognise tort liability in such situations, it would be easier to make the kinds of arguments that Hirsh does, see Chapter 8 in this volume.

3.3. Rights Compared to Other Options

However, rights-reasoning does not exist in isolation: there are alternatives. In addition, the rights formulation has limits both in theory and in practice. This is most apparent by the rights discourses not being firmly accepted across common law jurisdictions and, in particular, being more accepted in academia than in court practice.[9] In practice, often there is little substantial theory used; within academia the alternatives offered within tort law are quite extensive.

3.3.1. Rights Theories

One of the dominant approaches are forms of rights theory, of which corrective justice is the most developed form at present. 'Corrective justice is the idea that liability rectifies the injustice inflicted by one person on another' (Weinrib 2002: 349; Weinrib 1995: Chs 1 and 6; Coleman 1992: Ch 11, esp. 205–209; Weinrib 2001; Ripstein 2016; Stevens 2007: Ch 1, 4, 13 esp. 291–305, 320–328; Nolan and Robertson 2012.). As a species of rights-reasoning, it recognises underlying rights, and defines a wrong as an infringement of a right that the wrongdoer owed to the victim; it covers both tort liability and remedies not focused on compensating for a loss.

This has the advantages that it (1) explains why tort law links victim and injurer, since it takes the injurer to have the duty to repair the wrongful losses that he causes; (2) explains why tort law as a law of wrongs, which matches our intuitions; and (3) offers the first order duty (prohibitions) and second order duty (repair) scheme.

On the other hand, it has the disadvantages that (1) a lot of the work is devolved to a debate over which rights we have in fact, and the philosophical claims which might or might not underlie those debates; and (2) in practice, it does not appear to be how the practitioners and judges reason.

3.3.2. Civil Recourse

A different approach is to engage with how tort law holds wrongdoers to account, and one of the most impressive forms of this is the civil recourse theory championed by Goldberg and Zipursky (2020; 2006). Instead of thinking something like 'the breach of a primary duty creates a secondary duty to repair', the civil recourse formulation would be something like 'the breach of a primary duty endows the victim with a right of action'. The state's role in overwriting private vengeance generates the need to provide a state-organised alternative, with underlying rights as well.

This has the advantages that: (1) it explains tort's bilateral structure: a claim by the victim against the wrongdoer, and not by the state nor against the state; and

[9] See Tony Weir's famous statement 'Tort is what is in the tort books and the only thing holding it together is the binding' (Weir 2006).

(2) there are a range of tort remedies and that a defendant incurs a legal duty to pay damages only upon the tort action's successful conclusion: settlement or court order.

It has the disadvantages that (1) again, like rights theories, it does not itself explain which rights there are nor (2) which remedies necessarily flow from the breaches; (3) again, it does not appear to be the way that practitioners or courts always reason.

3.3.3. *Deterrence*

A third focus is not deontological as the first two described above have been, but instrumental: using tort law to achieve a particular purpose. That purpose is open to discussion, but normally focuses on avoiding harm. There are different ways to formulate this, but one of the dominant ways has been the Law and Economics movement in the USA (Posner 1973, as the original treatise, but more recently (and more digestibly) Posner 1995; Bingham 2010a). One example of how to put the point across was captured by Jules Coleman (2001), describing negligence:

> Imposing an unreasonable risk of injury is in turn a matter of failing to take precautions that a reasonable person would take … A precaution is reasonable when it is rational; a precaution is rational when it is cost-justified; and a precaution is cost-justified when the cost of the precaution is less than the expected injury.

This approach has the advantages that it (1) motivates effort to prevent harm generally, where the deterrence is viewed as incentivising society to take rational choices to reduce injuries and accidents it promotes an efficient allocation of harms and efforts to prevent those harms; and (2) at least to the extent that law and economics theory would be willing to be classed as a theory of deterrence, rather than one seeking optimal efficiency in general, it is a chance for legal realism to be felt in tort law.

It has the disadvantages that (1) members of society do not behave in a rational fashion, nor, necessarily, should they; not all aspects of "reasonableness" can be reduced to rationality; (2) it is entirely instrumental and lacking any deontological values; (3) if the deterrent is a money payment, how should its value be calculated and to whom should it be paid? and (4), it does not appear to be the way practitioners or courts appear to reason.

3.3.4. *Distributive Justice*

This approach considers the goods in society and sees tort law's role as part of the wider goal of distributing those goods fairly (Gardner 2014). As Rawls (1999: 3 and 6) powerfully put it:

> Justice is the first virtue of social institutions, as truth is of systems of thought … while the distinctive role of conceptions of justice is to specify basic rights and duties and to determine the appropriate distributive shares, the way in which a conception does this is bound to affect the problems of efficiency, coordination, and stability.

This approach has the advantages that (1) it promotes the allocation of resources proportionate to some objective good; and (2) if constructed around a neutral factor, like risk, there may be an explanation for at least some of tort law.

It has the disadvantages that (1) there is no agreement about what we should be distributing (e.g. goods and services, or happiness) and how that distribution should be carried out; (2) there is no obvious boundary between tort and tax, social security or other re-distributive systems; and again, it only covertly (and allegedly) underpins how practitioners and judges reason.

Some other approaches exist as well, though they are more marginal within tort law in the common law tradition. There is a small strand raising the possibility of retribution within tort law, for example (Honoré, 1995). There is also an approach that says tort law is simply compensatory, undoing, to the extent we can, the harm one causes another. That seems more to be a description of tort law's predominant function, rather than its purpose, so it has not been discussed here.

Perhaps the reality is that no single explanation works, certainly there is no single consensus for a universal theory. One practical point is to understand how much these theories can be mixed, yoked together, or, like a human body, one provides the bones against which the muscles of the other work. One example is Peter Cane's (2001: 413) thesis that 'corrective justice provides the structure of tort law within which distributive justice operates'.

3.4. What does Rights-reasoning Add?

Some legal systems seem to function without formulating their tort law around rights, the French for example (Viney 2019), and in others it is open to debate whether they do or do so fully, as in England. The formulation of rights provides a particular framework in which to have some of the debates that, arguably, would need to happen anyway. This framework offers some advantages, particularly in how to formulate the 'wrong' involved in civil wrongs expressed by tort, and some grammatical benefits for describing tort law, including for omissions. The key, then, is the relative advantage, if any, of the rights formulation, and the efficiency in getting there. It is not obvious that rights-reasoning is the only way those advantages, or sufficiently important other ones, might be achieved.

4. What Might We Use Rights to do in Criminal Law?

We might now consider what rights-reasoning can do for criminal law, and the immediate suggestions will be drawn from what it has done within tort law.

4.1. Rights, Duties and Wrongs

The same kinds of rights-reasoning described above could be used in criminal law, and in many cases, covering the same rights. Thus, many of the rights Lord Reed listed above in respect of tort might have groups of offences protecting them: bodily integrity (assault, sexual assault, homicide), liberty (kidnapping), property (theft, fraud, criminal damage) might all be protected. We might consider other formulations, such as rights to autonomy being protected by strongly by, amongst others, sexual offences and fraud offences.

There may be specific rights that are only recognised, or protected to different degrees and in different ways, in one area of law and not another. For the moment, we might note that a right to privacy and a right to reputation might not be protected by the criminal law to the same degree as in private law; though greater protection for private acts might be manifest in a number of ways, from aggravating the offence of burglary when of a dwelling, through to the non-applicability of public order offences to private spaces. The distinction has been said to turn on whether the relevant right-duty relationship is interpersonal, or public, in the sense of involving the state. That basis has strong historical roots, though is typically not fully cashed out across the system. For example, one of the traditional authorities for English law has been Blackstone (1765–9: vol III, Ch 1, p 2), writing over 250 years ago.

> Wrongs are divisible into two sorts or species; *private wrongs*, and *public wrongs*. The former are an infringement or privation of the private or civil rights belonging to individuals, considered as individuals; and are thereupon frequently termed *civil injuries*: the latter are a breach and violation of public rights and duties, which affect the whole community, considered as a community; and are distinguished by the harsher appellation of *crimes* and *misdemeanors*.

Under this approach there are therefore choices about what constitutes private rights and duties, and what constitutes *public* ones.[10] Unsurprisingly, a leading private law theorist has argued that private law should be the determinant of the content of interpersonal duties, even where criminal law also regulates that sphere (Stevens 2014).

As noted by Blackstone, under this conceptualisation, each interference with a right then generates a *wrong* by the person interfering. There is a difficult question here. Is it only interferences with claim-rights that generate wrongs? Or, in Hohfeldian terms, would an interference with a privilege or liberty, power or immunity also generate a wrong? (Singer 1982). The most likely position seems to be that interference with a right would be needed. Hohfeld tried hard to distinguish between rights and the other forms, and any attempt to generate liability for interfering with anything but a right, especially a liberty, might collapse that

[10] See further, the chapters by Lichtenthaler and Renzikowski, Chapters 10 and 13 in this volume.

distinction (Hohfeld 1913/17: 35).[11] But more generally, there is a question over the individualisation of these protections, and the role of the state. This is linked to Hohfeld's definition of legal liberty and privilege: 'Thus, if A has the privilege to do certain acts or to refrain from doing those acts, B is vulnerable to the effects of A's actions. B cannot summon the aid of the state to prevent A from acting in such a manner no matter how A's actions affect B's interests.' But is the summoning of the state a necessary element? For example, Kocourek (1920: 36) disagrees with Hohfeld's conception of liberty and no-right, on the ground that a legal relationship requires the state to be involved. He gives the example of the liberty to smoke a cigar in your own home: an outsider cannot sue you for doing so. If that outsider tried instead to interfere to stop you, the smoker could sue, but where would that action come from? Would it come from liberty, or from other rights in relation to the property in your own home, and the right to exclude, as well, perhaps, as personal bodily integrity rights? What is perhaps clear is that these kinds of issues are not simple to discuss, let alone answer. The role of the state is particularly unclear, beyond simply the recognition of particular rights through legislation or through the courts, and the provision of a mechanism to enforce them privately, criminally or through other means.

Private law in the common law tradition addresses these kinds of issues in part by conceiving of each interpersonal relationship as involving a bilateral duty: each car driver owes duties to each road user and pedestrian, who similarly owe duties back. Many crimes can be formulated in the same way, that we each owe duties to everyone else not intentionally or recklessly to cause them serious harm, for example.[12]

Yet clearly not all criminal offences are in the right–duty form, as there are victimless crimes, or at least, crimes where no victim actually suffers harm, or the class of victim is so large and unrealised that it would make no sense to speak of a victim. The strongest examples include the inchoate offences relating to terrorism, and various offences relating to endangerment (including some road traffic offences) and harm to the environment. At the least, one might either then have to expand the scope of the right to cover even remote threats of unlocalised harm, or consider rights as not being universally required. The option to engage in rights-reasoning only where certain conditions are met would necessitate a clear articulation of what those conditions are. They would seem to include, at least, that a legal person's rights are engaged.

[11] 'These two groups of relations seem perfectly distinct; and the privileges could, in a given case, exist even though the rights mentioned did not. A, B, C, and D, being the owners of the salad, might say to X: "Eat the salad, if you can; you have our license to do so, but we don't agree not to interfere with you." In such a case the privileges exist, so that if X succeeds in eating the salad, he has violated no rights of any of the parties. But it is equally clear that if A had succeeded in holding so fast to the dish that X couldn't eat the contents, no right of X would have been violated.' See, similarly, Edward Weeks adds to this idea with his concept of 'uncorroborated liberties' in his book *The Doctrine of Damnum Absque Injuria Considered in its Relation to the Law of Torts* (1879).

[12] In England, under the Offences Against the Person Act 1861, s 20.

But the issues that re-arranging criminal law around rights would raise are not just about the classes of the duties, they would extend to other conditions there are or should be for liability, let alone just who the rights-bearer is in each situation, if there is one at all. Are the duties themselves breached only when the defendant acted with fault, for example? Where a result is required, is the right formulated with reference to that outcome, or is the right infringed, and the outcome instead a question of actionability of the tort claim, as might be argued within tort law? These are difficult questions that would be possible to answer, though criminal law has not tended to do so until now (Duff 2014a).

4.2. Practical Claims?

There might be some practical benefits to using a rights-reasoning model. Obviously, some points are the same as in tort law, for example; as just discussed, some crimes do require a result before the criminal liability is created, while others do not. Similarly, omissions liability might be framed around rights and duties; where omissions liability is so framed, there is a simplicity in having all liability framed in that way. The downside might be that in those places where rights-formulations are particularly difficult or contested, relying on them might diminish the overall integrity of the legal system. One potentially interesting place is the role of consent.[13] One way of conceiving of consent is in a rights-model, that the victim can waive his or her right to the defendant doing a particular thing. Where the criminal law does not grant that right, as English law does not for anything more than the most minor physical harm,[14] and not at all in respect of property transfers,[15] that might be evidence against rights-reasoning being employed, at least, not fulsomely, as things stand. Similarly, while consent is central to the English law of most sexual offences, a consenting person might still be the victim of an impossible attempt: the defendant might believe the complainant does not consent to the defendant's sexual acts, but the complainant in fact does, so the defendant is liable for attempting the sexual offence. More generally, even where consent does negative a criminal offence, that does not necessarily mean that rights are the reason why. For example, the state might no longer be justified in acting where the complainant consented, for reasons separate to rights. Obviously not all criminal offences involve persons who might consent, though the rights-reasoning might just be more apt if there is such a person. More generally, legal actors might choose to criminalise conduct even where there is consent, for instance because society is harmed in some way, or some other value, such as protecting dignity or vulnerability, overrides the role of consent. It might not always be easy to express those issues in terms of rights.

[13] See further Hirsch, Chapter 8 in this volume.
[14] *R v Brown* [1994] 1 AC 212.
[15] For the purposes of theft at least, *R v Hinks* [2001] 2 AC 241.

In respect of those duties the state might be said to owe, whether directly through its agents, or where a right extends to requiring the state to act to safeguard the performance of the right against the efforts of third-party individuals, 'right' might take on another meaning: standing to enforce. It might be argued that at least some 'rights' in the criminal context might relate to the exercise of state power, and a limitation some legal systems deploy to prevent misuse is to require that the person claiming that power must be personally involved to a sufficient degree. That is the sense of "standing" used here. Examples might include the ability to bring a prosecution privately, or a claim that the state's exercise of power would be abusive because of their own failures.

4.3. Rights Compared to Other Options

For many criminal legal orders, the alternative to rights reasoning has been to rely on constitutional norms grounded in the Parliamentary imprimatur through which criminal law is created. The alternatives offered within tort law might have some purchase, about deterring certain conduct, perhaps a form of 'criminal recourse', rather than civil recourse, and echoing the seminal work Duff (2007) has done within criminal law.

4.4. What does Rights-reasoning Add?

One simple answer to whether rights-reasoning is needed is that it has not been the predominant model within criminal law so far, and yet what we have had has undeniably been criminal law. Of course, that just means we must think through what rights-reasoning being *needed* means for criminal law. It might mean that there is some greater clarity, structure or other benefit that the criminal law could have, while not being *necessary* to the system. Ultimately, this seems to come down to whether the benefits from rights-reasoning are sufficient and outweigh the costs, as well as the comparative benefits from the alternatives. That would take a lot of analysis to show, and might be specific to individual legal systems.

5. Reasonings within a Legal System

So far, we have examined what some forms of rights-reasoning might be within a legal system, and a key issue underlying this is how exclusive any one form must be. Put another way, can multiple forms of rights-reasoning co-exist, and what other forms of reasoning can be accommodated?

If parts of a legal system are sealed off from one another, there is no difficulty in having different and potentially contradictory reasoning apply in each. But the very idea of a 'legal system' presupposes sufficient coherence that the term 'system' is appropriate. That value is a matter deeply embedded in, for instance, jurisprudential discussions about what legitimacy a legal system has (Raz 1970). The question then becomes how much tolerance the system has for variations in underlying reasoning. For many common law legal systems, while at times formally employing a rights-based reasoning in private law, there has been no dogmatic insistence on a particular formulation or applying its consequences.

One answer, perhaps familiar to Germans, might run like this. First, criminal law should be the tool of last resort, the *ultima ratio*, so criminalisation should only happen when other modes of law are insufficient to protect the relevant interests (Jareborg 2005; Husak 2005b). This is also sometimes linked to a principle of 'subsidiarity', that the criminal law is there to provide support to existing interests within civil law: it is unclear whether subsidiarity is part of, derived from, or just closely related to *ultima ratio* (see also Dubber 2005: 692; Roxin 1997: 26–27; Vormbaum 2011: 667–69). The better view is that it is a separate principle, addressing what the content of the criminal law should be *after* the decision to criminalise has taken place (Dyson 2021). Second, a principle of unity of the legal system holds that the contents of the system should be coherent, though this does not, in fact, require that all objects have the same meaning in all areas of law (Kloepfer 2011: para 10.141; Deutsch 1976: vol 1, 89–97). What it does mean is that criminal law cannot criminalise what private law has said is lawful.[16] Third, in Germany at least, only constitutionally accepted purposes of the criminal law can justify criminalisation, in particular, that criminal laws protect 'legally protected goods' (*Rechtsgüter*).[17] However, even if those three principles are accepted, there are a number of gaps. It might be that the criminal law is thought necessary, and that the civil law identifies the conduct as unlawful. Should the criminal law adopt the same definitions as civil law? Criminal law could set a threshold of criminal liability higher than the civil law, so on a given set of facts there would be civil liability without criminal liability. Criminal law could also use concepts, and components for liability, which differed from civil law without infringing those first two principles. The third, on *Rechsgüter*, sits in an unclear relationship with the interests protected by delict, whether in § 823(1) of the BGB or any other provisions.[18] It is also the neatest parallel to rights-reasoning. It is therefore difficult to say that criminalisation in parallel to civil law applies in the same way as criminalisation when not so parallel, since the civil law interests might be imposing restraints on traditional criminalisation in practice and they are not being discussed there.

By contrast, in England, criminal offences and torts each have their own different substantive components; it is only recently that some comparisons have been made systematically across the areas of law. The default belief in the last 150 years has been that it is in no sense necessary for one branch of the law to employ the

[16] See also Renzikowski, Chapter 13 in this volume.
[17] See BVerfGE 92, 1, 13; BVerfGE 126, 170, 197.
[18] Or, indeed, via § 826. See also the discussion of Hellwege and Wittig 2015: 128–32.

substantive law of the other. What we see sometimes are claims that to do so would cause confusion.[19] When they are connected, it is only occasionally a reasoned process; normally it is grounded only in the very simplistic statement that there is 'no reason why not' have them the same.[20]

On its surface, English law does channel substantive questions of criminal law which might occupy the same conceptual space as tort law. However, in specific instances it might prioritise criminal law over civil law. It is also notable that the channelling most obviously happens through particular procedural means, rather than by direct reasoning or engaging in the same core values or norms.

Related concerns are about how well we can separate one area of law from another, and thus, indeed, what an 'area' of law is. Those issues are beyond the scope of this chapter.[21] One recent jurisprudential approach has claimed that, ontologically, 'an area of law' is a set of legal norms that are intersubjectively recognised by the legal complex in a given jurisdiction as a subset of legal norms in that jurisdiction (Khaitan and Steel 2023: 76–96; Khaitan and Steel 2022: 325–51).

We could face one particular and significant problem from starting to employ rights-reasoning for the substantive criminal law: the content of those rights.

First, would the criminal law use the rights other areas of law have developed, where those rights already exist? That is, the content of the criminal law is subsidiary (in the sense noted above) to other areas of law or, put in more everyday language, that the criminal law is piggy-backing on, for example, the civil law? The alternative is that there is some kind of autonomous criminal definition of each right, but that raises the question of whether there is any effect of each right formulation on the other area of law? In some other tort/crime contexts, English law might be described as operating via 'splendid isolation',[22] but it is doubtful that is a rational method which is viable in the long term. One possible approach is what gave this chapter its title, considering whether there are 'naked rights', rights which are then clothed by particular areas of law.

6. Naked Rights

One particularly interesting angle to consider is whether the rights that are referred to in tort law and might be referred to in substantive criminal law are, in fact, expressions of the same underlying root.

[19] See on automatism: *Mansfield v Weetabix* [1998] 1 WLR 1263 at 1266; 1268–79; on the civil law of ownership and theft: *Bentley v Vilmont* (1887) 12 App Cas 471 at 477, see also *R v Hinks* [2001] 2 AC 241 at 263–70.

[20] See *R v Stephens*, (1866) LR 1 QB 702, 708–10; *Crawford Adjusters (Cayman) Ltd v Sagicor General Insurance (Cayman) Ltd* [2014] AC 366 at [110].

[21] For the author's previous work see Dyson 2014: 115–37.

[22] See, e.g. *Ashley v Chief Constable of Sussex Police* [2008] UKHL 25.

Sometimes legal objects have a similar form to each other despite being placed in different parts of the legal system. The most common reason is that the objects share historical origins. The original object is only later placed as a junction between frameworks but started as a freestanding concept. The borderline between tort and crime has such instances. The English law against harassment is just such an example: the Protection from Harassment Act 1997 specifies a rule, not to harass, in s 1, and that rule is given the form of a criminal offence in s 2, and a means are provided of claiming damages in a civil court in s 3. The legislation describes the duty in neutral terms, only relating to the obligation on the individual. The duty does not relate to the conduct, to the procedures, or to norms or remedies associated with the duty. The fact that there are not many common examples is itself revealing, including that there are no specific torts for sexual battery, murder, theft and many other well-known offences which cause harm.

Another example is slightly older, from one of the Factories Acts of the nineteenth century, the precursor to the modern English Health and Safety legislation.[23] The Factory and Workshop Act 1878 required that machinery be securely fenced, enforcing this by both a fine and civil liability for death or bodily injury. The underlying prohibition, just like the machinery it applied to, was naked.

Sometimes the objects might arise from the same place, but the history is more clouded and the links less obvious. One example in English private law is an 'assumption of responsibility' generating some kind of obligation to act, often an obligation to take care.[24] This could arise in tort law, bailment and other areas, but it could not necessarily be said to be originally grounded in any one of them. There are historically significant instances of it, such as perhaps the first treatise engaging with the tort of negligence being one formally on bailment (Jones [1828] 2007).

Another example is directly to recognise duties which are expressed not as freestanding duties, but in some sense linked to the area of law they first appear in but have a junction with another area of law. In England, breach of statutory duty is a way of creating a civil claim for harm caused by the breach of a duty in a statute where the statute does not itself expressly create civil liability for harm caused by breaching the statutory duty. The statute will normally have an enforcement mechanism of some kind, just not a civil one. The claimant must show that, despite the absence of an express reference to creating civil liability in the statute, that is what Parliament intended. It is a factor against civil liability that the statute does impose a criminal penalty since it can be argued the criminal penalty alone shows that it is all Parliament wished to supply as an enforcement mechanism.[25] A famous

[23] See, e.g. the Health and Safety at Work etc. Act 1974.

[24] For recent argument in this direction, see e.g. Nolan 2019.

[25] *Carroll v Barclay (Andrew) and Sons, Ltd* [1948] AC 477 at 489–90; 493; *Biddle v Truvox Engineering Co* [1952] 1 KB 101 at 103; *Cutler v Wandsworth Stadium* [1949] AC 398 and see also Goodhart (1946) 62 LQR 316 at 317.

example of a more general integrative technique is §823(2) BGB. §823(1) requires anyone who intentionally or negligently injures the protected interests of German law, life, body, health, freedom, property, or another right, to pay compensation to that person. German law further adds, in §823(2), that the same duty to compensate is owed by someone who breaches a norm intended to protect another, so long as it is done with fault. A protective norm, or *Schutzgesetz*, will be found in many criminal offences which might not otherwise be fitted within §823(1) easily, and in any case civil liability is much easier to establish once the criminal liability has been found. However, in both the English and the German forms, the language is of an underlying duty. That duty might be expressed in a statute which concerns primarily criminal law, but the constituent duty is given expression in tort law.

One way to approach this, used by some legal systems, is to use a neutral term like an 'unlawful act'. This intermediate concept is, in a sense, the legal format that allows objects to transfer across relevant borders; pushing an object into that state and out again according to some priority and through the behaviour of ordinary users of the system. For example, Dutch law's key definition of an unlawful act is, amongst other things, 'an act or omission in violation of a duty imposed by written law' and all criminal laws must be in written form (in addition, breaching social standards of due care also generate liability).[26] This naturally means that every criminal act is also the base unit for then layering on the components for tort liability. French legislation does not do so expressly, but apparently began to do so as a free translation of the Roman '*damnum injuria datum*' (Halperin 2010: 80–81). It will be immediately apparent that what makes the act unlawful might be tightly bound up with other aspects of liability, especially, notions of fault and notions of individual rights.[27] That might be a way to think of a naked concept, potentially, if the underlying work was done in that way, a naked right underneath.

It might be that the 'clothes' put on by one part of a system have a particular effect on the underlying right, but only when expressed in that part of the system. An example would be a rule of interpretation within criminal law which held that any ambiguity had to be interpreted in favour of the defendant. The criminal liability under the Protection from Harassment Act described above would be affected,

The possibility that this conception not only would better represent the reality of some legal issues, but also that it might provide better answers about what the law should be, suggests further research is necessary. That should include both areas of law where rights-reasoning already exists, and where it is being considered, including criminal law. It might engender better coherence across the legal system as well. Ultimately, if there is no obvious answer for how unified the conceptions of rights are within the system, there will be greater pressures on other ways a system might maintain its cohesion, other than those determining unlawfulness. These

[26] Article 6:162, Burgerlijk Wetboek (Dutch civil code).

[27] The integrative techniques in contract law, whether through public policy, illegality or otherwise, are sadly beyond the scope of this chapter.

might be hard law, such as the role of specific doctrines from causation to defences, or soft law, such as through the choices of legal actors.

7. Conclusion

This chapter has explored what rights-reasoning within substantive criminal law could look like, and what it could offer. It drew from within tort law some ways that rights-reasoning has worked there, and sketched how that might apply within criminal law. It considered the problem of how to co-ordinate the rights formulations across both legal systems, and whether there might be 'naked rights' underneath the outer layers of different areas of law. If there might, they deserve more research, particularly as a way to get better answers, descriptively and normatively, as well as more coherent ones across the legal system. What is abundantly clear is that there is no 'off the shelf' version of rights-reasoning which can simply be applied within criminal law, even from within legal systems where some relevant part of the system uses rights-reasoning already. Much more work would be needed before any possible re-orientation of substantive criminal law around rights could be evaluated.

PART II

Rights and the Assessment of Criminal Wrongdoing

3

The Violation of Individual Rights as a Principle of Criminalisation

IVÓ COCA-VILA*

1. Introduction

After several years of intense discussion about the principles that should guide criminalisation, lately the idea seems to be gradually gaining ground – both among continental and Anglo-American scholars – that the search for a principle capable of precisely guiding legislatures on what they should criminalise is doomed to failure (see, e.g. Duff 2018: Chs 6 and 7). First, the two substantive principles of criminalisation favoured classically by criminal law scholars – the harm principle (or the *Rechtsgut*, in continental systems) and the legal moralist approach – have lost much of their support.[1] Both have been revealed as ineffective tools in curbing the expansion of criminal law. What is more, some scholars see the harm principle (or the *Rechtsgut*) as an engine that propels the expansion of criminal law.[2] Second, those who still insist on seeking substantive principles capable of guiding legislatures are accused now of arrogating to themselves a function that is not theirs: in democratic states, the decision of what to criminalise belongs exclusively to parliaments.[3] The allegedly expert opinion of criminal law scholars is no more relevant than that of any other citizen. The only limits on criminal law should therefore be procedural, not substantive.

* An earlier version of this chapter was delivered to the 'Interdisciplinary Conference on Rights in Criminal Law' at the University of Graz in July 2022. I am grateful to Philipp Hirsch and Elias Moser for inviting me to participate and to a number of persons at the conference for the useful discussion of my paper at the time.

[1] Regarding the harm principle (or the *Rechtsgut*) see Duff 2018: 266–272; Harcourt 1999; Hörnle 2019a: 211; Husak 2005b: 114–15. For a rejection of the legal moralist approach, see Chiao 2019: 168–81; 2016; Hörnle 2021: 86–89.

[2] Since everything can be explained as a *Rechtsgut* and every kind of behaviour can be expressed as a harm, both concepts, originally developed as limits, would encourage criminalisation. Regarding the harm principle, in this vein, see Dan-Cohen 2006/2007: 2421. The same paradoxical effect is attributed to the *Rechtsgut* principle; see e.g. Pawlik 2012: 131–37.

[3] This point is clearly made by Gärditz 2016; 2015: Chapter V; 2010. In a similar vein see Stuckenberg 2013: 37.

Consequently, the thesis is gaining ground, according to which criminal law scholars dealing with criminalisation issues face the following unconformable dilemma: either develop a minimal (thin) theory of criminalisation, accepting that it cannot give specific answers to legislators, but instead only provide a set of relevant guidelines to frame the political discussion on criminalisation,[4] or conclude that criminal law scholars must return to dealing exclusively with the doctrine of the positive (criminal) law. Questions of criminalisation, according to the latter train of thought, should be dealt with either by constitutionalists, who can determine which acts of criminalisation are constitutionally valid and which are unconstitutional (Stuckenberg 2013: 35), or by political philosophers (Chiao 2019: Ch 5) who have traditionally dealt with the theory of the legitimate use of public coercion and are therefore in a better position to enlighten legislators on criminalisation topics.

The widespread feeling of scepticism toward any substantive ambitious approach to the criminalisation issue has been reached, however, with little attention paid to an alternative proposal to the mainstream theories of criminalisation, namely the rights violation theory. In fact, within the Anglo-American debate about criminalisation, framing the discussion as a choice between the harm principle (or *Rechtsgüter*) and legal moralism has been very common (see Hörnle 2014a: 176). Although the rights violation theory has a long tradition in criminal law scholarship, and has always accompanied the criminalisation debate in the background, the rights rhetoric has not been discussed in recent times with the depth it deserves. My aim in this chapter is therefore to fill this lacuna.

In what follows, I begin in Section 2 by presenting a critical examination of the three most influential versions of the rights violation theory of criminalisation.[5] If I am correct, none of them satisfactorily fulfils the goal of providing a reasonably thick substantive principle of criminalisation. That is, none of them are capable of offering a principle so rich in its content that it allows us to apply it without having to make further normative judgments and leading at the same time to a highly uncontroversial delimitation of the scope of criminal law within the framework of contemporary Western societies.[6] In fact, I do not think any theory of criminalisation should aspire to do so much. However, in Section 3, I argue that the rights violation principle offers the best starting point for a liberal theory of criminalisation, since it places the figure of the individual as an autonomous, rights-holding agent at the centre of the criminalisation debate. After arguing that any theory of criminalisation must be understood as a thin theory, i.e. as a theory that merely

[4] This thesis is defended paradigmatically by Duff 2018.

[5] Although, in this chapter, I reduce the problem of criminalisation to the passing of a statute defining something as a crime ('criminal law on the books'), I am aware that the criminal law that governs a given society is shaped by many institutions, in particular, by the enforcement bodies and the judges called upon to interpret it. On this broader sense of criminalisation, see e.g. Lacey 2009: 941–47; Lacey 1995.

[6] On the distinction between thin and thick theories of criminalisation see Duff 2018: 253–55.

guides the way in which we should deliberate on criminalisation issues, I outline the core features of a thin rights-centred normative theory of criminalisation. In my view, we must embrace a supra-positive concept of rights, which must also be far-reaching, must be understood as a *pro tanto* reason for criminalisation, and should be the unique principle of a monist theory of criminalisation. I conclude in Section 4.

2. The Violation of Individual Rights as a Thick Principle of Criminalisation

The idea that criminal law ought (only) to protect individual rights against violations by others goes back to (at least) the nineteenth century. While among continental contemporary advocates of this approach, German Kantian criminal law theorist PJA Feuerbach is often credited as the intellectual father (Vormbaum/Bohlander 2014: 32–45), in the Anglo-Saxon debate, the *approach* is often traced back directly to Immanuel Kant's philosophy of law (see, e.g. Stewart 2010). The shared starting premise is the Kantian notion of law, i.e. the idea that the central purpose of law is to secure the external freedom of a person against obstructing actions of others.[7] Law demarcates personal spheres of freedom through the notion of the (subjective) right, and the state is called upon to protect such rights against interferences. The criminal law, according to this view, constitutes a particularly intense mechanism of granting respect for rights. From this viewpoint, a very simple theory of criminalisation can be formulated: only the violation of others' rights, as interference in another's sphere of freedom, ought to be criminalised.

The most important dissonances among advocates of the rights-centred approach begin, though, when it comes to defining what is meant when invoking 'rights' – in particular, when defining the source of these rights, defining their content or scope, and last but not least, when assessing what kind of rights violations are – wrong in a way, or to a degree, that provides sufficient reason to criminalise them. In general, the notion of right is not used to offer all-encompassing theories of criminalisation, but rather to show the inadequacies of classical theories of criminalisation, in particular the harm principle.[8] Although many scholars outline criminal wrongdoing as a rights violation, only a few have attempted to sketch a

[7] Other similar theories of criminalisation are built on the Kantian notion of law. Ripstein 2006: 229–25, resorts to the sovereignty principle, which holds that all violations of 'equal freedom' are criminalisable. Dan-Cohen 2014: 101–14, limits the scope of the criminal law on the basis of the notion of dignity, that is, 'the main goal of the criminal law ought to be to defend the unique moral worth of every human being'. Both authors claim that the harm principle is under-inclusive and fails to provide a rationale for criminalising certain harmless wrongs. For a case against Kantian criteria for ensuring fair criminalisation, however, see Baker 2016: Chapter. 4.

[8] In particular, the notion of right is generally used to offer an alternative to the under-inclusiveness of the harm principle dealing with 'harmless' rape and trespass. See e.g. Gardner/Shute 2000.

substantive (thick) theory of criminalisation. Here I will limit myself to outlining the three most influential approaches in the contemporary criminalisation debate.

2.1. Kant's Natural (Criminal) Law

The first approach is based on the violation of natural rights. This is the path paradigmatically explored in the continental debate by the German legal scholar Wolfgang Naucke.[9] Naucke's approach is decidedly supra-positivist and anti-relativist, since neither the rule of the majority nor the constitution is decisive when it comes to deciding what to criminalise. It is also substantive and thick, since it offers a closed catalogue of rights violations that should be criminalised, positively delimiting the scope of a liberal criminal law (Naucke 2015: 21, 23).

Starting from the Kantian conception of law, and inspired by the works of Feuerbach, Naucke claims that punishment can only be legitimately imposed to punish retributively a certain type of violation of the most essential personal rights. Specifically, it refers to the right to life, physical integrity, and liberty, thus limiting the scope of the criminal law to homicide, bodily harm, kidnapping, crimes against sexual freedom, and treason crimes.[10] Additionally, not every violation of such rights would be criminalisable, but only intentional, conscious, and violent infringements that cause harm to other persons.[11] Likewise, given the limitation of rights whose violation ought to be criminalised, Naucke not only rejects the criminalisation of immoralities or actions that cause an erosion of social taboos, but also of a large part of modern crimes of (abstract) endangerment, negligent crimes, and crimes committed in a mistake of law (Naucke 1993: 143–50).

Naucke's approach achieves particularly well the main task of a thick theory of criminalisation, i.e. to restrict the scope of criminalisable conduct: only the fully culpable violation of negative Kantian rights is legitimately criminalised. Naucke

[9] Naucke 1993, 1985. In a similar vein, see Wolff 1987: 211–13. In the Anglo-American debate, Wellman (2017), Chapter 4, supports a subject-matter constraint of the following kind: only those acts that amount to a forfeiture of one's natural right not to be punished in that way may permissibly be criminalised.

[10] Naucke 2015: 123–24; 1985: 195. In a similar vein, see Stewart 2010: 34.

[11] Naucke 2015: 81–98; 1985: 195. Wellman 2017: Chapter 4, distinguishes between rights infringements and violations. To violate someone else's rights implies a culpable breach of the right. Criminal law is an appropriate response, says Wellman, to rights-related culpability. Only rights violations should be criminalised. On the contrary, whoever breaches a right through no culpability incurs in a mere rights infringement. Rights infringement constitutes a non-criminalisable tort. Tort law is an appropriate response to mere rights-related harms. Wellman, however, does not articulate a theory of criminalisation based on the violation of someone's right. Nor does he determine which (moral) rights would be relevant, nor does he clarify the difference between violation and infringement. If 'culpability' is the only decisive factor in legitimate criminalisation, any right could be criminally protected; in fact, Wellman 2017: Chapter 7, accepts the criminalisation of *mala quia prohibita* offences. For a case against the infringement/violation distinction, see Oberdiek 2004.

even gives a closed list of these rights. Thus, the classic epistemic criticism that supra-positive theories of criminalisation are radically indeterminate does not apply in this case. Nor, in my opinion, is it a decisive argument against Naucke's approach that a supra-positive theory based on Kantian natural law lacks any (legal) authority in the framework of today's democratic and liberal societies.[12] A normative theory of criminalisation is not legally binding, so the fact that it is based on (Kantian) natural law does not disqualify it as a normative guide about what ought to be criminalised and what not. Nor is it a real problem that Naucke's theory is visibly contrary to the will of contemporary (democratic) legislatures: a (normative) theory of criminalisation, by definition, must not bend to the democratic will.[13]

However, the central weakness of Naucke's approach is that it is based on a purely negative conception of freedom that can no longer be endorsed within the framework of contemporary Western welfare states. By limiting the circle of criminalisable conduct to the violation of negative (defensive) rights, he leaves out conduct that also deserves to be criminalised – i.e. conduct that is detrimental to positive freedom, that is, to the basic conditions for personal development.[14] A good example is the crime of tax evasion: although a conception of law based on the liberal ideal of Kantian law would tend not to criminalise it, no one nowadays seriously doubts that serious tax evasion (in the framework of a welfare state) deserves to be punished.[15] Naucke's theory is likewise unsatisfactory insofar as it leaves out of criminal law the endangerment of important negative rights, as well as negligent violations of such rights, which deserve to be punished. In short, the ahistoricism of the catalogue of rights protected by criminal law makes Naucke's approach objectionable in the framework of a welfare state in which (criminal) law is not any more content with securing the external freedom of a person against obstructing actions of others.[16]

2.2. Criminal Law as an Ancillary Form of Shielding the Law

The second approach that I want to address here relates to the German legal scholars Joachim Renzikowski's and Voker Haas's claims that it is the primary

[12] For a different opinion, see Hirsch 2021: 200–01.

[13] For a different point of view, see Hirsch 2021: 201; Kubiciel 2018: a scholar who wants to influence the legislature cannot live in permanent genuine disagreement.

[14] In a similar vein, see Lauterwein 2010: 27; Stächelin 1998: 45–46.

[15] For discussion on the (moral) wrongfulness of tax evasion, see e.g. Green 2017. Attempts to explain crimes such as tax evasion on the basis of the notion of shared (individual) rights (see e.g. Hirsch 2021: 120–23, 194–97) avoid the criticism of under-inclusiveness, but deprive the Kantian approach of the restrictive force that Naucke succeeds in preserving. Whether violations of collective interests can be convincingly explained in terms of shared individual (negative) rights can be left open here.

[16] In this vein, see Wohlers 2000: 61–109. In general, for a critique of the decontextualised approaches to the limits of criminal law, see Farmer 2016: Chapter 1.

law – i.e. civil law and public law – that defines the spheres of freedom of citizens, via appeal to rights.[17] In other words, the non-criminal law defines the spheres of liberty through rights (rights that regulate life in society, these rights existing *prior* to the criminal law). The role of the criminal law is merely to *protect* these pre-existing rights; it does not *create* them (Haas 2002: 55). According to that view, criminal wrongdoing presents a double dimension: in its horizontal dimension, it represents a violation of the right as interference in a protected sphere of liberty of one citizen. In its vertical dimension, it means a violation of the conduct rule enacted by the state in an attempt to prevent the interference in others' spheres of liberty.[18] According to Renzikowski, this applies both to crimes against individuals and to victimless crimes. In the latter, it would be the collectivity represented by the state that holds the right violated by the offender (Renzikowski 2020: para 13).

From this conception of criminal law, limits on criminalisation can be derived. The rights principle, as Philipp Hirsch points out (2021: 215), is a negative principle of criminalisation:[19] although it does not offer criteria on what should be criminalised, it does exclude the possibility of criminalising those behaviours that do not violate rights. First, since there is no legal claim or right to the imposition of a moral standard or taboo, criminal law ought not to be used to restrain conducts eroding morality. Second, those collective interests that cannot be reconstructed as rights of the collectivity should not be criminalised. If there is no right to a feeling of security, it is wrong to criminalise such conduct that only erodes that general feeling of security (Hirsch 2021: 217). Third, by defining criminal wrongdoing as an individual rights violation that involves an attack against the status of the other as a legal subject, some proponents of this conception, such as Hirsch, in line with the Kantian-inspired theory of criminal law, further aim to reduce criminalisation to conduct committed with intent or deliberate recklessness. Inadvertent (unconscious) negligence, therefore, would not constitute a wrongdoing deserving punishment (Hirsch 2021: 217).

In my view, the theory of the ancillary nature of criminal law suffers from two major drawbacks if it is to be understood as a thick theory of criminalisation. The first involves its indeterminacy: even if it is accepted that criminal law should only protect rights founded in other branches of law, the identification of such rights is deeply controversial (Hörnle 2014a: 182). Even if the existence of a right can be indisputably assessed, the main question for any thick theory of criminalisation, as Renzikowski himself admits (Renzikowski 2020: para 18), remains unanswered, i.e. against what kind of attacks the right must be protected by punishment.

[17] The question of whether the primary legal system merely gives legal validity to pre-positive rights or whether these rights come into being at the very moment they are legally regulated can be left aside. For discussion, see Günther 2000: 491.

[18] Haas 2002: 105; Renzikowski 2007: 563–66. For a case against such a dual approach to criminal wrongdoing, see Hirsch 2021: 107–31.

[19] On the difference between negative and positive principles of criminalisation, see Duff 2018: 235–37.

In short, even on the basis of legal rights, it is impossible to determine, all things considered, the object of criminalisation without further normative judgments.

The second drawback is that, unlike Naucke's approach, since the criminalisation of conduct against collective interests could be criminalised as a collective rights violation, it is doubtful that the ancillary approach can effectively limit the expansion of modern criminal law.[20] Clarity about which collective or shared interests deserve criminal protection and which do not is of fundamental importance, and the ancillary approach does not offer the expected answer. In short, this approach is far from offering a thick substantive principle of criminalisation, because it does not offer sufficient criteria to delimit the circle of protectable collective interests.

2.3. Protecting Constitutionally Derived Rights

Finally, the third approach I will consider claims that the constitution is the source from which to derive the rights that the criminal law should protect. From the constitutional texts, it should be possible to excerpt valid reasons for and against criminalising certain conduct. This could be done either based on general clauses that make explicit which conduct should be banned,[21] or directly through the catalogues of basic rights that the state must protect.[22] Furthermore, it is commonly accepted that constitutional texts and treaties entrench some obligations regarding what has to constitute a criminal conduct. The constitution (or the ECHR), thus, not only tells us which rights *can* be protected by the criminal law, but also which rights *must* necessarily be protected through criminal punishment.[23] From here, the discussion focuses on whether victims have a right to have certain acts criminalised 'on the books' and then prosecuted, or whether the right extends to having the perpetrator effectively punished.[24]

The search in the constitution for a closed catalogue of conducts that the criminal law should protect has also been undertaken by some advocates of the theory of *Rechtsgut*[25] or, in the Anglo-American debate, of the harm

[20] On the legitimacy problems posed by modern criminal law (abstract endangerment offences, cumulative offences …), essential reading is Silva Sánchez 2008a.

[21] In Germany, see e.g. Hörnle 2005: 65–78; Wrage 2009: 370–74.

[22] See e.g. Altenhain 2002: 295–99; Nuotio 2010: 253.

[23] See Lazarus 2013. On the philosophical discussion defending a (constitutionally entrenched) duty to criminalise violations of rights to life and liberty, see Harel 2015.

[24] For discussion, see e.g. Silva Sánchez 2008b; and Hörnle 2019a: 218–19, who claims that individuals whose rights have been violated have a right against the state to obtain a statement about the wrong in the form of a criminal court's condemnatory message. See also in this volume Abraham, Chapter 11: 198–199.

[25] The radical thesis, paradigmatically sustained by the Italian legal criminal law scholar Bricola 1974, argues that only that value is criminalisable that is implicitly or explicitly included in the constitution. This is supposed to operate as a positive, thick, categorical principle for criminalisation. The most widespread thesis, however, simply seeks to constitutionalise the debate on the legal good, looking to the constitutional text as an anchor for the classic supra-positive criminalisation discussions. See e.g. Nuotio 2010: 252.

principle.[26] For the purposes that interest us here, the advantages of a theory of criminalisation anchored in constitutional texts are the same, regardless of whether 'rights' or '*Rechtsgüter*' are sought. First, the vagueness of constitutional texts makes it possible to elaborate a theory of criminalisation that is more flexible than the ancillary approach, without being fully exposed to the epistemological and authoritative problems inherent in supra-positive theories. Second, a theory of criminalisation based on constitutional texts has restrictive force: to the extent that declaring the unconstitutionality of a criminal statute implies its nullification, that is, it ceases to be (never was) valid law, it is a theory of criminalisation with capacity to bind legislatures (Wrage 2009: 372–73). Third, a recourse to constitutional texts of liberal inspiration also makes it possible to derive an essentially liberal theory of criminalisation: since only rights deriving from the constitution can be criminally protected, neither mere immoralities, nor taboos, nor mere feelings (of insecurity), or collectivist values are objects of legitimate criminalisation.[27]

Despite all of the above, the search in the constitution or treaties for a closed catalogue of rights that fixes criminalisation is unpersuasive. Andreas von Hirsch has argued that such a theory does not allow for discussions from the perspective of transnational criminal law theory,[28] which is true and applies to any positivist approach to a theory of criminalisation. However, there are two other main objections that are worth highlighting here. First, constitutional texts and, in particular, the catalogues of fundamental rights, are profoundly vague and indeterminate, making it chimerical to extract clear guidelines for criminalisation from them.[29] For example, whether a constitution recognises the right to property has little bearing on whether we should criminalise the illegal occupation of empty or abandoned property.

Second, the search for a closed catalogue of rights that could or must be protected by the criminal law confuses two different levels, that is, that of the constitutionality of a criminal statute law and that of its substantive legitimacy. The aim of a theory of criminalisation cannot only be to inform about which criminal statute laws are constitutionally acceptable – which is what constitutional theory deals with – but it must go beyond that. It is a matter of providing the legislator with the reasons for or against the criminalisation of a certain type of conduct. In other words, not every behaviour that can be criminalised according to the constitution should be criminalised.[30] The attempt to present substantive theories of criminalisation as constitutionally imposed, as some supporters of the theory of *Rechtsgüter* have done,[31] is therefore profoundly disturbing.

[26] On the relevance of the harm principle in constitutional judgments, see e.g. Berger 2014: 433.
[27] In that vein, see Hörnle 2005: 72–88, 108–15, 483; Wrage 2009: 374.
[28] Simester/von Hirsch 2014: 134; von Hirsch 2008a: 926.
[29] In this vein, see Jareborg 2005: 522–23.
[30] Hörnle 2014b: 685: 'Constitutional analysis cannot do the whole work.'
[31] See e.g. Bottke 2003: 488. See also Wrage 2009: 370–77, who tries to 'constitutionalise' a criminalisation principle based on the notions of autonomy and dignity. A critique of these approaches can be found in Stuckenberg 2013: 35–39; Du Bois-Pedain 2004: 322; Lagodny 2011; and Engländer 2015.

3. Towards a Thin Rights Theory of Criminalisation

As I have argued in the previous section, rights-based theories of criminalisation either do not pretend or fail to offer a thick theory of criminalisation based on the violation of rights. Nevertheless, this does not mean that we should entirely abandon the notion of rights violations in the discussion of criminalisation. As I will show, the violation of rights is an appropriate starting point for the construction of a liberal theory of criminalisation. To that end, however, it is essential to abandon Naucke's pretence of offering a substantive thick theory and to assume – following Antony Duff – that the most to which we criminal law scholars can aspire is to offer a somewhat more modest (thin) theory – one that is able at most to guide the way of thinking and debating about criminalisation.

3.1. The Liberality of the Violation of Others' Rights Approach

Mainstream criminalisation theories based on the notion of legal good (or harm) and those based on legal moralism have an essentially collectivist inclination.[32] The state avoids harms and protects goods that it recognises to be valuable to maximise the sum of those goods from a holistic perspective, and it protects a moral or civic order that is supposedly valuable for a peaceful and flourishing community. In fact, as Knut Amelung shows (Amelung 1972: 43–51), the concept of *Rechtsgut* was introduced in the nineteenth century as a theoretical tool to overcome the prevailing restrictive rights approach defended by Feuerbach in order to criminalise some acts against the conventional morality. Surely, there are liberal-orientated interpretations of the concept of legal harms and legal goods (see e.g. Peršak 2007). In fact, the harm principle should be one of the two considerations that a liberal state should have in mind when criminalising a certain conduct, according to Joel Feinberg's well-known criminalisation account (Feinberg 1984: Chs. 1 and 3). However, not even those *liberal* interpretations can fully capture the notion of persons having rights. The main objective is still the avoidance of damage to a physical entity that has a positive value in the eyes of the state.

Conversely, taking individual rights as the main object to be protected by the criminal law automatically means placing the citizen at the centre of the debate on criminalisation – as an autonomous agent capable of sovereignly deciding how to conduct his or her life, i.e. deciding what is right and wrong for him- or herself and doing what he or she believes to be right even when this is adverse to a legal interest.[33] Or, as Tom Campbell states, 'rights are attractive because they express the great moral significance of every individual human being. A society

[32] See e.g. Dan-Cohen 2006/2007: 2420–21; Hörnle 2014a: 169–70 and Chapter 5: 97–98 in this volume; and Renzikowski, Chapter 13: 234–237 in this volume.

[33] In a similar vein, see also Moser 2020: 60.

that is based on rights is believed to manifest and affirm the dignity of each and every human life as something that is deserving of the highest respect'. (Campbell 2006: 3). Meir Dan-Cohen also points in the same direction, arguing against the harm principle when he states that: 'The distinguishing characteristic of criminal offenses is not the harmful end result, but the fact that the result is brought about through intentional human agency, since only such agency can convey a proper, respectful, or improper, disrespectful, attitude to people and is therefore the appropriate object of moral concerns' (Dan-Cohen 2006/2007: 2424). Dietmar von der Pfordten defends a convincing view of this personal-centred approach to the legitimacy of norms under the label of 'normative individualism'.[34] According to von der Pfordten, 'normative individualism' can be specified by three sub-principles: (a) the principle of individuality: only individuals are ultimately to be considered, (b) the all-principle: all affected individuals are to be considered, and (c) the equality-principle: all affected individuals ought to be considered equally.

This individualistic and anthropocentric understanding of the object of protection of the criminal law is not only fundamental to politically legitimise state coercion, but is also characteristic of modern Western constitutions, all of which are based on the notion of individual rights (Hörnle 2014a: 170). Here, I do not try to justify the liberal thesis.[35] For the purposes of this chapter, it is sufficient to note that if we want a criminal law in accordance with the dominant philosophical liberalism and Western constitutions, there is no better starting point than the logic of individual rights.

Moreover, the individualistic perspective of rights offers a good parameter for restricting the scope of modern criminal law, i.e. to keep it from constantly expanding. Whoever assumes the violation of individual rights as a starting point when discussing criminalisation cannot feel comfortable with criminalising any legal infraction or any distortion of a diffuse social institution. Contra Vincent Chiao,[36] criminalisable conduct – that is, conduct that is susceptible to being responded to by the state with censure and hard treatment – must present some dimension of direct or indirect injury to an individual right.[37] The further we move away from the direct violation of an individual right, the greater must be our reluctance to criminalise such conduct. The protection of (public) institutions, in general, is something that should be achieved with regulatory sanctioning law, but not with criminal law.[38] From this point of view, of course, many of the new crimes against collective interests come to be viewed with suspicion. The goal is not to limit the scope of the criminal law to the injury of purely individual interests, but to force

[34] For a case of 'normative individualism' see von der Pfordten 2012, 2010: 23–27.

[35] For a strong case of a liberal rights-based approach to criminal law, see e.g. Murphy 1973.

[36] Chiao 2019: Chapter 5. In a similar vein, see Kubiciel 2018: 176.

[37] See also Silva Sánchez 2008a: 165–82.

[38] For a compelling case against the reduction of criminal law to just another public policy and against its use to protect public institutions or public procedures, see Silva Sánchez 2008a; 2023.

us to think carefully about how conduct against a collective interest affects private citizens as rights-holders.[39]

3.2. Features of a Theory of Criminalisation Based on the Violation of Individual Rights

Anyone who accepts that a theory of criminalisation must respond to a liberal logic will wonder how such a theory could be developed without incurring the defects attributed above to the classic thick theories based on the violation of the rights of others. Here, I will content myself with outlining the five essential features on which to build such a theory of criminalisation. I recognise that there is still a lot of work to be done and that here I am simply outlining some under-developed arguments on how such a theory should look. A theory of criminalisation based on the violation of others' rights must (a) be constructed on a rather thin principle, (b) be supra-positive in nature, (c) take as its reference point a far-reaching concept of rights, (d) operate as a *pro tanto* parameter, and (e) be built around one single principle of criminalisation (i.e. a monist rather than pluralist theory).

3.2.1. A Thin Principle of Criminalisation

I agree with Duff that it is impossible to offer a thick substantive theory of criminalisation test capable of delivering satisfactory results by limiting to zero the margin of normative discussion for its application.[40] The question of criminalisation in a Western (moral pluralist) society is far too complex to reduce the debate to an exact formula. This, however, does not mean that all reflection on criminalisation by criminal law scholars is superfluous.[41] Virtue lies in the middle ground. A theory of criminalisation can still aim, in the context of contemporary pluralistic societies, to offer a thin principle of criminalisation, i.e. a principle that guides the way to deliberating about criminalisation while leaving space for its application for further normative judgments.[42] As Hörnle states, 'Legal theorists should not expect to have considerable influence on lawmaking, [but they should] provide rational, coherent, and principled arguments, arguments which are (or should be) necessary in the deliberative stages that precede the casting of ballots in parliament' (Hörnle 2014b: 700).

[39] This thesis is not at all new, since it has been presented in the continental world by the so-called defenders of the personal concept of legal good. Essential reading is Hassemer 1973; Hassemer/Neumann 2017: paras 131–48. In a similar vein, see Peršak 2007: 130–31.

[40] Duff 2018: 262–76. For a non-persuasive case for a thick substantive theory, see Wrage 2009: 377.

[41] For discussion, see Dworkin 2011; Husak 2023: 1–6; Kleinig 2008: 21–22. I develop an extensive critique against the thesis that denies the desirability of developing substantive theories of criminalisation in Coca-Vila 2023.

[42] In depth see Coca-Vila 2023: 100–06.

In my view, the theory of rights violation ought to be understood as a (moderately) thin theory of criminalisation: we have reason to criminalise a conduct if it constitutes a violation of individual rights. Obviously, a thin theory of criminalisation such as this one is far from offering decisive answers to all questions about criminalisation. Unlike the approach advocated by Naucke, such a theory leaves the substantive normative task to be done in working out which conduct should be seen as infringing rights, and what kind of rights violations deserve to be criminalised. However, that does not mean that this principle of criminalisation is superfluous. As Duff points out, a thin principle, even if it does not provide substantive criteria, can show what kinds of criteria will be relevant (Duff 2018, p. 254). In particular, a thin theory of criminalisation based on individual rights violations ensures that the conduct to be criminalised affects the protected freedom of an individual, as the fundamental point of reference in a liberal state. Unlike the radically thin master principle presented by Duff (2018, Ch 4), the rights-centred approach is only a moderately thin principle: although it does not eliminate the normative discussion for its application, it does delimit it in a non-deniable form.

3.2.2. A Supra-Positive Principle of Criminalisation

The violation of others' rights theory of criminalisation must adopt a supra-positivist (normative) perspective. Since the aim is to provide arguments to legislatures to assist them in deciding what to criminalise and what not, there is no reason to limit the scope of rights that can be protected by the criminal law to those already recognised in other branches of law (civil or administrative law) or in constitutional texts. Clearly, a persuasive theory of criminalisation will avoid making overtly unconstitutional proposals and will seek to build bridges with constitutional doctrine. This, however, does not force us to reduce the catalogue of rights to those specifically contained in the constitution. Its abstraction and vagueness, added to the deference of the constitutional courts to the legislator, allows a very broad space for play within the framework of the constitution.[43] Criminal law scholars, instead of hiding behind the constitution, must be able to offer good legal or philosophical reasons to specify the kind of legal (not necessarily positivised) rights that should be protected.[44] In short, it is necessary to find 'arguments in a pre-positivistic stage that are, however, embedded in the framework of considerations what the law has to achieve' (Hörnle 2014a: 178).

Against the supra-positive approach to the theory of criminalisation, it cannot be argued that criminal law scholars undemocratically arrogate to themselves a

[43] On the deficiencies of (German) constitutional control as a way of limiting criminalisation, see e.g. Du Bois-Pedain 2004: 310–314.

[44] On the difference between moral rights, pre-positivistic legal rights, and positivistic legal rights, see Hörnle 2004: 178.

function that belongs to legislatures.[45] No one claims that legal scholars have the power to criminalise conduct or to bind the democratic legislature by pointing out pre-constitutional theories. It is not a question of parliament being bound by expert opinion. It is, as Jesús-María Silva Sánchez points out, about parliament being able to rely in its deliberations on expert opinions about what should be criminalised and what should not (see Silva Sánchez 2018: 29–39). Therefore, what a normative theory of criminalisation aims to offer legislatures are rational *prima facie* grounds for or against criminalising certain types of conduct.[46] Understanding criminalisation as a pure act of authority (majority rule) free from any substantive debate and value judgments may be an accurate description of some contemporary pathological criminalisation processes, but it does not at all represent the ideal of democracy and (criminal) law to which we should aspire.[47]

3.2.3. A Far-Reaching Concept of Rights

To outline a thin theory of criminalisation based on the notion of rights violations, it is essential to clarify what we mean by 'rights'. However, I do not intend to offer a detailed analytical definition of rights here,[48] nor to address the classic discussion between the two main theories, i.e. the so-called interest or beneficiary theories and the will theory of rights.[49] Although I endorse the will theory – that is, the theory that sees the meaning of rights in respecting, protecting, and enforcing the autonomous will of the rights-holder[50] – in what follows I am primarily interested in dealing with the scope of the concept of rights from a strictly philosophical–political perspective.

Once we have abandoned a positivist approach to the notion of rights, it is clear that a theory of criminalisation based on the notion of rights requires a commitment to some underlying moral, philosophical, or legal foundation.[51] Among the proponents of the theory of rights, it is common to reduce the circle of rights that can be protected by the criminal law to the so-called negative or Kantian rights.[52] Criminalisable conduct would only be that which involves an interference in the legal sphere of an individual detrimental to the classic liberal (negative) freedoms (life, private property, freedom from violent crime, protection against being defrauded, etc.). It is only in connection with these negative freedoms that we can

[45] In depth see Coca-Vila 2023: 100–06.
[46] In this vein, see Hörnle 2014b: 684.
[47] For a case against the anti-democratic critique, see Coca-Vila 2023: 100–04; Silva Sánchez 2018: 29–39. Also see Moore 2014: 184: the procedural approach to criminalisation 'both overvalues democracy and undervalues a sense of restraint that even the most ardent democrats should feel'.
[48] See e.g. Kramer/Simmonds/Steiner 1998; Moser 2020: 55–60.
[49] For discussion, see e.g. Arel 2005: 193–97; Edmundson 2012: Chapter 7; Stewart 2012.
[50] For a case for a normative account of the will theory of rights, see Moser 2020: 56–60.
[51] For discussion on the different political approaches to rights, see Campbell 2006: Chapter 4.
[52] See Naucke 1993. In a similar vein, see Hörnle 2014a: 181–84; Moser 2020: 60.

properly speak of rights, since only here can we identify a specific rights-holder (the victim) who exercises control over the corresponding duty.[53]

What kind of freedom the criminal law should protect is another fundamental question that I cannot answer in depth here. Thus, I shall content myself with arguing that, to shape a theory of criminalisation, it is preferable to assume a broad concept of individual rights that also encompasses the positive dimensions of freedom. In other words, the concept of rights must encompass both negative and positive rights.[54] By positive (or welfare) rights, I mean those that individuals have against the state to receive a benefit that is fundamental for them to be able to really live as normative agents, choosing autonomously and freely, pursuing their own conceptions of worthwhile lives.[55] In short, the freedom that contemporary (criminal) law must provide is somewhat more complex than the strictly negative Kantian freedom.[56] Thus, for example, from the positive right to health care of every citizen derives the possibility of criminalising tax evasion. The fact that the duty to pay taxes is not directly correlated with a specific right to benefit from it does not prevent this type of individual right from being protected by the criminal law. Likewise, the criminalisation of certain omissions to effect (an easy) rescue is also legitimate, inasmuch as it constitutes a grave violation of a positive right of the imperiled person. Opening the object of protection to positive rights, whose foundation and scope is highly controversial, makes it more difficult to determine the realm of what can be criminalised. This, however, is not a decisive objection once the thin nature of the proposed theory of criminalisation has been conceded.

3.2.4. *A Pro Tanto Reason for Criminalisation*

From my point of view, the rights of others principle should not be understood as a categorical one, i.e. it is not a principle that tells us what must or must not be criminalised without room for reasons for and against. Instead, it should be understood as a *pro tanto* principle of criminalisation. A *pro tanto* principle only informs us about what constitutes good reasons for criminalising certain conduct,[57] but leaves room for good reasons to refrain from doing so. There can be, all things considered, (side-constraint) reasons for refraining from criminalising certain conduct even if it violates a right.

Surely, certain violations of basic (negative) rights offer very powerful reasons for criminalisation; think, for example, of the malicious violation of a child's right

[53] Moser 2020: 60. See also Renzikowski, ch 13: 238–239 in this volume.

[54] In fact, this thesis is not in its practical conclusions contrary to what is held by the contemporary advocates of the strictly negative concept of rights, who resort to other principles of criminalisation to give protection to the violation of positive rights. See e.g. Hörnle 2014a; 2014b; Moser 2020: 60–1.

[55] In a similar vein, see e.g. Fredman 2008: Chs 1 and 3; Griffin 2008: 180.

[56] For discussion, see e.g. Coca-Vila 2016: 248–75; Günther 2016.

[57] On this dichotomy, see Duff 2018: 249.

to life.[58] The criminalisation of this type of conduct may even be constitutionally mandatory by virtue of the doctrine of positive obligations to criminalise developed by the ECtHR.[59] However, the fact that certain conduct is almost universally regarded as deserving of punishment does not imply that a normative theory of criminalisation must operate categorically.[60] In fact, there can be, in a specific case, strong reasons that speak against the criminalisation of conduct that violates others' rights: the minor violation of the right, the purely private nature of the right's infringement, the possibility of resorting to non-criminal sanctions, the costs of law enforcement, etc.[61] Even in the face of violations of the most basic negative rights, we should approach punishment with suspicion and emphasise the exceptional character of criminal law.[62]

Therefore, contrary to AP Simester and von Hirsch's argument, a theory of criminalisation based on the notion of rights in no way requires criminalisation of every infringement of a right, constricting 'the moral space within which to account for mediating factors that should constrain the criminalisation decision' (Simester/von Hirsch 2014: 136). The question is whether the violation of the right is a categorical or *pro tanto* reason. I believe the second option is the right one. The identification of the right to be protected is just as important as examining the appropriateness of effectively criminalising its violation.

3.2.5. Rights Violation as a Unique Principle of Criminalisation

A pluralistic theory of criminalisation assumes that two or more principles determine what should and should not be criminalised. Hörnle is a well-known advocate of a pluralistic theory of criminalisation,[63] based on two principles: the violation of rights of individual persons, and the endangerment of collective interests. In fact, Hörnle develops two different theories of criminalisation, each based on partially different logics. For example, while the criminal law would have a categorical and responsive function in the face of violations of basic rights, it would have an essentially preventive function in the face of endangerment of interests, the endangerment being merely a *pro tanto* criminalisation ground (Hörnle 2019a: 213–18).

[58] For a republican defence of the duty to criminalise, see Harel 2015: the state has a duty to criminalise violations of basic rights to life and liberty and this duty ought to be constitutionally entrenched.

[59] For discussion, see Malby 2019: Chapter 6; Lazarus 2013.

[60] For a different opinion, see Hörnle 2019a: criminal law must be categorical when it deals with violent attacks against the most important rights to non-intervention. Beyond the core, a right is only a *pro tanto* reason to criminalise behaviour.

[61] On the different ways (and reasons in favour) of responding to a public wrong, see e.g. Duff 2018: 280–92. For discussion on relevant factors in criminalisation other than blameworthiness, see Jareborg 2005: 527–30.

[62] For a defence of the exceptional character of criminal law, see Husak 2005b: 117.

[63] Hörnle (2019a), p. 210; and ch 5 in this volume. In a similar vein, see Moser 2020: 60. See also Stewart 2010, who advocates a pluralistic theory based on the principle of harm and the violation of rights.

This pluralistic approach has two important advantages. First, it is perfectly compatible with contemporary criminal law because, by going beyond the violation of personal rights, it makes it possible to legitimise the multiple offences of endangerment existing in Western criminal systems. Second, at least as far as the criminalisation of the violation of personal rights is concerned, Hörnle's approach makes it possible to hold on to a strict concept of rights. In other words, since the criminalisation of, for example, tax fraud does not have to respond to the logic of rights, Hörnle does not have to force the idea of a right abandoning the conceptual requirement of a specific rights-holder in order to criminalise certain forms of tax evasion. As Elias Moser points out, the 'duty to pay taxes does not correlate directly with a right to benefit from it', but this is irrelevant because the tax offence does not sanction the infringement of any right (Moser 2020: 60).

However, there are also strong reasons to prefer a monistic theory of criminalisation based on the idea of the individual rights infringement. In fact, I believe that we must pay the price of assuming a broad or improper concept of rights. The object of criminalisation should not only be those rights that have a concrete, identifiable rights-holder (Moser 2020: 60), but also the violation of positive or participation rights. To the extent that there is a right, for example, to have the state provide certain public assistances, a tax offence can be criminalised as an infringement of this right of a plurality of beneficiaries to benefit from governmental expenses. I do not think that the main reason in favour of a monist theory is purely aesthetic; it is not just a matter of offering a homogeneous and well-rounded theory of criminalisation.[64] A pluralist theory loses restrictive force insofar as it multiplies the principles of criminalisation to accommodate to existing law. Only by passing all acts of criminalisation through the individualistic filter of rights infringements can the theory be expected to deploy a certain restrictive force. Where the act to be criminalised cannot in any way be seen as a form of infringement of citizens' individual rights, the legislator should avoid resorting to the criminal law. This, however, does not detract from the usefulness of developing further derivative or non-foundation principles.[65] It certainly makes sense to compartmentalise discussions on the criminalisation of positive rights and negative rights, as long as one does not lose sight of the fact that the central point of reference for criminalisation in a liberal state is the individual rights as the foundational principle from which deliberations about criminalisation are to begin.[66]

Against my approach, it might be argued that it makes no sense to blur the notion of rights in order to redirect the whole theory of criminalisation to a single principle; this objection has some truth in it. However, I am convinced that the mere fact of being forced to consider every act of criminalisation from the individualistic perspective of personal rights – even accepting the criminalisation of positive rights – is a better way of dealing with questions of criminalisation than

[64] However, see Hörnle 2019a: 211 and ch 5: 89 in this volume.
[65] In that vein, see Hörnle 2019a: 216–19.
[66] Also defending a monist approach, see e.g. Duff 2018: 234.

that proposed by pluralist theories. At the very least, we aspire to develop a theory capable of limit the expansion of criminal law. It is the tension of having to legitimise criminalisation on the basis of the interests condensed in a personal (moral) right that endows the theory of criminalisation with a certain restrictive force. In any case, I recognise that in their consequences a monist and a pluralist theory can be largely coincident. The important question is which positive rights one criminalises and which collective interests the other does.

4. Conclusion

The purpose of this chapter is to explore what rights theory can offer as a principle of criminalisation. Although it is also doomed to failure as a thick theory, I have argued that the violation of individual rights is a good starting point for thinking about criminalisation in liberal states. Having shown that any theory of criminalisation – including one based on the violation of individual rights – must be understood as a thin theory, I have outlined the core features of a thin rights-centred normative theory of criminalisation. In my view, we need to adopt a supra-positive conception of rights, which must also be far-reaching, be understood as a *pro tanto* reason for criminalisation, and be the only principle of a monist theory of criminalisation.

4

Interpersonal Abuse and the Right to Freedom from Domination in Criminal Law

GALIA SCHNEEBAUM*

1. Introduction

The mainstream legal theory of modern criminal law is a liberal theory, which focuses its attention on the individual subject as a bearer of rights, interests, and duties (Lacey 1988). While the individual rights of offenders occupy a dominant role in criminal law theory (as well as criminal doctrine), the place of victims and their rights has become the subject of much debate and controversy in recent decades. The oft-mentioned 'neglect' of victims' rights is heavily discussed in the context of criminal process and punishment (Doak 2005; Katz-Dahan 2022). Yet the difficulty persists in substantive criminal law. Particularly, there seems to be a mismatch between the conceptualisation of criminal wrongs as public wrongs (Blackstone 1796; Marshall et al. 1998: 7) on the one hand; and the acknowledgment that core criminal wrongdoings address individual victims, and involve the violation of individual rights, on the other hand. Certainly, not all criminal offences provoke the same difficulty. Some wrongdoings, often referred to as victimless crimes – bribery, perjury, treason – are all about harm to public interests. Yet other core offences – murder, theft, assault, rape, to name just a few – engage individuals rather than some communal entity, society at large, or indeed 'the public'. If what is at stake, in these offences, is individual rights and/or interests, in what sense do they constitute public wrongs? (Duff 2018: 26; Moser 2019: 182). The complexity is allegedly even weightier, whenever the criminal law vests potential victims with legal power to turn an otherwise lawful act into a crime (i.e. when non-consent by

* I thank Tamara Castiel and Aya Kadur for excellent research assistance. Previous drafts of this chapter have been presented in the Rights in Criminal Law Workshop at the University of Graz (2022); at the Criminal Law Discussion Group, the University of Oxford (2022); at the ICON-S International Annual Conference (2022); and at the Criminal Law Workshop at HUJI (2024). I thank participants in these forums for their helpful feedback.

the victim is recognised as a formal element of the offence) (Hirsch, Chapter 8 in this volume, 2–5).

The purpose of this chapter is not to resolve in any direct or systematic manner the puzzle of reconciling individual rights with criminal law as public law. My aim, rather, is to investigate the display of this conundrum in the context of a defined group of emerging criminal offences – which I refer to as *interpersonal abuse* offences. Rather than a problem to be solved and settled, I consider the principal tension between individual rights and the criminal law as an interpretative tool; A guiding question, that may help to verify the features of a distinct category of criminalisation and illuminate its wrongfulness. Interpersonal abuse offences, I argue, are unique among standard 'offences against the person', as they are not best understood as negative-liberty violations. Therefore, they cannot be analysed within existing, liberal-oriented frameworks that attempt to reconcile the individual autonomy of victims and criminal law as public law (Hirsch 2024: 9–13). Drawing on neo-republican political theory, I suggest that interpersonal abuse should be understood as violating a right to freedom from domination – a wrongdoing that affects individuals but also concerns the public and implicates societal interests. Methodologically this type of inquiry may provide inspiration for future investigations in different fields and diverse subject matters of criminal law – a point I shall return to towards the end of the chapter.

One group of offences I discuss, have been introduced in recent years in the US, Israel, and elsewhere, as a sub-category of sex offences, also known as 'abuse of position', offences. They prohibit abusive sex in a host of hierarchical relationships, such as abuse by police officers, educators, workplace supervisors, healthcare professionals, or the clergy (Green 2020: 165–8; Schneebaum 2015: 350–7). Another field of criminalisation under my inquiry covers non-sexual forms of abuse (including mental and economic abuse) in intimate or in custodial relationships (Schneebaum 2021b). A third area of growing regulation I shall discuss is workplace bullying, also known as moral or psychological harassment. Such regulations prohibit repeated mistreatment of an employee, which often takes the form of verbal abuse or behaviour that is threatening (Namie 2009). While the above-mentioned offences and regulations are usually not discussed together, this chapter points to their common features and addresses the distinct question they raise, in terms of the tension between individual rights and criminal law. The gist of my argument will be that offences of interpersonal abuse are best understood as vindicating a right to freedom from domination, which is distinct in important aspects from a right to individual autonomy. While an autonomy-based theory preserves an image of human beings as essentially free unless episodically coerced, a neo-republican theory acknowledges that, in major social institutions and relationships, people are often vulnerable to domination (Shapiro 2016: 22). Importantly, while a liberal framework tends to portray negative liberty violations in terms of limiting the range of options available to a person (Tadros 2005: 998), wrongful domination implicates being at the mercy of another person or having one's options subject to the authoritarian control of another. I argue that this type of liberty violation implicates public interests beyond the individual right to freedom from domination.

Before diving into the details of the argument, a few remarks on method are due. First, I should clarify what I mean by *drawing on* neo-republican theory. This body of scholarship encompasses an entire domain of writing and writers, among whom exist as many disputes as there are consensuses (Harel 2015: 10). The current chapter does not purport to present the full scope of this literature, but rather to make use of parts of it that are relevant to the issue at hand. Considering this, the version of neo-republican theory presented here may not coincide with some readers' presumptions regarding republican theory. Some readers may assume that the analysis to follow would deal with positive as opposed to negative liberty (Berlin 1969: 118–72), which is the focus of liberal theory. Others may associate Republicanism with civic virtues and political participation. These preconceptions regarding Republicanism are not incorrect. The argument developed below, however, focuses specifically on the concept of freedom from domination, which has been developed in recent decades within a *neo-republican* political theory (Pettit 1997; Skinner 1998). As we shall see, freedom from domination cannot be categorised under the dichotomies of positive versus negative liberty (Pettit 1997: 27) nor the traditional division between the private and the public sphere.

The analysis presented hitherto also differs in important respects from certain Neo-republican accounts of the criminal law, that have gained influence in recent years (Braithewate & Pettit 1992; Dagger 2011; Pettit 2014). While such accounts often make the case for freedom from domination to be recognised as *the* conception of justice underlying criminal law, this chapter presupposes a pluralistic, rather than monistic approach to criminal law theory (Horder 2021: 197). I do not claim that freedom from domination should be viewed as the ultimate protected interest in criminal law, nor that freedom from domination should completely alter the prevailing liberal-oriented conception of autonomy in criminal law. Instead, I discuss freedom from domination in the context of a specific group of offences, for which the liberal notion of autonomy is simply inadequate. Importantly, I do not discuss 'freedom from domination' in an abstract fashion (as is often found in Neo-republican philosophical texts) but rather explore the features of interpersonal abuse as a specific form of violating freedom from domination. I ask what precisely is wrongful about interpersonal abuse, and I argue that this type of wrongdoing is best captured with the help of neo-republican notions and ideas.

Having said that I deal with specific offences, my argument does include some level of generalisation and abstraction. In previous research I have considered some of the offences discussed in this study, separately: the criminalisation of sex in authority relations (Schneebaum 2015); anti-bullying regulation (Schneebaum 2021a); and the criminalisation of non-violent abuse in intimate partner relationships (Schneebaum 2021b). The purpose of this chapter is to induce from these discrete inquiries; to work from the bottom up, to capture mutual conceptual elements. I also aim to transcend national boundaries. Obviously, the offences under inquiry are not found in all jurisdictions. Some of the offences I study are criminalised in Israel[1] and in the US (sexual abuse of position);[2] some are criminalised in England and Wales (mental abuse in intimate partners' relationships),[3] and others in France (workplace bullying).[4] My argument, however, is that these distinct instances share similar conceptual features. The purpose of this chapter is to explore these elements with the help of Neo-republican theory and its conception of freedom as non-domination.

The chapter proceeds as follows. Part I will survey the offences under study and will point to the challenge they pose for a standard liberal theory of criminalisation. Part II will elaborate on the conception of freedom from domination in neo-republican theory. Part III will utilise the legal and philosophical materials presented thus far, to construct an understanding of interpersonal abuse offences as vindicating a right to freedom from domination. Part IV will explore the private and public aspects of the wrong of interpersonal abuse.

1.1. Contemporary Prohibitions against Hierarchical Abuse and Harassment

Scholars who study the theory of 'the special part' of criminal law (Duff et al. 2015, Farmer 2017) have identified, in recent years, several areas of criminalisation for which standard liberal theory is scanty. What I have in mind here are not crits, anti-carceral, or abolitionist scholars, who question the entire project of the criminal justice system. I rather refer to theorists who are generally sympathetic to the project of the criminal law, but nevertheless are critical of the imperialism of mainstream liberal criminalisation theory (Dubber 2018; Loughnan 2019: 6–7). Also, in recent decades, an array of criminalisation initiatives have opted to broaden the scope of criminal law to punish exploitation of the vulnerable. This 'next generation' of criminalisation includes such offences as prohibitions against human trafficking and modern slavery, the criminalisation of sex work clients, and interpersonal abuse offences. While such criminalisation could potentially be justified under an extended meaning of the liberal 'harm principle' (Mill 1859; Feinberg 1984), it essentially challenges the minimalist approach to criminalisation, and arguably contests entrenched ideas about confining the criminal law's scope to preventing negative liberty infringements – coercion rather than exploitation (Green 2007: 96). While the numerous criminalisation initiatives mentioned above may be subsumed under the general title 'defending the vulnerable' or protecting 'lifestyle autonomy' (Horder 2022: 50), this chapter focuses on

[1] E.g. the offence of 'forbidden intercourse despite consent', Israel Penal Code, Art. 346(b).

[2] E.g. the offence of 'sexual exploitation by therapist', North Dakota Code § 12.1-20-06.1.

[3] The offence of 'controlling or coercive behaviour in an intimate or family relationship', Serious Crimes Act 2015, c. 9 § 76.

[4] The offence of 'moral harassment', Article 222-33-2 du Code Penal.

a narrower terrain within this landscape. This terrain – which I title 'interpersonal abuse offences' – includes three sub-categories: sexual abuse of position, workplace bullying, and intimate abuse.

An emerging category of criminal offences in various jurisdictions makes it a crime for a person in a position of authority to have sex with a person under their care/authority. These offences are new to the Common Law (Schneebaum 2015: 346–7; Green 2020: 163). Conceptualising the wrongdoing involved in them has been challenging from the perspective of standard liberal theory. Some portion of abuse of position offences apply only to juvenile victims,[5] which has been easier to justify. However, many abuse-of-position offences address adult victims; they seem to criminalise consensual sex between competent adults (Green 2020: 163). The specific types of authority figures and relationships that are covered under abuse-of-position offences, vary among jurisdictions. In the US the most common relationships covered, are those between law enforcement officials and persons under their control or custody,[6] and between healthcare professionals and patients.[7] In Israel a main category of criminalisation is that between workplace supervisors and subordinate employees.[8] Under Israeli law, moreover, not only are sexual physical acts criminalised, but also verbal sexual harassment. Thus, whenever repeated sexual advances, comments, or suggestions are made towards a subordinate employee by a supervisor, to a student by a teacher, or to a patient by a healthcare professional, the harasser might face criminal charges, punishable by up to two years' imprisonment.[9] Showing the victim's non-consent in these hierarchical settings is, again, not required.

A second type of prohibition which I consider under the interpersonal abuse category, covers *non*-sexual harassment. This type of wrongdoing is also known as moral harassment or workplace bullying. While there is no universally accepted definition for workplace bullying, most definitions refer to it as repeated mistreatment of an employee, often involving psychological abuse, humiliation, or attempts to undermine or sabotage an employee's work (Namie 2009). Typical scenarios

[5] E.g. in the UK, the law proscribes 'abuse of position of trust' when the victim is a child. Sexual Offences Act 2003 ss 16–24.

[6] E.g. Alaska Stat. §11.41.425(a)(2), which prohibits a person who is 'employed in a state correctional facility or other placement designated by the commissioner of corrections for the custody and care of prisoners' to engage in 'sexual penetration with a person who the offender knows is committed to the custody of the Department of Corrections to serve a term of imprisonment or period of temporary commitment'. The current proposal to amend the sexual offences section of the Model Penal Code also includes a provision that prohibits sexual exploitation of people in custodial settings. See ALI Council Tentative Draft No. 6 (Apr. 2022) Section 213.3(2).

[7] E.g. North Dakota Code § 12.1-20-06.1, which prohibits 'Any person who is or who holds oneself out to be a therapist' from intentionally having sexual contact with 'a patient or client during any treatment, consultation, interview, or examination'. The provision further specifies that 'consent by the complainant is not a defense under this section'.

[8] Israel Penal Code, art 346(b). The article proscribes the actor from having intercourse with a woman over the age of 18 within employment supervisory relations 'by exploiting [his/her] authority in employment or in service'.

[9] Prevention of Sexual Harassment Law, art 3(a)(6).

include verbal abuse, excessive monitoring, overly harsh and unjustified criticism, threats, or intimidation (Schneebaum 2021a: 67). In several European countries, workplace bullying is currently actionable as a civil wrong and, in some jurisdictions, it is prohibited as a criminal offence[10] (Lerouge 2010: 129).

A third category of interpersonal abuse offences prohibits psychological or economic abuse in intimate-partner, inter-generational, or guardian relationships. England and Wales have taken the lead in criminalising non-physical intimate-partner abuse, by introducing, in 2015, a novel offence titled 'coercive or controlling behaviour'.[11] It proscribes a person (A) from 'repeatedly or continuously' engaging 'in behaviour towards another person (B) that is controlling or coercive'. The offence applies only if A and B are involved (or have engaged in the past) in an intimate or a family relationship. While the statutory language abstains from defining 'coercive or controlling behaviour', it clearly sets out to capture a unique wrongdoing, dissimilar to the ones recognised for decades by the common law offences of assault and battery (Bettinson et al. 2015: 180). The Home Office Statutory Guidance[12] stipulates that 'controlling behaviour' includes such conduct as:

> controlling or monitoring the victim's daily activities and behaviour, for example making them account for their time, dictating what they can wear, what and when they can eat, when and where they may sleep, who they meet or talk to, where they may work, restricting access to training/development etc … Making and enforcing rules and regulations that the victim is expected to follow and using punishments to make them comply.

England and Wales have also amended and updated in recent years the traditional offence prohibiting child cruelty.[13] The offence of child cruelty applies in guardian relationships – whenever an act of cruelty is committed towards a child by a person aged 16 or over, who has responsibility for a child under that age. In 2015 this offence was amended[14] so as 'to make it absolutely clear (…) that cruelty which causes psychological or physical suffering or injury is covered'[15] and 'the behaviour necessary to establish the ill treatment limb of the offence can be non-physical'.[16] While there may be significant differences between child- and adult abuse, the criminalisation of non-physical abuse in both contexts exceeds the

[10] Article 222-33-2 du Code penal: 'Harassing another person by repeated conduct which is designed to or which leads to a deterioration of his conditions of work liable to harm his rights and his dignity, to damage his physical or mental health or compromise his career prospects is punished by a year's imprisonment and a fine of E 15,000'.

[11] Serious Crimes Act 2015, c. 9 § 76 (UK).

[12] Home Office, Controlling or Coercive Behaviour: Statutory Guidance Framework (2023), www.gov.uk/government/publications/controlling-or-coercive-behaviour-statutory-guidance-framework/controlling-or-coercive-behaviour-statutory-guidance-framework-accessible.

[13] Sec. 1 to the Children and Young Persons Act (1933) ('cruelty to persons under sixteen').

[14] Serious Crimes Act 2015 Sec. 66.

[15] Serious Crimes Act 2015 Fact Sheet: Clarifying and updating the criminal law on child cruelty, www.assets.publishing.service.gov.uk/media/5a80beb9e5274a2e8ab51eaf/Fact_sheet_-_Updating_the_law_on_child_cruelty_-_Act.pdf.

[16] The Code for Crown Prosecutors, Legal Guidance, Child Abuse (Non-Sexual), 16 August 2023, www.cps.gov.uk/legal-guidance/child-abuse-non-sexual.

traditional limits of criminalisation in liberal states. First, psychological abuse does not seem to qualify as 'harm' in the relevant sense to criminal law. Feinberg, for example, distinguished between harm and mere 'hurt feelings' (Feinberg 1984: 86; Brake 2023: 46–7). Moreover, emotional abuse is often perceived as consensual (or not non-consensual) since the victim supposedly *chose* to stay rather than leave, particularly in long-term relationships. Under these assumptions, the criminalisation of emotional abuse might be suspected as a form of paternalism.[17] Finally, prohibitions against mental abuse mostly imply the criminalisation of speech, which is generally disfavoured under liberal regimes.

Cumulatively, the offences mentioned above share important common elements. First, they all presuppose a certain type of relationship between offender and victim, that precedes the criminal act. Mostly, they apply in asymmetrical or hierarchical social relationships. Secondly, the above offences employ similar terminology to denote the legal wrong involved. Either in formal statutory language, or in legal discourse surrounding their enactment and enforcement, the terms 'abuse' or 'harassment' are brought up to describe the wrongdoing. Figuring out the essence of abuse and harassment as a criminal wrong, however, has proven to be challenging from the perspective of conventional criminalisation theory.

At first glance, these offences 'reside' in the chapters of the criminal code that are conceived through the idea of autonomy violation. For example, the mainstream criminalisation theory of sex offences predominantly employs the concept of protecting sexual autonomy (Hörnle 2018: 236–7). This criminal theory draws on a rich philosophical tradition that, as it was applied to criminal law, mainly endorses a 'negative liberty' understanding of autonomy (Green 2020: 24), and considers the criminal law as justified (perhaps even necessary) to prohibit person A from interfering with a person B's choices within a protected sphere of sovereignty (Brudner 2009: 28–9).

Yet interpersonal abuse offences fundamentally misfit the conventions of a liberal conception of criminalisation, and often stretch criminalisation beyond what would normally be acceptable, under a liberal theory. For example, the commonplace assumption that sex offences are intended to protect the right to sexual autonomy (Schulhofer 1998) is seriously contested whenever abuse of position sex offences are concerned, since they do not require non-consent as an element of the offence, and at times explicitly mention that consent shall not be a defence.[18] Additionally, workplace bullying prohibitions criminalise certain speech acts, which is considered contrary to the freedom of expression (Coenen 2017). New offences of intimate partner abuse go beyond physical assault and criminalise 'controlling behaviour' that does not necessarily involve

[17] This argument is admittedly weaker when child abuse is concerned, as children's immaturity requires and even justifies paternalism, hence, the criminalisation of child abuse may be classified as 'soft' rather than 'hard' paternalism (Feinberg 1986a). Yet as elaborated below, due to the hierarchical relationship between parents/guardians and children, I argue that the notion of freedom from domination is much more suited than the conception of negative liberty, to conceptualise the wrong of intergenerational abuse.

[18] North Dakota Code § 12.1-20-06.1.

violence against the body. To be sure, liberals do not focus exclusively on bodily integrity, and may support the criminalisation of certain types of speech (e.g. pornography and hate speech) under the 'offence principle' (Feinberg 1985: 1). Yet the criminalisation of workplace bullying and psychological abuse in the family, are hard to justify under the framework of 'offence', which traditionally focused on speech in the public sphere (Farmer 2011: 282–3), rather than in interpersonal relationships. Finally, many abuse or harassment offences require proof of a pattern of behaviour, repetition, or course of conduct by the offender. This stands in contrast to the conventional liberal-oriented, criminal law jurisprudence, which usually focuses on discrete acts as the *actus reus* of the offence (Kelman 1981: 594).

A possible response to this difficulty would be to preclude the criminalisation of abuse offences (or some portion of them) as exceeding the permissible limits of the criminal law in a liberal state (Green 2020: 175). This chapter advises a different route, namely, to search for a theoretical basis for criminalisation outside the liberal framework. I consider such exodus to be a necessary step in accounting for this emerging criminal category, since, as will be demonstrated shortly, the hierarchical settings within which these offences flourish, and the assumptions they make on human relations within such settings, are simply inconsistent with the liberal paradigm. I consider the Neo-republican framework to be a most relevant source of inspiration in that direction, so I shall turn now to explore its contents.

1.2. The Right to Freedom from Domination

Republican theory has its roots in ancient Greece and Rome, but in recent years it was revived by neo-republican scholars (Lovett 2022: 4). In its contemporary mode, Neo-republican theory positions itself as an alternative to liberal theory, by anchoring its conception of justice on freedom from domination, rather than autonomy or negative liberty (Lovett 2022: 7–8). How is freedom from domination distinct from autonomy? Importantly, the starting point of the Neo-republican conversation is not the assumption of freedom (which occasionally might be disrupted by episodes of coercion), but the reverse assumption of domination – a state of un-freedom that is emblematic rather than exceptional, in certain social arenas. Domination is a type of social power that people hold over other people. To be sure, social power is a broad term (Wrong 1995: 32). Everyone at some point holds power over other people and is probably subjected to the power of others. Yet domination is a distinct type of social power. The master-slave relationship is often mentioned as the most obvious case of domination (Pettit 1997: 31). What is unique about social power in this paradigmatic case? Masters possess almost complete control over what slaves will do and the conditions of their lives (McCammon 2018: 2). Hence, Domination is described in the Neo-republican literature as a power which is in some sense unconstrained, or unchecked. Being dominated entails being subjected to vast discretion, to a capricious will or judgment, or to the arbitrary power of others (Pettit, 1997: 31–2). It is up for masters to decide if, and how they will use their power over slaves (McCammon 2018: 2–3). Hence, it is often said that being a slave entails being at the mercy of another person (Pettit 2014: 137).

To understand how freedom from domination is distinct from autonomy, and how domination is distinct from coercion, requires some elaboration. Under the above characterisation, it might seem as though being subjected to domination, and having one's autonomy violated, are two ways of representing the same evil (Lovett 2022: 7–8). In both the vice seems to involve having one's choices dictated by others. To deal with this difficulty, it has been suggested by some Neo-republicans that, as opposed to violation of autonomy, which requires the actual use of power, domination is concerned with the very potential for use of power. What makes domination unique (the argument goes) is that it denotes being subjected to the *potential* for interference, even if in any given situation force was not actually used and no interference took place (McCammon 2018: 7). This sort of analysis, however, has been heavily criticised by other neo-republicans as over-inclusive. If domination simply marks a capacity for interference, then 'given that such capacities seem ubiquitous, domination may be ordinary to the point of triviality, 'as merely 'sitting around minding their own business, physically strong people have the capacity to overpower weaker people' (McCammon 2018: 10). Specifically in the context of criminal law theory, the above understanding of domination seems unable to account for important differences. If we test the idea of 'potential of power' as opposed to 'actual power' against traditional core criminal offences against the person – such as assault – the potential of use of power as opposed to actual use of power does not seem to capture something significant. Surely, the point of a theory of domination is not to portray the person who merely goes around with a gun (Gädeke 2020: 199) as exercising an offence which is more severe, or even as severe, as a person who points a gun at someone.

Domination, then, is not best captured as any type of potential superiority or impending threat over human beings. More productively, it has been suggested that domination is a form of power that is typical of certain social structures (Thompson 2013: 283–4), wherein power is distributed asymmetrically among hierarchical positions (Hasan 2021: 1–2). It signifies a systematic pattern of power wherein certain people routinely wield power over others, who are regularly subjected to their control. This stands in contrast to situations wherein human beings are occasionally equipped with power over one another, so that A can wield power over B, but B can also wield power over A. Moreover, it has been suggested that domination marks a position of power which is certified by a set of norms or rules that are regarded as legitimate. This trait may be referred to as the normativity of domination (McCammon 2018: 13–5). Those who dominate, never simply exercise their will over others. They are rather vested with an authority to rule (Thompson 2013: 284–6). It is in this sense, that the state of domination is independent of any specified act of coercion, since domination marks the very position of those who are authorised to make decisions for others, to guide, and to issue commands. Pettit's famous discussion of the considerate master effectively illustrates the point (Pettit 1997: 32): a slave is unfree due to the very position of being a slave, even if the master happens to be too respectful to violate his/her freedom through designated acts of interference.

The characteristic of domination as grounded in legitimate norms – the normativity of domination – is crucial to identifying its pervasiveness in contemporary societies. As mentioned above, slavery manifests a paradigmatic historical case of domination. But the question arises as to the contemporary social and political arenas in which speaking of domination is of relevance. The modern revolution in government and politics, particularly within regimes that consider themselves democratic, is often understood as having eradicated the tyrannical institution of slavery and having transformed monarchic or absolutist political regimes. What bearing then, if at all, does an illustration of the master-slave relationship carry to contemporary societies? (Thompson 2013: 281–2).

Neo-republican thinkers presume the danger of domination is very much alive in modern societies. A central field in which they identify domination is the relationship between political government and citizens, including liberal democratic regimes. They conceptualise the power of political government as domination and in fact claim that some of the familiar democratic mechanisms – such as judicial review and other 'checks and balances' – are best understood as (proper) responses to the danger of political domination (Pettit 1997: 206–40). Thus, the separation of powers among distinct branches of government (the legislative, the executive and the judiciary)–which was famously advocated by Montesquieu – is an expression of the neo-republican ideal of freedom from domination, as 'the consolidation of functions in the hands of one person or group would be likely to allow that party to wield more or less arbitrary power over others' (Pettit 1997: 177). Yet, according to Neo-republicans, the problem of domination is not confined to the political sphere. It exists in relationships between individuals and non-governmental social institutions as well (Pettit 1997: 62; Dagger 2011: 47).

A primary issue Neo-republicans address in this context is work relationships (O'Shea 2019, Bogg 2017). On this point, Neo-republicans fundamentally disagree with liberals in their perception of the modern employer-employee relationship. Liberals view slavery as grossly distinct from modern labor relations, the former constitutes hierarchical status relations while the latter are (supposedly) based on 'employment at will' and 'freedom of contract' (Maine 1861; Radin 2007: 196). In contrast, Neo-republicans assert, that while modern work relations originate in contracts, they nevertheless involve a significant measure of domination. Elizabeth Anderson, for example, suggests that modern employers enjoy domination over employees, because they exercise authority that is 'sweeping, arbitrary, and unaccountable,' while employees occupy 'a state of republican unfreedom, their liberties vulnerable to cancellation without justification, notice, process, or appeal' (Anderson 2017: 54, 64). Additional social arenas that have been identified as involving domination by neo-republicans are contemporary health institutions, immigration authorities (McCammon 2018: 31–2), education systems and the modern family (Shapiro 2012: 308).

1.3. Wrongful Domination and Interpersonal Abuse

While all neo-republicans perceive domination as a pressing danger in contemporary societies, they intriguingly diverge on what is wrong about it. To be sure, to speak of domination is to complain about an injustice (Shapiro 2012: 293). But what precisely is wrongful about domination? To an important stream of neo-republican thought, the key to understanding the wrongfulness of domination requires attending, again, to its normativity – the insight that domination always involves power exercised through norms and rules that are regarded as legitimate (McCammon 2018: 24–31; Thompson 2013: 278). While this may appear at first glance paradoxical (if domination is legitimate, how is it problematic?), the legitimacy of domination is crucial to account for its wrongfulness.

Ian Shapiro articulates the relationship between the legitimacy of domination and its potential wrongfulness in a particularly convincing way. Much like Pettit, Shapiro maintains that freedom from domination, as opposed to equality, or negative liberty, is the main conception of justice that should guide political regimes (Shapiro 2012: 294). However, in contrast to Pettit, Shapiro emphasises that power over others, in and of itself, does not constitute an injustice (Davidov 2017: 376). Instead, focus should be placed on instances wherein those in a position of power *abuse* it (Shapiro 2012: 308):

> Our freedom is often curtailed when we are in the power of others, but this is not domination unless that power is somehow abused or pressed into the service of an illegitimate purpose. Children are in the power of parents, students of teachers, workers of employers; in all these cases, their freedom is limited. But we only think of it as domination if those in positions of authority abuse their power in some way, as when an employer or teacher demands sexual favours as a condition for promotion or a good grade.

Shapiro is not a sexual harassment scholar, nor is sexual harassment the focus of the text cited above. Shapiro simply mentions sexual harassment as an example of wrongful domination. Extrapolating from the above passage to a more generic theory of interpersonal abuse, we may conclude that this type of wrongdoing requires two elements. First, it must take place within a relationship of domination – a hierarchical relationship wherein one person holds a legitimate position of power or authority over another. Indeed, offences of interpersonal abuse apply in various hierarchical relationships: employer-employee, teacher-student, parent-child, etc. But hierarchy alone is not sufficient to constitute domination, according to Shapiro. A second required element is that the powerholder needs in some way to abuse his/her power. We need to inquire more thoroughly into the possible manifestations, and the distinct wrongfulness of such abuse of power, in the context of interpersonal abuse offences.

The notion of abuse of power is obviously not alien to criminal lawyers. It is a familiar concept in the context of public corruption offences. As Jeremy Horder observed in a recent book, misconduct in public office is an instance of wrongful domination. Public misconduct offences censure the use of public position by public officials, in Chief Justice Coke's words, 'to do according to their wills and private affections',[19] rather than using their authority to further the public good (Horder 2018: 59). Yet abuses of power by public officials are mostly perceived in terms of their wrongfulness towards public interests. They form an archetypal public wrong. Is this type of conceptualisation apt for offences of interpersonal abuse?

Reviewing the jurisprudence of abuse offences, certain arguments indeed go in that direction. For example, British law seems to have adopted, in recent years, a public conception of sexual abuse of position, prosecuting it as a public misconduct whenever it is perpetrated by public officials (mostly police officers), and conceiving the wrong in terms of harming the proper administration of public office (Green 2020: 170). Yet such accounts seem inadequate to capture the core of the wrongdoing of interpersonal abuse. First, they limit the criminalisation of sexual abuse to positions of public office. However, as described above, offences of interpersonal abuse apply to authority figures in the public as well as the private sphere. More importantly, whenever we consider interpersonal abuse – be it in the public or the private sector, be it sexual or non-sexual – our sense of injustice seems to refer to the human beings involved in the superior-inferior relationship, rather than some public or bureaucratic interest in the 'proper administration of office'. The wrongfulness of workplace sexual harassment, for example, is not exhausted by the fear that professional decisions or roles will be contaminated by the biases of subjective whims and desires. We rather think of the offender as infringing in some sense on the rights of people who are subordinated to him or her. If we consult ordinary language – it reflects and reaffirms the intuition that interpersonal abuse cannot be reduced to a public wrong, serious as it may be. Otherwise, we would not have used the term – as we so often do – to refer directly to an individual victim who *has been abused* by an authority figure.

But what is encapsulated in that statement? What does the judgment 'she/he was abused' morally signify? If it is the right to autonomy which is vindicated through the traditional prohibitions against assault, or rape, what is being vindicated through prohibitions against interpersonal abuse? The standard neo-republican response would be 'the right to freedom from domination'. Yet this response would have to be inferred rather than found in neo-republican political theory, as interpersonal abuse is not the typical wrongdoing they had in mind in contemplating freedom from domination. Moreover, further reflection is required to comprehend what precisely is at

[19] Rooke's Case (1599) 5 Coke Reports 99, at 100.

stake in the violation of freedom from domination through an act of interpersonal abuse.[20]

The following does not purport to provide an exhaustive answer to such an inquiry. But (I hope) it will take us an important step further. I suggest that interpersonal abuse should be understood as a form of authoritarian behaviour within authority relations – conduct which is carried out under the colour of an office, or a role, but nevertheless rejects the very idea that power should be confined to a given sphere of legitimacy. Consequently, it casts subordinates with a heightened sense of submissiveness – an affect[21] that is experienced by individuals and violates their right to freedom from domination. At the same time, this infringement also concerns the public in a distinct way. As will be elaborated below, abuse performed by authority figures disrupts society's ability to preserve vital social institutions as legitimate and functioning.

The most obvious form of such authoritarianism takes place whenever a person in a position of domination explicitly extorts a subordinate for some personal service or benefit, which clearly reside outside the scope of his position or role ('have sex with me or lose your job'; 'have sex with me or you'll be denied medical treatment'). Yet this type of extortionate behaviour is not the most common case of interpersonal abuse or harassment that are currently discussed within criminal law. What is more, criminalising such conduct could probably utilise, or had already been covered by, existing criminal offences such as coercion, extortion, or possibly even rape (having sex under threats could without much stretch be conceived as sexual non-consent under conventional liberal standards). It would not have required the invention of new offences. Moreover, many abusive acts are not extractive in nature – they are not intended to extort any tangible benefit from the subordinate. Hence, they cannot be conceived through the liberal conceptions of autonomy-violation in the sense of transgressing one's sovereignty over body or property (Brudner 1995: 230). The core of the offences discussed in this chapter is abusive, rather than non-consensual sex. It is not the unwanted imposition of some act (either sexual or not), but the exposure to a domineering attitude that is the heart of the wrongdoing.

The domineering attitude the criminal law has in mind here is importantly not limited to an ultra vires type of transgression. Going back to Shapiro's remarks, a case in which promotion was denied due to an employee's refusal to acquiesce with sexual advances by a workplace supervisor, is a clear transgression of the legitimate outlines of the office, and an obvious case of wrongful

[20] Victor Tadros offers a thoughtful conceptualisation of the wrong involved in domestic abuse, based on the notion of freedom from domination. Considering the case of a jealous husband who obsessively monitors his wife, Tadros submits that domestic abuse results in the victims having her options subject to the unwarranted and arbitrary control of another person (Tadros 2005: 996–1002). The account suggested in this chapter is likewise premised on the idea of freedom as non-domination, but unlike Tadros, I emphasise the authoritarianism involved in domestic abuse and its hierarchical nature, rather than its arbitrariness.

[21] For a survey of theories of affect, see Gregg, M. et al. 2010; Rosenberg 2024.

domination. Yet interpersonal abuse stretches beyond this ultra-vires sense of being subjected to the legal decision-power of others. Criminalising abuse is not mainly concerned with reclaiming for subordinates a deserved legal right (such as reinstituting a deserved grade or promotion). It is rather about condemning the power holder for the demonstration of an authoritarian attitude toward subordinates. The criminal law demonstrates here something akin to what Jeremy Horder referred to in another context, as an austere republican approach (Horder 2018: 22), under which what we need to prevent is not only the actual transgression of the permissible outlines of authority by power holders, but also a kind of expressive transgression. The very manifestation of a despotic approach by power holders is wrongful. The criminal law assumes here, that already in being exposed to a quid-pro-quo offer by an officeholder, the subordinate – and perhaps also her fellow subordinates who have witnessed such offers – are offended. Their offence persists even if promotion was ultimately not denied, and even if no sexual contact eventually took place.

1.4. Interpersonal Abuse between Private and Public Wrongs

With the help of Neo-republican insights, we are now able to formulate more clearly the wrong involved in interpersonal abuse along the private/public dichotomy of criminal wrongdoing. As mentioned above, there is an ongoing debate among criminal law theorists regarding the public aspect of criminal wrongdoing (Abraham 2024: 1–2; Hirsch 2024: 9–13). Particularly those who hold non-utilitarian views of criminal law, feel obligated to formulate the contents of criminal wrongdoing in terms that, in one way or another, refer to public interests or values (Thorburn 2014). The demands of such reconstruction have been easier to meet with regards to victimless crimes, which are more readily conceived in terms of disturbing public peace or unsettling civil order (Farmer 2017: 37). Offences involving individual victims have, naturally, been harder to conceptualise in those terms, particularly under a liberal criminalisation theory, which speaks the language of individual rights and liberties. While there have been attempts to conceptualise the public aspect of criminal wrongdoing within an autonomy-based framework (Brudner 1995: 229–30) or a will theory (Hirsch 2024: 2) my attempt here is to discuss a host of wrongdoings that break away from the liberal framework altogether. It is my view that these wrongdoings – which I refer to as interpersonal abuse – carry both private and public aspects that are derived from a neo-republican understanding of freedom. In accordance with my methodology throughout this chapter, I do not rely on some general republican argument regarding the role of the state in guaranteeing freedom from domination (Braithewaite et al. 1990; Pettit 2014; Dagger 2011). My project is interpretative rather than prescriptive: it seeks to uncover the wrongfulness of interpersonal abuse and to show that it has a double meaning – at the level of individual victims, and at the socio-political level.

The neo-republican literature helps us see, first, the individual wrong inflicted on those who are abused by authority figures. Being dominated is depicted in the neo-republican literature as being cowed (Horder 2018: 59), experiencing oneself as pliant and servile (O'Shea 2019: 3), and not being able to walk tall among one's fellows, or to look to powerholders squarely in the eye (Pettit 1997: 71; Horder 2018: 59). Allegedly, the very position of being under the power of others – as is the case with being a pupil, a child, an employee – involves domination. Yet when we move from a philosophical contemplation of 'freedom from domination' to the legal landscape, we see that the law does not condemn domination qua domination. The law is only after instances wherein domination is exercised in an illegitimate manner toward subordinates, turning their experience from being vulnerable to domination, to being consumed in domination. Criminal law does not prevent employers from directing, demanding, or disciplining employees; it does not preclude parents from disciplining children altogether. It rather seeks to condemn the physical and mental abuse of employees/children respectively, since such abuse is clearly not required for legitimate purposes (Pollard 2002); It is rather a manifestation of despotism. In the face of such authoritarianism, subordinates can no longer imagine their freedom outside their positions as subordinates, as the abuser expresses profound disrespect for the confines of his/her own power. Having to put up with such an attitude, deprives subordinates of the possibility of experiencing themselves as un-dominated. Whenever authority takes on the pejorative form of authoritarianism, the criminal law seeks to defend the right of subordinates to freedom from domination.[22]

Authoritarianism embedded in interpersonal abuse also has a significant public aspect. As mentioned above, some forms of abuse of power are par-excellence public wrongs. If we wished to illustrate an overt instance of such public abuse of power involving sex, we would depict a case of sexual bribery – wherein a person holding public office accepts sexual favours from a subordinate citizen, or an employee, in exchange for acting or withholding action as an official. The proper administration of office, which concerns the public, will be harmed by such conduct, as well as the more fluid 'public trust' in government institutions. But this chapter considers instances of abuse of power, in which subordinates come out as victims rather than as accomplices. How is the public implicated in such wrongdoings? Should we think of the public as wronged, in addition to individual victims, in every instance of interpersonal abuse? And if so – in what sense?

The neo-republican understanding of freedom as non-domination should inspire us to acknowledge the public significance of the wrong of interpersonal

[22] I leave for future research the question of whether, on this account, individuals should be viewed as mere beneficiaries of the criminal justice system's duty to protect freedom from domination or should be viewed as holding a more robust right vis-à-vis the state in the criminal law. The main point of the present study is to initially carve out the outlines of the wrong of abuse through a conception of freedom from domination, as opposed to autonomy.

abuse.[23] This public meaning is not limited to abuse perpetrated by public officials. In non-governmental institutions too, the wrongdoing of interpersonal abuse has a societal dimension that goes beyond the harm suffered by individual victims. In fact, the marks of public infringement are prevalent even in the most private arena of abuse – the family. This is so, because interpersonal abuse disrupts society's ability to preserve social institutions of authority as functioning and legitimate.[24]

On this account, the criminalisation of abuse, its condemnation through public enforcement and punishment, is not intended merely to condemn the negative effects of domination, it also aims to uphold authority relations, perceived here as valued social institutions. Under this understanding, authority should not be viewed as a necessary evil that may only be tolerated through its restraint (Luxon 2013: 31–2). It should rather be acknowledged as a valuable social institution, whose contempt through the act of abuse concerns the public beyond those who have been directly affected. Whenever parents or educators abuse children or students, at stake is not only the well-being of those who have been abused, but also institutions of authority. Think, for example, of parental or educational authority which, as Hannah Arendt observed, have always been accepted not only as a natural necessity but also as a 'political necessity, the continuity of an established civilisation which can be assured only if those who are newcomers by birth are guided through a pre-established world into which they are born as strangers' (Arendt [1968] 2006).

This, of course, is not to say that all contemporary criminalisation of interpersonal abuse is justified. The analysis presented here, beyond providing a principal justification for criminalisation, also allows or even requires developing critical tools to differentiate between justified and unjustified criminalisation initiatives, in this emerging field. A full discussion along these lines exceeds the scope of this chapter. To demonstrate its potential briefly, we may consider the question of criminalising intimate partner abuse, as opposed to criminalising intergenerational abuse in the family. If physical violence is involved – no question it should be criminalised in both contexts, but this will have readily been achieved through prosecuting traditional offences such as assault or homicide. Yet such offences do not cover non-physical abuse and are not adapted to consider abuse as a pattern of behaviour or course of conduct. To capture patterns of abuse, including mental or economic abuse, we see the emergence of new criminal offences.

[23] The same structure of argumentation – i.e. that the violation of individual right may also carry a societal/political dimension and hence justifies criminalisation, is present also in core liberal accounts of the criminal law as public law. E.g. Thorburn 2014. Note, however, that the contents of individual and public rights discussed here diverge from the liberal ones.

[24] I realise that in the above articulation of the public dimension of interpersonal abuse, I read into neo-republican accounts meanings that may not have been intended by their original authors. The main difference is that while adherents of the right to freedom from domination tend to stress the danger in power relations, and refer to domination institutions as inherently suspicious, the account presented here stresses also the value of domination – understood as legitimate authority. I thank Leora Katz-Dahan for bringing this different emphasis to my attention.

Among these initiatives, the criminalisation of intimate partner verbal abuse is currently more controversial than the criminalisation of inter-generational psychological abuse.[25] I suggest that a main reason for these disparate moral intuitions, is that while parents possess legal authority over children, husbandly authority over wives is no longer acknowledged as a valid legal institution. Consequently, women are no longer dominated in intimate partner relationships under the conception developed here, and the criminal law should not seek to preserve such relationship as an institution of authority by condemning its contempt (Schneebaum 2021b: 73–79). The authority of parents (or other guardians) over children, on the other hand, is still valued in contemporary society, though we seek to confine it to certain limits and prevent its misuse. Therefore, parents' abuse of children should be criminalised even if it does not involve physical violence.

Of course, liberals too may support the criminalisation of psychological child abuse in the family, for example by extending the meaning of 'harm' under the harm principle, to include psychological harm (Clark Miller 2022; Salzberger 2024). Liberals who support the criminalisation of child abuse may at the same time object to the criminalisation of intimate partner abuse. They might represent the latter as an instance of hard paternalism which violates women's autonomy and diminishes women's agency (Coughlin 1994). One may therefore inquire about the upshot of a neo-republican account vis-à-vis a liberal account, in this context. The point is that, as an essentially relational concept, domination (or freedom from domination) allows for more nuanced distinctions that better fit the social arenas of interpersonal abuse than the liberal framework. While both frameworks may lead to similar conclusions in some cases, they rely on different reasons, and may lead to contrasting conclusions in other cases.

To account for the distinct normative judgments of child abuse v spousal abuse, liberals would have to rely on a non-relational vulnerability appraisal, which tends to presume that children are immature and vulnerable while adults are not (unless they suffer from some severe disability or incapacity). Hence, they would authorise the criminalisation of child abuse and reject the criminalisation of (non-physical) spousal abuse. In contrast, under a neo-republican account, adults too may, under certain circumstances, be vulnerable to domination. On the account presented here, intimate partner abuse does not warrant criminalisation – not because its victims are adults, but because spousal patriarchal authority has ceased to exist as a valid legal institution in contemporary modern societies. Wherein domination, understood here as legitimate authority, is non-existent, the right to freedom from domination is not violated in its so-called 'abuse'. In contrast, sexual harassment in workplace supervisory relationships does merit criminalisation under the analysis presented here, because workplace authority was not abolished as a valid legal institution. Thus, while

[25] For example, while non-physical intimate partner abuse is criminalised in the UK, it is not criminalised in the US. In contrast, both jurisdictions criminalise some version of child cruelty.

virtually no liberal account would permit the criminalisation of (verbal) sexual harassment in the workplace, a neo-republican account would merit such criminalisation in hierarchical workplace settings.

2. Conclusion

To conclude, interpersonal abuse offences provide a unique case study for some of the prominent questions in criminal law theory today. One question concerns the place and role of individual rights within criminal law as a branch of public law, which supposedly deals with public wrongs. The question has become more acute with the so-called privatisation of criminal law, particularly the success of victim rights movements. A second question concerns the dominance of classic-liberal criminalisation theory which revolves around the concept of negative liberty (or autonomy). Neo-republican political theory is a useful source of inspiration to deal with both questions. First, this chapter assumes – together with further republican-inspired accounts (Duff 2018) that all criminal wrongs – even those involving individual victims – should be conceptualised with a conception of the public in mind. To use Antony Duff's language, public wrongs always *concern* the public, otherwise they would not (or should not) be criminalised. Recovering how exactly they concern the public requires a work of interpretation. This chapter postulates that such labor cannot be performed in the abstract. Attempts to come up with a singular, or even several, master-principles of criminalisation have largely failed in recent decades (Duff et al. 2014: 5–6). It is therefore advisable to work within narrower criminal categories and to pay close attention to context (Lacey et al. 2012). This should not drive us to the conclusion that criminal law is always contingent on specific social, cultural, and geographical conditions, or that we should never try to construct any account of criminalisation that exceeds the boundaries of a specific time and place. As this chapter shows, neo-republican theory provides a useful framework to theorise offences across several jurisdictions, that share mutual conceptual elements.

Substantively, neo-republican theory offers fresh perspectives of the individual harm and wrong involved in interpersonal abuse, whereas the appeal to a liberal, autonomy-based, or harm-based conception has failed to satisfy that need. One final lesson of this study is that, whenever we explore the conjunction of individual rights and criminal law, there is no singular, but a plurality of individual rights to be considered. The study of interpersonal abuse offences cannot bear direct lessons or be transplanted as is, in other areas of criminalisation. It is my hope, however, that it may provide inspiration for future studies of criminalisation, whatever their doctrinal context or philosophical stimulation might be.

5

Victims' Rights and Obligations – Why these Concepts Should be Central to the Assessment of Criminal Wrongdoing

TATJANA HÖRNLE

1. Why Focus on Victims' Rights?

I will defend the thesis that victims' rights and obligations should play a more prominent role in criminal law theory in general and, more specifically, in the assessment of events as criminal wrongdoing in individual cases. I will come back to the notion of victims' obligations as a component for the assessment of crimes at the end of this chapter, but most of the discussion will be on victims' rights. The decision to focus on victims' rights means venturing away from well-trodden paths in the German and the Anglo-American traditions. The traditional German approach has been and continues to be decidedly non-individualistic: even in the case of serious crimes against persons (classic mala in se crimes), criminal wrong is *not* defined as something done to the victim (Hirsch 2021: 13–18). Instead, criminal law scholars describe the essence of wrongdoing as conduct that 'harms the validity of norms' (*Normgeltungsschaden*) (Jakobs [2000] 2017; Frisch 2015: 77–85; Pawlik 2017: 29). Others rely on the notion of 'social harm' (*Sozialschädlichkeit*, Roxin and Greco 2020: 316). Criminal law theory in English-speaking countries also shows non-individualistic tendencies, in the tradition of legal moralism, with a focus on violations of moral prohibitions (Moore 1997: 72–72) or on the notion of 'public wrongs' (Duff 2018: 75–101).

Within the Anglo-American discussion, however, there is also a strong individualistic strand: references to the harm principle in the tradition of John Stuart Mill are common (Feinberg 1984; Husak 2008: 65–77; Simester and von Hirsch 2011). According to this approach, the assessment of a specific crime should focus on the harm (or risk of harm) for the individual victim or victims. I share the individualistic starting point that does not conceptualise all criminal wrongs as (potential) damage to the validity of norms or some other not clearly specified 'social' harm.

However, I argue that criminal law theory needs to integrate the notion of rights beyond the notion of harm. Looking for damages, injuries, or suffering – or the risk of such outcomes – is not always the best way to evaluate conduct that involves an attack on another human being. In some cases with individual victims, the judgment need to be 'serious wrongdoing' despite the fact that the victim did not suffer and the act did not cause tangible harm.[1] A different, in my view preferable approach explains the common core of such criminal wrongs as a violation of another person's defensive rights (*Abwehrrechte*).[2] The focus on the notion of rights is an alternative to *both* non-individualistic *and* 'tangible harm/risk of tangible harm' concepts of wrongdoing. This does not mean that judgments about the seriousness of crimes will always be different if the violation of a right is considered to be the essence of wrongdoing. Usually, disregard for another person's defensive rights will *also* result in harm or the concrete risk of being harmed, and the weight of harms or endangerment plays a role at the sentencing stage, when a fine-tuned assessment of a specific event is required. With a rights-based approach, however, harm is not a necessary component of criminal wrongdoing.

The individualistic approach, with its focus on rights, has the advantage of being a 'better fit' with foundational concepts in both political and constitutional theory. Modern constitutions that have been shaped by liberal political philosophy are built around individual rights. This focus on individuals' rights is a characteristic feature of 'normative individualism' (von der Pfordten 2005; von der Pfordten and Kähler, 2014), and it can and should be replicated in criminal law.[3] Choosing this path does not require the existence of written constitutional texts or constitutional courts in systems of positive law. As criminal law theorists, we can assume that the basic idea of normative individualism is well anchored today (not in all, but in many countries). Political theory based on normative individualism provides common ground for transnational criminal law theory.

A move to a stronger focus on victims' rights in criminal law theory requires complex theories of punishment and criminalisation. After all, criminal law in modern societies must also protect indivisible shared goods (such as our physical environment) and genuine collective interests (such as administrations that are free of corruption). Rather than speaking of 'the theory of punishment' and 'the theory of criminalisation' in the singular, the alternative is to develop pluralistic theories: one for crimes that disregard defensive rights of individuals and thus create individual victims, and another set of considerations regarding crimes against collective interests. Criminal law theorists disagree if proposing pluralistic theories is desirable. Alec Walen, in his new book (Walen forthcoming), proposes to distinguish between criminal law and penal law, the latter encompassing

[1] See Gardner and Shute 2000, who make this point for the raping of an unconscious woman and other examples of 'harmless rape'.

[2] Hörnle 2014b; see for the relevance of subjective rights also Hirsch 2021; Coca-Vila, Chapter 3 in this volume.

[3] See for this point also Coca-Vila, Chapter 3 in this volume.

regulatory offences that are unavoidable in modern, highly complex states. Others insist that criminal law theory should be derived from one singular axiom (see Pawlik 2012: 86). Aesthetic reasons might explain a preference for a unified theory and deductive reasoning beginning with only one axiom: describing separate constructions is less satisfying than developing a seamless, holistic theory. This kind of reasoning does, however, not have much convincing force. Mastering complexity is more important than pleasing criminal law theorists' preferences for the beauty of minimalist constructions. Ivó Coca-Vila points out in this volume that there are other reasons to be sceptical of pluralist accounts: opening a second route to justify the criminalisation of conduct might take out some of the critical bite of a rights-based analysis. A plurality of theories for criminalisation gives politicians more opportunities to find a rational explanation for trends that expand the scope of criminal prohibitions. I would respond to this concern that pluralistic does not mean plethoric, or unfettered discretion for law-makers. Rather, the challenge is to pay closer attention to the second strand of criminalisation theory, too, which focuses on collective interests, and to develop criminal policy guidelines for this field as well.

2. Which Rights?

Before discussing in more detail my proposal that victims' rights deserve more attention in criminal law theory, a few words about the basic notion of rights are necessary (see also Coca-Vila, Chapter 3 in this volume). Invoking 'rights' means introducing a highly complex, historically shaped concept (Wenar 2021; Wenar 2005) that can be understood in the sense of natural rights, constitutional rights, or claims of rights. It is not possible to cover these discussions extensively in a sub-section of one chapter, thus, I will only briefly sketch some assumptions. With regard to the idea that rights can be deduced from a theory of natural law, scepticism is in place, particularly if this approach is rooted in the assumption that the way humans organise their coexistence must be shaped by their relation to God (or some other version of higher power). Classical treatises on natural law and natural rights have drawn such connections (Finnis 2011), but legal reasoning should not presuppose religious beliefs that are no longer widely shared. Beyond references to God, proponents of natural law also talk about basic goods that are essential for a good human life (Finnis 2011: 59–89). The problem with such lists of essential goods is that they are described as universally valid and that they are based on a particular version of a good life to be defended against other visions and practices. If this makes sense in moral philosophy, it must be left open here, in any case, it should not be transferred into the field of law. In fragmented societies, law must be pragmatic and realistic and must bridge different conceptions of what various subsets of the population regard as a good life.

A more promising alternative to claims about 'natural rights' focuses on rights granted in constitutions. Some question this approach, arguing, first, that the high status of constitutional rights makes it more difficult to criticise demands for criminalisation (Simester and von Hirsch 2011: 136). The fear is that references to constitutional rights within criminal policy debates would more or less automatically lead to the conclusion that the conduct in question should be made a criminal offence. However, this worry can be attenuated: after all, almost all constitutional rights are subject to a process of balancing against countervailing reasons. Second, Simester and von Hirsch point out that throughout history human rights were rights of human beings against the state.[4] But this is neither state of the art – at least not in German constitutional theory – nor can one develop a plausible portrayal of the modern state on this basis (see Volkmann 2021: 1076–80). Constitutional rights include the right to be protected against the actions of others, and thus the state must also protect human rights against interferences by fellow citizens.

In transnational debates, another obvious objection is that references to constitutional rights might work well in a national legal system such as the German, which has both a written constitution that includes a comprehensive catalogue of fundamental rights and a well-established tradition of constitutional theory and jurisprudence that recognises protective rights. But what if this is not the case? And would we not lose important perspectives if discussions in criminal law theory were restricted to legal scholars who focus solely on their own system of law (Simester and von Hirsch 2011: 134)? I agree that it cannot suffice for criminal law theory to point to national constitutional law, but the conclusion should not be to forego categorically a set of arguments that might actually help convince politicians and lawmakers. If, for instance, there is a rich discussion about privacy rights as constitutional rights, this can be the starting point (not a conclusive argument) for developments in criminal law theory. In addition to national constitutional law as a source of inspiration, guidelines for the protection of rights through criminalisation of conduct can also be derived from international human rights law (Malby 2019).

There are, however, limits to making constitutional references, particularly if a given constitutional text does not contain an extensive list of individual rights. Other obvious sources for identifying individuals' rights are civil law and public law. Ivó Coca-Vila describes this approach with the expression 'Criminal Law as an Ancillary Form of Shielding the Law' (Coca-Vila, Chapter 3 in this volume). In many cases, this will be a promising approach: if the law grants rights, and if these rights serve to protect fundamental interests of human beings, also in their role as citizens, this can be a *pro tanto* reason in favour of criminalisation. However, a simple reference to an existing legal right will not always be a sufficient starting point to argue that it should be protected with the means of the criminal law. The

[4] Simester and von Hirsch 2011: 134; see for a distinction between negative and positive constitutional rights and scepticism regarding positive rights also Currie 1986: 890.

scope of legal rights (*all* legal rights granted somewhere in a legal system) is wide, too wide to give even a *pro tanto* reason for applying the criminal law as a protective shield (Coca-Vila, Chapter 3 in this volume). Another problem can be that neither civil law nor public law do yet acknowledge an individual right despite the fact that the conduct in question might be highly detrimental for individual victims. For instance, this can become relevant if conduct using new technologies or other recently emerged phenomena are discussed as a matter of criminalisation before other legislative projects have been begun or concluded (for example, because debates about the adequate regulation in civil or public law take a long time on the European or other supra-national level). Therefore, it can be necessary and plausible to base a *pro tanto* argument in favour of criminalisation on the claim that a right *should* be acknowledged.[5] The term 'rights claims' means 'should be acknowledged as a right' in contrast to the descriptive statement 'has been acknowledged as a right' in, for instance, constitutional or other laws. Even if one is sceptical about a strong, ontological or quasi-ontological claim that persons *have* certain rights 'just in virtue of being a person' (Stewart 2010: 19), the basic reasoning can be rephrased as 'we should acknowledge mutual rights that we all have as citizens or as human beings'.

Arguments in criminal law theory that are based on a rights claim need a more complex structure than rights already granted in constitutions or other legal documents. Reasons must be given as to why a right not to be treated in a certain way should be acknowledged; in further steps, conclusions must be drawn for the field of criminal law. A plausible rights claim is not sufficient to support the demand for criminalisation. Often, the crucial questions are, first, whether a defensive right really needs to be supported with the expensive and harsh instrument of criminal justice rather than with other measures and, second, whether countervailing rights of other parties or compelling collective interests might topple the initial *pro tanto* argument.

With this very short sketch of rights and rights claims I hope to have made it plausible enough that the concept can be employed in a meaningful way for the purpose of criminal law theory. In order to argue that an individual does have the right not to be treated in a certain way, it can suffice to point to an acknowledged constitutional right or to another source in the legal system that grants individuals an important right. If this is not the case, arguments must be more complex, beginning with arguments in favour of a rights claim.

3. Mapping the Landscape

In treatises on criminal law and criminal law theory, in Germany and elsewhere, rights and obligations of individuals do not play an important role. My plea is to

[5] Hörnle 2014b: 183–85; see for the notion of rights claim in general Zivi 2011.

re-construct criminal law theory on the basis of the concept of victims' rights and (to a lesser degree) victims' obligations, see Section 4.5 below, in all areas that make up the broader field of criminal law theory. These are

- theories of punishment;
- theories of criminalisation;
- criminal law doctrine;
- criminal procedure; and
- sentencing.

3.1. Theories of Punishment

A theory of punishment has to justify the prohibitions (norms of conduct) and the threat of sanctions in criminal laws as well as the practices of criminal proceedings, censure in the form of convictions and criminal punishments. Scholars occasionally discuss victims' rights within the framework of punishment theories (Whiteley 1998; Silva-Sánchez 2008b; Hörnle 2019b). However, most answers to the question 'How can criminal punishment be justified?' focus exclusively on public interests (our shared interest in the prevention of future crimes) (see Roxin and Greco 2020: 151–54), or they dismiss, in the form of pure retributive approaches, the idea that punishment for crime needs any justification at all (Moore 1997: 104–52). Expressive theories of punishment mostly emphasise the belief that the message delivered with a criminal conviction serves to reaffirm 'the validity of norms' (Jakobs [2000] 2017; Frisch 2015: 77–78). My position is that victims of serious crimes have a right to obtain a censuring response from the state[6] and that this must be a central element within a sufficiently complex approach to justify criminal justice systems and the criminal punishment of individual offenders.

Obviously, victims' rights cannot be the only consideration that supports the existence of criminal punishment as an institution. To justify this expensive and intrusive system, public interests should play an important role, too, that is, citizens' shared interests in the prevention of certain conduct. Strengthening the role of victims' rights in punishment theories does not mean excluding the public dimension of criminal law and criminal justice.[7] We share the interest in preventing exploitative behaviour that harms collective achievements and goals, such as tax evasion and corruption, or that endangers natural resources. With regard to conduct which targets individuals, prevention likewise is in our collective interest, as we are all potential victims of future crimes. Environments that are characterised by high levels of violence and other forms of disregard for the rights of others not only have an impact on individual victims but also on everyone who takes

[6] Hörnle 2019b; see for a stronger focus on victims' rights also Hirsch 2021: 228–41.
[7] See, for this conclusion also, Hirsch 2021: 235–236; see Hirsch, Chapter 8 in this volume.

precautions against high risks of victimisation. Also, social cohesion and social solidarity in societies with a high prevalence of serious crimes against persons might well decrease.[8]

The usual framing of discussions about punishment theories as a matter of 'either prevention or retribution' or 'absolute versus relative theories' misses a crucial point – preventive considerations are important, but do not exhaust the reasons that are needed to justify complex practices of prohibiting behaviour, enforcing these prohibitions and acknowledging that individuals' rights have been violated. Criminal law judgments *also* serve important functions for victims of crime. Victims have the right to obtain a judgment, a judgment stating that wrong has been done to them. Public disinterest would imply that the victim was struck by misfortune (rather than another human being's wrongful, rights-violating conduct) or that responsibility lies with the person who wrongly claims to have been a victim.

Emphasising the relevance of criminal law judgments for victims of crimes does not presuppose empirical proof that every crime victim, or at least a majority of them, in fact feels the desire to see offenders punished. In terms of the overall degree of civilisation within societies, it is a good sign if individual victims are willing to accept restorative measures and if they prefer mild rather than hard expressions of disapproval. Emphasising victims' rights does not amount to a demand for severe sentences. The argument, rather, is a normative one that addresses the basic rationale of criminal punishment in contemporary legal systems. Violations of defensive rights should not simply be ignored. Putative victims can demand that state officials, acting on their behalf, examine the possibility of a serious violation of their rights by others and then, once the requisite facts have been established, censure wrongdoing. The German Constitutional Court grants victims the right to have state authorities investigate crimes against life, bodily integrity, liberty, and sexual autonomy as well as crimes that occurred while the victim was in the custody of the state (see Hörnle 2017b: 41–42).

3.2. Theories of Criminalisation

Theories of criminalisation aim to provide a framework for decisions concerning the kinds of conduct that should be criminalised and the kinds that should not. The notion that the rights of individuals should play an important role in this context is as underdeveloped as it is in the field of punishment theories. In the German tradition (see Roxin and Greco 2021: 24–62; Dubber 2005a: 682–96), the general guideline as to what to criminalise focuses on the vague notion of a legal good (*Rechtsgut*). Within this framework, it is common to distinguish between collective legal goods (*Universalrechtsgüter*) and individual legal

[8] See, for the concept of social cohesion, Schiefer and van der Noll 2017.

goods (*Individualrechtsgüter*). The basic underlying idea is not to focus on the relations between individuals and defensive or subjective rights but on the argument that certain goods are valuable and thus should be protected by criminal laws.

In Anglo-American criminal law theory, references to the harm principle are frequent, see Section 1 above. The main reason for evoking the harm principle is to rebut legal moralism, that is, the idea that moral disapproval is a sufficient reason to prohibit conduct. At the same time, however, it is obvious that the detrimental consequences of an act for another human being are not always a sufficient reason for a criminal prohibition. Criminal law theorists thus argue that the harm principle needs to be supplemented with the category 'wrongfulness' (Husak 2008: 65–77; Simester and von Hirsch 2011: 19–32; Tadros 2016). With this move, the main question becomes how to determine whether conduct is wrongful or not. The idea to point to moral wrongfulness again requires connecting legal reasoning with moral arguments. Antony Duff tries to draw some boundaries by insisting that criminal prohibitions should target only public and not private wrongs (Duff 2018: 75–101). I propose keeping more distance from common concepts and relying neither on the notion of *Rechtsgüter* nor on the harm principle filtered by the notion of a public wrong. The alternative is to focus on the violation of individual rights as one major area where strong prima facie reasons support the criminalisation of conduct. Again, this cannot not be the only reason, as collective interests can also be deserving of the protection of criminal laws.[9]

Another clarification might be called for: speaking about victims' rights should not be understood as referring to rights that cannot be subjected to balancing with countervailing reasons. Victims' rights are merely *pro tanto* rights, that is, they must be open to balancing against other considerations and factual constraints. Not even well-funded criminal justice agencies in states with ample financial resources would be able to carefully investigate and assess every case of a rights violation.

3.3. Criminal Law Doctrine

The term 'criminal law doctrine' (*Strafrechtsdogmatik*) is used to describe the rules that govern the assessment of individual cases. In most legal systems, these rules are written down, in part, in criminal codes and criminal laws, complemented by case law and, in the German tradition, by criminal law scholarship as well. The rules of criminal law doctrine determine, for instance, which outcomes will be attributed to which agents and whether a justification is applicable under the circumstances of the case. The suggestion to emphasise victims' rights and obligations in this context might sound peculiar. Victims' rights usually do not play a

[9] Hirsch 2021: 217 uses an extended view of rights, speaking of collective subjective rights as rights of the 'legal community', see also Hirsch, Chapter 8 in this volume.

notable role in standard accounts of national criminal law doctrine in textbooks or case books. They figure in the chapter of textbooks that deals with the relevance of consent as justification of conduct that fulfils the elements of an offence description. However, within criminal law theory (and based on it, criminal law doctrine), the notion of subjective rights and the relational features of the event that is examined as a crime should play a stronger role. Recognising theses relational features is important for defining the boundaries of permissible conduct, see in more detail Section 4 below.

3.4. Criminal Procedure and Sentencing

In the field of criminal procedure theory, it is most obvious that the rights of individuals must play an important role. Defendants' rights – the right to privacy, for instance – can provide protective shields, and intrusive investigative measures must be justified as a proportionate interference with defendants' rights. This point is universally acknowledged, as 'rights' here often refers to well-established legal rights that are part of positive law (constitutions and/or codes of criminal procedure) rather than merely points of discussions within criminal law theory.

More debated are issues of victims' rights. Positive law commonly acknowledges victims' rights in the form of rights that *all* witnesses in criminal trials have – those, for instance, that limit the scope of permissible questions in order to protect core privacy rights.[10] Beyond the functional role as (possible) witness, the role of victims in procedural laws is limited, and it is controversial as to which degree of involvement would be desirable within a theory of criminal procedure. To what extent should individual victims have a say regarding the initiation and termination of criminal proceedings and decisions during proceedings? Should they be able to influence sentencing decisions – either directly or indirectly – with victim impact statements? In recent decades, procedural laws have given victims a somewhat more active role. In Germany, for instance, they may assume the role of accessory prosecutor in the case of certain serious crimes,[11] and in the US and the UK they may submit victim impact statements (Bandes 1996; Roberts and Manikis 2011). The basic structure is not designed, however, to give victims comprehensive decision-making powers. The historical evolution of our criminal justice systems took responses to crimes away from victims and their social groups and established state prosecution and adjudication. This emergence of public criminal law and criminal procedure is considered an important step towards more civilised, less violent ways of communal existence (Baldwin 2021). It is not my intention to radically question this development, to the contrary: attempts to reintroduce the victim as an actor with real power deserve close scrutiny.

[10] Rape shield laws are examples, compare for the current state of law in the US Cassidy 2021: 151–58.
[11] Described as a 'renaissance of the victim', Jung 2020.

My point is that it is possible to strengthen the perspective of 'a victim' in criminal law theory, that is, in the general, not case-related discussions about the basic structures of criminal law and criminal law doctrine, without necessarily making the commitment to give individual victims' personal needs and personal assessments decisive weight on the individual case level. Victims of real crimes and the role of 'a victim' within criminal law theory should be distinguished. The latter is a not-yet-individualised figure in the social role of a citizen with defensive rights against other citizens.[12] When discussing criminalisation theory or punishment theory, it is obvious that we can only refer to 'a victim' in a non-individualised way: we can only refer to the 'typical' interests or status of potential victims. The same is true with regard to criminal law doctrine. However, when dealing with cases in criminal procedure and sentencing, the victim is a unique human being, an individual with personality, attitudes, needs, and emotions.

Giving this individual a stronger position would imply opening the door to personal assessments beyond the narrow legal framework that aims to hedge the impact of personal opinions and emotions and the social and biographical factors that shape them. A crucial question is whether it is desirable to introduce victims' personal perspectives. This question cannot be resolved here. There is a large body of literature discussing the advantages and disadvantages of giving victims a say in criminal proceedings (see Mendlow 2021, Roberts and Erez 2004; Crawford and Goodey 2000; Bandes 1996). It could be argued that listening to the assessments and needs of individual persons might counterbalance the alleged detachment of criminal justice professionals from the real world. Giving extensive decision-making powers to individual victims would, however, unavoidably clash with principles and goals that should structure criminal procedure and sentencing: the equality principle (equal treatment of offenders who have committed similar crimes) and the purpose of criminal convictions, namely, as the uniform, consistent reaffirmation of the norms of conduct. Emphasising victims' rights does not mean *excluding* all other considerations, such as our collective interest in maintaining an equality-based system of criminal justice and norms of conduct. Within the scope of this contribution, it is not possible to discuss these tensions comprehensively. Emphasising victims' rights in criminal law theory *does* require the re-examination of procedural rules.[13] It does not, however, force us to conclude that each individual victim must be entitled to determine whether and how criminal proceedings should be conducted and what sentence is adequate.

[12] As used here, the term 'citizen' refers to all persons who live within a jurisdiction, beyond the formal legal status of nationality; see for the broader notion of 'denizens' in political theory for instance Turner 2016.

[13] See, for this point also, Hirsch 2021: 241–324.

4. Rights and Obligations in Criminal Law Doctrine

4.1. A Critique of the German Collectivist Approach

One purpose of this chapter is to defend a strong role for victims' rights and victims' obligations within the basic structures of criminal law doctrine. In Germany, criminal law scholars have traditionally devoted considerable effort to passionate debates about how these basic structures should be conceptualised, compare Schünemann 1984. Recently, discussions have become somewhat less intense, but central chapters in textbooks and handbooks on criminal law still describe the 'general doctrine of crime' (*Allgemeine Verbrechenslehre*) or 'the system of criminal law', see, for instance (Roxin and Greco, 2020: 288–333; Hilgendorf 2020).

A general doctrine of crime serves two functions. First, it helps grasp the essence of 'a crime', that is, the general features of criminal wrongdoing that apply to *all* crimes or important subgroups of crimes. Describing what constitutes the core of criminal wrongdoing overlaps with theories of criminalisation, but treatises on German law outline the general doctrine of crime separately from the sections in which criminalisation and the *Rechtsgut* doctrine are discussed (see Roxin and Greco, 2020: 20–100; 288–333). Second, consent about 'the system' helps structure the path by which to proceed when assessing a specific case. A systematic approach does have advantages, particularly for the education of future lawyers and judges: it can contribute to a more consistent and predictable application of law.[14]

I propose reconsidering the basic abstract notion of the essence of crime. Within German criminal law doctrine, this means questioning the assumption that wrongdoing can be described in a uniform way, a way that is suitable for both offences against collective interests as well as for crimes against individuals.[15] From this viewpoint, crime is *exclusively* a matter between the state or the collective of citizens and the offender. Victims have no relevance for these kinds of theories. But, as Eric Hilgendorf (2020: 7) commented: "A rape cannot plausibly be seen as an act of communication between the offender and the state about the content of law." Wolfgang Frisch recently admitted that it is not plausible to reduce the 'essence of crime' to disrespect for the law (Frisch 2019: 195).

The idea of focusing on offenders' disrespect for the law as the essence of criminal wrongdoing is neither helpful on a descriptive level, if one seriously tries to grasp the effect of crimes, nor is it convincing from a normative viewpoint. Authors who use terms such as 'harm to the validity of the law' (*Normgeltungsschaden*) do

[14] On a more critical note, one could add that German legal scholars sometimes spend too much time retelling the story of how the system evolved, see Hilgendorf 2020: 4.

[15] See, for this approach, for instance, Pawlik 2012: 151–56, and other authors who emphasise that criminal acts show disrespect for the norms of conduct, e.g. Frisch 2015: 67–68; Rostalski 2019: 97–98.

not make an effort to operationalise this kind of harm. These words are not meant to refer to a state that can somehow be measured. This is not to say that the broad, general idea is implausible: if the public authorities were to ignore a significant number of crimes, detrimental effects on persons' willingness to respect prohibitions seem likely, and vengeance and blood feuds might occur. But this allows only a crude sketch of cumulative effects after many crimes remain uninvestigated or offenders unpunished. This way of defining criminal wrongdoing can work only if crimes are seen in the plural, as a group of incidents with cumulative effects.

The notion of a *Normgeltungsschaden* is equally problematic from a normative perspective. First, as mentioned above, the basic features of many contemporary legal systems are shaped by normative individualism. Individuals' subjective rights play a fundamental role in national constitutional law and international human rights law. It seems odd to maintain a basic understanding of crime that ignores individuals and their rights and to focus exclusively on the cumulative effects of a multitude of crimes rather than on the relations between individuals. Second, the use of lofty and misty concepts in criminal law theory can have negative effects on criminal justice practice. It opens the door for judgments about crimes that are at best intuitive, at worst moralistic, but which claim to be the best solution for defending 'the validity of the law'. Third, it is also not convincing to insist that criminal law theory has its place as an academic, scientific enterprise if we work with terminology that sounds rational and impressive but on closer examination turns out to be fuzzy.

4.2. A Critique of the 'Harm Plus Moral Wrongdoing' Definition

English literature that begins with the harm principle concedes that the finding of criminal wrongdoing cannot be based *solely* on the diagnosis that the offender caused harm but needs to be supplemented with a determination of moral wrongdoing. Emphasising *moral* wrongdoing, however, invites the objection that assessments in criminal law differ from moral assessments. According to Antony Duff, only a subset of moral judgments is relevant for criminal wrongdoing, namely, the category of public wrongs that excludes merely private wrongdoing (Duff 2018: 75–101). With this idea, the relevant questions are moving in the same direction as a rights-based concept. I would assume that deliberating about the question: 'Was this a public wrong?' will mostly lead to results similar to those arrived at when the question is discussed whether a person in this situation should be granted a defensive right. The shared assumption is that judgments in criminal law should track only a small subset of morally problematic conduct. The reasons as to *why* a certain kind of intrusion should concern all other citizens can be expected to be similar to the reasons why the claim 'a citizen should not be required to accept this as something that others might rightfully do' should be accepted and a defensive right granted. Conceptually, however, the move from 'wrongfully harming others' to 'violating the rights of others' makes it clearer that legal judgments should be rooted in political philosophy rather than being a subset of assessments stemming from moral philosophy. Starting point for understanding the general essence of 'a crime' should not be moral considerations that point to moral wrongs, even if the moral wrongs are narrowed down in a second step as Duff proposes, by excluding the merely private moral wrongs. Rather, starting points for describing what 'crime' means should be citizens' defensive rights against each other and important genuinely collective interests.

4.3. The Importance of Perspectives

Not only punishment theory and criminalisation theory, but also the assessment of criminal offences should be rooted in the notions of normative individualism and equal relations between citizens. This requires paying more attention to perspectives when discussing the general concept of crime (*Allgemeine Verbrechenslehre*). If one looks into criminal law textbooks, the question 'Which perspective should be taken when assessing criminal wrongdoing?' does not play a role. The most likely reason for the lack of attention to the relevance of perspectives is that authors implicitly and automatically, *without thinking about it*, step into one particular vantage point: the third-person perspective. If one takes it as a given that assessments must be made from a third-person viewpoint, this point is not even worth mentioning. Only if one pays attention to the existence of a possible alternative, that is, the second-person viewpoint, can awareness grow that the third-person perspective is not natural and unavoidable when assessing human conduct. In contemporary moral philosophy, arguments are made for the 'second-person standpoint' (Darwall 2006) and a relational perspective (Wallace 2019). This important shift deserves more attention in mainstream criminal law theory.[16]

What is there to criticise about a third-person perspective? As far as it means that events should be evaluated in an objective, impersonal way, I certainly do not wish to raise objections. Criminal judgments are and should remain judgments by state officials, expressed on behalf of the individual victim, but not adopting this individual victim's *personal* assessment of the event. To be taken seriously by everyone, not just victim and offender, criminal law must strive for high standards of objectivity. This also means relying on the current state of scientific knowledge. For example, an ill-founded assumption about the cause of a disease (voodoo or poisoning with an otherwise innocuous substance) must be irrelevant for criminal law, even if both offender and victim believe in it.

[16] See, for an adaption of Darwall's arguments about recognition, Hirsch 2021: 147–56 and Chapter 8 in this volume.

The idea of a third-person perspective becomes problematic if it is meant to adopt a detached, other-worldly perspective that assumes an evaluator who is not on eye-level with humans but who assesses our conduct from a superior vantage point. In societies that have been shaped by monotheistic religions, not only moral judgments but also criminal law theory have been influenced by belief in God as the evaluating instance. Our ordinary moral judgments are still deeply anchored in Judeo-Christian thinking and thus take the third-person perspective as the undisputed vantage point for moral judgments.[17] The belief that our sins are recorded and assessed in the Last Judgment has shaped the more general idea of a moral ledger where moral merits and moral shortcomings are recorded. Criminal law theorists have mentioned the picture of a moral ledger as a notion that also matters for legal assessments (see Alexander and Ferzan 2009: 179).

While scholars in our contemporary secularised constitutional states would certainly agree that criminal law theory should not be based on an *explicit* reference to God or other religious concepts, the point I want to make is that we should also be more attentive to *implicit* assumptions. The link from religious convictions to traditional moral judgments, and from there to the assessment of crimes within the institution of state punishment, has left traces in criminal law theory and criminal law doctrine. Traditional moral judgments, which are imbued with the idea of God's moral ledger, are retained in the field of criminal law theory, not in the form of open, explicit references to religious commands or traditional moral demands, but with regard to the poorly reflected foundational choice of 'whose perspective'. The input of traditional moral judgments is most likely particularly strong if influential voices within moral philosophy rely on their intuition, that is, if they spend their energy on the invention of ever more bizarre factual scenarios while trusting the soundness of their intuition for the moral assessment of each scenario.[18]

Meanwhile, our societies – their legal frameworks, that is, and to a great extent their extra-legal norms of conduct – have moved on from the norm 'obey God's commands' to a different kind or relational morality. The second-person viewpoint of equal citizens and the rights and duties inherent to these relations are part of what has been introduced above as normative individualism. This foundational shift requires us to scrutinise both the older foundations of judgments about moral wrongdoing as well as implicit assumptions that underlie retrospective assessments in criminal law. It should no longer be taken for granted that criminal law doctrine should be constructed in correspondence with traditional moral judgments based on a third-person perspective. Rather, the logical conclusion is that judgments in criminal law should consciously adopt a relational perspective that focuses on the second-person perspective, that is, on the perspective of a victim.

[17] See Casey 1990 for the connection between Christian teaching and the formation of our moral practices.

[18] See, for an example of this approach, Kamm 2007.

As mentioned above (see Section 3.4.), this does not mean relying on the personal assessment of the individual victim. Applying a victim's perspective requires judges and jurors to slip into the shoes of actual victims, but to put an emphasis on the social role of the victim rather than on his or her individual personality. This social role will often be 'thin' as most incidents charged as crimes happen between strangers, that is, in contexts without a preceding 'thick' web of mutual duties and rights between offender and victim. The 'thin social role' refers to the offender's status as a fellow citizen and the resulting duty not to interfere with other citizens' right to X, X being property, bodily integrity, etc. In contrast, some crimes are committed within the context of more substantial versions of pre-crime rights and duties, for instance, within families or other relevant social relations.

Criminal justice officials who assess a crime should ask themselves whether a reasonable person or, more precisely, a reasonable person in the social role of the victim in relation to the offender would consider certain circumstances as factors that enhance or diminish wrongdoing. The crucial point is to adopt a second-person viewpoint and to avoid moral reasoning that is based on a third-person (God's) viewpoint and, in particular, to avoid the idea of a ledger and a Last Judgment. Criminal courts should neither attempt to pass judgment about the entire life of a defendant nor should they strive to grasp every detail that might be called morally significant. The decisive question should be whether a citizen in the social role of the victim (typically a stranger, sometimes not) had a defensive right or whether such a citizen had to accept what the defendant did.

4.4. Consequences for Criminal Law Doctrine: A More Limited Role for Intentions

The deliberations above concerning the superiority of a second-person versus a third-person perspective might sound highly abstract and theoretical. However, I hope to show that the choice of perspective matters for the details of criminal law doctrine, for instance, when ruminating about the question if and how much a defendant's *mental state* influences the seriousness of a crime. My thesis is that applying a victim's perspective should lead to an overhaul of criminal law doctrine because less weight should be given to the subjective world-view of offenders (what they thought and intended) and more to objective factors (such as the deviation from standards of care that citizens have to abide by).

One issue that needs to be reconsidered is the relevance of intentions for criminal law assessments. We should ask why criminal laws often assign (much) higher sentences to acts if harmful consequences were intended compared to objectively reckless or careless behaviour without this intention. Scholars and criminal justice officials tend not to question the assumption that intentional crimes are much more serious, probably because this assessment dovetails with traditional, deeply rooted moral intuitions. Some argue that without inner mental states such as intention or knowledge of substantial risk, objective carelessness should not be considered a criminal wrong at all.[19] Why human beings' inner mental states should be considered so important can be explained with the logic inherent to Christian theology: the inner act of disobedience alters the relevant relationship with God, and the crucial wrong lies in humans' evil, insurgent will.[20] The theological tradition of focusing on evil will survived the period of Enlightenment – and was re-affirmed in a modified version as Kant's famous dictum that nothing but good will can be called good in itself without reservations (Kant [1785] 2016: 18). The idea that an agent's will should be the focus of moral assessments still plays a significant role in present-day moral judgments.

A victim's perspective is based on a different concept of 'relational'. From a second-person viewpoint, the focus of attention would shift from the 'evil will' as something occurring in the offender's mind to other ways of describing the wrong done, namely the social meaning of an interaction and the tangible aspects of the incident. This is not to say that offenders' mental states would become entirely irrelevant for criminal law theory and criminal law doctrine. I do not propose to revert to older systems of evaluation that responded only to harm (*Erfolgsstrafrecht*). Indeed, it is unclear if there ever was a criminal law system that paid no attention to the difference between intended and unintended consequences.[21] Rather, the point is to ask the right question, and this question is: 'To what extent do offenders' intentions and attitudes matter to a hypothetical reasonable victim?'

They do matter if they alter the social meaning of an act that disregards the victim's rights. Antony Duff has drawn attention to the difference between an attack and endangerment (Duff 2009: 147–58). This distinction is relevant from a victim's perspective. If two offenders' degree of carelessness and the outcomes of their conduct are identical, the fact that one of the acts was an intentional attack adds an additional element. For instance, purposely hurting another person expresses targeted disrespect for the individual victim and that person's rights. A point that needs more attention, however, is the *relative weight* of the difference between cases of gross carelessness and cases of intentionality. Sentencing ranges deserve scrutiny if they prescribe much higher punishments for intentional acts than for cases of gross carelessness: from the victim's perspective, the additional feature 'intentional attack' will not always make a pronounced difference compared to a 'merely' reckless act, if the latter was committed in a way that showed a particularly high degree of indifference for fellow citizens.

[19] See, for instance, Alexander and Ferzan 2009: 71, who claim that humans are not morally culpable for taking risks of which they are not aware.

[20] See Maihold 2005: 154–55 for the central role of free will in Thomas Aquinas' theological concept of crime and punishment.

[21] See for the argument that seemingly pure harm-based Medieval practices actually presupposed intentions as typical phenomena: Schildt 1997: 388.

The relevance of subjective and objective factors for assessing the weight of wrongdoing plays a role at many places in criminal law doctrine, for instance, in discussions about the appropriate sentencing of attempted versus completed crimes. Philipp-Alexander Hirsch, who also proposes the second-person viewpoint, argues that the difference between attempts and completed crimes does not influence the degree of criminal wrongdoing, as the (completed) attempt as such expresses the full amount of disrespect for the victim (Hirsch 2021: 219–24). This conclusion does not seem evident to me. Disregard for the victim's defensive rights has indeed been fully expressed with the completion of the attempt. However, from a victim's perspective, it also matters for the retrospective assessment of wrongdoing that and how much harm has been done.[22] If one reconstructs defensive rights and mutual duties of citizens, the crucial point is that outcomes can be attributed to offenders' careless behaviour. More ambitious versions of 'control about everything, including all consequences of one's acts', usually discussed under the heading 'moral luck', are too demanding if the task is to regulate relations between citizens.[23]

4.5. Victims' Obligations

Evaluating criminal wrongdoing from a second-person viewpoint entails paying attention to the notion of victims' rights. However, a change of perspective should not lead to resorting to a one-sided, partisan evaluation of incidents. *Mutual* rights and obligations that structure the relations between citizens matter, and for this reason, judgments in criminal law can also include obligations of potential victims. This thought is even more alien to standard views in criminal law theory and criminal law doctrine, which concentrate exclusively on the wrong done by the offender. In German sentencing theory, a few authors have argued that punishment should be mitigated if victims could easily have done more to protect themselves against the kind of crime in question (Hillenkamp 1981; Schünemann 1982). Their reasoning was different, however, from mine: for them, the argument that criminal law should be 'ultima ratio' was central, that is, the expensive and intrusive machine of criminal justice should only be used if crimes cannot be prevented by other, cheaper and less intrusive means, including self-protection by potential victims. My aim is not to challenge the *ultima ratio* idea in principle, but I would emphasise a different aspect: when assessing criminal wrongdoing, it should be considered whether the other person in an interaction, the subsequent crime victim, disregarded the obligation to behave in a reasonable way.

This notion of victims' obligations should figure in lawmakers' decisions on how to formulate the legal description of offences and should also play a role at

[22] See, for a more extensive development of this argument, Duff 1996.

[23] See, for a discussion of the moral luck problem, Burghardt 2018: 395–404, 418.

the sentencing stage. Victims' obligations can become a topic in the process of drafting or altering prohibitions in criminal law if the criminal act is typically preceded by interactions between the future offender and the future victim. In the reform of sexual assault law, for example, the appropriate scope of criminalisation depends on what is considered to be necessary communication between persons in a sexualised interaction. This debate is summarised with the keywords 'no means no' or 'only yes means yes'. Conceptual deliberations that are necessary when reforming sexual assault law, moving away from the old-fashioned focus on offenders' violence and towards a consent-based model, should include a clear idea of how citizens need to communicate if a prior interaction could be considered ambivalent (typically in contexts that might be called 'date rape'). Another example are laws that mitigate sentences for cases of provocation. A traditional approach focuses on the mental state of the offender, that is, the intensity of the offender's anger and related emotions. However, if mental states as such are not the key but rather victims' obligations, the laws on provocation must be based on a different logic. Under this premise, it is not sufficient to argue that the offender acted in a very agitated state; rather, the decisive question should be whether the victim violated a legal duty towards the offender. If the victim's conduct did not conflict with legal obligations, the offender's mental state (annoyed, furious, etc.) should not be relevant for assessments in criminal law. For instance, a victim's announcement of the intention to seek a divorce should not lead to the finding that the victim's spouse, who was deeply emotionally affected by the announcement, should receive a milder sentence for a violent attack on the victim (Grünewald 2010: 243–61).

5. Conclusion

The purpose of this chapter is to argue for a conceptual reorientation in both criminal law theory and criminal law doctrine. We should question the traditional, religiously grounded, virtually exclusive fixation on the offender, particularly the offender's evil mind. This requires us to recognise the deep impact of traditional moral evaluations that still shape widely held intuitions. In societies based on the idea of normative individualism and with constitutions that emphasise the rights of individuals, criminal law theory needs to be rebuilt. This affects all the questions that criminal law theory should address: Why maintain the institution of criminal punishment (punishment theory)? What should be prohibited (criminalisation theory)? How should individual conduct be assessed (criminal law doctrine and sentencing theory)? Once it is accepted that judgments in criminal law should track citizens' rights and duties from a second-person point of view, victims' rights and obligations must play an important role.

6

Rights, Reasons, and Culpability in Tort Law and Criminal Law

GREGORY ANTILL*

1. Introduction

There has been a recent renaissance in private law theory, due in large part to both the explanatory and justificatory power of the notion of private rights in tort law. Harnessing rights-based accounts, recent civil recourse and corrective justice theorists of various stripes have pushed back against attempts to 'recast private law as public law',[1] making a compelling case that 'rights-discourse in tort theory promise[s]' both 'foundational, normative justifications' and a descriptive 'analysis of the structure of tort law' that offers an 'integrated account' of both its 'structure' and 'substance'. (Goldberg and Zipursky 2012: 252).

The contributions of civil recourse and corrective justice theorists toward understanding tort law in terms of private rights has been so successful in reclaiming 'private law' from the realm of 'public law' that a similar approach has begun to attract interest among theorists in the paradigmatically public realm of criminal law, to recast public law as private law. In recent work, philosophers of criminal law have begun questioning the common conception of criminal law as grounded in offences against the state, attempting instead to provide an alternative

* Earlier versions of this material were presented to audiences at the University of Graz and Yale Law School. I am grateful to everyone who commented on those occasions, and in particular to Philipp-Alexander Hirsch, Tatjana Hörnle, and Hamish Stewart. This material has also benefited enormously from written comments and conversation from Gideon Yaffe, Douglas Kysar, Pamela Hieronymi, Mitch Berman, Amin Afrouzi, Pinchas Huberman, Samantha Godwin, Ethan Seidenberg, Tomas Churba, Arthur Lau, and Fiona Furnari.

[1] See Goldberg and Zipursky 2012: 251–52. Examples of such civil recourse and corrective justice theorists, broadly construed, include Coleman (1992); Weinrib (1995); Stevens (2007); Honore (1988); Perry (1992); Cane (2002). Importantly, as I discuss in more detail below, not all rights-based approaches fall under this categorisation. In particular, this critique does not extend to 'rights-based views' that hold merely that rights-violations are the proper object of *criminalisation* by the state, (see e.g. Hörnle (2014) or rights based views, such as that proposed by Philipp-Alexander Hirsch see Chapter 8 in this volume, which emphasises not the restoration of the object of the victim's rights, but rather the restoration of the legal status of the victim, by affirming the community's regard for the victim as a rightsholder.

grounding in terms of victim's rights and the principles of corrective justice, whereby criminal liability involves duties of a defendant not to violate the rights of the victim and secondary duties to repair the harm (or restore the object of right) caused by violations of the primary duty.[2] In doing so, this contemporary work builds upon at least one prominent strand of earlier restorative justice theories, understood as theories according to which 'crime is defined by the harm it has caused to victims, and the primary function of the reaction against it is . . . to repair or compensate for the harm'.[3] As proponents of this new movement have been clear, this project is not primarily 'descriptive'.[4] Certain parts of criminal law – victimless crimes and non-relational duties; the absence of victims' consent as a requirement for prosecution; and punitive harms to offenders that exceed that required for reparation of violated right, are, on a corrective-justice perspective, difficult or impossible to accommodate.

Nonetheless, much of the moral 'core' of criminal law is thought to be compatible with a corrective justice picture, and the rest easily jettisoned, leading to a normatively superior revisionary account of criminal liability and procedure. Indeed, as Elias Moser has recently argued, this moral core of criminal law may appear *better* explained by such a 'private law' picture (see Chapter 1). While there are some victimless crimes, most crimes – homicide, rape, assault and battery, or theft – seem closely associated with the violation of an important victim's right. On a public law account, this relationship appears at best indirect. The fact that the object of criminalisation is a relational duty to other individuals (e.g. a duty not to steal) is merely a contingent result of the fact that the public has a particular general interest in ensuring individuals do not steal from one another. As Moser argues, a victim-rights account of criminal law, as opposed to the standard public-rights account, 'allow[s] for the more common-sense interpretation' of such criminal offences (idem). On the victim rights view, the explanation for why the law picked out this particular duty was that 'people owe *each other* the performance of a duty not to steal and that this duty holds *because* individuals have a right to property against other individuals' (idem). Such a direct explanation allows for a 'more adequate description' of the relationship between rights-violations and criminalisation without the more 'counter-intuitive' indirect account by way of public interest in private rights (idem). On the normative, revisionary side, a corrective or restorative justice approach to criminal law has been thought to be more humane to both victims and offenders. By focusing on principles of restorative justice, a victim-centric approach will give victims more control over the process of prosecution (idem at 188), providing them the possibility of ending prosecution by waiving their right (idem at 188–92). It will also ensure that criminal law focuses

[2] For recent proponents of such views in criminal law, see Bronsther (2021); Moser (2019); Poama (2018).

[3] Braithwaite 1999: 1734. See also Dolinko (2003); Garvey (2003).

[4] See Moser 2019: 191–92.

on compensating or restoring the victim, as best we can, unlike the current criminal procedure which can, too often, contribute to the secondary victimisation of the survivor of the crime, by forcing them to traumatically relive the harm at trial. Finally, and most importantly, a victim-centric approach promises the end of some of the more draconian punitive punishment of the criminal justice system that focus on retribution or deterrence toward offenders, rather than more productive methods of restoring or repairing relations between the offender and victim.[5]

This chapter argues that while restorative and corrective justice approaches to criminal law are often motivated by the view that, by eschewing punitive punishments, such approaches are less harmful toward defendants, this conclusion is too quick. In fact, the restorative logic of such victim's rights account, by focusing on the degree of harm suffered by the victim (or the magnitude of the infringement of the victim's rights) rather than the degree culpability of the defendant in causing the harm (or violating the right), threatens to demand disproportionately severe punishments toward minimally culpable defendants. Such corrective-justice-based approaches thus violate a principle of weak proportionality which lies, I argue, at the heart of criminal law.

The chapter proceeds as follows. Section 1 describes the *weak proportionality principle*, laying out the ways in which criminal liability is, and ought to be, at least weakly proportional to the culpability of offenders who perform the same action with different degrees of *mens rea*.

Using the American Tort system as an illustrative example, Section 2 explains how a system of legal liability grounded in the rights of victims not to be wronged and in their secondary rights for repair when their right is violated, is unable to conform to the principle of weak proportionality and unable to apportion liability according to the degree of *mens rea* of the defendant.[6]

Section 3 explains how the offender-centric foundations of liability in the Anglo-American system of criminal law differ from the rights-based picture of liability in tort law and are thus able to provide protection to defendants which a corrective justice approach to criminal law may be unable to accommodate.

[5] idem, see also Garvey 2003: 309 ('restoritivism is said to prefer milder punishments like restitution … while retributivism is said to prefer harsher punishments like imprisonment').

[6] In doing so, I build upon, and draw out in greater detail, an objection about moral luck and inequality in treatment of similarly situated offenders that has been levelled in the past by retributivists against analogous restorative justice views. See e.g. Dolinko 2003: 331 ('restorative justice … resemble[s] rehabilitation in its high potential for giving similar offenders strikingly disparate treatment. … [The central aim in its handling of an offender is to repair the harm that her crime inflicted, and the extent of that harm can vary greatly because of factors beyond the offender's foresight or control and irrelevant to her culpability.'); Ashworth 1993: 290–91 ('offenders acting with equal culpability could by chance cause markedly different consequences [and so] … find themselves confronted by two differently disposed victims.'). In particular, I hope to spell out in greater detail the contours of the *mens rea* regimes which would naturally follow from the respective theories of justice, and to thereby address possible replies which more sophisticated civil recourse and corrective justice theories in tort law may have been thought to have provided in answer to this retributivist objection.

Finally, Section 4 concludes by using the comparative analysis of *mens rea* in tort law and criminal law to raise two particular challenges to further attempts to ground criminal law in principles of corrective or restorative justice: explaining and justifying attempt liability; and explaining and justifying the Model Penal Code (MPC)'s *mens rea* criminal liability grading system of reduced criminal liability for lessor *mens rea*.

Before continuing the argument further, an important dialectical point. The target of this chapter is a particular strain, or conception, of rights-based or restorative approaches to criminal law: the conception which understands criminal law as functioning to vindicate the rights of the victim by correcting the rights violation through repairing the harm or restoring the object of the right that was infringed upon by the actions of the offender, and so undoing or correcting (as far as possible) the initial wrongdoing. However, this is just one among a number of possible conceptions that a restorative or rights-based approach to criminal law might employ. As proponents of restorative justice approaches have pointed out, 'no single definition of restorative justice commands universal assent' and there is no consensus on 'who is supposed to restore what to whom' (Garvey 2003: 307). In addition to the view of restorative justice as concerned with restoring the victim, 'restorative justice' might also refer to a view that seeks to restore or repair the *relationship* between the victim and offender, or to restore the community as a whole (and the victim's status as an equal community member). Similarly, victim's-rights-based accounts might seek not to vindicate the object to which the victim had a right, but rather the victim's community status as a rights holder.[7] My critique does not apply to these other conceptions of a rights-based approach to criminal law. Indeed, one goal of the paper is to show the importance of keeping clear what precisely we mean by 'restorative justice' or 'rights-based' approaches, by showing how the corrective justice conception is importantly different from, and may face distinctive problems compared to, a theory of restorative justice or a rights-based approach that is focused on restoring the relations between the victim and offender, in ways that have sometimes been overlooked in discussions where such views have been allowed to be run together.

2. Criminal Law, *mens rea*, and Proportionality

Part of the standard picture of contemporary Anglo-American criminal law is a commitment to a principle of what we might label 'weak proportionality'.[8] Criminal liability ought not to treat substantially less culpable agents as substantially more

[7] See e.g. Philipp-Alexander Hirsch's contribution, Chapter 8 in this volume.

[8] I discuss this weak proportionality picture and its relationship to the MPC *mens rea* regime in more detail elsewhere. See Antill (2022).

criminally liable than substantially more culpable agents for the same criminal offence.

This principle is weak in several ways. First, it does not require that a criminal law system perfectly apportion criminal liability to the subjective culpability of the agent. Criminal law has never attempted to distinguish all the fine grained-differences in culpability among defendants who have committed the same criminal act.

Second, it is weak in the sense that it does not require any strong assumptions about, or commitments to, any particular picture of the fundamental function or justification of criminal law. It is consistent with both expressivist, retributivist, rehabilitative and all but the most extreme deterrence-based theories and so intended to be broadly ecumenical about the underlying function and justification of criminal law.[9]

Third, it is weak in the sense that the principle of weak proportionality does not purport to provide *sufficient* conditions for a justifiable criminal system. Instead, this principle provides a necessary *minimal standard* of normative acceptability for any theory of criminal liability. A theory of criminal law where the resulting system of criminal liability does not conform to the principle of weak proportionality, whatever else the theory's merits, is an inappropriate basis for grounding criminal law.

This principle is both normative and descriptive. In American law, for example, the ban on 'greatly disproportioned' punishment has roots in both Eight Amendment jurisprudence, where the 'cruel and unusual punishment clause' has been held to 'prohibit … sentences that are disproportionate to the crime committed',[10] and in a line of United States Supreme Court jurisprudence, originating in *Morisette v United States*, where the Supreme Court has suggested that proportioning *mens rea* elements to criminal liability is a 'universal and persistent' feature of 'mature systems of [criminal] law'.[11] While the focus here will be on American Law, similar (and often even stronger) proportionality principles are common in various jurisdictions across the world. The European Union Charter of Fundamental Rights, for example, holds that '[t]he severity of penalties must not be disproportionate to the criminal offence'.[12] In English Law, Lord Woolf CJ in *R v Offen (No 2)* interpreted the European Convention of Human Rights prohibitions against arbitrary, cruel, and degrading punishments

[9] It is sufficient for the purposes of this chapter that such weak proportionality is, at minimum, a desiderata for a justification of criminal law, even if there are some doubts about whether, and to what degree, each of these various underlying standard justifications of criminal law really are compatible with such a principle. See Berman (2021) for a sceptical account.

[10] *Solem v Helm*, 463 US 277 (1983). See also *Graham v Florida*, 560 US 48 (2010) ('the concept of proportionality is central to the Eighth Amendment'); *Harmelin v Michigan* 501 US 957 (1991) (recognising a weak proportionality principle banning punishments that are 'grossly disproportionate').

[11] *Morissette v United States*, 342 US 246, 251 (1952). Accord *Liparota v United States* 471 US 419 (1985); *United States v X-Citement Video*, 513 US 64 (1994); *United States v Flores-Montano*, 541 US 149 (2004); and *Rehaif v United States* 588 US (2019).

[12] Art 49(3) of the Charter of Fundamental Human Rights of the EU, 2012/C 326/02.

as enshrining a similar 'constitutional' requirement against grossly disproportionate punishments.

To ensure conformity to this principle, US federal criminal law, along with most US state jurisdictions,[13] follows the American Law Institute's MPC in adopting a *mens rea* grading regime whereby the criminal liability of an agent who commits some criminal offence is proportioned to the culpability or blameworthiness of the mental state they were in with respect to that offence at the time the crime was committed.[14] Agents who act to create some harm to a victim purposefully or intentionally, and are thus thought to be more culpable for that harm, are typically subject to greater criminal liability than those who are merely reckless or negligent with respect to that harm.

In this chapter, I will argue that this *weak proportionality principle* is incompatible with a corrective-justice approach to criminal law that grounds criminal liability in the violation of victim's rights and a duty to repair the material rights violation.

The argument, in short, is as follows. The culpability of an offender is primarily a function of an offender's reason-responsiveness. On the reason-responsiveness conception of culpability, an agent who commits some criminal offence – such as stealing property – is culpable because he or she has failed to appropriately respond to the reasons he or she has to respect other people's property. Their actions evince a lack of sufficient concern for the reason giving force of other people.

Because two different agents might perform the same action for different reasons, two agents who cause the same criminal harm might be differently culpable, based on the reasons they had for causing that harm. This is captured, at least roughly, in the MPC *mens rea* hierarchy of purpose, knowledge, recklessness, and negligence.[15] As philosopher Peter F Strawson has observed, the agent who shoves and harms another person purposefully, and makes the harm their 'conscious object'[16] out of a 'malevolent wish to injure', is more blameworthy than the knowing or reckless agent who harms them to the same degree when shoving them out of the way 'in contemptuous disregard of [their] existence'(Strawson 1962). And the agent who knowingly tolerates a harm or risk of harm is more culpable than the negligent agent who shoves 'accidentally' without taking due care for the foreseeable risks it might involve (idem).

But a victim-centric rights-based approach to criminal law, where criminal liability is determined by the magnitude of a material rights violation, will be

[13] See generally Robinson and Dubber 2007: 26–29 (showing that over two-thirds of states have adopted the MPC).

[14] See Model Penal Code § 2.02(5) (Am L Inst 1962). For example, Criminal Homicide under MPC section 210.1 classifies a killing as a murder if the action was purposeful. But a defendant will typically be guilty merely of manslaughter if they were only reckless, and the less-severe crime of negligent homicide. A similar ordering by *mens rea* exists in non-MPC regimes that follow the alternate 'Penn System' of homicide grading. See Keedy (1949).

[15] I discuss the relationship between the MPC *mens rea* regime and the reasons-responsiveness picture of culpability in much greater detail elsewhere. See Antill (2022).

[16] Model Penal Code § 2.02(2)a (Am L Inst 1962).

unable to track the degree to which the rights-violator did or did not respect the reasons they had to refrain from harming the victim.

The magnitude of a rights-violation is, of course, relevant to an offender's culpability. The stronger the right being violated, the more reason the offender has to refrain from acting in ways that violate it. So, all else being equal, two similarly situated agents who engage in rights-violative activity will be equally culpable.

The problem is that not all else will be equal. One agent who engages in the activity might be merely reckless or negligent toward the rights violation, another knowing, and yet another might violate the right intentionally or purposefully. These different *mens rea* states will all have consequences for the degree of failure in reasons-responsiveness manifested by the agent (which grounds, in turn, the degree of culpability of the agent). The agent who takes the rights violation as a reason which counts in favour of acting will manifest worse modes of reasons-responsiveness than will the knowing or reckless agent who takes the rights violation, or risk of rights violation, as an insufficiently strong reason to refrain. And so, these agents will all be differently culpable with respect to their actions.

But (as I will argue in the next sections) the duty of repair generated by a rights violation, and the strength of that duty, will not align with those differences in reasons-responsiveness. Because the demandingness of the duty to repair is a function of the harm (or magnitude of the rights violation) that needs repairing, its strength can be largely orthogonal to the degree to which the defendant appreciated the reasons they have to respect the right or refrain from the harm.

This problem can be illustrated by considering liability in both criminal law and tort law doctrine for the same underlying actions. By looking at how the natural logic of a victim's-rights-centred approach to wrongdoing shapes tort law and seeing how tort liability differs from criminal liability, we can see more clearly how such logic is insufficient to vindicate the weak proportionality principle. While a picture of criminal law grounded in rights violations can make sense of a requirement that the defendant must have been culpable or have violated some duty of care toward the victim, there is no reason why the *degree of culpability* of the offender in breaching the duty should make a difference to the degree of criminal liability.

3. Culpability and *mens rea* in Tort Law

Suppose D violates V's right to bodily integrity – say by kicking V in the shins as in *Putney v Vosburg*.[17] How might this rights violation give rise to legal liability? What role does D's culpability play in the process? While private law theorists differ in the details, recent private law theorists have given us a plausible general account of how the story might go.[18] In kicking V in the shins, D violates a legal

[17] 80 Wis 523, 50 NW 403 (Wisc, 1891).

[18] This particular account draws heavily from that of Goldberg and Zipursky (2012). However, as we will see, it's general contours are common to any of the target views.

'duty-imposing rule'.[19] This rule is *relational* in the sense that it 'enjoin[s] actors not to act in certain ways toward others or upon others'.[20] These duty-imposing rules connect to rights in at least two ways. First, they are legal recognition of pre-legal natural rights to be free from injury at the hands of others, as well as political rights of recourse by the government for harms suffered (idem at 268–71). Second, these laws also generate 'legal rights' for victims (idem at 261–63). In particular, they generate both a primary claim-right by the victim not to be mistreated (along with a corresponding duty for agents not to mistreat the victim) as well as a secondary right of the victim, consisting of the power to demand repair (along with corresponding duties by the wrongdoer to comply with such demands and provide reparations) (idem at 271–73).

One benefit of this rights-based approach to analysing tort law, according to its proponents, as opposed to approaches which understand tort as instantiating broader principles of distributive justice, is that it can explain why the defendant must be *responsible* for the harm suffered by the victim. As Goldberg and Zipursky have put the point: 'tort law does not simply redistribute or re-allocate losses according to a principle of justice. It assigns liability as a way of holding a person responsible for certain consequences that his or her conduct has had for another. In tort, liability is a form of responsibility. Hence, any tort theory that aims to take Tort Law seriously on its own terms must include a robust notion of responsibility' (idem at 257–58).

By grounding tort law in rights-violations generating secondary duties by the rights violators to repair the injury of the primary rights-violation, we can understand why legal liability in tort law must involve some such 'robust notion of responsibility' for the liable party. It may be that when D kicks V, the person best situated to compensate V is not D, but rather some third party, P, who is best placed to minimise costs and avoid harms going forward.[21] However, if P has not interacted with V so as to put P in the proper relationship with V, by violating a duty to V and causing the injury, P is not responsible for violating V's rights, and so cannot be liable – either morally or legally – for a special duty of repair.

How much this captures a culpability requirement on the part of the defendant depends on the kind of responsibility required for a primary rights-violation. Different versions of corrective-justice approaches have employed different conceptions of 'responsibility'. There is, for example, a very weak sense of responsibility in which all that is required to show that D is responsible for some harm is to show that D is merely causally responsible for the harmful outcome.[22] This 'outcome responsibility' is an explanatory or descriptive, rather than a moral, notion of responsibility. It is the same question we might ask when we are asking

[19] Hart (1994).
[20] Goldberg and Zipursky 2012: 261. See also Coleman (1988).
[21] See e.g. Calabresi (1965).
[22] See Honore (1988) and Perry (1992).

whether some lighting strike was responsible, or not, for the house burning down. To say that the lightning is responsible is to say it was the cause, perhaps the proximate or direct or primary cause, of the fire. But it is not to say that the lightning is morally blameworthy, or culpable, for the results.

It is clear that such outcome responsibility will be too weak to capture a culpability requirement on the part of a criminal defendant. Defendants can be entirely blameless while still causally responsible for a harm or rights infringement. However, corrective justice is plausibly compatible with a thicker notion of moral responsibility as well. While some theorists have argued that this minimal sense of responsibility is all that is, in principle, required for a wrong to be inflicted, and so all that is in principle required to generate a duty of repair,[23] many others have argued that a rights-based account requires a more stringent, moralised, responsibility requirement.[24] For a right to be violated, rather than merely infringed upon, in the sense that makes the violator accountable to the victim in the right way to generate a duty of repair, the violator must be blameworthy, or at fault, for the harm.[25] They must have failed to fulfil some duty of care. It is not enough, for me to be responsible in the sense necessary for a breach of a duty of care, if I kick you in the shin involuntarily, say while sleepwalking or suffering an epileptic fit.[26] Breaching a duty of care requires not just that the defendant be causally responsible – that the defendant be the proximate cause of the harm – but morally responsible. The agent must have engaged in some faulty conduct, which, in turn, requires that the harm have been foreseeable by the agent, and that there be some culpable failure by the agent in failing to avoid that foreseeable harm.

If we adopt this second approach to responsibility, as the American legal system arguably has,[27] then we can see how a rights-based account of liability could involve at least some culpability requirement. Like the criminal legal system, anyone who is liable must be liable in virtue of a voluntary act or omission.[28] Moreover, like the criminal legal system, anyone who is liable must have some 'guilty mind'.[29] In causing injury, a tortfeasor's act or omission must involve some culpable mental state, such as purpose or negligence.[30] However, while this feature of corrective

[23] And so compatible with a 'strict liability' tort regime like that of England. See *Rylands v Fletcher*, LR 3 HL 330 (1868). For recent defence within a similar corrective-justice theory on which culpably-caused harm is neither necessary nor sufficient for wrongdoing, see Ripstein (2016: 130–48). Unsurprisingly, Ripstein predicts an even larger gap between tort-doctrine grounded corrective justice and analogous provisions in criminal law. Idem at 143 ('it is only if the basis of liability is thought to be some form of moral condemnation, punishment, or sanction that it looks as though there is anything exceptional about regarding the realisation of a substantial risk as wrongful').

[24] See especially Coleman (1992).

[25] See Feinberg (1986b); Thomson (1986).

[26] See *Lobert v Pack*, 9 A 2d 365 (Pa 1939).

[27] In contrast to the English system, American tort law typically requires at least negligence with respect to the harm in order for the defendant to be liable. See *Brown v Kendall*, 60 Mass 292 (1850).

[28] See Model Penal Code § 2.01 (Am L Inst 1962).

[29] ibid § 2.02 (Am L Inst 1962).

[30] There is some debate about whether negligent conduct, for torts, really does require any culpable state of mind. See Ripstein 2016: 130–50. I will assume for the purposes of my argument that a

justice may be able to incorporate some culpability requirements into a theory of liability, these requirements will be too weak to conform to the principle of weak proportionality.

The important thing to note is that while a rights-based account may require that the defendant be morally responsible for the rights violation, this notion of moral responsibility is still very thin. It is a threshold notion, that is required for D to count as violating, rather than merely infringe upon, V's primary right, and so on the hook for the duty to repair. But responsibility in this sense is all or nothing. So long as the defendant was sufficiently culpable to violate the right, he or she has thereby incurred a duty of repair. A duty either is or is not breached. If the duty was breached, then the victim's right was violated and the violator is now under a duty to repair. The content of this reparative duty is established by considering the magnitude of wrong done to the victim. Once a breach is established, the blameworthiness of the actor typically does not factor into the reparative calculus.[31] That is, particularly blameworthy actors will still only be required to make the victim whole. And only slightly blameworthy actors will, likewise, still be required to make the victim whole.[32]

Thus, on a corrective-justice account of liability, responsibility is a condition for being 'on the hook' for liability, but what one is 'on the hook for' is not a function of *how* responsible one is. Once one is past a certain threshold of responsibility, to count as violating a duty of care, one has breached their primary duty not to violate the victim's rights, and so incurred a new secondary duty of repair. This means, first, that it does not matter, with respect to amount of liability, whether the breach was negligent, reckless, or purposeful. Regardless of the *mens rea* of the tortfeasor, the tortfeasor will be responsible for restoring the victim for the harm incurred. Second, it does not matter *how* reckless, how negligent, or how malicious, the tortfeasor was. Consider the classic Burden vs Probability of Loss (B/PL) formula for determining negligence.[33] According to Learned Hand's famous formulation:

> To provide against resulting injuries is a function of three variables: (1) the probability of the loss (2) the gravity of the loss and (3) the burden of adequate precautions … Possibly it serves to bring this notion into relief to state it in algebraic terms: if the probability be called P; the injury L; and the burden, B; liability depends upon whether B is less than L multiplied by P: i.e. whether B < PL (idem).

negligence standard does require culpability, since my aim is to show that even if we accept such a claim, a corrective justice theory will still be unable to capture an adequate proportionality requirement.

[31] This is, of course, not to deny that legal realist observation that juries are often influenced by such culpability judgments in calculating damages. However, if juries are so influenced, they are acting contrary to the formal structures and spirit of the law. Contrast this with a judge who, in criminal sentencing, may be required to be influenced by such culpability judgments.

[32] I put aside, for now, the issue of punitive damages. See the discussion in Notes 61–63 and accompanying text.

[33] *United States v Carroll Towing Co* 159 F 2d 169 (2d Cir, 1947).

The BPL formula can be understood as a model for the agent's reason-responsiveness. If an agent acts to cause some harm, the strength they gave the victim's well-being as a reason to avoid causing a risk of loss to the victim must have been less than the strength they gave the force of avoiding their own burdens as a reason to act. When B<PL, the agent who still acts to avoid the burden is failing to give appropriate weight to the reason-giving force of the rights and well-being of others.

On this picture, the greater the difference between B and PL, the worse reasons-responsiveness is manifested by the actor, and the more culpable they are. But on the classic B<PL formula, liability for the *entirety of the loss* is generated as soon as the agent demonstrates any failure in reasons-responsiveness.[34] An agent who is grossly negligent, and an agent who is only barely negligent, will be equally liable. While the result may be that liability is disproportionate to the culpability of the tortfeasor, the system makes sense from the logic of a corrective justice perspective. Since the victim has still been wronged, they have a claim to repair, irrespective of the quality of the reasons the defendant had for so acting. As John Goldberg has noted, the corrective aims of tort law can also help explain why Tort law refuses to acknowledge many exculpatory excuses that form an essential part of criminal law.[35]

While it is true that many tort law regimes take into account the degree to which an agent's negligence contributed to the harm, this calculus is again typically orthogonal to the degree of culpability of the respective tortfeasors, often because of a desire to vindicate the goals of corrective justice. While comparative negligence regimes can sometimes take into account the 'degree' of culpability, the comparative calculus also factors in other considerations such as the percentage of causal responsibility which the agent's negligence had for the harm. See *Kingston v Chicago & N W Ry Co*, 211 NW 913 (Wis 1927). Moreover, however the percentage of liability is apportioned amongst the tortfeasors, the ultimate amount of liability is fixed, irrespective of their collective culpability. That contributory negligence does not function to track relative culpability judgments is perhaps clearest in cases like *Nash v Port Auth of NY & NJ*, 2008 856 NY S. d 583 (App Div 1st Dept) where, in the 1993 terrorist bombing of the world trade centre, the Port Authority was held to be 68 per cent responsible for the harms, for negligently failing to prepare for terrorist threats, while the terrorists themselves who carried out the bombing were held to be merely 32 per cent responsible. However this liability was apportioned, it was clearly not intended to track the relative moral responsibility of the terrorists and the Port Authority for the attacks.

It is also true that, while tort law does not distinguish between negligence and recklessness, it does distinguish between intentional and unintentional

[34] Though, again, it is possible that there may be alternative rights-based accounts, less centred on restoring the object of right, and more centred on addressing failures of respect for the right, which might take an alternative approach. See, e.g. Hirsch, Chapter 8 in this volume.

[35] See Goldberg (2015).

tortfeasors.[36] Assault and Battery, for example, are intentional torts, which require (in the language of criminal law) either purpose or knowledge. However, crucially, liability does not require that the actor intend the harm. The majority rule in tort law follows a principle of single intent, rather than dual intent.[37] The defendant must intend *to contact* the plaintiff but need not intend *to harm* the plaintiff, let alone intend the harm which actually occurs (idem).

Indeed, the majority rule in tort law follows the colloquially named 'eggshell skull rule' according to which the harm not only need not be intended, it need not even be reasonably foreseeable.[38] In *Vosburg*, for example, the kick to the shins caused an unforeseeable loss of the use of the plaintiff's leg.[39] Despite the fact that that the plaintiff neither intended, foresaw, or even could have reasonably foreseen, the risk of such harm, the defendant was liable in virtue of intending to violate the plaintiff's right to bodily integrity through intending a non-consensual contact.

In this way, intentional torts are actually *closer to* strict liability (where the agent is liable regardless of any fault) than are negligent torts which at least require the violation of a reasonable person standard, if not subjective awareness of the harm.[40]

In contrast, an intentional tortfeasor can be minimally culpable. They may have, e.g. gently brushed aside another shopper's hand in order to get to the final beanie baby toy on the shelf at the shopping mall. Still, if in doing so, they cause, unforeseeably to them, enormous harm to the person, they will be liable for that entire harm. Even though they neither intended any harm, or foresaw the risk of any such harm, or even *could have reasonably foreseen the risk of any such harm*.

In a negligence tort, in contrast, breach requires a certain level of (a) foreseeability and (b) unjustifiability on the part of the tortfeasor.[41] On a typical B<PL analysis, breach requires that the agent's reasons for acting be weaker than the

[36] Unlike criminal law, however, it does not require for intent that the agent actually had a subjective intention to bring about the harm. Under tort law, knowledge is typically sufficient for 'constructive intent' and so sufficient for tort liability for intentional torts. See e.g. *Garratt v Dailey*, 46 Wash 2d 197, 279 P 2d 1091 (Wash1955).

[37] See Restatement (Second) of Torts.

[38] There are exceptions. The tort of intentional infliction of extreme emotional distress (IIEED), for example, requires 'dual intent'. See *Leichtman v WLW Jacor Communications*, Inc. 634 NE 2d 697 (1994). However, IIEED is in a minority among intentional torts and perhaps reflects some lingering scepticism about emotional harms, rather than the internal logic of tort law. See Chamallas (2000). In any event, the 'dual intent' standard has been enshrined as the dominant approach for intentional torts in the most recent restatement (third) of intentional torts, which re-emphasises the 'single intent' approach as the dominant and 'most defensible' doctrine. See, Simons (2006) (arguing that 'the single intent approach is much more defensible, and indeed is the only plausible interpretation of the case law in this area').

[39] *Putney v Vosburg*, 80 Wis 523, 50 NW 403 (Wisc, 1891).

[40] Though the eggshell skull rule can apply to certain negligent harms as well, insofar as they are liable for the full extent of a foreseeable harm, even when the degree of harm was not itself foreseeable. See e.g. *Benn v Thomas* 512 NW2d 537 (Iowa 1994) (upholding an 'eggshell skull rule' even in the case of harms due to negligent rear-ending of plaintiff in motor accident). This is, again, consistent with the idea that even when there is a culpability requirement, that requirement is a mere threshold notion.

[41] See e.g. *Palsgraf v Long Island Railroad Co*, 248 NY 339, 162 NE 99 (1928).

reasons to refrain. If the burdens to the agent from refraining are greater than the foreseeable loss to the victim (weighted by the probability of that loss), it isn't negligent and there is no liability. Moreover, the harm that they cause, in failing the B<PL analysis, must be foreseeable by the actor. No such unreasonableness is required for an intentional tort. It is possible that I had some compelling reason to intentionally push you out of the way. Perhaps by doing so, I will prevent far greater burden to myself, such that the burden is greater than the probable (or even the actual) loss. Still, if I intentionally violate your bodily integrity without your consent, I am liable to correct all the injury that befell you. Second, no foreseeability requirement is in place. The dominant rule in intentional torts is the 'eggshell skull rule'. If I intentionally hit you in the head, and unforeseeable to me, you suffer far greater harm than a reasonable person would have foreseen, I have a duty to correct all those harms.

Despite superficial similarities, then, this system is actually quite different from the standard *mens rea* regime in criminal law, where a purposeful defendant must typically be purposeful *with respect to the criminalised harm*, not merely with respect to the action that causes that harm, in order to be held more liable than a negligent agent. In fact, the intention/negligence distinction in tort law, properly understood, is actual *the opposite* of the standard criminal law hierarchy, which treats those who deliberately cause a criminalised harm as more liable than those who cause that same harm inadvertently. From the perspective of culpability, where we look to the blameworthiness of the wrongdoer to determine liability, the ordering enshrined in tort law makes no sense. But from the logic of a victim-rights-centred corrective-justice account, the system of liability in tort law makes perfect sense. The role of responsibility is to connect the tortfeasor to the harm in the right way, so as to generate a duty of repair. In cases of indirect harm, this requires some connection in terms of breach of duty. But if the agent violated the right directly (i.e. if the rights violation was the content of the agent's intention) then no more linkage needs to be provided.[42] The agent is therefore on the hook for whatever repair is required, regardless of how culpable they were with respect to the harm.

It is, of course, true that American tort law does allow for punitive damages on top of compensatory damages. Such damages are often explicitly tied to the culpability of the tortfeasor, typically requiring that the tortfeasor's conduct be 'grossly negligent' or 'intentionally malicious'. However, the exceptional and controversial nature of these damages makes them, in some ways, an exception that proves the rule. Many private law theorists are deeply sceptical of the place of punitive damages in tort law, precisely because they appear so inconsistent with the corrective function of tort law generally.[43] Punitive damages are an outlier. A place where

[42] See e.g. Ripstein 2016: 39–51. Thanks to Pinchas Huberman for helpful discussion on this point.

[43] Idem at 260–21. 'The inability to explain such awards is not, however, a limitation of [a corrective justice] account, but rather the vindication of it: The practice of U.S. courts with regard to punitive damages gives up on the idea that a tort is a private wrong.'

tort law departs from its corrective justice function and turns its gaze from the victim to the offender. And so, the existence of punitive damages in American tort law does little to help show that such punitive functions follow from a corrective-justice-based legal system.

It is worth noticing that, even in the case of punitive damages, tort law's general function of promoting a victim-centered corrective justice hampers the ability for punitive damages to function properly as a means of tracking the culpability of the tortfeasor. The United States Supreme Court has held in *State Farms v Campbell* that due process restraints require proportionality in punitive damages.[44] But what the court has held punitive damages must be proportional *to* is the underlying compensatory damages. But as we have seen, the compensatory damages are necessarily a poor proxy for culpability. Compensatory damages in a legal system grounded in corrective justice can be dramatically disconnected from the culpability of an actor, even for the same wrongful act. This means that any secondary retributive function of punitive damages in torts will be distorted by the primary aim of achieving corrective justice. Maximally culpable defendants who, by luck, caused minimal injury, will face minimal punishment; whereas minimally culpable defendants who, by luck, cause maximal injury, may now face potentially enormous punishment in the form of punitive damages.[45]

4. Culpability and *mens rea* in Criminal Law

There was a time when Anglo-American criminal law looked much closer to contemporary American tort law. Historically, through the nineteenth century, many criminal offences under the pre-MPC Anglo-American common law regime required only 'general intent'. Under this general intent standard, it was sufficient for criminal liability that an actor performed a criminal act that caused the criminalised harm with some malicious intent, whether or not the intent corresponded to the criminalised harm.

Thus, in *Regina v Cunningham*, a defendant attempting to illegally tamper with the family gas meter in the basement and thereby inadvertently causing gas to seep into his mother in law's room was charged with malicious endangerment of her

[44] *State Farm Mut Auto Ins Co v Campbell*, 538 US 408, 426, (2003).

[45] Aggravated and nominal damages have also been thought to pose a similar difficulty for corrective justice theorists, since, in cases of nominal damages, there is no tangible harm to the victim in need of repair. It may thus appear that such damages must be functioning to express the culpability of the tortfeasor, rather than the wrong suffered by the victim. Traditionally, the response on the part of corrective justice theorists is twofold: first, that wrongs can consist of bare rights violations, rather than tangible material harm; second, that damages help vindicate a victim's rights by allowing the victim to demand recognition, in the courts, of their rights, and acknowledgement that those rights have been violated. See e.g. Ripstein 2016: 254–60. Some cases of purportedly punitive damages may actually be understood as providing a similar victim-centric expressive function. See e.g. *Jacque v Steenberg Homes, Inc*, 209 Wis 2d 605.

life. He was charged with this offence despite having either no *mens rea* or, at worst negligence, with respect to that element of the crime.[46] The trial judge instructed the jury that the defendant 'has not got to intend' (idem) the statutory element of 'maliciously administer[ing] ... any poison or other destructive or noxious thing, so as to thereby endanger the life of such person' (idem) provided that the person intended *some* 'unlawful' or 'wicked' act which caused the harm (idem).

In *Regina v Faulkner*, a sailor attempting to steal rum from the cargo of a ship lit a match to see better in the dark. The match set fire to some of the rum, the fire spread, and the ship was ultimately destroyed.[47] The sailor was charged with violating the Malicious Damage Act for 'maliciously' destroying the ship. The trial judge issued jury instructions to the effect that the defendant should be found guilty even if they had 'no actual intention of burning the vessel' as long as he intended to steal the rum and that the theft did, in fact, cause the fire (idem).

As long as the defendant acted 'wickedly', it did not matter (a) how wickedly they acted and (b) whether their wickedness was directed at the criminalised harm in the appropriate way. As then leading criminal law theorist Francis Bowes Sayre described the situation, '*mens rea* doubtless meant little more than a general immorality of motive' (Sayre 1934: 411–12).

As in *Faulkner* and *Cunningham*, appellate courts began to reject such trial court interpretations, in favour of *mens rea* requirements that required the defendant 'intend to do the particular kind of harm that was done' or at least that they 'must foresee that the harm may occur yet nonetheless continue to recklessly do the act' (idem)

This evolution culminated in the mid-century Model Penal Code (MPC). One of the major advancements in the MPC was a shift in criminal law from a conception of *mens rea* in terms of 'general' wickedness – whereby the agent must have had some guilty mind while committing the material acts of the crime – to the current 'element-analysis' of *mens rea*.[48] On the contemporary element analysis, a defendant must have one of the four MPC *mens rea* states – purpose, knowledge, recklessness, or negligence, with respect to each of the criminalised material elements of an offence.[49] Moreover, if the requisite *mens rea* is present (i.e. if the agent intended or was reckless with respect to a harm constituting the material element of some criminal offence), the MPC often criminalises even the *inchoate* version of the crime when the material element is absent, providing either attempt liability or reckless endangerment liability when a harm to a victim was absent.[50]

[46] [1957] 3 WLR 76; 2 QB 396, 41 Crim App 155.

[47] 13 Cox CC 550 (1877).

[48] See Robinson and Grall (1983).

[49] See Model Penal Code § 2.02(1) (Am L Inst 1962).

[50] While the specifics of how and whether attempt liability conforms to the weak proportionality principle in criminal law is a subject of active debate, the important thing to note (as discussed in the next section) is that the very idea of inchoate liability, however it is ultimately cached out, will be difficult to explain or justify on a corrective justice account, since no victim's rights will have been violated and, even if it were, the duty to repair will be empty.

5. Two Challenges for the Rights Based Approach

The Model Penal Code's approach to harms of Battery and Assault (combined into the category of assault in the MPC) is illustrative of both this element analysis and the approach to attempt liability. MPC Section 2.11.1 divides up crimes of assault, for example, into the misdemeanor crime of 'simple assault' involving more minor bodily injury[51] and the more serious felony crime of 'aggravated assault' involving more serious bodily injury.[52] Simple assault requires not just intentional 'wrongful contact' but that the agent 'purposefully, knowingly, or recklessly' causes bodily injury (idem). Aggravated assault, in contrast, requires not just that the agent 'caused serious bodily injury to another' but that they did so either 'purposely, knowingly, or recklessly under circumstances manifesting extreme indifference to the value of human life' (idem). Moreover, each category of assault includes 'attempts to cause' bodily injury or serious bodily injury to another, respectively (idem).

We can compare this approach to the approach of tort law as illustrated in *Vosburg*. In *Vosburg*, the defendant, Putney, intended unwanted contact with another person and caused serious bodily injury. Under the corrective justice approach of tort law, the fact that he intended unwanted contact, and so had 'general *mens rea*', sufficed to make him responsible, which sufficed to violate, not merely infringe upon, the rights of his victim to bodily integrity. At that point, we look to the victim's right of repair, which is determined here by the harm caused to the victim. The defendant is then duty-bound to repair the entirety of the harm and would be under the most degree of liability.

In contrast, under the MPC approach, we look to the offender. Putney did intend unwanted contact with Vosburg and so is culpable for failing to respect the reasons he had to refrain from doing so, given by the victim's right to be free of such unwanted contact. However, Putney was neither purposeful, knowing, or reckless with respect to the serious physical injury. Because he was not purposeful, knowing, or reckless, his action did not manifest a culpable lack of concern about injuring Vosburg, and so criminal law would provide him with a proportionately minor degree of criminal liability. He would not be liable for aggravated assault and, depending on the risk of minor injury that Putney foresaw, he might not even be liable for simple assault.

Suppose, instead, an alternative offender, call him Putney Prime, did kick Vosburg with the intent to cause serious injury but failed in his attempt. Again, on the reasons-responsiveness approach, we look to Putney Prime's culpability. Like Putney, Putney Prime intended unwanted contact, and manifested a culpable failure to respect the reasons he had to refrain from violating Vosburg's rights. However, because he believed his kicking would cause serious harm, he also

[51] Model Penal Code § 2.11.1(1) (Am L Inst 1962).

[52] ibid § 2.11.1(2) (Am L Inst 1962).

manifested the even more culpable lack of concern for Vosburg's well being. He is, as a result, more culpable, and thus more liable, on the MPC system.

In contrast, Putney Prime would have much less tort liability than Putney. Under the victim-centric approach, we look to the victim, Vosburg Prime. Like Vosburg, Vosburg Prime's right to bodily integrity was violated when Putney Prime intentionally kicked him. This violation will trigger a secondary right to repair, and a corresponding duty to Putney Prime. However, to determine the scope of the duty, we look to the harm Vosburg Prime suffered. Because he suffered little or no harm, there will be little or no liability for Putney Prime. Vosburg only has the right to make Putney answerable to the harms he caused to Vosburg, and those harms are minimal. Because he is a private individual, he does not have the right to make Putney answerable for his ill-will toward Vosburg, in the way the state, on a retributivist, expressivist, or deterrence picture, would be entitled to hold Putney to account for such culpable vicious will. A criminal law whose *mens rea* regime was structured, like tort law, to realise the principles of corrective justice would thus be both under- and over-inclusive. It would violate the principle of weak proportionality by apportioning too little liability to a defendant guilty of attempt-crimes, while, at the same, time, apportioning too much liability to defendants who engaged in wrongdoing with only minimal ill will, by abandoning the specific *mens rea* elements required by the MPC to safeguard against disproportionately severe punishment, regressing to the more draconian, 'general intent' standards of older common law approaches to Anglo-American criminal law.

6. Conclusion

In this chapter, I have considered how a system of *mens rea* growing out of principles of corrective or restorative justice, taken by many theorists to underly tort law, would differ from the kind of *mens rea* regimes which arise in a system of public criminal law grounded in more traditional retributivist, expressivist, or deterrence-based principles. I have argued that, perhaps counter-intuitively, an 'offender-centric' criminal law focused on the degree of blameworthiness of the defendant actually affords less culpable defendants more protection than would a victim-centric criminal law grounded in principles of corrective or restorative justice.

In so doing, I have shown that a certain conception of a victim's rights or restorative approach to criminal law, grounded in principles of corrective justice or civil recourse familiar to private law, faces potentially fundamental challenges: in particular, that a system of criminal law grounded in principles of corrective justice would be incompatible with the *mens rea* based hierarchy of criminal liability and attempt liability, both of which are core features of a mature system of criminal law. I also hope to have thereby provided at least some additional motivation for *alternative* conceptions of victim's rights approaches to criminal law, such as those explored in some of the other chapters of this volume.

While these challenges may not be insurmountable, I do hope to have shown that they are perhaps larger than many corrective-justice theorists have previously appreciated. An adequate victims-rights-based account of criminal law must be able to explain how the ensuing system of criminal liability, grounded in principles of corrective justice, can conform to the *weak proportionality principle*. This appears to require showing how the system can be sensitive to the *mens rea* of the offender in ways that provide a plausible account of both attempt liability and the *mens rea* element analysis and *mens rea* grading regimes of the MPC. Because culpability appears to factor in only as a threshold requirement on a corrective-justice account, it is unclear how such a story could be told.

These challenges are particularly important given the motivation of many of those advancing a corrective-justice account, to provide a more humane system of criminal justice that divorces criminal liability from punishment, understood as legal sentences whose function is to make the defendant suffer some harm or be made worse off than they would otherwise have been. On the corrective justice account, the losses or harms which befall the defendant are simply a side-effect of the underlying function of criminal liability to restore the victim.

What I hope to show in this chapter is that the offender-centric proportionality requirement functions just as much as a shield as it does a sword. The kind of 'corrective' demands which a system so grounded in rights violations would possibly have the potential to be much more burdensome than the culpability of the wrongdoer would have demanded under a more traditional approach.

7

Why Victims' Rights are Irrelevant to Paradigmatic Justifications

MARK DSOUZA

1. Introduction

Responding to reports of a dangerous gunman in a residential area, Beckford, a police officer, saw Barnes fleeing with what appeared to be a gun. Beckford gave chase and then shot Barnes dead. When he was shot, Barnes was on his knees, unarmed, with his hands in the air, begging to be spared. But Beckford believed (let us accept, honestly) that Barnes was about to shoot him dead, and that he therefore had to shoot Barnes to save himself.[1] Should Beckford be entitled to a justificatory plea of self-defence?

What if we slightly modified the facts? Say, Barnes-2 was indeed armed and, had he not been shot first, would have fired at Beckford-2. Should Beckford-2 be entitled to a justificatory plea of self-defence? (I deliberately leave open the question of whether Beckford-2 was aware of these facts about what Barnes-2 was about to do.)

In both these 'Beckford variations', the defendant commits a *pro tanto* offence (the *actus reus* performed with its *mens rea*), but there are also some key differences. Consider in particular, the issue of whether, objectively and all things considered, the respective victims suffer a wrong, i.e. a violation of their rights. It is plausible to think that because Barnes posed no actual threat to Beckford, objectively speaking, Barnes suffered an all-things-considered wrong. His right to life was violated insofar as, objectively, there existed no all-things-considered-wrong-denying reasons for Beckford to shoot Barnes. Barnes-2, on the other hand, did pose an actual threat to Beckford-2, and so objectively speaking, he was liable to Beckford-2's defensive force. Therefore, all things considered, he was not

[1] *R v. Beckford* [1988] AC 130 (PC). On these facts, the Privy Council ruled that Beckford was entitled to succeed in his plea of self-defence; even though he was mistaken – even unreasonably so – about whether Barnes posed a threat to him, the facts as he perceived them did entitle him to defend himself, and the force he used was not disproportionate on those (perceived) facts.

objectively wronged by being killed by Beckford-2. Objectively, there were all-things-considered-wrong-denying reasons for Beckford to shoot Barnes. If you subscribe to what I call the 'wrongness hypothesis' (Dsouza 2017: 3–6), this difference dictates whether a justificatory defence to criminal liability is available. Here's what the wrongness hypothesis states:

> Justifications exculpate by negating (at least) the objective all-things-considered wrongness of the defendant's *pro tanto* offence whereas excuses leave this undisturbed, and instead exculpate the defendant based on personal blameworthiness-denying factors. Where the defendant's *pro tanto* offence is a victimising one (as in the Beckford variations), the wrongness hypothesis implies that if, objectively, a victim's rights were violated by the *pro tanto* offence, then a plea of justification should never succeed.

In other words, if you subscribe to the wrongness hypothesis, you think that Beckford's plea of justification should not succeed, because Barnes' rights were violated. Beckford-2's identical plea is not disqualified for that reason, though you may perhaps think it is disqualified for other reasons (the one typically cited is that to successfully plead a justificatory defence in respect of a *pro tanto* offence, the defendant needs to have been motivated by justifying reasons). Thus understood, the wrongness hypothesis is one feature of criminal defences that a majority of theorists, including George Fletcher (1975: 320), John Gardner (2007a: 92–5), Andrew Simester (2021: 401–10), Benjamin Sendor (1990: 766), Douglas Husak (1989: 516–7) (1999: 52–3, 55), Miriam Gur-Arye (2003: 21), Albin Eser (1976: 621–3, 635, 637), Paul Robinson (1975: 272–3) (1990: 749–50) (1997: 394–9), Peter Westen (2006: 306), Suzanne Uniacke (1994: 12, 14–22), and Antony Duff (2007: 264–6, 270, 273–6, 281–4), agree upon.

But there is reason to doubt the central place that the wrongness hypothesis occupies in theories of defences.[2] In previous work, I have argued that what I call the 'quality of reasoning' hypothesis is a plausible, well-founded alternative to the wrongness hypothesis and that it gives rise to desirable liability outcomes (Dsouza 2017). But even while raising doubts about wrongness hypothesis-based models of justification, I had stopped short of suggesting that they should be rejected. I take up that task here. Specifically, I argue that we should reject the wrongness hypothesis when theorising criminal justifications. In the context of victimising offences, this means that a defendant, D's, entitlement to a justificatory defence should not depend on whether the putative victim, V, of a *pro tanto* offence (i.e. the *actus reus* performed with *mens rea*) suffered an all-things-considered wrong at D's hands. So, the fact that, objectively, Barnes' rights were violated, should not disqualify Beckford from succeeding in his plea of self-defence. Conversely, it also means that the fact that a *pro tanto* offence happened not to violate the

[2] Greenawalt and Baron separately theorise the availability of justificatory defences based broadly on subjective perceptions of facts, and therefore hold that even someone who commits an objective all-things-considered wrong can be justified. See Greenawalt 1986: 91–99, 102; 1984: 1903, Baron 2005: 393, 396–8; 2009: 124–30. I agree.

apparent victim's rights does not contribute to the success of a justificatory defensive plea. The fact that, objectively speaking, Barnes-2's rights were not violated, does not help Beckford-2 in his plea of self-defence. (That said, as will become clear presently, in no way do I deny the importance of victims' rights to questions of criminalisation, or to exercises of discretion before and during a trial, and to sentencing.) I defend these claims by showing that basing one's theory of defences on the wrongness hypothesis limits the ability of these defences to perform their distinctive role within the criminal justice system, whereas basing it on the quality of reasoning hypothesis facilitates defences in their performance of that distinctive role.

To this end, I begin in Section 1 by identifying the distinctive role that justifications play within the criminal justice system, and demonstrating, in Section 2, that incorporating the wrongness hypothesis into a theory of justification limits the ability of justifications to perform that distinctive role. In Section 3, I survey the arguments made in support of the wrongness hypothesis and argue that they do not convince. Then, in Sections 4 and 5, I illustrate how a theory of justification based on the quality of reasoning hypothesis can allow justifications to essay their distinctive role, while generating plausible liability outcomes. Section 6 concludes.

2. The Distinctive Role of Supervening Defences

Not all defences are alike. Pleas such as infancy, automatism, and insanity deny D's status as a responsible moral agent at the time of the offence; pleas of alibi, inadvertence, consent, and intoxication deny the elements of an offence's *actus reus* or *mens rea*; and pleas such as limitation, diplomatic immunity, and double jeopardy invoke procedural objections to trying D. None of these defences are justificatory. Justificatory defences belong to the set of 'supervening' defences – defences that do not dispute D's responsible moral agency, or that she committed the charged offence's *actus reus* with its *mens rea*, but instead invoke additional factors that 'block the presumptive transition from responsibility to liability' (Duff 2007: 263; Simester 2021: 400; Dsouza 2017: xv). The set of supervening defences includes justifications such as self-defence, the defence of property, and necessity (which can, in some forms, be justificatory), and some excusatory defences like duress. Accordingly, let us focus on identifying the distinctive role of supervening defences in substantive criminal law.

The distinctive (though not necessarily sole) role that supervening defences play in the criminal justice system seems to relate to conduct evaluation (as contrasted with conduct guidance). This is most clearly true of supervening excuses. It is generally accepted that supervening excuses are not conduct-guiding – they do not tell us what we should or may do; instead, they tell the decision maker what to tolerate from us (Thorburn 2008: 1095; Greenawalt 1984: 1899–1900;

Dsouza 2017: 87–92). Merely tolerated behaviour is not encouraged or permitted behaviour, and although we can probably infer from previous grants of excuses what behaviour we are likely to get away with (Duff 2002: 61–8; Lee 2009: 137–8), excuses are not meant to offer conduct guidance as to what we should, or may, do. Their distinctive role is in helping with conduct evaluation.

Justifications are different. They do seem to offer some conduct guidance – they tell us what behaviour is permissible (Stewart 2003: 333–6; Gardner 2007a: 106; Dsouza 2017: 88). So, Robinson treats them as being 'rules of [conduct] guidance' (along with offence stipulations) rather than 'principles of adjudication' (along with doctrines of excuse) (Robinson 1990; Robinson 2013: 237). But that is too quick. Both justifications and offence stipulations do offer conduct guidance, but both also influence adjudication; adjudicators must refer to them in deciding whether their guidance was followed. So, the real issue is whether the *distinctive* roles of justifications and offence stipulations are the same, *va.*, offering conduct guidance. Justifications and offence stipulations differ enough to suggest that that's not obviously the case (see for instance, Tadros 2007: 103–15). Offence stipulations are imperative – 'Do this; don't do that', whereas justifications are permissive – 'You may do this, you may omit to do that'. Additionally, the imperative guidance in offence stipulations narrows the set of conduct choices available to us, while justifications expand them by creating exceptions to guidance contained in offence stipulations (Dsouza 2017: ch 4). And these differences matter: on any plausible theory of justification, claiming a justification is not the lawmaker's 'Plan A' for how things should go; it is a contingency plan – 'Plan B'. Plan A is to prevent *pro tanto* offences from being committed, via the guidance contained in offence stipulations. When that plan fails because a specified contingency has arisen, then Plan B – the justificatory guidance comes into play. All things considered, when planning ahead, the lawmaker would rather that Plan A was followed (i.e. that nobody committed a *pro tanto* offence), than that Plan A was abandoned and Plan B was followed (i.e. a *pro tanto* offence was committed with justification).[3] This may even be the case when the contingency has arisen – even though D is permitted to use fatal force to defend herself against a child innocently aiming a gun at her, there is no reason to assume that the lawmaker *prefers* that D kill the child, rather than vice versa. So, the conduct guidance contained in offence stipulations applies *imperatively* to *all persons* from the time the offence is created, and it continues to apply until and unless the offence is repealed. But when an agent who was following Plan A encounters the specified contingency, the guidance in Plan B *also* becomes applicable, as *optional* guidance, for *that particular agent*, from that moment, and it ceases to apply as soon as the justificatory option is either adopted or precluded. In sum, a justification's guidance has a limited audience – it speaks only to agents

[3] Gardner put it thus: 'Legal justifications are not there to be directly followed by potential offenders. They merely permit one to follow reasons which would otherwise have been pre-emptively defeated.' (Gardner 2007a: 117).

that find themselves in the situation identified as the justification-triggering contingency; and it has only a brief conduct guiding lifespan – starting from when the specified contingency is encountered, and ending when the justified option is exhausted or ruled out. Typically, this lasts just a few moments, though exceptionally, it can be longer. This contrasts sharply with not only an offence stipulation's conduct guiding lifespan (which I have previously discussed), but also with a justification's conduct *evaluating* lifespan, which begins from the time a potentially justified action is performed and can last as long as it takes to exhaust the agent's final appeal against a conviction. At the very least, it lasts until an investigating body decides that the justification so clearly applies that further investigation is unnecessary.

On balance then, although like offence stipulations, justifications assist with both, conduct guidance and conduct evaluation, unlike offence stipulations, the distinctive role of justifications seems to relate to conduct evaluation (Dsouza 2017: 85–8; Duarte d'Almeida 2015: 77; Hart 1948).[4] In this, they are more like supervening excuses; they guide those tasked with evaluating an agent's conduct after it has been performed.

The particular conduct evaluation with which supervening defences assist is performed at trial.[5] The aims of a criminal trial shape the sort of conduct evaluation that is performed during the trial, and not all matters that could possibly be relevant to conduct evaluation are in fact relevant to conduct evaluation during a trial. There are several things a criminal trial aims to do, but probably the most important in the present context, is reaching a just verdict of 'guilty' or 'not guilty'. The central judgement in these verdicts is what Michael Zimmerman (2002: 554) calls 'hypological' – a judgement *about the laudability, culpability, or moral neutrality of the defendant* in respect of her conduct. Hypological judgements are a type of agent evaluation that can be contrasted with 'deontic' judgements, which are often thought to be a type of act evaluation involving judgements about moral rightness or wrongness of the agent's act (Zimmerman 2002: 554).[6] They can also be contrasted with 'aretaic' judgements, which are judgements about the agent's character – her moral virtue and vice (Zimmerman 2002: 554). Whereas a deontic judgement may be concerned with whether the agent's *act* was morally good, and an aretaic judgement may be concerned with whether the agent has the *character* trait of bravery, a hypological judgement is concerned with whether an *agent acted* praiseworthily or blameworthily in respect of *this* particular conduct token.

[4] Hart later retracted his 1948 essay, but Duarte d'Almeida has sought to reinvigorate Hart's claims from that essay in his monograph.

[5] Even when investigators and prosecutors consider the availability of a defence prior to trial, they do so in order to predict the defendant's chances of success should the defence be raised at trial.

[6] Although Zimmerman expresses some doubt about the precision of this characterisation of deontic judgements, the proposition that they are a type of act evaluation captures their essence adequately and distinguishes them from those that are hypological.

The central judgement in a verdict is this last sort of judgement – one that is hypological.[7] It follows therefore, that the distinctive role of supervening defences is to assist with the making of hypological judgements at trial. Any consideration that interferes with the ability of supervening defences to perform this distinctive role ought to be excluded.

3. The Distorting Effects of the Wrongness Hypothesis

In what follows, I argue that one such consideration is the content of deontic judgements about the objective all-things-considered wrongness (or rightness, or neutrality) of D's act, which, proponents of the wrongness hypothesis, insist shapes justificatory defences. But first, let me clarify that I am not suggesting that the substantive criminal law should be *uninterested* in whether we judge what happened as to be welcomed, lamented, or greeted with indifference. It seems plausible to think that such deontic judgements can matter at stages other than when applying supervening defences. For instance, it seems likely that they matter when deciding what sorts of conduct to make criminal in the first place. Perhaps they matter pre-trial, in the exercise of any discretion an investigator or prosecutor has as to which matters to investigate, or prosecute, respectively. They may also matter during the trial, but prior to applying the supervening defences, when establishing whether D is *eligible* for a criminal law hypological judgement. Apart from showing that D performed her conduct as a responsible agent, this may entail showing that her conduct was deontically objectionable (by showing that a *pro tanto* offence was actually committed). Additionally, deontic judgements may well matter for post-conviction sentencing decisions. At all these stages, it may well be appropriate to be guided by concerns about the victims' rights. At least some scholars would dispute the relevance of victims' rights in at least some of these domains (see e.g. Alexander and Ferzan 2009), but here, I need not take a firm stance on those debates. My immediate focus will be to show that they should be excluded when applying supervening defences.

Note first that our hypological judgement about an agent (let's call this judgement$_a$), and our deontic judgement about the act (let's call this judgement$_e$) can diverge. One clear example is when an agent performs the *actus reus* of an offence without its *mens rea*. Consider someone who has non-consensual sex with another,

[7] No doubt, a victim (assuming there is proved to have been one), will have an interest in knowing the verdict, and especially if the verdict is 'not guilty', she will have an interest in knowing *why*. (Interestingly, some common law systems – specifically those in which juries try criminal cases and are not required, or indeed permitted, to give reasons for their verdicts – will be unable to cater to this latter interest in knowing why a verdict was returned.) But this does not mean that the judgement contained in the verdict itself is a judgement about whether she was recognised as having suffered a wrong, i.e. a deontic judgement about the rightness or wrongness of the defendant's act. The verdict remains a hypological judgement. As such, it need not be determined by a deontic judgement about the rightness or wrongness of the defendant's act. My thanks to the editors for pushing me to clarify this point.

while reasonably believing that the latter was consenting. Here, $judgement_e$ is adverse but $judgement_a$ is not. Gardner explains that while we are tempted to think that we can avoid authoring any wrongs if only we are careful and clever enough, this temptation stems from the overly optimistic assumption that the perfection of our rational faculties will allow us to perfect our lives (by, in this context, never authoring a wrong) (Gardner 2007a: 81). But we are only human; we have limited epistemic access to objective truths, and limited control over the uncertainties of the physical world. So, despite our best efforts, we will inevitably author tragedies and fortuitous events. But the example above shows that even when objectively terrible things happen, an agent may not commit a *pro tanto* criminal offence, and so may not be liable to the adverse hypological judgement contained in a conviction.

$Judgement_a$ and $judgement_e$ can also diverge when a *pro tanto* offence has been committed. Here's how: The criminal law works in stages. *Ex ante*, it identifies conduct that should be avoided so as to prevent some specific *pro tanto* wrong from occurring. Then, *ex post*, it evaluates cases in which the proscribed conduct was performed anyway, to determine whether the agent was blameworthy for having performed the conduct (Simester and von Hirsch 2011: 3; Dsouza 2017: 8). The major part of the *ex-ante* conduct guidance is found in offence stipulations, which are typically, a combination of *actus reus* and *mens rea* elements. But some *ex-ante* conduct guidance is contained in justifications, rather than offence stipulations. So, an agent may commit a pro tanto offence, but still have chosen her actions entirely in line with the criminal law's advance conduct guidance, if she acted in a manner that was open to her under some justificatory criminal law rule. In this sort of case, the agent has, after all, behaved as the criminal law told her she was required or permitted to behave, and so $judgement_a$ is not adverse (Dsouza 2015). But again, because the agent has limited epistemic access to objective truths, she may nevertheless have authored a wrong such that $judgement_e$ is adverse. *Beckford*[8] was a case in which this happened. Here's another example:

> D reasonably believes that V is threatening her life, and so, she chooses to defend herself by pushing V. This is the minimum amount of force that would be effective against the threat thought to be posed by V. Choosing in this way is permitted by the justificatory rule governing self-defence. But it transpires that despite appearances, she was not being attacked, and therefore her 'defensive' action victimises an innocent V.

Since D has chosen her actions entirely in line with the criminal law's advance guidance, we have no reason to make an adverse $judgement_a$ about her. Yet, since V has been wronged, our deontic $judgement_e$ about what happened is adverse.

In short, persons who perform deontically problematic conduct need not have behaved in a manner that calls for an adverse hypological judgement. To be clear, adverse deontic judgements are strongly correlated with adverse hypological judgements insofar as when we set our minds to performing a task (including one that merits a deontically adverse judgement), we usually succeed. But even

[8] *Beckford* (n 1).

the most skilled, careful, and clever of us will sometimes fail, because we do not control all of life's variables. In those cases, $judgement_a$ and $judgement_e$ will pull in opposite directions.

Now recall that all wrongness hypothesis-based theories of defences reserve the label 'justification' for instances in which $judgement_e$ and $judgement_a$ are both at least neutral and use the label 'excuse' for instances in which $judgement_e$ is adverse, while $judgement_a$ is neutral or positive. But if the distinctive role of supervening defences is to assist with making hypological judgements, then it is inappropriate to deny a justification when $judgement_a$ is neutral or positive. To do so conveys false information about our hypological judgement of the agent, and we do not want the criminal law to speak untruths (Simester 2021: 10–1). What's more, wrongness hypothesis-based theories of defences also use the label 'excused' for agents who offend under duress. In duress cases, $judgement_e$ is clearly adverse; where D commits a victimising *pro tanto* offence, an innocent V has suffered a wrong. Additionally, insofar as D (knowingly) does not act as the criminal law permits,[9] D deserves an adverse $judgement_a$ as well. This means that some agents who respond perfectly to the criminal law's guidance (i.e. those who deserve a positive or neutral $judgement_a$, although $judgement_e$ is adverse) are clubbed with others who do not (i.e. those who successfully plead duress). Again, wrongness hypothesis-based theories deploy the terminology available to convey misleading, or at least, insufficiently nuanced, information about defendants. In fact, any theory of defences that tries to use the labels 'justification' and 'excuse' to accurately state both hypological and deontic judgements asks too much of these labels.

Duff's solution is simply to expand our vocabulary (2007: 264–6, 270, 273–6, 281–4). He says that people for whom $judgement_e$ is adverse and $judgement_a$ is not, should be said to have acted with 'warrant'. I have no especial theoretical objection to this general approach, but I doubt it is a good idea because:

(a) labels like 'warranted' do not carry the same social significance as the labels, 'justification' and 'excuse', so they may be less able to convey our hypological approval of an agent who responded perfectly to the criminal law's guidance;
(b) introducing new terminology increases the complexity of our system of defences solely to convey information about whether an all-things-considered wrong occurred. In victimising offences, this amounts to information about whether the victim, in some sense, deserved what happened to them. We should be uncomfortable with embedding this sort of victim-evaluation (and potentially, victim-blaming) into our criminal justice system. Besides, information about whether something objectively wrong happened is gratuitous; the verdict is meant to state a hypological judgement about the defendant. The added complexity associated with creating new labels is not justified by any added value.

[9] As distinct from tolerated, or 'not censured or punished'. As I use these terms, one may tolerate impermissible action, but if action is permissible, there is no need for anyone to display toleration.

In sum, the wrongness hypothesis, with its insistence on considering the deontic merits of D's conduct, hinders supervening defences in the performance of their distinctive role by distorting the labels 'justification' and 'excuse'. Rejecting it (and connectedly, the idea that justifications should depend on deontic judgements about D's conduct), may enable us to deploy these labels, with their existing social significance, to convey accurate hypological judgements about D.

4. Arguments for the Wrongness Hypothesis

So why do so many people, theorists and lay, have such strong intuitions in favour of the wrongness hypothesis? One reason might be that in ordinary speech, it seems natural to want to communicate whether a wrong happened even if it was occasioned non-culpably. A person suffering a wrong may also want that fact to be recognised in an authoritative judgement issued by a court considering the facts. It is possible to communicate this by reserving the language of justification for instances where the agent acted non-culpably, *and* no wrong happened. Doubtless, the ease with which we can slip between two senses of a statement like, 'D pushed V with justification' – the first, a judgement about whether the agent was justified, and the second, a judgement about whether the pushing was justified – also helps. But *pace* Gardner (2007a: 95), I doubt that the rationale for using the term 'justification' like this survives the transition from ordinary speech into speech made in the context of a criminal verdict, for reasons that are hopefully clear by now. While in ordinary speech, we can afford to be promiscuous about the sorts of judgements we try to convey by our usage of terms like 'justification', in the context of a criminal verdict, our focus is unambiguously on making hypological judgements – judgements about the merit *of the defendant* in light of her conduct. When we use terms like 'justification' and 'supervening excuse' in this context, we should focus only on judgements about the agent.

Nor does the sheer ubiquity of the supposed intuition favouring the wrongness hypothesis offer any support for its truth. Constant repetition of a plausible proposition (which the wrongness hypothesis undoubtedly is) can convert the proposition into received 'wisdom', and then, into gospel. As Ralph Waldo Emerson (2015: 136) observes, when that happens, the proposition can masquerade as intuition when actually, it is an instance of a 'tuition' – a learned belief that circumvents scrutiny. In other words, the familiarity of the wrongness hypothesis may not evidence its correctness so much as reflect its pervasiveness. So, discard intuition. Consider instead the occasional attempts to argue for the wrongness hypothesis from logic.

For Robinson (1975: 271–2; 1990: 740–2, 749–52; 1997: 399–400), justifications are simply negative offence elements that cannot conveniently be included in the offence stipulation. Since we criminalise *actual* wrongful harms rather than merely intended or risked ones, justifications must work by negating the objective wrongness (or harmfulness) of what happened. It will be clear from my arguments in Section 1, that I reject the claim that justifications can, in principle, be collapsed into the same category as offence stipulations. If my arguments for doing so convince, then the premise of Robinson's argument falls, and with it, his support for the wrongness hypothesis.[10]

A different strategy is to start with some intuited claims about how justifications and excuses should function and argue back from those features to the wrongness hypothesis. Those arguing in this way often identify one or more of the following intuited claims about justifications and excuses:

(a) justifications cannot conflict with each other;
(b) third parties should be permitted to assist justified, but not excused, agents;
(c) nobody should be permitted to resist justified action (Robinson 1996: 51–54, 59–60) (Robinson 1997: 404–6) (Fletcher 1978: 759–69).

Additionally, some people using this argumentative strategy also make assumptions about which defensive claims can properly be called justifications. For instance, Robinson (1996: 45; 1997: 391) assumes that both, police officers making arrests, and persons acting in self-defence, make justificatory defensive pleas. That assumption is at least controversial – Gur-Arye (2011; 2021) and I (Dsouza 2024) have argued that police officers making ordinary arrests exercise a power or act within the realm of a rights-displacement. They do not commit a *pro tanto* offence. Therefore, they need offer no supervening defence to a criminal court. But my concern here is about the broader tactic of arguing backwards from expected features of the justification/excuse divide to its structure.

However deployed, this tactic is weak. There is considerable disagreement on the features that justifications and excuses should have, so this sort of argument cannot convince anyone with different intuitions. Besides, this style of argument arguably proceeds in the wrong direction – our theory of justification and excuse should decide further questions about third-party consequences, conflicts of justification, and the right to resist; not the other way around (Husak 1999; Tadros 2007: 119–20, 281–2; Greenawalt 1984: 1919–27).

Another approach, which Fletcher (1974: 1272, 1274-6, 1304; 1985: 958) introduced into Anglo-American thinking from German criminal law theory (Eser 1976: 626–30) appeals to the pleasing symmetry that the wrongness hypothesis sets up between the *actus reus*/*mens rea* distinction and the justification/excuse distinction. On this view, just like the *actus reus* refers to the objective elements of a *pro tanto* offence and the *mens rea* to its subjective elements, justifications negate the objective wrongness of the *pro tanto* offence and excuses negate the subjective

[10] Incidentally, Alexander and Ferzan (2009) also think that there is no substantive difference between justifications and offence stipulations but instead argue that the criminal law should actually focus on culpability rather than wrongs and harms. They therefore argue that neither offence stipulations nor justifications, should focus on the fact-relative wrongness of what happened. So, even if we agree with Robinson's initial premise, his conclusion does not necessarily follow.

wrongness (or culpability) of what D did. Now, undoubtedly this elegant symmetry does lend some appeal to the wrongness hypothesis and, additionally, it offers a straightforward way to distinguish between justifications (which must, at a minimum, deny that D authored an all-things-considered wrong) and excuses (which do no such thing). However, the logical leap in assuming that thinking of offences and defences symmetrically will help us work out how criminal laws ought to function is unsubstantiated. There is no particularly good reason to think that the claimed *actus reus*-justification and *mens rea*-excuse symmetry can offer any normative support for a theory of how the criminal law should function. True, offence and defence definitions (and within them, *actus reus*, *mens rea*, justification and excuse stipulations) perform different functions within the criminal law, but they are not *how* the criminal law functions – or at least, they do not set up the only account of how the criminal law functions. I described one plausible alternative in Section 1. On this account, the criminal law functions by *ex-ante* stipulating conduct that should be avoided, and *ex post* evaluating cases in which the conduct nevertheless occurs, to determine the actor's blameworthiness. The distinctive role of offence stipulations (i.e. the *actus reus* and *mens rea*) relates to the *ex-ante* stage of criminal law, and so the *ex-ante* function of the criminal law, viz. providing prior conduct guidance with a view to avoiding identified harms, shapes their features. Conversely, since the distinctive role of supervening defences relates to evaluating conduct after it contravenes an offence stipulation, the *ex-post* function of the criminal law, viz. evaluating D's blameworthiness, shapes the features of supervening defences. Accordingly, all supervening defences should work by negating (at least some aspects of) the defendant's blameworthiness, and none of them should work by negating the occurrence of a wrong (Dsouza 2017). This would mean we need a new way of distinguishing between justifications and excuses, but plausible options exist (e.g. Dsouza 2017: 109–20). In sum, the argument from symmetry too does not give us compelling reasons to accept the wrongness hypothesis.

5. Outlining an Alternative

Rejecting the wrongness hypothesis simplifies our task; if information about judgement$_e$ is superfluous to a criminal verdict, we need not convey it. We can reserve the label 'justification' for all and only cases in which our hypological judgement (i.e. judgement$_a$) is positive or neutral, such that justifications turn on the defendant's culpability/blameworthiness, and not (at all) on the wrongness of the defendant's deed. The flip side is that now we need a new way to distinguish between justifications and supervening excuses. Elsewhere (Dsouza 2017), I have defended one model, based on what I call the 'quality of reasoning' hypothesis, that rejects the wrongness hypothesis, but can still distinguish between justifications and excuses. I use it here to demonstrate that viable alternatives to wrongness hypothesis-based theories of supervening defences do exist. In outline, my quality-of-reasoning-based model of defences:

- is limited to supervening defences. Nobody suggests that the wrongness hypothesis explains the exculpatory pull of other defensive claims, including those that deny the court's jurisdiction, D's responsible agency, the *actus reus*, or the *mens rea*, (Dsouza 2017: xv) and so they can be defended on their own terms;
- distinguishes between the quality of D's 'functional-reasoning', i.e. how well she meets expected standards of acuity in perceiving facts and drawing appropriate conclusions from them, and her 'norm-reasoning', i.e. whether she chooses her conduct in a manner that aligns with the normative guidance applicable to her volitional conduct, including normative guidance as to how much care she should take when exercising her capacities to perceive facts and draw appropriate conclusions from them, where such guidance is provided (Dsouza 2017: 24–8). In general, the criminal law's hypological judgements should track the quality of D's norm-reasoning; poor norm-reasoning should attract 'norm-blame'. The quality of D's functional-reasoning (and correspondingly, her desert of 'functional-blame') is relevant primarily outside the criminal law, where a finding of liability does not automatically suggest any morally adverse judgement about D;
- distinguishes between norms contained in the criminal law's system of conduct-guiding rules (criminal conduct norms) and broader societal conduct-guidance (societal conduct norms) (Dsouza 2017: 110–1). These often overlap substantially, but occasionally societal conduct-norms require something that criminal conduct norms do not (e.g. politeness), and vice versa;
- accepts that since some criminal conduct norms are contained in justifications rather than offence stipulations, D may deliberately violate an offence stipulation but still have chosen her conduct in line with the criminal law's (justificatory) conduct norms. In such cases, D is entitled to a justification. Having conducted herself in line with the criminal law's advance conduct guidance, she has displayed no culpable norm-reasoning in respect of criminal conduct norms. In short, justifications negate any blameworthiness flowing from poor norm-reasoning in relation to criminal conduct norms (Dsouza 2017: 96–9). But (assuming perfect knowledge of the law's conduct guidance[11]) when D's choice of conduct in violating an offence stipulation reveals an inappropriate attitude towards the criminal law's (overall) conduct guidance, she is not entitled to a justification. Having deliberately chosen to act contrary to criminal conduct norms, D deserves, pro tanto, to be called a criminal;

[11] This is so unlikely an assumption that it is better to think of it as a deeming fiction. See Dsouza 2017: 26. Insofar as it simplifies the analysis, it will serve for the present purposes. The (de)merits of this fiction, and what should replace it, are questions for another piece.

- allows an unjustified D to nevertheless have a claim to a supervening excuse, also based on a denial of blameworthiness; albeit blameworthiness flowing from poor norm-reasoning in relation to societal conduct norms. This may happen when, say, she deliberately contravenes the criminal conduct norms because she is wrongfully subjected to a serious threat. On such occasions, D's conduct, notwithstanding its deviance from criminal conduct norms, may be in line with societal conduct norms governing how one may respond in light of the threat. She will not therefore, by her conduct, have shown herself to have norm-reasoning that compares poorly to the normative gold standard for societal norm-reasoning. It would therefore be hypocritical for a criminal court, as representative of that society, to single D out as being especially deserving of a criminal conviction. This objection to hypocritical blaming is an objection to the blamer, rather than the content of the blame – a blaming judgement may be both hypocritical, and true. Therefore, the hypocrisy-based objection to a conviction is not conclusive – hypocritical, but true, blaming decisions may well be justifiable despite their hypocrisy, by reference, for instance, to overriding policy considerations. These overriding considerations may also permit the imposition of additional conditions (which may well be motivated by a consideration of victims' rights, and may, for instance, require that the agent's functional reasoning have met a specified standard of quality) for the grant of an excuse. In sum, when D claims a supervening excuse, she has a good blameworthiness-denying case for (but no entitlement to) the defence (Dsouza 2017: 109–20); and
- treats necessity as a non-paradigmatic form of justification, with its own exculpatory logic. Briefly, on this view, 'best interests intervention' necessity[12] is not a supervening defence at all; it negates the (often implicit) non-consent element of an offence's *actus reus* by legally recognising a substituted consent (Dsouza 2017: 123). Lesser-evils justificatory necessity[13] is a supervening justification, that functions like an excuse, except that, because the evil averted was so much greater than the evil caused, the law deems D to have acted with justification.

The differences between the outcomes generated by this model of defences and wrongness hypothesis-based models are set out below.

[12] This is the form of necessity in which an agent (D) appears to victimise another (V), but does so in the best interests of V, in circumstances in which it was impracticable to ascertain whether V consented to D's intervention, because, for instance, V was temporarily or permanently incapacitated, or there was no time to ask. See Winnie Chan and Simester 2005: 124–7; Stark 2013: 950, 952–56; Dsouza 2017: 122–3.

[13] This form of necessity is premised on an act-utilitarian comparison of the evil brought about by an agent's *pro tanto* criminal intervention, as compared to the evil that would have occurred in a counterfactual world in which the agent did not intervene. See the judgment of Brooke LJ in *Re A* [2001] Fam 147; Stark 2013: 957–9; Dsouza 2017: 123.

Table 7.1 Supervening Defence Outcomes: Wrongness Hypothesis-Based Models v The Quality of Reasoning Model

#	**All-things-considered wrong? (A)**	**Followed criminal conduct guidance believed applicable?[14] (B)**	**Mistaken about what criminal conduct guidance was applicable?[15] (C)**	**If mistaken re (C), reasonable mistake? (D)**	**Followed societal conduct guidance believed applicable?[16] (E)**	**Mistaken about what societal conduct guidance was applicable?[17] (F)**	**If mistaken re (F), reasonable mistake? (G)**	**Outcome: Wrongness hypothesis (H)[18]**	**Outcome: Quality of reasoning (I)**
1	N	Y	N					Justified	Justified
2	N	Y	Y	Y				Justified/ Excused	Justified
3	N	Y	Y	N				Excused/No Defence	Justified
4	N	N			Y	N		Excused	Can be Excused

[14] If the answer here is 'N', then no justification is available even on (most) wrongness hypothesis-based models.

[15] I refer only to cases where D is mistaken about the facts, so believes some inapplicable legal guidance applies. I exclude mistakes as to the content of the law.

[16] I refer here to potentially exculpating reasons, whether or not they are accepted in a legal system. Where the answer is 'N', no defence is available even on (most) wrongness hypothesis-based models.

[17] I refer only to cases where D is mistaken about the facts, and so believes some inapplicable societal norms apply. I exclude mistakes as to the content of societal norms.

[18] Alternative entries in this column reflect differences in the details of the main wrongness hypothesis-based models. These details are not material to my argument here.

5	N	N			Y	Y	Y	Excused	Can be Excused
6	N	N			Y	Y	N	No Defence	Can be No Defence[19]
7	N	N			N			No Defence	No Defence
8	Y	Y	N[20]					Excused	Justified
9	Y	Y	Y	Y				Excused	Justified
10	Y	Y	Y	N				Excused/No Defence	Justified
11	Y	N			Y	N		Excused	Can be Excused
12	Y	N			Y	Y	Y	Excused	Can be Excused
13	Y	N			Y	Y	N	No Defence	Can be No Defence
14	Y	N			N			No Defence	No Defence

[19] I use different words here (and in Row 13) than the words in Rows 4, 5 etc, because although nothing in my view commits us to treating these cases differently from others in which there is a *pro tanto* reason to excuse, I recognise that matters external to my view (i.e. policy considerations) may favour the withdrawal of a defence here.

[20] Such wrongs can occur because we humans are not in perfect control of all variables that determine the outcomes of our actions – e.g. *R v Scarlett* [1993] 98 Cr App 290.

6. Comparing the Models of Defences

So, how does the quality of reasoning model's way of using the terms 'justification' and 'excuse' compare with that of wrongness hypothesis-based models? Consider the outcome columns in Table. 7.1. In a full model of defences, the outcome column(s) can contain three possible definitive values – Justified, Excused, or No Defence.[21] With just those options, there is only limited information one can convey.

On the quality of reasoning model:

(1) A 'Y' (for 'yes') in column (B) means that D displays the proper attitude towards the criminal law's guidance, and so D acted with justification. Of course, since norm blame depends on D's attitude towards the norms, I refer here to the criminal law norms applicable in the facts as D perceives them. Being justified in the criminal law does not preclude non-criminal liability, for instance, for poor functional reasoning.

(2) A 'Y' in column (E) indicates that D has a defeasible case for an excuse based on having responded appropriately to the societal (though not criminal) conduct norms applicable in the facts that she perceived. Since her conduct shows her normative reasoning to be no worse than that of the normatively acceptable member of society, it would be hypocritical for the criminal justice system representing that society to single out D as meriting the stigmatising label, 'criminal' (Dsouza 2017: ch 6). However, this argument may be defeated by, for instance, overriding policy considerations. Moreover, a criminal law excuse does not preclude non-criminal liability, for instance, for poor functional reasoning.

(3) We always convey accurate information about criminal norm-blameworthiness when granting D a justification. The grant of an excuse is less definitive, though even there, since one would rather be justified than excused (Gardner 2007a: 108–13, 133; Baron 2005: 389; and for a survey of the literature on this claim, see Husak 2005a: 557), the model virtually guarantees that an excused D's conduct did not conform to criminal conduct norms, although it conformed to societal conduct norms. Despite conforming to societal conduct norms, some people may not be excused from criminal liability, since there is no entitlement to being excused – while one *asserts* a justification, one only *asks* to be excused (and so, can be refused). Of course, the state cannot refuse an excusatory defence groundlessly – there must be reasons. But these reasons flow not from the structure of criminal law defences, but

[21] In Table 7.1, there are also two non-definitive values in these columns, viz. 'Can be Excused' and 'Can be No Defence'. I have used these non-definitive values to recognise that the outcomes in these cases are under-determined by our theory of the structure of defences. Each criminal law system will need to take a definitive stance on these cases, and its stance will be dictated by the matters that fall under the broad heading of public policy. But whatever the dictates of public policy in any given system, the available definitive stances remain these three identified in the main text.

rather, from broader policy considerations, like the seriousness of the offence, the standards of epistemic reasoning we expect people to display, and the need for judicial consistency.

(4) whether an all-things-considered wrong occurred is extraneous to deciding what type of supervening defence D can plead. This considerably simplifies the analysis, allowing us to drop column (A), and retain what remains of Rows 1 to 7 to address all relevant variations of cases.

On standard wrongness hypothesis-based models:

(1) The labels 'justification' and 'excuse' attempt to convey information about both, judgement_e and judgement_a. The most prominent such models allow a justification when there was no all-things-considered wrong (i.e. judgement_e is at least neutral), no criminal norm-blame, and no functional-blame. They grant an excuse when a justification is unavailable, but some other factor negates either criminal norm-blame, or societal norm-blame (coupled, on some accounts, with an absence of functional-blame).

(2) We need twice the number of rows, and one extra column, in our table to describe the outcomes in various factual permutations because of the added complexity.

(3) The message conveyed by the verdict is distorted by obscuring information about the hypological judgements we can make about the agent in respect of her conduct. The labels 'justification' and 'excuse' cannot reliably convey information about either D's criminal norm-reasoning, or her societal norm-reasoning. Instead, some agents who respond appropriately to criminal norms (Rows 2 and/or 3) are clubbed with agents who do not (Rows 4, 5, 8, 9, 11, 12 and possibly also 10). While this problem is starkest in relation to agents who complied with norms applicable to the facts as they reasonably, but mistakenly, believed them to be, the Table shows that it also affects several *other cases.*

One apparent weakness of the quality of reasons model vis-à-vis wrongness hypothesis-based ones is that is seems insensitive to the fault associated with being unreasonably mistaken as to facts; it does not distinguish between Rows 2 and 3 (and correspondingly, Rows 9 and 10) and Rows 5 and 6 (and correspondingly, Rows 12 and 13). But on closer examination, this objection rarely bites. Consider first, Rows 2 and 3 (and correspondingly Rows, 9 and 10). The objection does not apply whenever the law has a criminal conduct norm guiding agents, in advance, to take care that their functional reasoning conforms to a specified standard (usually, reasonableness) when they choose to commit a *pro tanto* offence and then plead justification. Such a norm is not built into the structure of the criminal law, but lawmakers can choose to impose it (Dsouza 2017: 40–45).[22] Where they do, and

[22] I take no stand on whether, and in what circumstances, lawmakers should require agents to take care to ensure that their functional reasoning conforms to a specified standard. My thesis here is not

D does not choose to take the requisite care, she displays poor criminal conduct norm-reasoning. Her case is a Row 4 (or correspondingly, Row 11) case, rather than a Row 2 or 3 case. Now consider Rows 5 and 6 (and correspondingly, Rows 12 and 13). A similar argument can be made here. The objection does not apply whenever social morality contains advance guidance requiring agents to take care that their functional reasoning conforms to a specified standard when they choose to commit a *pro tanto* offence and then plead a defence. Again, while this guidance is not a necessary feature of societal morality, a given society's morality may include it. Where that is the case and D does not choose to take the requisite care, she displays poor societal conduct norm-reasoning, and so there is no reason to excuse her. Her case is a Row 7 (or correspondingly, Row 14) case instead of a Row 5 or 6 case.

The objection still bites in respect of the few cases in which

(a) there was no advance guidance in criminal or societal conduct norms requiring the agent to take special care in exercising her capacities for functional reasoning when she chooses to commit a pro tanto offence and then plead a supervening defence, and the agent reaches conclusions that we, *post facto*, judge to have been unreasonable; or
(b) the agent tried to obey the relevant advance conduct guidance but fell short where a reasonable person would not have, because she has certain personal traits that the law refuses to attribute to the 'reasonable person'. I refer here to cases in which D is less able to meet the standard of the reasonable person because she is on the autism spectrum or has a lower-than-normal IQ (but is ineligible for an irresponsibility defence). D may even be undiagnosed at the time of her alleged offending, and therefore unaware that she ought to calibrate her efforts to account for her divergent attributes.[23]

I have argued elsewhere (Dsouza 2015) that such agents do not exhibit shortcomings of a nature that merit criminal consequences (though perhaps non-criminal law responses may be appropriate). For that reason, I consider it a strength of the quality of reasoning-based model that, unlike wrongness hypothesis-based models, it does not impose criminal law consequences in these cases.

7. Conclusion

The wrongness hypothesis commits us to the view that justifications are unavailable whenever an all-things-considered objective wrong has occurred (or in the

about what norms lawmakers ought to include in the criminal law system, but rather, about the proper way to internally organise those norms that they do include.

[23] See *R v B (MA)* [2013] EWCA Crim 3, in which the defendant argued that the facts were precisely of this sort. The court disbelieved the defendant but ruled, obiter dicta, that even if it had believed him, it would have been appropriate to convict him.

context of a victimising offence, someone's rights have been violated. But this consideration obstructs supervening defences (including justifications) in their performance of their distinctive role, viz., contributing to making fair hypological judgements about defendants who have committed pro tanto offences. We should therefore abandon the wrongness hypothesis, and accordingly, treat any consideration of whether, objectively, an all-things-considered wrong occurred (or whether a victim's rights were violated), as irrelevant to whether the defendant acted with justification. Doing so considerably simplifies our analysis of which defence is available and in what circumstances, while helping us to convey more accurate hypological verdicts about the defendant.

PART III

Individual Rights and Public Sanctions

8

Individual Consent and Shared Normative Authority

Conceiving of Crimes as Violations of Individual Rights and Public Wrongs

PHILIPP-ALEXANDER HIRSCH

1. Who is Wronged when Crimes Occur?

Let me sketch out an – admittedly somewhat rough – answer to this question from the perspective of criminal law theory. Many authors[1] seem to readily subscribe to the position that criminal law serves a genuinely public function, equating crimes with public wrongs. Consequently, it is the polity or the legal community that is wronged when a crime is committed. This can be dubbed the *public-wrong conception of criminal law*. According to this conception, the distinctive feature of criminal law that distinguishes it from other areas of the law lies in responding to public wrongs, whereas the function of civil law is to respond to private wrongs (e.g. Pawlik 2004: 75 et seq.; Lamond 2007; Renzikowski 2007: 563 et seq. and Chapter 13 in this volume:; Husak 2008: 135 et seq.; Edwards and Simester 2014; Lee 2015).[2] Where public and private wrongs cannot be distinguished at a primary level (e.g. crimes and torts), criminal law's distinctive function is seen in responding to wrongs *on behalf* of the legal community as a whole, whereas the function of civil law is to respond to wrongs *on behalf* of a specific individual (see Duff 2011: 140, 2014: 164, 170 et seq. and Chapter 15 in this volume or Stevens 2014: 112 et seq. and 121 et seq.). This often corresponds to the underlying normative justification of criminal law. According to communitarian approaches, for example,

[1] In this chapter, I will not consider approaches that see themselves as alternatives to state criminal law, such as abolitionist or restorative justice approaches.

[2] The notion that criminal wrongdoing is of a genuinely public nature is also not a new development but historically well-founded, to be found for instance in Blackstone, *Commentaries on the Laws of England* (1765–9), Bk IV, ch. 1; Hegel, *Grundlinien der Philosophie des Rechts* (1820), §§ 95 et seq., 220 or Kant, *Metaphysik der Sitten* (1797), § 52, Anm. E.

the values or interests pursued by criminal law are of a genuinely public nature, which is why it falls to the community – or rather its agent, i.e. the public prosecutor – to prosecute crimes and to hold offenders accountable (see Duff 2001: 56 et seq.). That said, more individualistic approaches (such as Kantian approaches), according to which criminal law upholds a system of equal freedom, are not substantially different in this respect. This is the case because while these theories refer to the value of individual rights to freedom, they are always concerned with the protection of the *totality* of individual rights. The latter can only be upheld by a public agent that can speak for all: i.e. the state. Consequently, the enforcement of criminal law must remain in public hands (see Thorburn 2011b: 96 et seq. or Ripstein 2009: 308 et seq.).

In the following chapter, I would like to propose an alternative model to this *public-wrong conception of criminal law* that meets two criteria: It is able to explain the public character of crimes whilst simultaneously allowing us to conceptualise crimes directed against individuals as violations of their rights. To this end, I will first argue that, at the level of substantive law, crimes are primarily concerned with the rights of the victim. This is the case since deontic control over the primary duty whose violation constitutes the crime lies with the victim (II.). I will go on to show that criminal law – unlike civil law – is particularly concerned with one aspect of the violation of rights: the offender's disregard for the legal status of the victim as a holder of rights (III.). Finally, drawing on relational theories of morality, I will demonstrate that understanding crimes as status violations not only substantiates attributing rights to individuals, but also identifies crimes as a public matter, in turn justifying public prosecution (IV.).

2. Consent and Rights in Substantive Criminal Law

Anyone attempting to discuss rights in criminal law should first clarify what rights actually are. However, it would exceed the scope of this chapter to adequately address this question, which has been disputed for decades. Instead, I will focus on *legal* rights and conceptualise them in the tradition of the *will theory*.[3] This appears justified, as legal practitioners and scholars – notwithstanding the

[3] Sometimes also called *choice theory of rights*. Its elaboration by Hart 1955, 1982 in particular has remained influential to this day. Other will-theory approaches can be found, for example, in Wellman 1985; Sumner 1987; Steiner 1994 or more recently Weissinger 2019. But see (even older) German literature, e.g. von Savigny 1841: 331 et seq. or Kelsen 1960: 130 et seq. Adopting an understanding of rights based on the *will theory of rights* naturally entails a number of conceptual limitations and problems inherent in the *will theory*. On the 'conceptual baggage' of the *will theory* (also in comparison to other approaches), see specifically Campbell 2006: 43 et seq.; Edmundson 2012: 98 et seq. and Wenar 2021. These conceptual limitations concern in particular the question of who or what can be the holder of rights, which in turn raises the question of who or what constitutes a legal subject. Since a concept of rights informed by the *will theory* only considers those entities to be potential rights-holders that are able to exercise power in the Hohfeldian sense (e.g. by being able to consent or

academic dispute about the correct theory of rights – still largely determine legal rights based on considerations rooted in *will theory*. Judges and other legal officials do not consider a putative right to be a legal right unless the presumptive rights-holder has specific powers with regard to the obligation of a legally obligated party. This makes a legal right a Hohfeldian (see Hohfeld 1913/17) molecule consisting of a claim-right in combination with a power pertaining to the legal duty correlative with the right.[4] Different forms of power can be distinguished following Steiner's classification:

1. to waive compliance with the duty (i.e. extinguish it);
2. to leave the duty in existence (i.e. demand compliance with it);
3. to waive proceeding for the enforcement of the duty (i.e. for the restraint of, or compensation by, the duty-holder in the face of threatened or actual breach) and thereby forgive its breach;
4. to demand proceeding for the enforcement of the duty;
5. to waive enforcement;
6. to demand enforcement.[5]

For an attribution of rights, it seems sufficient for one of these forms of power to be applicable, either on an individual level or in connection with others.[6] Thus, prima facie, it is not impossible that the power to waive rights and the power to (judicially) enforce rights are attributed to different subjects within a legal system.[7]

However, I see the question of whose rights are wronged by criminal offences (the victim or the legal community) as a matter of substantive criminal law, which defines criminal offences and potential defences. This, in turn, limits the scope of

to enforce rights in court), animals, for example, are excluded; in the case of children or legal persons, a more or less comprehensive proxy model is required. See also Hart 1982: 184, fn 86, but critical of the resulting inconsistencies of the will theory, e.g. Wellman 1995: 116 et seq. and MacCormick 1976. Of course, this has implications for the rights-based conception of criminal law developed below, where criminal law is invoked to protect, for example, animals, children or corporate identities.

[4] The ensuing question of whether we should add to the full description of rights a privilege in Hohfeld's sense – being allowed to exercise a power (to which the distinction between validity and legitimacy is coupled) – cannot be addressed here.

[5] Steiner 1994: 69, following the fundamentally similar distinction made by Hart 1982: 184.

[6] However, this is controversial: While the levels of compensation (levels 5 and 6) are ignored by most will theorists, many emphasise the aspect of (judicial) enforceability (levels 3 and 4; see, e.g. Kelsen 1960: 139 et seq. or Wellman 1985: 136). For others, the mere possibility of the right's addressee to be released from the correlative duty (levels 1 and 2) suffices to be attributed rights (e.g. Sumner 1987: 43). I agree with the latter view because subsequent levels, i.e. levels 3–6, are contingent upon and justified by the existence of a power at the first two levels; firstly, there is a logical precedence in that the question of enforcement only arises if the obligation has not been waived (i.e. no waiver of rights at the first level) and the obligation or right continues to exist; secondly, the fact that a person has the power to insist on or waive a right is a *pro tanto* reason to give them the power to enforce the right if it is infringed. This does not preclude assigning the enforcement of the right to someone else for other reasons. However, this goes hand in hand with an increased need to justify assigning downstream levels of power (enforcement) to someone other than the person who has primary power over the duty of conduct.

[7] Similarly, it is conceivable that a right may be assigned to more than one person (either individually or collectively) at the first, second or third level. See also Kelsen 1960: 141.

consideration to the first two levels of power. Indeed, an act does not need to be prosecutable as part of criminal proceedings to qualify as an offence under substantive criminal law.[8] On a descriptive level, we can distinguish substantive criminal law from criminal procedural law because the latter only entails the mechanisms by which the former is enforced. Therefore, the attribution of rights on a substantive level can be considered independently of the procedural reaction to a criminal wrong. It follows that who is wronged by a criminal offence depends solely on who has power over the existence or non-existence of duties, the violation of which is punishable under criminal law (i.e. level 1 and 2 in the above list). Now, most offences affecting individual interests can be justified or excused by an individual's consent. This corresponds to the (potential) victim executing a legal power to waive compliance with a duty (i.e. extinguish it) or to leave the duty in existence. This means that, focusing on substantive criminal law and thus on power on the first two of the aforementioned levels, the *will theory of rights* conceptualises consent as an instance of discharging someone from his or her duty; hence, it designates the (potential) victim as the rights-holder. To put it differently: Individuals hold legal rights against possible offenders not to be criminally battered, robbed, raped, or otherwise encroached upon their interests, precisely because *they* have the power to waive compliance with the duty in question.

Some objections might be raised against this line of argument. For one, criminal law does not recognise an unlimited power of consent. For example, major assaults against individuals, such as killing someone, cannot be legally justified by a victim's consent. Admittedly, this is a bullet I have to bite.[9] However, this does not call into question rights in criminal law in general. Justifiable restrictions on consent (e.g. in cases of incapacity to autonomously determine one's own affairs) at best prove that the scope for the legal system to assign power over obligations relevant to criminal law to individuals is limited.[10] However, this should not come as a surprise and is not specific to criminal law. There are also limits to private

[8] Effective criminalisation, of course, requires procedural enforcement. It would hardly be conceivable for behaviour X to be criminalised by a legislature passing a law that defines X as a crime, only for them to add that X-ing will not attract criminal liability – that those who engage in X-ing must never be prosecuted. However, the procedural question of whether and how an act of X-ing is to be prosecuted does not arise until, on a substantive level, the violation of a duty backed by criminal sanctions comes into play (see n 6). Since the question of who is wronged by a crime depends primarily on the direction of this duty, this is a matter of substantive law. For partly similar considerations, see also Stevens 2014: 119 et seq.

[9] At least against the background of the will theory of rights, which has difficulties in conceptually accounting for inalienable rights that cannot be waived.

[10] Admittedly, incompetent consent is a relatively uncontroversial example; most would agree that, in general, only competent consent may waive a duty. The more difficult examples are those where criminal law does not sanction even competent, informed consent to negate an offence, e.g. in the case of consensual homicide. This raises the question of whether criminal law should refrain from defining as criminal what is done with the consent of the person concerned, restricting itself to *injuria* – and *volenti non fit injuria*. I cannot explore this question in depth here, but I would like to propose two possible solutions: First, one could take a strictly positivist stance and reject the question entirely. Restrictions on consent are nothing more than restrictions on the attribution of rights within a positive

autonomy in civil law along the lines of those in criminal law – for example, void contracts that cannot be enforced by either party, even when both had agreed. However, no one would doubt the existence of rights in civil law because of this.[11]

A second objection could be that the outlined argument is only cogent insofar as it concerns the violation of individual interests. How do victimless crimes, which clearly affect only public interests, fit into the picture? In the context of criminal offences that aim at protecting public interests it makes little sense to speak of individual rights in criminal law. However, this does not stand in the way of applying the concept of crimes as violations of rights to them as well. In victimless crimes, all members of society are the joint holder of a right. To exercise this public right, society has created a public agent, the state. It follows that state authorities only have a derivative legal power, which they exercise vicariously for the members of the legal community. So, even if the power of consent in criminal law is only a strong argument in favour of individual rights, there is nothing to be said against adopting the concept of violations of rights in the context of victimless crimes, the legal community being the entitled person.[12]

Finally, one could object that my approach leads to a problematic privatisation of criminal law. This objection can be understood in two ways: On the one hand, it seems that it would lead to a levelling of the differences between civil and criminal wrongs, and thus between civil law and criminal law. On the other hand, my approach seems to be incompatible with the idea that crimes – even where they impair individual interests – concern us all; that is, that they are always a public matter. I would like to investigate these two objections separately in an attempt to reject them.

3. Crimes as Status Violations

What is the difference between civil and criminal wrongs anyway if crimes affecting individuals are understood as violations of individual rights? There can be no

system of criminal law. Whether these legal restrictions – provided that higher law (e.g. the constitution) allows them – can in turn be morally justified, cannot be meaningfully answered from a legal perspective. Secondly, the principle of *volenti non fit injuria* could be recognised as a moral principle constitutive of criminal law (I personally think that competent and informed consent should always be recognised in criminal law as negating the crime). If this were accepted, then the criminalisation of the killing of another human being upon their request might only be justified if it can be shown that not only the person killed is affected; for example, by citing the protection of the rights of third parties (or of collective legal interests) as the fundamental reason for criminalisation (for this line of reasoning, see, e.g. Stevens 2014: 117 et seq.; McConnell 2000: 29 et seq. and Hruschka 1977: 198, fn 16). Yet if this cannot be convincingly justified (and I think there is much to be said for that position), then criminalisation itself cannot be justified.

[11] For a similar rebuttal, see Stevens 2014: 119 et seq.

[12] In fact, this is what adherents of a *public-rights conception of criminal wrongdoing* advocate when they conceive of criminal wrongdoing as violations of rights of the state. See, e.g. Steiner 1994: 66 et seq. or Renzikowski 2007: 563, 569 et seq. While this is particularly odd when it comes to explaining violations of individual rights (see Moser 2019: 182 et seq.), it works quite well for victimless crimes.

meaningful distinction between civil and criminal wrongs unless there are also differences in the way criminal law and civil law each conceptualise the violation of individual rights. In the following section, I would like to argue that this can be achieved by invoking the concept of a *status violation*. This is the case as a culpable status violation, i.e. the disrespect of claims to legal recognition, is constitutive only of criminal wrongdoing. More specifically: Criminal wrongs are characterised by the fact that one culpably disregards the normative authority that rights endow to a rights-holder. To support this argument, two things need to be shown: first, that rights have this recognitional function; and second, that this recognitional function is only relevant in criminal law.

3.1. The Recognitional Function of Rights

One notion of the recognitional function of rights is rooted in the fact that the attribution of rights often serves as a way of recognising the worth of individuals or groups (e.g. in the gay rights movement).[13] However, this is not the notion I am concerned with. My point is that holding rights comes with a special normative authority to which legal recognition refers. Whoever has a right, exercises a practical de jure authority vis-à-vis the obligated party to make a demand with regard to the object of the right. And vice versa: Whoever considers himself or herself obligated because of another person's right, stands in an accountability relation to the rights-holder; he or she must recognise and respect this authoritative status. Therefore, rights have a recognitional function that goes beyond claiming a certain behaviour from someone else.[14] For this reason, I would like to distinguish between the material and the formal aspect of rights:[15] The *material* aspect of a right is about its content. The *formal* aspect of a right is about the status that someone has as the holder of the right. Let us take the example of my property right to my car. If Peter takes possession of my car, then I can demand a certain behaviour from Peter, namely, to hand over the car. This is what my right consists in *materially*. At the same time, I can demand that he recognises my normative authority as the owner: I alone, and no one else, can assert this authoritative status in relation to Peter. This is what my right consists in *formally*.

[13] On the recognitional function in this sense, see Edmundson 2012: 113 et seq.

[14] This recognitional function of having rights is naturally associated with *demand theories of rights*. Like *will theories*, they focus on the agency of the rights-holder; unlike *will theories*, they place a special emphasis on how the status of a rights-holder plays out in intersubjective relations. The *locus classicus* for this approach is Feinberg 1980: 151, labelling rights as 'especially sturdy objects to "stand upon" […]. Having rights enables us to "stand up like men", to look others in the eye, and to feel in some fundamental way the equal of anyone. […] Indeed, respect for persons (this is an intriguing idea) may simply be respect for their rights […]. To respect a person then, […] simply is to think of him as a potential maker of claims.' Various elements of a *demand theory* can also be seen in the work of Wildt 1992: 148 et seq., Waldron 2000: 128 et seq. or Darwall 2006: 18 et seq.

[15] As far as I know, the distinction I want to make was first systematically developed in Kant's philosophy of law. See Kant, *Metaphysik der Sitten* (1797), § 42 with fn * and, on this, Hirsch 2017: 305 and Hirsch 2021: 162 et seq.

As the example shows, these two aspects of a right correspond to two different claims: the *material* claim to fulfil a certain duty which is the content or object of the right; and the *formal* claim to be recognised as the holder of a right with a special normative authority to make that material demand. It is the latter, the formal claim, that comes with a recognitional function. This is nicely illustrated by Feinberg's distinction between two ways of claiming one's right which he describes in his widely acclaimed essay 'The Nature and Value of Rights':

> One important difference then between *making legal claim to* and *claiming that* is that the former is a legal performance with direct legal consequences whereas the latter is often a mere piece of descriptive commentary with no legal force. Legally speaking, *making claim to* can itself make things happen. This sense of "claiming", then, might well be called "the performative sense". [...] Claiming that one has a right [...] as opposed to "performative claiming" [...] is another sort of thing [...]. To claim that one has rights is to make an assertion that one has them, and to make it in such a manner as to demand or insist that they be recognized (Feinberg 1980: 150).

Following Feinberg, I will refer to the performative and assertoric claiming of a right. A right is claimed *performatively* when Φ – i.e. the content or object of the right – is claimed. In contrast, a right is claimed *assertorically* when the recognition of the status as rights-holder (i.e. of being entitled to demand Φ from the obligor) is claimed. Only the latter is a claim to recognition.

However, it is important to emphasise that this recognitional function is not merely an insignificant, commendable by-product of rights ownership. Rather, it is a constitutive element of it. Without it, it would be impossible to understand what it means to be the owner and addressee of a right. Indeed, the recognitional function of rights is crucial to understanding why duties correlative with rights are *directed* duties. It is characteristic of rights that they correlate with duties directed to or owed to the rights-holder. However, I am obligated to the rights-holder precisely because he or she exercises practical authority in relation to me. If I want to fulfil my duty *as* a directed duty, then I must recognise this status. The reverse is true for violations of rights: The violation of a directed duty is more than just *a wrong*: It is *a wronging* of the being to whom the duty is owed (see e.g. Hart 1982: 184; Waldron 1984: 8; Jones 1994: 36 et seq. or Thompson 2006). Hence, flouting of a directed duty always expresses disrespect for the person entitled to it (see also Darwall 2006: 18 et seq., 140 et seq.; Wallace 2019: 82 et seq., 156 et seq. and Vandieken 2019: 293 et seq.).

3.2. Criminal Wrongs as Violations of Rights in the Formal Sense

How does this help us to distinguish between criminal and civil wrongs when both see the individual as the rights-holder? On the surface, there seems to be no difference. The same protected interests and the same primary duties underlie torts and crimes, e.g. in the case of tortious battery and criminal battery. In both cases, the content of the right, i.e. the claim not to be harmed and the corresponding duty to refrain from harming, is the same. However, if we consider the formal aspect of a right and the recognitional function that comes with it, civil law and criminal law take different paths. This is the case because civil law does not attach any decisive importance to a culpable status violation, i.e. to the offender's disregard for the practical authority of the rights-holder.[16] On the one hand, tort law does allow for strict liability (i.e. liability regardless of whether someone is at fault for disregarding the rights of others[17]). On the other hand, the disregard of the rights of others is not in itself sufficient to trigger civil liability. Thus, tort law neither recognises liability for attempts nor liability for endangerments. Rather, civil liability presupposes that the object or content of the right was actually impaired. Let us again take the example of tortious battery: Civil liability requires that harm to bodily integrity was actually caused. The situation is different in criminal law. In Germany, for example, there is no strict liability at all; in common law jurisdictions, there is a strong presumption against strict liability.[18] It follows that only a person who culpably disregards the rights of others can be held criminally liable. In fact, such a status violation is not only necessary (at least in most crimes),[19] it is also sufficient for criminal liability. This is the case because even if no harm or

[16] For a partly similar verdict – although not related to a culpable *status violation* – see Sullivan 2014 and Antill, Chapter 6 in this volume, who argue that tort law focuses on compensation for harm and therefore does not place the same emphasis on culpable wrongdoing as criminal law: It does not differentiate between levels of wrongdoing as subtly as criminal law does, and also ignores some forms of criminal wrongdoing, such as attempts, altogether.

[17] This is, of course, controversial and there has been an ongoing debate as to whether strict liability can be justified in tort law. However, although there are many torts in both civil and common law jurisdictions that require fault (at least negligence) on the part of the defendant in order to be liable for causing harm, there remains a considerable number of torts in tort law that do not require fault. See, e.g. Flume 2021 for German and Austrian law; and for a survey of European tort law, Dam 2013. For English law, see Oliphant 2017; Sullivan 2014 and in particular Gray 2020. For a comparative law perspective, see Bussani, Sebok and Infantino 2022.

[18] Admittedly, the situation is not clear-cut in common law jurisdictions: On the one hand, there is a certain opposition towards strict liability due to the commitment to the *mens rea* principle rooted in common law. On the other hand, there are many offences, particularly in statutory law, which either (in part) do not require fault or where this has not been stipulated, leaving the matter to interpretation. In English law, for example, there has even been a presumption against strict liability since 1960, unanimously established by the House of Lords, according to which 'the common law presumes that, unless Parliament has indicated otherwise, the corresponding mental element is an unexpressed ingredient of every offence' (*B* v *DPP*, [2000] 2 AC, 428, 460). However, this presumption of *mens rea* can be (and has been) rebutted by the courts when interpreting statutes, and English criminal law now probably contains more offences which impose strict liability than ones which require fault – as well as more offences of this kind than most other European countries. Nevertheless, the moral objections to holding people criminally liable when they have not been proven to be at fault are deeply anchored in the common law criminal law theory and theoretically well-founded. For an overview of the problematic relationship between strict liability and criminal law, see the contributions in Simester 2005 and also the overview in Horder and Ashworth 2022: 100 et seq., 192 et seq. and in particular 199 et seq.

[19] This naturally leads to the question whether criminal liability should depend solely on such status violations. If so, this would argue for treating attempted and completed crimes in the same way. Moreover, criminal liability would be excluded in the case of (inadvertent) negligence. I cannot explore

damage has been caused, one can be liable to prosecution solely for attempting to undermine the legal status of another person or for culpably creating a risk for this to happen.

Now one might ask why it is the culpable *status violation* that is characteristic of criminal wrongdoing: Why is it not sufficient to refer to the culpable violation of a duty as the distinguishing factor between criminal and civil wrongdoing? The answer is that only the concept of a status violation captures the fact that criminal offences are about the violation of rights correlative with directed duties. If we were to only refer to the culpable breach of duty, it would not matter to whom this duty is owed and who is wronged by its breach. The formal aspect of a right and the associated recognitional function alone express that rights correlate with directed duties. It is this directedness that matters in criminal law,[20] as demonstrated by the power of consent. Consent in criminal law demonstrates that criminal wrongdoing depends precisely on the offender disregarding the victim's special normative authority to decide on the permissibility of harmful conduct.[21] Let me present this argument again in a slightly more formalised version:

1. If consent in criminal law requires us to conceptualise criminal offences as culpable violations of rights or of the duties that correlate with them;
2. And if the directedness of duties correlative with rights presupposes that the obligor and the obligee stand in a relationship of authority and accountability, so that the breach of a directed duty owed to the rights-holder shows disrespect for his/her authoritative status;
3. Then a culpable status violation is constitutive of criminal offences.

If this is correct, and if, in turn, such a culpable status violation is neither necessary nor sufficient for civil liability, then a meaningful distinction can still be made between torts and criminal offences, even with both involving the violation of individual rights. Thus, individual rights in criminal law do not lead to a privatisation of criminal law in the sense of cancelling out the difference to civil law.

this question in detail within the scope of this paper and must contend myself here with a Solomonic response: If one wants to advocate a rights-based approach as a monistic theory, then this involves treating attempted and completed crimes equally and decriminalising crimes of negligence (see Hirsch 2021: 219 et seq. for details). However, my approach does not seem prima facie incompatible with a *pluralist theory* of criminal law that recognises other criteria for criminal behaviour (e.g. harm) in addition to status violation, which might allow for different treatment, for example of completed and attempted crimes.

[20] This does not mean that there is no bipolarity and directed duties in private law. I am merely arguing that civil law does not attach any importance to bipolarity in the context of rights (i.e. the recognitional function) in what constitutes a wrong.

[21] Insofar as the offender must cognitively understand that a harmful act is not being performed with consent. If the offender erroneously believes that he or she is performing a harmful act with the consent of the person concerned, there is no criminal liability. See Dsouza, Chapter 7 in this volume.

4. Special and Shared Normative Authority

However, this only helps us to avoid the first prong of the aforementioned 'privatisation objection'. The other prong aims at the alleged fact that conceptualising criminal offences as violations of individual rights would mean that crimes could no longer be understood as a public matter. The need for a public prosecution of criminal offences directed against individuals would thus become obsolete. However, this objection fails to recognise that the violation of the victim's authoritative status, which is constitutive of criminal offences, always has a supra-individual and thus society-wide dimension.

To demonstrate this, I would like to take a closer look at the metaethics of directed duties correlative with rights, drawing on Stephan Darwall's conception of second-personal reasons (Darwall 2006).[22] In his acclaimed book, 'The Second-Person Standpoint', Darwall argues that directed duties have an essentially interpersonal character. According to him, those duties implicate a distinct class of practical reasons, 'second-personal reasons [...] whose validity depends on presupposed authority and accountability relations between persons and, therefore, on the possibility of the reason's being addressed person-to-person' (Darwall 2006: 8, italics omitted). Thus, second-personal reasons are agent-relative (as opposed to agent-neutral) reasons for action. This means that these reasons for action only apply because and insofar as someone else has normative authority over me, and I am accountable to him or her. As Darwall shows, however, second-personal reasons are subject to certain felicity conditions. If, for example, A demands something from B, then this constitutes a second-personal reason for action for B if and only if:

1. A has de jure legitimate authority to make this demand on B (*normative authority*).[23]
2. B is accountable to A, insofar as A is entitled to blame B, complain to B or otherwise demand responsibility from B in case of refusal or non-fulfilment (*accountability*).[24]

[22] Darwall's approach is one of several approaches that seek a relational justification of morality and that have gained some traction in the moral philosophical literature. See, e.g., Wallace 2019 and Zylberman 2021. I use Darwall's approach here because – unlike Wallace and Zylberman, for example – he does not attempt to trace all moral duties back to bipolar duties but recognises that bipolar and impersonal duties coexist and are inextricably linked. This is what makes him interesting for the relational interpretation of criminal wrongdoing that I am trying to defend.

[23] This normative authority must not be misunderstood as a legislative authority, according to which the authority would consist in creating obligations that would not otherwise exist. Darwall's theory of morality illustrates this point: According to Darwall 2006: 277 et seq., 300 et seq., the origin of moral duties are the demands of the moral community, which he justifies in terms of hypothetical contractualism (as demands on behaviour that no one could reasonably reject). Therefore, authority – and this idea can also be transferred to other, non-moral normative duties – is rather an authority in terms of validity (according to which it depends on the authority of the entitled person whether an obligation remains in force or is maintained) and an authority in terms of justification (according to which one is able to demand accountability from others for breaches of duty). See also James 2007: 915 et seq. and Yaffe 2007: 949 et seq.

[24] See Darwall 2006: 15 et seq., 65 et seq.

3. B is normatively competent, i.e. B can comprehend the demand asserted by A as a justified reason for action and – on the basis of this – to consider himself or herself responsible to act in accordance with the demand (*normative competence*).[25]
4. Authority, accountability and competence are, in principle, claimed or attributed reciprocally, so that the authority claimed by A is not forcefully imposed on B, but is acceptable by the latter as a free and equal agent of the normative community (*reciprocity*).[26]

These felicity conditions for successfully addressing second-personal reasons and, likewise, for being bound by directed duties reveal a central feature of those reasons: Individual authority can only be claimed between two persons if, *ceteris paribus*, it can, in principle, be claimed by every member of the normative community (including the accountable person).[27] This has the effect that second-personal reasons must always be considered under two aspects. For one,

[25] Darwall 2006: 22 et seq., 107 et seq. In this respect, he refers to *Pufendorf's Point*: '[I]n holding people responsible, we are committed to the assumption that they can hold themselves responsible by self-addressed demands from a perspective that we and they share, [...] the standpoint of free and rational members of the moral community.' Here, Darwall recalls Pufendorf's insight that '[t]o be obligated [...], we must be able to take a second-personal standpoint on ourselves and be motivated by internally addressed demands whose (second-personal) authority we ourselves accept' (Darwall 2006: 23).

[26] See Darwall 2006: 20 et seq., 243 et seq.

[27] This claim, of course, requires some explanation, which Darwall has given in great detail – and I think convincingly – in his book and other papers on the subject. For the purpose of this chapter, however, I will attempt to summarise Darwall's argument for the 'entailment claim', i.e. that bipolar obligations always already entail a moral obligation period (i.e. an obligation that is not owed to a specific person and thus not agent-relative) and, hence, that individual authority must inherently entail representative authority. Darwall's argument is based on the premise that the determination of moral obligations is not within the purview of particular individuals, even when those obligations are owed to them (i.e. bipolar obligations). To illustrate this, Darwall examines the process of blame from the perspective of the victim. Consider a scenario in which a blatant breach of duty to you occurs; for example, I step on your foot for no good reason. Your blame, which subsequently manifests as an implicit moral demand for a better course of action, is more than a simple expression of emotion. Rather, it is an attempt to highlight my blameworthy actions and hold me accountable. The essence of your blame is to initiate a dialogical interaction, an 'implicit R.S.V.P.' that requires recognition on your part (see Darwall 2006: 145). However, the process of acknowledging and accepting your blame, culminating in feelings of guilt and remorse, requires that I accept your blame as justified and agree that a different course of action would have been more appropriate (see Darwall 2006: 28, 2013a: 139). It is not simply because of you, the victim, having said so that I would accept your blame as justified. Rather, it is the realisation that the implicit demand in your blame could be made by any member of the moral community, including myself, that triggers my acceptance of your blame and subsequent guilt. In essence, it requires understanding that my actions against you constitute a universal moral transgression, or in Darwall's terms: a violation of an *obligation period*. Darwall refers to this as *Pufendorf's Point* (Darwall 2006: 23, 112), which is expressed by the third of the aforementioned felicity conditions (*normative competence*, fn 25) and posits that in order to legitimately obligate and hold others accountable, there must be an assumption that they can hold themselves responsible and accountable for the same reasons from a shared perspective (see Darwall 2013c: 37 et seq.). Darwall sees this shared perspective as the impartially disciplined perspective of the moral community, rather than a simple normative implication between two individuals. The application of *Pufendorf's Point* illustrates that when one assigns blame, one reinforces a claim that is assumed to be universally applicable within the moral community. Consequently, according to Darwall, the act of blaming, whether directed at oneself or others, implicitly communicates a demand, not out of individual discretion, but as a representation of the moral community.

second-personal claims express a *bipolar* authority/accountability relation; in turn, this constitutes a particular instantiation of a *general* authority/accountability relation within the normative community of equal agents. The following diagram helps to understand the normative relations at issue:

Bipolar normative claim	*Instantiation of* →	Impersonal normative claim
↕		↕
Individual Authority	*Instantiation of* →	Supra-individual authority[28]

Individual second-personal authority vis-à-vis an accountable person (corresponding to a bipolar normative claim) thus implies that the accountable person as well as uninvolved third persons have what I would like to call a supra-individual second-personal authority as members of the normative community (corresponding to an impersonal normative claim).[29] Nevertheless, despite this derivational connection, individual authority – compared to supra-individual authority – is accompanied by a special, privileged status, since it establishes claims of a different kind, as Darwall vividly shows using the example of rights:

> Right holders […] have a distinctive authority to hold others answerable for violations of *their* rights that third parties do not have. The point is not that third parties

[28] Following Darwall 2013c: 39: 'Bipolar normativity [*sc.* bipolar normative claim] involves a distinctive individual authority that obligees have to make demands of and hold obligors responsible. And moral obligation period [*sc.* impersonal normative claim] entails a representative authority that anyone shares as a representative person or member of the moral community.' The elements in each column entail each other, and each of the elements in the left column entails the element in the right column that is in its row. Since general claims can exist without corresponding bipolar claims, the elements in the right column do not entail the elements in the left column in their rows.

[29] I would like to deviate from Darwall's terminology in order to follow a differentiation rooted in norm theory – particularly common in German legal scholarship – according to which criminal sanctions presuppose the violation of a norm of conduct. A distinction must be made here between a violation of a concrete duty of conduct (i.e. the norm of conduct already concretised for a specific case) and a violation of the general norm of conduct (i.e. as it expressed in criminal law provisions in an abstract-general way): If A commits an assault on B according to Section 223(1) of the German Criminal Code, then the punishable violation of the duty of conduct in the bilateral relationship between A and B constitutes a violation of the right (i.e. the bipolar normative claim) of B because the existence of the duty of A not to assault B depended on B's (non-)consent, and thus it was precisely B who was wronged. At the same time, however, this breach of duty constitutes a violation of the norm of conduct as an abstract-general rule (i.e. the one from which the specific duty of A in relation to B was derived), whereby A acted 'objectively' wrongfully. This 'objective wrongdoing' consists in the fact that all other addressees of the norm enshrined in Section 223(1) of the German Criminal Code (C, D, … *n*) may demand compliance with the rules of conduct subject to criminal sanctions (i.e. the impersonal normative claim) because the special authorisation of B is only the concrete instantiation of a supra-individual authority from which every member of the legal community can hypothetically derive a special authorisation – i.e. if they themselves are affected. Or, to put it differently: Since every member of the legal community may potentially derive individual claims from norms of conduct that are enforced by means of punishment due to their nomological structure, every member may generally demand that everyone should comply with these norms. On this in detail, see Hirsch 2021: 187 et seq.

> have no authority. To the contrary, I [...] claim that any special authority right holding obligees have can exist only if there is also an authority, *representative* [in my terms: *supra-individual*] *authority*, which they share with third parties, as well as with any obligor who might violate their rights. The point is that there is a special *individual* authority an obligee has to hold the obligor personally answerable that can, like the power of consent, be exercised only by the right-holding obligee herself at her discretion (Darwall 2013c: 30).

Let us again take the example of Peter who takes possession of my car: In the bipolar relationship with Peter, I have a special, individual authority with regard to the car. This is reflected, for example, in the fact that I can demand its return or consent to it being damaged. However, I only have this individual authority because I am part of the legal community with Peter and other persons, which assigns this authority to each owner. As members of the legal community (and potential owners), they therefore have a supra-individual authority. They, too, may demand that my individual authority (i.e. ownership powers) is respected, although they have no individual authority – and thus no bipolar claims – regarding my car. However, this connection between individual and supra-individual authority also holds true in the case of a status violation, i.e. the disrespect of one's authority. If Peter destroys my car against my will, he not only violates my special status, i.e. my normative authority as the rights-holder with the power to consent, but also the general status of every member of the legal community. This is the case because my special authority to consent to harmful acts concerning my property exists only because and insofar as all members of the legal community (including Peter) may claim it, *ceteris paribus*, with regard to their legal interests.

Since, in my understanding, the violation of individual rights in criminal law amounts to the disregard or non-recognition of the victim's legal status as a rights-holder, this meta-ethical analysis of rights and directed duties following Darwall allows criminal offences to be considered as a private *and* a public matter. The clou of my approach is to conceptualise criminal wrongdoing intersubjectively all the way through. When it comes to their private dimension, crimes are violations of individual rights, or more precisely: of the special legal status constitutive of the ownership of rights. However, since this special legal status is an instantiation of the general status that each member of the legal community holds, crimes retain a public dimension. Public prosecution is justified by the fact that not only the special legal status of the victim is violated, but also – albeit in a different way – the underlying general legal status of every other member of the legal community (including the offender). Thus, the public dimension of crimes, i.e. crimes being a matter of general public concern, is derived from the plurality of the violated subjects.[30] In this dual wrongfulness of crimes, understood as status violations, lies

[30] I must admit that this analysis differs from Darwall's position in two respects: First, Darwall himself draws a parallel between the distinction between bipolar obligations and obligations periods and the distinction between civil law (more precisely: tort law) and criminal law. For Darwall – and he shares this view with many other advocates of bipolar normativity – tort law is the proper realm in

the deeper normative reason why criminal proceedings – unlike civil proceedings – allow for both public prosecution and individual participation by the victim.

5. The Twofold Nature of Crimes

Let me summarise my argument again: The power of consent in criminal law demonstrates that the normative authority to decide on the (non-)existence of a duty – the violation of which is punishable under criminal law – lies with the potential victim. It follows that crimes are primarily a violation of individual rights, the distinctive feature of criminal liability (as distinguished from civil liability) being that the offender culpably disregards this particular *individual authority*. However, this individual authority to consent is vested in the individual by the legal community, as I have attempted to demonstrate drawing on Stephen Darwall's conception of second-personal normativity. It can exist only if there is also a *shared authority*, which the potential victim possesses together with third parties, as well as with any obligor who might violate his or her rights. This explains why crimes necessarily have both a supra-individual and an intersubjective dimension. The former justifies public prosecution, the latter justifies victims' participation rights in criminal proceedings.

Compared to the *public-wrong conception of criminal law* mentioned at the beginning, this perspective on crimes has the advantage of providing a normative explanation of why consent may justify crimes against individuals. It can also provide a normative explanation of why victims should be involved in criminal proceedings, as victims' participation rights are not merely charitable benefits that

which bipolar obligations have their place. See Darwall 2013d: 176 et seq., but also Thompson 2006: 343 et seq. or Wallace 2019: 98 et seq. I fear, however, that in doing so Darwall overestimates the bipolar internal structure of tort law, at least if – as I have attempted to show above – we take the recognitional aspect of bipolar obligation seriously and categorically understand the flouting of bipolar obligations as a failure of recognition. At a minimum, and this is all I need for my argument, bipolar normativity has its place in criminal law if we understand crimes as status violations. Second, Darwall seems to paint a different, less individualistic picture of impersonal obligations and supra-individual authority than I do when he says that 'it is up to the people and their representatives, e.g. prosecutors, to decide whether and how to hold people accountable for violations of criminal law' (Darwall 2013b: 84 and likewise Darwall 2013c: 31). This suggests that criminal wrongdoing concerns the polity ('the people') as such, rather than its constituent citizens individually. According to this view, the public dimension of criminal wrongdoing is due to the genuinely collective character of the people (the normative community). I, on the other hand, would like to conceptualise the public dimension of criminal wrongdoing in a thoroughly intersubjective way. I see no need for prosecution by a public prosecutor on the grounds that the public ('the people') has been wronged as a collective. Rather, the public character of criminal justice is fundamentally a matter of pragmatism. Since each individual member of the community has had his or her supra-individual status violated, it is easier to provide for a kind of class action on behalf of all individuals than for all members of the legal community to have to deal bilaterally with the offender because of the violation of their supra-individual authority. Supra-individual authority is indeed a public status in that it can be claimed by anyone as a member of the normative community. However, this does not change the fact that individual claims correspond to this status.

we hand out to victims so that they may better cope with a crime. Rather, they reflect the fact that victims of crime – from the perspective of substantive criminal law – have their own rights violated. At the same time, this approach enables us to retain the public dimension that justifies public prosecution. Hence, acknowledging this dual nature of crime does not replace the *public-wrong conception of criminal law*, but adds another layer to it, which allows us to paint a more comprehensive normative picture of crime.

9

Reconciliation as a Sufficient Response to Crime

MICHAŁ DEREK*

1. Introduction

One of the fundamental dilemmas of criminal justice is the search for an appropriate response to the crime committed. In essence, the appropriate response to a crime has been strictly linked to the finding of guilt of the perpetrator and the imposition of punishment. It seems to be undeniable that there are good reasons, even if not sufficient ones, to punish the offender when the victim is looking for a criminal response to the crime that has been committed. Sometimes, however, the victim's attitude towards the offender and the crime itself may be different: the victim may simply wish to obtain compensation for the harm caused by reconciliation with the offender (Westen 2004). When discussing individual rights in criminal law and their possible impact on the state's right to punish, it is worth considering the following question: should the state refrain from punishing the offender if such a wish is expressed? The dilemma behind this question is the following: does the attack on the interests of the individual concern only that individual, or does it also concern society as a whole? Does reconciliation and reparation alone satisfy the requirements of justice? Or is it essential to preserve the conservative system of the public right to punish the perpetrators in every case of the commission of a prohibited act, regardless of the victim's wishes?

The answers to these questions are not obvious for a number of reasons. The lack of punishment for the prohibited act due to the reconciliation between the offender and the victim can be seen as a consequence of the recognition of the right of the victim to decide on his or her interests. One of the means of expressing this right is consent. Such a relationship between the right to respect for private life

* I am grateful to Philipp-Alexander Hirsch and Elias Moser for their valuable feedback on this chapter, which helped me identify ways to improve it.

and consent has also been recognised by the courts.[1] By virtue of the valid consent, the act is not unlawful and therefore criminal liability is excluded. Consent may be prior (when the victim allows the second person to violate his or her interests) or subsequent (when the victim subsequently accepts the violation of his or her interests). The position of the victim, who does not demand punishment for the offender with whom she has reconciled, can be seen as an expression of the specific form of subsequent consent. However, some commentators do not even recognise prior consent as a defence in certain cases. According to such a view, the individual's right to privacy does not allow him or her to determine, for example, the question of the protection of life or health. Thus, the relevance of prior consent to, for example, euthanasia, voluntary sadomasochistic behaviour between adults or homosexual intercourse has been questioned (Devlin 1965; Stephen 1873). Secondly, the concept of retrospective consent has been challenged on the grounds that the victim cannot consent to the violation of her goods after the crime has been committed (Feinberg 1986a). Finally, it can be argued that reconciliation, although positively valued by society, does not generally mitigate the harm of the conduct to the extent that punishment can be completely waived.

Thus, the consideration of the individual's right to decide on the waiver of the criminal reaction to the wrong requires a clarification of the criminal significance of reconciliation. As can be seen, this is a problem of substantive criminal law (the legitimacy of the state to punish), which has its source in the scope of the individual's right to decide on his or her personal life, and at the same time implies consequences in procedural criminal law (the discontinuation of criminal proceedings). I will argue that there are good philosophical and ethical reasons for claiming that, if the victim does not seek the punishment of the perpetrator, the sufficient response to the prohibited act in certain cases can only be compensation for the damage resulting from the reconciliation between these parties. My aim is to show that, in such circumstances, the state may not be legitimate in punishing the offender. I will also argue that the resolution of the conflict between the offender and the victim may be important for society as a whole, since it is not incompatible with both the expressive and the retributive functions of criminal law.

2. 'From dawn to dusk': Article 59a of the Polish Criminal Code

To illustrate the dilemma, I will briefly outline the discussion in Poland on how to ensure justice in cases where reconciliation between the victim and the offender has taken place after the crime. In 2013, the Polish Parliament introduced the so-called

[1] See, e.g., judgments of the European Court of Human Rights: *Dudgeon v the United Kingdom*, application no 7525/76; *Laskey and others v the United Kingdom*, application nos 21627/93, 21628/93, 21974/93.

'great reform' of criminal procedure and substantive criminal law. The main goals of the reform were, in particular, to make the criminal justice system more adversarial and to strengthen the position of the victim. The latter involved increasing the importance of compensation and giving the victim and the offender greater influence in the proceedings. One of the basic assumptions was the belief that the response to the crime should not only be retrospective – consisting of public condemnation of the crime and retribution – but also prospective – allowing the conflict between the perpetrator and the victim to be extinguished (Kardas 2019: 22–24). Compensation for the damage caused by a crime and reconciliation between the victim and the perpetrator were found to be the means to achieve this goal.

One of the regulations expressing a new perspective of criminal justice was Article 59a of the Polish Criminal Code. It stipulated that criminal proceedings may be discontinued under the following conditions:

(a) the aggrieved party (victim) submits an application;
(b) the offender reconciles with the victim and makes amends or compensates for the damage before the start of the court proceedings;
(c) the offence was a property offence punishable by imprisonment for up to five years, an offence under Article 157 § 1 of the Penal Code (causing a disorder in the functioning of a bodily organ or a health disorder lasting more than seven days but not serious) or another offence punishable by imprisonment for up to three years;
(d) the perpetrator has not previously been convicted of an intentional crime involving the use of violence; and
(e) there are no special circumstances that make the procedure inconsistent with the need to fulfil the purposes of the punishment (Majewski 2015).

The regulation had been highly controversial even before it came into force. Its supporters stressed that not every crime deserves punishment. The behaviour of the offender after the crime should be taken into account when considering the response to the crime. The public, communal response to the crime committed – understood in the way Duff presents it (2003a: 61) – should be necessary in order to be justified. In other words, punishment, as a severe means of protecting goods, should only be applied when the social conflict could not be resolved outside the criminal proceedings, according to the *ultima ratio* principle of criminal law (Wróbel 2012). Furthermore, in some cases, the ethical need to satisfy the public sense of justice may be satisfied by accepting the victim's choice between punishment and restitution. The reason for dropping the case is not only reparation or compensation, which are specific elements of restorative justice, but also reconciliation. The latter fulfils an educational function, which is usually sufficient not only to repair the relationship between the victim and the offender but is also positively valued in society and reduces the social tension caused by the crime (Królikowski 2014: 79–84).

At the same time, the provision of Article 59a of the Criminal Code has been strongly criticised. According to its opponents, the primacy of restorative justice may lead to the exclusion of an appropriate response to the crime. The main justification for punishment is the affirmation of certain values and their binding force. The commission of a crime is always a violation of public order, regardless of the victim's opinion. Therefore, reconciliation between the victim and the perpetrator – even together with compensation – does not eliminate the need for punishment (Sepioło 2013: 114–15; Sakowicz 2013: 32–34). In addition, critical voices in the discussion pointed to the possible risk of pressure on the victim to submit the application and to the (too broad) scope of the crimes for which the proceedings could be discontinued. Opponents also emphasised that the regulation had unduly divided perpetrators into rich and poor, with only the latter able to protect themselves from punishment.

After its introduction into the Criminal Code, the provision of Article 59a was repealed by the new majority in the Polish Parliament in 2016 after less than 10 months. In the bill amending the Criminal Code, the authors noted that the provision had not achieved the goals of criminal law, especially in the form of retribution. The perpetrator's behaviour after committing the crime, as well as his attitude towards the victim, should not absolutely exclude punishment. In addition to the belief in 'buying justice', the authors underlined the risk of pressure on victims to 'absolve' perpetrators of criminal responsibility.

3. The Rights of the Individual and the Models of Criminalisation

As I have already pointed out, the discontinuation of criminal proceedings at the request of the victim who has reconciled with the offender should be seen as the result of the recognition of the victim's right to decide on his or her own interests. However, the scope of this right is disputed. It is therefore not surprising that consent in criminal law, as a means of expressing an attitude towards a particular interest, is sometimes called into question. The scope of individual autonomy, which affects both the validity of consent and the victim's ability to decide on the criminal consequences of wrongdoing, depends on the philosophical model of criminalisation. Models of criminalisation show the relationship between the rights of the individual (here: the victim) and the power of the state to punish (*ius puniendi*). Following the division into the harm principle, legal paternalism and legal moralism (Bayles 1974: 187), I would like to distinguish three models for justifying criminalisation: the liberal, the paternalistic and the communitarian. Depending on the model, it may or may not be legitimate for the state to punish if the victim consents to the act committed by the offender. At the same time, and more importantly in this chapter, each model indicates the specific limits within which the victim may choose other means of responding to the offender's crime (such as reconciliation). I will argue, however, that despite many significant differences between the models, each of them can, to a considerable extent, lead to the recognition of consent as a factor that excludes the legitimacy to punish.

In the liberal model, the restriction of an individual's freedom is only permissible if the individual's behaviour causes harm to others. Therefore, it is the individual who is the best judge of his own case (Mill 1859; Witmer-Rich 2011). Mill's division of social reality into two dimensions, the public and the private, can lead to the belief that the 'self-realising individual' (Taylor 1992: 28) is free to decide what is moral or immoral as long as the behaviour only affects his or her interests (Hart 1963; Lyons 1985). Any society based on liberal ideas must be neutral in its understanding of the good life. As is characteristic of all concepts based on nominalism, defined by Pinckaers as 'a system of thought that affirms that nothing is real except the individual and his singular acts' (2001: 115), freedom becomes 'an enclosed atom, an isolated island, a monad' (2005: 168). An individual simply has 'a right to do wrong' as long as the wrong affects only himself (Waldron 1981). It is therefore not surprising that the liberal model recognises the voluntary consent of the victim as a defence in criminal law (Feinberg 1984: 115; Williams 1957). As a result, acts such as attempted suicide, euthanasia or voluntary sterilisation may no longer be considered crimes. If the basic aim of criminal law is to protect the individual from the harm caused by another, the community cannot punish behaviour that is not considered harmful by the victim. The state's right to punish violations of individual values seems legitimate only as a simple consequence of an individual's choice to violate his or her rights.

However, it can be argued that the action against the individual always violates the public rules that guarantee freedom to all. Mill avoided this dilemma by taking a narrow view of the harm that justifies punishment: if the behaviour neither violates a specific duty to the public nor harms another individual, then the consequence of the action is that 'which society can afford to bear for the greater good of human freedom' (1859: 76). Feinberg, on the other hand, advised caution in using the 'public interest' argument to limit the validity of consent. There is a degree of affection for the public interest that still does not outweigh the harm caused by the state's encroachment on the liberty interests of its opponents (1984: 222). In the liberal model, then, the harm to the public resulting solely from the wrong to which the victim consents cannot a priori justify punishment.

The second model – the paternalistic one – asserts that criminalisation is legitimate even when it is necessary to prevent harm (physical, psychological, economic) to the actor himself (Feinberg 1986a). Freedom is understood here in a different way than in the liberal model – as subject to restrictions that go far beyond the mere prevention of harm to others. Freedom guides people towards objective goodness 'in order to confer upon the will the power to act with perfection' (Pinckaers 2005: 172); it is based on something unchangeable and external to the individual's faith. In the case of paternalism, this authority to judge what is right or wrong for others opens up the discussion of the possible role of law, especially criminal law, in the protection of values. Paternalism describes people as either placing 'an unreasonably high negative weight on what is at most an inconvenience, or discount unreasonably the probability or seriousness of future injury' (Dworkin 1988: 125), so that the state can protect them for their own – objectively viewed – goodness. It is worth noting, however, that criminal paternalism is a nuanced concept that can be further divided into 'hard', defined by Feinberg as aimed at 'protection of the competent adults, against their will, from the harmful consequences even of their fully voluntary choices and undertakings' for their own good, and 'soft', which prevents self-regarding harmful conduct only when that conduct is essentially involuntary (1986: 12). It is easy to see that a defence of consent is of little use in the case of hard paternalism. As long as the harm is objective and absolute, the individual is not entitled to decide on the scope of criminal law protection (Husak 2008: 68). Under soft paternalism, the range of behaviour to which the individual may consent is much broader.

The use of criminal law based on paternalism differs from the third of the above models, the communitarian model. What distinguishes the former from the latter is that in the communitarian model, criminal intervention is enforced not to protect the individual who is the victim of a criminal act (not 'for his sake' – Feinberg 1986a: 12), but rather to protect society as a whole. According to communitarians, liberalism ignores the implications of the assumption that the individual is not alienated from others, but forms certain communities with them: a family, a commune or a state. As Sandel wrote, 'to deliberate well about the common good requires more than the capacity to choose one's ends and to respect others' rights to do the same' (2001: 5). In the communitarian model, 'I' is replaced by 'we' (Duff 2003a: 51), while the state is supposed to provide 'civic virtues' (Sandel 2001: 6).

It is not obvious, however, what the consequences of the above statements are for criminal law. The absence of harm is not an obstacle to the state's right to punish. The evil to be condemned is not subjective; it is an objective 'evil in any case' (Feinberg 1988: 125–26). Devlin argued that we cannot say that there is a 'realm of privacy' for the individual, so that society, as a 'community of ideas', can judge his behaviour in terms of good and evil. At the same time, it is possible to punish immoral acts that are 'beyond the limits of tolerance' (1965: 16–17). This idea has been strongly criticised, inter alia, for failing to define the meaning of 'moral conviction' and for relying on premises that may be arbitrary (Dworkin 1966: 994–1002; see also Hart 1964; Lyons 1985). On the other hand, Duff argued that not all moral wrongdoing is worth criminalising, but only that which demands a collective response and is salient; such a form of 'modest legal moralism' 'does not demand even that all public wrongs must be criminalized', because 'we will sometimes do better to focus on repairing harm, or dissuading risky conduct, or resolving conflicts, rather than calling wrongdoers to account' (2014b: 230). The communitarian model should therefore not be seen as a basis for the direct incorporation of morality into criminal law (although there is always a risk of this happening), but it does open the door to the introduction of offences for which consent is not a defence.

The liberal model is considered dominant in mainstream thought (Bloom 1987: 25–43; Taylor 1992: 14). David Johnston has observed that Western political thought has evolved 'from a low estimate of the efficacy of human actions in the world and a low regard for the value of social relations based on individual consent to a vision of society in which virtually all such relations would stem from the wills of individuals through consensual agreements' (2010: 49). On the other hand, this insight is not consistent with social practice, since 'Anglo-American criminal law takes the position that there are numerous harms that all persons are incompetent to inflict or allow to be inflicted upon themselves, regardless of how much they consciously desire them' (Westen 2004: 129). The latter author concluded that existing provisions (e.g. criminalising killing as an act of mercy or maiming someone for perverse aesthetic reasons), at least in part, reject the notion that the mature person knows best what is good for him or her. These prohibitions can be based on both paternalistic and communitarian models, depending on the reasons for the restrictions.

However, as the above description shows, despite various differences between liberal, paternalistic and communitarian approaches, they all make consent valid under certain conditions. Disagreement about the philosophical foundations of consent does not imply different consequences for its use in criminal law. In other words, although each model is based on different principles, there are a considerable number of cases in which the normative consequences of the individual's consent are the same. An analysis of the models not only explains the various approaches to difficult cases, but also demonstrates the universal recognition of consent as such. First, in none of the models does consent affect decisions that lead to the violation of other people's goods or supra-individual values (e.g. the environment, public safety, public health). The essence of consent is to decide only on the goods of the person consenting. In any model, therefore, it is essential to determine whether it is only the goods of the individual that are violated by the consensual assault. Secondly, even the most liberal concepts do not recognise consent as a defence unless it is given voluntarily and consciously (Dworkin 1983: 20).[2] Since in each model the basis for recognising consent as valid is the individual's right to self-determination derived from the concept of freedom, the consent of the person whose capacity for self-determination is limited or absent is irrelevant. Therefore, neither the liberal, nor the paternalistic, nor the communitarian model provides a basis for validating consent given by a minor, an incapacitated person, or a person who is in a condition that prevents him/her from making free choices (e.g. under torture, coercion or threat). Moreover, the communitarian model in a liberal state has much in common with the liberal model, as these societies share values such as freedom, autonomy and privacy. In this case, the society does not abandon its principles of shared public morality but treats the criminal law as 'a weapon of last resort' (Duff 2003a: 67). The communitarian attitude towards the criminalisation of behaviour despite the victim's consent can be observed to be largely the same as the liberal one, especially in the case of goods such as: property, personal freedom, physical integrity, honour.

It turns out that major differences between the consequences of the applied models result from the adoption of hard paternalism or the total incorporation of

[2] See also the judgment of the Polish Constitutional Tribunal of 9 July 2009, no SK 48/05, section 4.6.

morality into criminal law ('ambitious criminal moralism'; Duff 2014b: 222). The tension between the liberal model and hard paternalism or ambitious legal moralism is the factor that provokes discussions on issues such as the criminalisation of euthanasia, incest or voluntary infertility. In liberal democracy, however, the state should avoid both hard paternalism and ambitious legal moralism as a basis for criminal provisions (Husak 2008: 151–52; Bayles 1974: 183; Duff 2014b: 223). Such a point of view tends to be acceptable even to protagonists of Devlin's view, who argued against the reasons for decriminalising certain behaviours rather than actually punishing them (1965: 116–17). Leaving aside the extreme variants of communitarianism and paternalism, consent can be a good defence in most cases for all three models of criminalisation. The controversial cases are actually exceptions. Despite the fact that they attract attention and arouse emotions in public debate, it is worth remembering that the significant range of behaviour to which one can consent is undisputed.

4. The Post-Crime Position of the Victim and the Impunity of the Perpetrator

The recognition of the individual's consent as a factor rendering the act lawful, according to various models of criminalisation, is not sufficient when considering the importance of reconciliation between the offender and the victim for the criminal consequences of the crime. The assertion of the right to decide on the way of resolving their conflict when the crime has already been committed assumes that it is possible for the individual to express a legally valid wish about his or her interests after the prohibited action. But is this actually possible? The dilemma has been discussed when considering the significance of retrospective (subsequent) consent in criminal law. Feinberg noted that consent cannot be retroactive; the forgiveness expressed by the victim 'cannot change history, or magically recreate the past' (1986a: 182). Therefore, retroactive consent 'in the best case will come too late' to have the moral significance of prior consent (1986: 187). Husak also contested the retrospectivity of consent, claiming that the victim's subsequent assessment that the treatment he or she disliked at the time was to his or her benefit 'should not be mistaken for consent' (2010: 114). The same position was taken by Dripps, for whom *ex post* acceptance of the violation of interests does not mean that the offence was not committed (1992: 1809).

On the other hand, Westen treated retrospective consent as valid and the conduct as not harmful from the moment the victim voluntarily and retrospectively consented to it, as 'something that chooses for herself and, hence, something that not only is no longer a wrongful harm, but that is no wrongful harm at all' (2004: 257). The similarity between prior and subsequent consent stems from the fact that in both cases the individual is in a 'state of not minding' the violation of his or her goods (Chwang 2009: 121). The debate about the validity of retrospective consent therefore depends on what purpose the consent serves (Witmer–Rich 2011: 392). Feinberg was right to argue that retrospective consent cannot change the past. Obviously, the individual cannot retrospectively determine the behaviour of the perpetrator. Nevertheless, consent is normative, which is why it is considered "morally transformative" (Hurd 1996: 121–46; Wertheimer 2003: 119–21). If we then respect consent because individuals are the best judges of their own interests, retrospective consent can change the moral meaning of past events (Witmer-Rich 2011: 395; Westen 2004: 263). The victim does not consent to the violation of his or her interests in a strict sense, but rather waives the legal protection provided by criminal law.

From this perspective, it is not surprising that even Feinberg did not deny that subsequent consent may express forgiveness or 'the lack of a sense of grievance' on the part of the victim (1986: 187). It can then be argued that the position of the victim, expressing a desire not to punish the offender after the crime has been committed, can under certain conditions lead to the offender's impunity. At this point, it is possible to make one thing clear. Since the need to respect the victim's position stems from the fact that the offender has not violated the interests of the former, the post-crime renunciation of criminal protection cannot exceed the limit of what could be the subject of prior consent (Wróbel 2012: 763), taking into account the limitations of a liberal, paternalistic or communitarian model, respectively. Note, however, that, in the simple case of classic acquiescence, the victim accepts the fact that his or her interests have been violated. Conversely, the case of withdrawal from the protection of the criminal justice system is more complex as the victim does not accept the violation, but only chooses other means of resolving the conflict (e.g. civil compensation). It is thus evident that the following section should focus on the pivotal role of reconciliation as a factor capable of transforming the normative assessment of the crime committed.

5. Reconciliation as 'Game Changer' in the Criminal Justice System

In the preceding section, I presented a theoretical argument for the admissibility of impunity for the offender, derived from the post-crime position of the victim. It was necessary to justify this general claim in order to address the specific case of the post-crime conduct, in which a change in the normative assessment of criminal conduct would result from the victim's position regarding reconciliation. This is an appropriate moment to pose a clear question: can reconciliation between the offender and the victim exclude punishing the former, as expected by the latter? Prima facie, the answer seems to be no, since punishment is the classic response to crime. Why does reconciliation after the crime seem to be a much less obvious factor in the impunity of the perpetrator than the prior consent of the victim? In the oft-cited case of *Holsey v State* (1908), the court overturned the conviction of a defendant who had ridden a mule without its owner's permission. The owner gave the defendant the choice of being flogged or paying for the mule. Does the choice to pay exonerate the defendant? The court recognised that the owner had the right to determine the legal consequences of the defendant's behaviour, 'in that class of cases where the offense involves no crime against society or good morals but relates solely to the redressing of private property wrongs'.[3] Paradoxically, the case is seen as proof of the rule that the victim – in general – has no power to determine the consequences of the crime (Witmer-Rich 2011: 394). The only reason for the court to respect the victim's decision was the fact that the wrong in the concrete case was exclusively of a private nature.

Therefore, the basic reason for rejecting the idea of reconciliation as a sufficient response to crime may be the existence of a public dimension in criminal law. Crime is a public wrong. It seems uncontroversial to admit that crimes against the individual always involve more than the violation of the individual's goods. Not only the victim but the whole community is affected by the offender's wrongdoing. The former 'was harmfully wronged: but the political community as a whole is also owed something, since it shares in the victim's wrong as a violation of its public values' (Duff 2003b: 48). Thus, in principle, the crime is not seen as a private matter, since the action affects every member of society. Accordingly, one of the functions of punishment – although not the only one – is to satisfy the social sense of justice. Moreover, attaching criminal consequences to the commission of a crime confirms the validity of legal norms. Even if the victim and the offender were to reconcile, the conflict between the offender and society would still exist. Although the victim 'has chosen not to facilitate [the offender's] punishment, others may – and not because of any personal resentment on their part, but because what [the offender] did was wrong and therefore [deserves] punishment' (Kleinig 2023: 605).

In other words, even if the relationship between the victim and the perpetrator is restored, the tension in the community will not disappear. This does not mean, of course, that the victim cannot forgive the offender. However, the modern state distinguishes between the wronged individual, who is able to forgive and reconcile with the offender, and the public authority, which has the right to punish (Kleinig 2023: 597). Although the victim has the right to reassess the past violation of his or her interests, the violation of public order remains. From this point of view, every crime seems worthy of punishment, regardless of the bilateral conflict resolution between the parties. Consequently, the idea that the victim determines the legal consequences of the crime deprives society (including the state authorities) of its right to punish. Indeed, the interests of the victim, who – in accordance with the liberal model of 'soft' paternalism and 'modest' communitarianism – can decide on the means to promote their way of life, can be seen as in discord with the public interest in punishing acts defined as crimes (Kardas 2019: 101). I will

[3] *Holsey v State* 61 SE 836, 836 (Ga App 1908).

argue, however, that the victim's right to decide on the consequences of the crime committed may be legitimate, at least to some extent, based on the offender's post-crime behaviour.

How, then, is it possible to express disapproval of the public wrong without punishment based on the victim's status? According to Duff, the public nature of crimes does not necessarily mean that they are:

> wrongs against 'the public' rather than the victim. We could, however, say that they are 'public' in the sense that, while they are often wrongs against an individual, they properly concern 'the public' – the whole political community – as wrongs in which other members of the community share as fellow citizens of both victim and offender. They infringe the values by which the political community defines itself as a law-governed polity: they are therefore wrongs for which the polity and its members are part-responsible in the sense that it is up to them, and not just up to victim and offender as private individuals, to make provision for an appropriate response (Duff 2003b: 47).

The recognition of crime as a matter of public concern does not preclude the right of the victim to decline criminal protection. The public interest in punishing minor offences against individuals may be viewed primarily as supporting the interests of the individual rather than as a fully independent value. In most cases it is not legitimate for the political community to direct the criminal reaction towards the perpetrator against the wishes of the victim since we recognise the right of the individual to valuing his or her goods. Reconciliation between the victim and the offender should be seen as a means of asserting the victim's right to decide on his or her private life by choosing the form of conflict resolution. As I have shown in the previous section, this right not only provides the basis for valid prior consent, but also changes the normative meaning of past events. Since we reject the extreme forms of criminal paternalism or criminal moralism, there is a wide range of cases in which the individual can assess the harmfulness of the violation of his interests.

Certainly, it can be argued that even in cases of post-crime reconciliation between the offender and the victim, the wrong against the state remains, relating to the breach of the legal rule introduced by the public authority. As Thorburn suggests, by failing to conform to the legal rules, the offender 'usurps the state's role in setting the terms under which he may interact with others' (2017; 9). However, the sole disobedience to the legal provisions, particularly in the case of minor crimes, seems to be insufficient basis for punishment. What is more, the 'remaining' part of the public interest in punishing the crime, which does not result from the protection of the individual interests of the victim, can be satisfied by calling the wrong a wrong. A response to the crime that is limited solely to the reconciliation resulting from the recognition of the normative authority of the victim, although it appears to be the weaker form of a symbolic response to the wrongdoing, can still, in certain cases and under certain conditions, fulfil the role of public condemnation traditionally associated with punishment. An 'appropriate response' to the crime is not the same as a 'severe punishment'. Not every wrong, even a public wrong, deserves punishment. Public condemnation of wrongdoing can take various forms in a society. The reduction of the penalty presupposes the existence of an important and socially acceptable reason; the reason that is 'of a particular kind' (Kleinig 2023: 598). The confession of guilt by the offender, who voluntarily takes responsibility for his actions as a result of reconciliation, can be such a reason. The crime is still treated seriously (Walgrave 2023: 620). No one claims that the act never happened or that it was not wrong; the apology is supposed to express 'the wrongdoer's recognition of the wrong she has done, her implicit commitment to avoid such wrongdoing in future, and her concern to seek forgiveness from and reconciliation with the person she wronged' (Duff 2003b: 51). Therefore, reconciliation still affirms the protected values, and their binding force is not questioned. Incidentally, such a view is not inconsistent with the expressive function of criminal law (Feinberg, 1965), since the offender's apology and restitution still retain their symbolic significance in showing disapproval of the wrongdoing (Walgrave 2023: 625).

It seems to be a great deal for the offender, but not only for him. The victim wins – as he wished – the end of the conflict, including compensation for the wrong. In return, the community's anger can be soothed by the offender's good behaviour after the crime. This view is linked to the idea of restorative justice (e.g. Christie 1977; Walgrave 2023), but it also has a symbolic function for the offender as a member of a community, since 'undertaking reparation can focus the wrongdoer's attention on the meaning of his wrongdoing, so inducing him to repent it as a wrong, and to see the reparation as an appropriate way of expressing that repentance' (Duff 2003b: 52). As noted above, the public nature of criminal justice does not imply that every wrongdoing is met with punishment. Conversely, the recognition of the individual's right to determine the discontinuation of criminal proceedings does not lead to the conclusion that the state accepts 'private criminal justice' in such cases. The privatisation of criminal law occurs when the individual is entitled to prosecute a crime and enforce the law (Bessler 2023: 27–28). Since the victim's right is only a factor to be taken into account by the court, criminal justice remains strictly 'public'.

Thus, even if crimes necessarily have a public dimension, we should not overestimate this feature as leading to the necessity of punishment. It is worth remembering that 'the public interest objection' can also be raised in the case of prior consent (Kleinig 2017: 36). According to the described models of criminalisation, the individual's decision on the criminal consequences of the offence can be questioned based on the idea that individual interests have social significance. However, if we are willing to narrowly define harm to others (Mill, Feinberg) and criminalise only salient public wrongs (Duff), there is a place for the freedom of individuals to decide what best promotes their interests. The communitarian model, in its modest version, seems quite helpful in defending my point: even if we establish that there is a public dimension to the crime, punishment should only be applied in cases that exceed the limits of social tolerance. Finally, it may turn out that, at least in certain cases, the community is able to cope with the offender's impunity by accepting the victim's right to resolve the conflict in another way. Since the recognition of reconciliation between victim and perpetrator promotes the concept of 'the judge in the individual's own case', this idea may also not be difficult for liberals to accept. It also avoids treating the victim in a way that is characteristic of 'hard paternalism' or 'ambitious criminal moralism'.

The normative authority of the victim to decide on the response to a crime can also be challenged by claiming that it conflicts with retribution as the aim of criminal justice. The principle of retribution as the legitimacy of punishment may well be described by the *ius talionis*; retribution is the only principle that predetermines punishment and its severity. This way of thinking about punishment is made particularly clear by Kant. He proposed that punishment should be proportionate to the offence, 'equal for equal' ([1797] 1996). The concept of retribution – derived from the idea of desert – shows the ethical relationship between the crime and the punishment and requires us to weigh the wrongness of the perpetrator's action (Królikowski 2005: 113). Nevertheless, it does not necessarily imply that punishment is the optimal response in every situation. Retributive justice is not an obstacle to taking into account the attitude of the victim or the behaviour of the offender expressed after the commission of the crime (Walgrave 2023: 625–26). The amount of wrongdoing that retributivists believe should correspond to the legal consequences may be seriously reduced because reconciliation is a highly positively valued factor. As a result, retribution is seen as the appropriate means of restitution (Duff 2003b: 58).

It is worth noting that reconciliation may be a sufficient response to a crime even when the normative authority of the victim to forgive the offender is questioned. In such a case, the offender's apology and efforts to make amends may be recognised by a society as mitigating his or her guilt. Such a view treats reconciliation as a factor recognised by the political community as important for the decision not to punish, because it reduces tensions in society and corresponds to the community's expectations regarding the response to a crime. Reconciliation through forgiveness is a value that has been appreciated and deeply rooted in European thought since antiquity. Suffice it to say that we can observe the renunciation of revenge as presented by Priam during his reconciliation with Achilles in the Iliad. From Homer's work which has undoubtedly had an overwhelming cultural impact on the understanding of justice – we can derive the conviction that reconciliation can bring order, harmony and consolation. In the New Testament, which can be seen as influencing the moral foundations of criminal justice, there are calls for forgiveness (Matthew 18:21-22; Luke 17:3-4), while the offender should quickly reconcile with his adversary and before the prosecutor delivers him to the judge (Matthew 5:25).

The above does not call for punishment to be completely replaced by reconciliation. In any model of criminalisation described, it is not legitimate to claim that the offender can never be punished even if he has reconciled with the victim. It is important to recognise that circumstances may vary, thereby

> [f]orgiveness that involves the cancellation of punishment may sometimes express a lack of self-respect on the part of the wrongdoer or a devaluing of the wrong that

> was involved. At other times it may express an admirable generosity on the part of the forgiver, to the extent that punishment of the wrongdoing lies within the power of the wrongdoer (Kleinig 2023: 609).

The adoption of any model of criminalisation therefore makes it possible to abolish punishment through reconciliation between the parties in the case of less serious crimes against individual goods, e.g. acts against property or liberty, as well as crimes such as insult or minor bodily injury. Consideration should also be given to cases where the *mens rea* takes the form of unintentionality. On the other hand, crimes that attack strictly supra-individual goods (e.g. war crimes or attacks on public officials) should make it impossible to discontinue proceedings. Clearly, controversies will arise in cases where prior consent is disputed. Furthermore, the reconciliation between the victim and the offender should be voluntary and conscious, analogous to prior consent, and the criminal court should protect both parties from exploitation or harassment. The court should establish the relevant circumstances of the case beyond reasonable doubt, bearing in mind that in some cases the interest of the community as a whole will lead to a return to the traditional way of dealing with the crime committed (Duff 2003b: 56).

6. Conclusion

In a number of crimes, reconciliation between the victim and the perpetrator can be a strong argument for saying that the conflict has been appeased, not only between individuals but also in the community. Furthermore, compensation can be seen as a sufficient symbol of condemnation: the offender voluntarily acknowledges that he is responsible for the wrong. Of course, not all crimes can be dealt with in this way. But not only in liberal, but also in communitarian and paternalistic thinking about criminal law, there is ample room to recognise the right of the victim to decide, at least to some extent, about the consequences of the crime.

The idea of reconciliation as a sufficient response to crime is based on the following premises:

- foregoing criminal proceedings at the request of the victim is an expression of the victim's right to decide on his or her private life;
- the grounds and scope of the right to decide on one's private life in the case of an attack on the interests of the victim can be explained by three concurrent models of criminalisation: liberal, communitarian and paternalistic;
- each model (with the exception of cases of hard paternalism and ambitious legal moralism) accepts the wide scope of the right to decide about wrongfulness of the action;
- the decision of the victim after the crime counts to some extent, because it has the power to change the normative character of the act;

- there are a number of crimes (especially minor crimes against individual interests) for which post-crime reconciliation between victim and offender has a normative significance, irrespective of the public (supra-individual) interest in punishment; and
- the public interest in punishing the crime in the case of reconciliation between the victim and the offender may be limited to showing disapproval of the wrongdoing.

10

The Role of Rights in Criminal Law and Theories of Punishment

SÖREN LICHTENTHÄLER

1. Introduction

To address the question of the role of individual rights in criminal law, a look at the offences typically considered worthy of punishment in modern criminal law systems seems to suffice at first: theft, murder, rape, property damage, and many more presuppose the violation of another's individual rights. It can therefore be said that a criminal act also wrongs the person whose rights it violates. But does this mean that it is precisely this violation of rights that is at stake in criminal law? In the following, I would first like to show that this question cannot be answered without dealing with what one considers to be the meaning and purpose of punishment in the first place, that is, which normative theory of punishment one holds.

To support this thesis, I will first outline the role of individual rights in criminal law as per the conventional perspective and confront this standpoint with the idea of crime as a violation of rights, as Hirsch has recently developed it. In discussing this concept, I will show why we should draw on theories of punishment in this matter. My argument essentially proceeds as follows: Even if some crimes involve an infringement of individual rights, it does not necessarily imply that the criminal conduct, insofar as it is criminal, inherently wrongs the respective holder of these rights and that criminal law is thus (also) concerned with their violation resulting from the offence. Whether this is the case can only be said if one recurs to what criminal law is supposed to be about in the first place, and to do this, one must look at the specific legal consequences of criminal law, i.e. what the meaning and purpose of state punishment is.

Following this, I shall therefore take a look at the mainstream theories of punishment to see what role they attach to eventual individual rights violated as a result of the crime in question.

2. The Role of Rights in Criminal Law from the Conventional Perspective

Before getting into these topics, it is necessary to clarify the meanings of 'criminal law' and '(legal) punishment', along with their essential features. However, addressing this question poses at least two methodological challenges. First, we must determine whether we aim to define the essence of criminal law as an ideal, timeless concept or merely identify the specific features of the social practices referred to as 'criminal law' in a particular time and place. I opt for the more modest approach, aligning with Hegel's belief that '... each individual is in any case a child of his time ...' (1991: 21) and that it is therefore impossible to transcend the perspectival boundaries inherent to this condition. So, when referring to criminal law in this context, we are talking about what is termed as criminal law in modern, state-based Western societies. In the quest of the essential characteristics of punishment, then, a new challenge emerges. For distinguishing what one considers to be 'essential' or 'characteristic' features requires a value judgment, which can introduce preconceived assumptions about the purposes of punishment into the definition of what punishment 'truly' is (see McPherson 1967). Depending on one's prior understanding in this regard, certain elements of actual legal punishment practices might be deemed unessential or even seen as privations of the very idea of criminal law.[1] While this danger cannot be entirely eliminated, it can be mitigated by focusing on paradigmatic instances of what modern Western societies, in accordance with their self-perception, consider as criminal law and legal punishment (see Fletcher 2010: 505). Against this background and in rough accordance with what McPherson (1967: 21) called the Flew-Benn-Hart definition, we describe legal punishment as the intentional interference with the rights of an alleged offender by state authorities, grounded in blame for violating a legal rule (see Binder 2016: 6–12; Hart 1968: 4–5; Walen 2021, Hoskins and Duff 2022), or, as Grotius (1680: Liber I, Caput XX, § 1) put it: '*poena est malum passionis quod infligitur ob malum actionis*'.[2] The rights, that punishment abridges in reaction to the supposed crime usually include, in modern states, the right to freedom of movement or the right to property, and sometimes even the right to life. Criminal law, then, is the body of law that governs which violations of the law may be met with punishment, specifying the responsible authority and the appropriate

[1] In some sense, you might say this is the complement problem to what Hart called a 'definitional stop' (1968: 5–6).

[2] Because I confine myself to what modern Western societies themselves understand by the institutions of punishment and criminal law, it is not a question here whether (or to what extent) empirical reality always corresponds to this self-understanding. Fassin 2018: 44, 59 doubts this, which is why he also rejects the usual definition of punishment and reduces it to simply one element: the infliction of pain. I think that this makes an immanent critique of the existing system of criminal law impossible and, therefore, throws out the baby with the bathwater (see Garland 2018: 163–68).

punishment methods (see Binder 2016, 2). Roughly speaking, it comprises what Hart calls 'primary rules of obligation' directed (at least in the classical view) at citizens specifying their permissible conduct and 'adjudication norms', a subset of 'secondary norms' empowering state agencies to identify breaches of these 'primary rules' and impose corresponding punishments (2012: 94–8).[3] In conditionally formulated criminal law statutes ('If someone does so and so, she will be punished so and so.') only the latter rules are explicitly stated, while the former can only be inferred to the extent that their violation is a necessary condition for imposing punishment.[4]

Describing punishment as a state reaction reflects a modern understanding that sets it apart from revenge. In cases where the breach of a primary rule also harms another individual, it is not the latter who faces the offender as in civil proceedings, but the entire political community. This is evident in adversarial criminal proceedings where the plaintiff is identified as the 'People', the 'State', 'Regina' or 'Rex'. Punishment is imposed and enforced by public authorities, including the public prosecutor's office and the courts, and this in principle regardless of, and if necessary, against the will of the crime victim. Against this background, the development of modern criminal law can be interpreted as a 'deprivatisation' of the conflict underlying the crime. The process, in which this conflict becomes a public matter, runs parallel and is closely linked to the emergence of the modern state and the formation and consolidation of its monopoly on the use of force (Greenberg 1984: 78–9, 83–4; Kirchengast 2006: 4, 10–19; Sarhan 2006: 54–64).

The individual victim on the other hand, is removed from the focus of criminal law and justice – a development famously criticized by Christie (1977) and others in the burgeoning victimology and victims' rights movements of the twentieth century as a kind of dispossession of the victim of 'her' conflict.[5] Nevertheless, this 'neutralisation' of the victim as the origin of public criminal law (Hassemer 1990: 72) can be and is usually regarded as progress, because this shift not only strictly separates state punishment from individual revenge and civil satisfaction

[3] The substantive norms specifying the content of possible penalties the state agency may inflict can be referred to as penal sanction norms (see Mañalich 2021: 40–8, Renzikowski, Chapter 13 in this volume: 233, and already Bentham 1970: 134: 'sanctional part' of a law). Of course, this distinction between primary rules or rules of conduct and sanction norms is just one way to interpret the structure of criminal law. For an overview on the diversity of different approaches in the German as well as in the English-speaking discourse see Grosse-Wilde 2018: 215–43.

[4] Thus, as Binding [1922] 1965: 4 stated, the criminal does not violate the penal sanction norm but fulfils its requirements (the breach of the primary rule).

[5] Kirchengast 2006, however, challenges the widespread assumption whereafter the monopolisation of criminal law and justice by the state or the King led to the complete removal of the crime victim, leaving her utterly powerless. On the ground of a Foucauldian 'genealogy', he argues instead that the victim has always played a fundamental role as a participant in the discourse of criminal law because the power to prosecute and punish belonged originally to the victim and has only been transferred to the state officials throughout the historical development of criminal law.

offered by tort law but also relieves the victim from the burden of taking the law into her own hands (Greenberg 1984). Since then, the fact that criminal acts such as theft may violate the rights of individuals has usually been regarded as an *occasion* rather than the *reason* for the intervention of criminal law (Renzikowski 2015: 218). While a criminal act may presuppose a violation of individual rights for criminal law to intervene, it is not necessarily for the sake of these individual rights that punishment is inflicted.

From a formal point of view, any violation of an individual right relevant to criminal law can be considered a public matter, because it involves the breach of a state-issued commandment, such as: 'Thou shalt not steal!'[6] Certainly, a primary rule like this, also referred to as 'Verhaltensnorm' (norm or rule of conduct) in German legal theory inspired by Binding ([1922] 1965),[7] is, according to its content and purpose, intended to protect some right of an individual, be it her right to property or life, and you can therefore say, at least from a non-collectivistic point of view, that the respective individual's right at stake is the very reason why the rule exists in the first place (see Renzikowski, Chapter 13 in this volume).[8] Nevertheless, the state still sets the rule, which is, due to its origin, public law (Haas 2000: 76–79; Kleinert 2008: 103–04; Renzikowski 2015: 217–18; Hirsch 2021: 108).[9] Consequently, the criminal act as a breach of these public-law obligations can be seen not only as a private but also as a public conflict.[10]

[6] The selection of commandments, whose breach is to be responded to with punishment, is up to the legislator. Which ones ought to be chosen is a question of the normative principle of criminalisation, which I will not pursue here.

[7] Bentham, however, has already distinguished between the 'directive' and the 'sanctional' or 'incitative' part of a law (1970: 134).

[8] It would possibly be different in a collectivist-authoritarian social order. There, it could be that primary rules such as the prohibition of killing do not exist for the sake of the individual, but to provide the sovereign with the resources, it needs.

[9] One might object that in this perspective many tort offences then also would constitute violations of public law. That is correct, after all, crimes can, of course, at the same time be tort offences – it is just that tort law is not concerned with this 'formal' aspect, but only with the 'material' violation of the right of the individuals, associated with it (see Renzikowski 2015: 217–18 – that Renzikowski 2021: 8 in contrast calls the former aspect the 'material' one and the latter the 'formal' one seems to be a clerical error).

[10] Prima facie, this approach sounds rather authoritarian and like what Dubber 2010: 198–210, 2018: 99–120 called the police model of criminal law because it suggests that a crime consists essentially in disobeying some state order and has nothing to do with an interpersonal event. However, this is not (necessarily) the case. If one considers the rights and freedoms of the individual as the ground for the duties imposed on all others by the state (see Renzikowski, Chapter 13 in this volume), then in the violation of such a duty there is at the same time an interpersonal as well as a public conflict. 'Materially', as Renzikowski 2015: 217–18 puts it, or substantially, the offence violates the rights of another person, 'formally' it violates a state requirement. However, whether the transgressed state norms or duties are about delimiting the freedoms of individuals and securing their rights, and whether they are otherwise appropriate to modern democratic societies, depends on their concrete content and purpose, on how they came about, as well as the general degree of social freedom achieved, and thus lies beyond the formal perspective adopted above (see Pawlik 2012: 90–99, 2020: 22–26). The same holds for the question of for what reason criminal law transforms an interpersonal event into one in which the general public is involved. In my opinion, the answer to this question depends on the theory of punishment one prefers.

3. Crime as a Violation of Rights?

Hirsch (2020, 2021, and Chapter 8 in this volume) critically examines the conventional understanding of crime. While he concedes that primary rules, even if they protect individual rights, have their origins in public law, he argues that this does not necessarily imply that it is the state which is wronged by a crime. Hirsch aims to assert that crime fundamentally constitutes a violation of rights. This includes the violation of an individual's rights in cases of crimes directed against individuals and the violation of the state's rights in the context of 'victimless' crimes. Methodologically, he refrains from attempting to develop a pre-positive theory of crime. Instead, he adopts the (German) substantive criminal law currently in force as his starting point, submitting it to a legal-theoretical structural analysis to substantiate his thesis. Hirsch's analysis is founded on a will-theoretical concept of individual rights, as also supported by Hart. According to this view, rights are seen as claims of the right holder, to which directed obligations of others correspond and over which the right holder has a sufficient degree of control (Hirsch 2021: 23). The last-mentioned condition of 'deontic control' means that only the person who can be considered as right holder is the one who has a special authority or power to decide concerning the duty of the obligor, i.e. who can demand, but who can also waive its fulfilment (Hirsch 2021: 45, 48, 109). That is the one to whom the respective right is assigned, and if the duty corresponding with it is breached, accordingly that is the one who is wronged. From this, Hirsch concludes that a crime directed against an individual does injustice not to the state or the general public but to the respective holder of the right thereby violated (the owner, for example, in a case of theft). For only she has the power of consenting to actions that would otherwise be prohibited by the primary rule of conduct, thereby rendering them permissible (see Hirsch 2021: 105; Moser 2020: 64). Consequently, according to Hirsch, crime can be 'functionally' or 'structurally' defined as a violation of rights (see Hirsch 2021: 44, 122, 132).

It appears clear that the idea of a right implies that its holder should be able to dispose of it. Moreover, it seems to be logically true that a violation of a right does injustice to its holder. When a criminal act, such as damaging someone else's property, infringes upon the rights of another, that individual is wronged as a consequence.

However, all this implies is that the conduct constituting a crime against an individual can also be described as a violation of the victim's rights. The question is whether this description encompasses the criminal conduct insofar as it is a crime, or if it solely applies when considering it as a tort under civil law. After all, Hirsch, too, does not deny that a criminal act, beyond the possible violation of the right of another, violates a state-issued prohibition and therefore also implies a conflict between the perpetrator and the public, represented by the state (2021: 106–7, 115, 126–7). Thus, it appears that two distinct aspects can be discerned. In one respect, the conduct constituting a criminal offence directed against an individual breaches a duty exclusively owed to that individual, and in another respect, a duty owed to the state. (for the following: Mañalich 2009: 80–93; Kindhäuser 2021: 481–98). A crime (directed against an individual) can, therefore, be understood as implying a breach of two different duties. Like the duty owed to the individual, the duty owed to the state is also 'directed', so the state holds a corresponding claim against the obligor of the duty.[11] This claim entails the obligation not to infringe the respective right of the other party. Putting aside any potential constitutional duties to prohibit specific acts, the state, however, has the authority to waive this obligation at its discretion simply by decriminalising the violation of that individual right or the specific manner of its violation, that is, by abolishing the corresponding rule of conduct. If the duty owed to the state (exclusively) aims at protecting the individual's right (e.g. the prohibition to violate another's property), its content is interconnected with the duty owed to the individual. The breach of the latter is a prerequisite for the possibility of breaching the former duty as well. If the right-holder consents to the infringement of her right, she effectively waives the duty owed to her (constituting her individual right), with the result that (in this specific case) the duty owed to the state also ceases to apply.[12] Individual rights are thus important in criminal law because their violation can be a precondition of a crime (as part of the *actus reus* requirement), or because they are objects of protection of the state's rule of conduct, the violation of which by the crime is reacted to with punishment. In this respect, they play a role in criminal law. Contrary to Hirsch, however, the relevance of consent in criminal law does not force us to conclude that a crime directed against an individual does (*qua* crime or insofar as it is a crime) injustice precisely to the victim and thus consists in the violation of an individual right. For a crime can be conceived solely as a violation of a duty owed to the state, while still providing a coherent explanation for the exempting effect of consent in criminal law. This does not negate the possibility that there are other reasons why a crime directed against an individual (*qua* crime) might wrong that very individual and not just the state, and that individual rights therefore play a role in criminal law or at least should play a role. Nevertheless, it appears that positive law does not provide us with any such reasons, prompting us to look elsewhere. It may initially seem plausible to try to fathom 'the essence' of crime, i.e. the aspects that make a wrong a criminal wrong. The problem is that in constructing such a pre-positive concept of crime, one is typically already guided by a prior understanding of the meaning and purpose of punishment – after all, it is about the specific characteristics of the behaviour that can legitimately be punished (see Pawlik 2012: 57). So, one seems to be trapped

[11] Whether one therefore likes to speak of a 'right' of the state being violated by the crime or whether one wants to limit the talk of rights to individuals and rather speak of 'competences' or the like with regard to state is a matter of terminology.

[12] However, as stated, this is the case only if the obligation to the state (the primary rule) aims exclusively to protect the right of the individual right-holder. If the duty exists (at least also) for supra-individual reasons, the victim's consent can have no significance in criminal law (see Kindhäuser 2021: 494). In Germany, for example, this is the case with consensual homicide, where the victim's consent to her own killing does not change the criminal liability for the killing (see Mañalich 2009: 96–99).

in a circle as the concepts of crime and punishment mutually refer to each other: crime is what demands punishment, punishment, what reacts to crime (Gallas 1965: 2). Nevertheless, it appears more reasonable to me to begin with the question of the justification of state punishment and develop the concept of crime within the horizon of the respective theory of punishment. For this approach compels us to reveal and justify our own normative pre-understanding that inevitably guides our perspective in this matter.

In other words: To ascertain the role the individual right violated by a crime plays in criminal law, it strikes me as necessary to address what criminal law is supposed to be about in the first place and, more precisely, what the meaning and purpose of state punishment is supposed to be, that is, which normative theory of punishment one holds.

4. The Theories of Punishment and the Role of Rights in Criminal Law

As is known, these theories can be categorised in various ways. Typically (and also here) they are divided in two main strands, which are ideal-typically contrasted: consequentialist and retributive approaches (see Rawls 1955: 4–5; Melissaris 2014: 372–7; Binder 2016: 57–93; Fassin 2018: 63–90; Hoskins and Duff 2022).[13]

4.1. Consequentialist Theories of Punishment and the Role of Rights in Criminal Law

A classic consequentialist justification of punishment can be found in Bentham's utilitarian account. From this standpoint, the institution of punishment is deemed justified only to the extent that it enhances social welfare or, as Bentham famously put it, by producing 'the greatest happiness of the greatest number' ([1789] 1970: 5). Accordingly, the negative consequences of punishment, such as the pain it inflicts or the pleasure it diminishes, must be outweighed by its utility, that is, its positive effects, like the pain it prevents or the pleasure it gives (see, for example, Bentham [1789] 1970: 170–203). The purpose of punishment is to prevent the harms caused by crimes. The most effective means to achieve this, however, remains a subject of disagreement. Some argue that the threat of punishment functions as a general deterrent by creating negative incentives for potential offenders, dissuading them from committing crimes (see Bentham [1789] 1970: 170–1; Feuerbach 1799: 45–47, 1801: 13–20; Farrell 1985). Others focus on the impact of punishment on the individual offender (special deterrence). This perspective

[13] The expressive theories are here subsumed to the retributive ones – whether one proceeds in this way or marks them as a third option is, in my opinion, a terminological question.

involves either incapacitating the offender by incarceration, thereby removing the immediate threat to society, or aiming for the offender's rehabilitation through imprisonment.[14]

In this paradigm, the essence of a criminal act, the reason for its invocation of criminal law, is not the wrong it inflicts. Instead, the crime must be punished because it entails the danger that others might imitate it, or because it is symptomatic of the dangerousness of the criminal himself. Individual rights hold significance only to the extent that punishment is intended to prevent their future violation. Thus, what is at stake, if at all, is the protection of the rights of each individual citizen (including those of the offender and the victim), but not those of the person injured by the criminal conduct. For their violation cannot be undone by subsequently infringing upon the rights of the offender – diminishing her happiness, intentionally harming her interests, and so on. Even if one were to consider the satisfaction the victim may derive from the offender's punishment, this does not necessarily outweigh the suffering the offender experiences due to the punishment, and the circumstance that the losses incurred by the offender are 'deserved' while those of the victim were not, falls outside the purview of consequentialist considerations.[15]

4.2. Retributivist Theories of Punishment and the Role of Rights in Criminal Law

With that said, it seems, that a retributive theory of punishment might be a more promising avenue for assigning a role to the individual rights of the injured person in criminal law. While the grand title of retributivism encompasses a diverse array of approaches (see only Cottingham 1979, Ten 1987: 38), those retributive theories that aim to justify punishment (as opposed to solely limiting a utilitarian justification based on its effects)[16] generally share the idea that individuals who commit crimes may be punished precisely because of, and in proportion to, the nature of their crime (Rawls 1955: 4–5; Walen 2021; Hoskins and Duff 2022). Unlike consequentialist or preventive approaches, retributivists consider the crime thus not only as the occasion but as the (or at least as a central) justifying reason for the punishment. In these theories, the crime itself plays a pivotal role in the justification and imposition of punishment. Consequently, it becomes possible that any violation of rights associated with the crime also holds significance.

[14] See the work of German legal scholar Liszt 1883, for an overview of such approaches see Raynor and Robinson 2005: 16–31.

[15] Apart from the fact that, even if it were otherwise, punishment would still not concern the rights of the victim violated by the crime, but rather the maximisation of her pleasure at the expense of the offender.

[16] Excluded in this context, thus, are the variants of retributivism, which merely advocate limiting the otherwise utilitarian-based punishment to the maximum of what the offender deserves (on the different variations of retributivism see Walen 2021, Hoskins and Duff 2022).

Anyone who – like the utilitarians – perceives crime and punishment merely as two 'evils', that is, as actions that diminish certain interests and reduce happiness (see Bentham [1789] 1970: 170; Hart 1968: 234–5), may find such an approach lacking in reason (see Pawlik 2020: 27–28). From this perspective, since one 'evil', the crime, has already occurred and cannot be undone, punishment, as the other 'evil', only compounds an existing injury, thereby increasing unhappiness and the perceived lack of reason. Nietzsche, although certainly not a utilitarian, also characterised revenge, which he viewed as the essence of punishment, as the 'will's unwillingness toward time and time's 'it was' (2006: 111) and, quite similarly, Martha Nussbaum speaks of magical thinking in this context (2015: 47–48).

To avoid this objection, a retributive theory must reimagine both crime and punishment. It must identify an aspect of the crime committed that is not yet irretrievably past once the damage is done but is still current and to which the state may reasonably react with punishment. Hegel termed this the 'positive external existence of the injury', which 'consists solely in the particular will of the criminal' (1991: § 99). In other words, it lies in the criminal's actuated maxim to commit wrongdoing. When interpreting the actions of a rational being, one can discern a broader message that these actions convey – a message suggesting that it is generally acceptable to act in such a manner (see Pawlik 2020: 4–10). Committing a crime would also manifest the statement that it is all right to act this way (see Pawlik 2020: 16–19) – that infringing upon another's rights as well as the right 'in itself' is acceptable. The specific function of punishment then is to contradict this implicit assertion, thereby 'cancelling' the crime, 'which would otherwise be regarded as valid', and restoring the right (Hegel 1991: § 99). Hegel, however, sees the essence of the crime, as distinguished from civil injustice, in the fact that the former violates 'the right as right' (1991: § 97), that it attacks the legal order itself, whereas the latter only violates the individual right of another. The 'restoration of right' (1991: § 99) sought through punishment, therefore, does not refer to the violated individual right, but to the integrity of the legal order as a whole.

The vindication of individual rights, by contrast, is the task of civil law, whereas in criminal law, according to Hegel, they play no role. Therefore, when it comes to our quest for a retributive theory that associates the purpose and meaning of punishment with the rights of the person harmed by the crime, Hegel's theory of punishment offers little assistance and requires no further discussion in this context.[17]

[17] For the same reason, approaches such as that proposed by Morris (see Morris 1968; Sher 1987: 69–90; Pawlik 2012: 82–90, 2020: 20–25), according to which the offender achieves an unfair advantage by committing the crime, which she would be deprived of by the punishment, are disregarded here. This advantage is indeed unfair to the individual victim, but only insofar as it is unfair to all other law-abiding citizens.

4.3. Victim-centred Retributivism and the Role of Rights in Criminal Law

A more suitable candidate for such a theory might be Jean Hampton's approach, along with the heterodox interpretation of the Hegelian metaphor of the restoration of right that she proposes (1988). According to her view, the offender degrades the victim through her crime, implicitly expressing that she places a higher value on herself than on the victim, thus viewing the victim as inferior (Hampton 1988: 124–5). In this context, punishment is intended to counter this presumption by degrading the offender, restoring the victim's worth, and affirming the equality of both offender and victim, contrary to the offender's opinion expressed in the crime (Hampton 1988: 125–6). A similar approach has been developed by Fletcher (1999; 2010). He, too, seeks to integrate the actual victims[18] of the crime into a retributive theory of punishment. In his view, the essence of crime lies in the offender's establishment of dominance over the victim, which continues even after the crime has been committed. Consequently, the purpose of punishment, as he sees it, is to dismantle this dominance and reinstate equality between the offender and the victim (Fletcher 1999: 57–59, 2010: 508).[19]

According to these forms of what Lippke (2003) called victim-centred retributivism, punishment is imposed also and precisely because of the person violated by it.[20] Yet, whether this implies that the individual rights violated by the crime also hold significance in criminal law hinges on the interpretation of punishment's aim to restore equality between the offender and the victim. If this means that punishment aims to compensate the victim for the harm suffered, then the individual right violated by the crime would indeed be of central importance in criminal law. However, this raises the question of why criminal law would be necessary apart from tort law, which also serves to provide compensation for harm.[21] Of course, one argument could be that tort law may not adequately address immaterial damage, especially in cases involving the violation of highly personal rights such as bodily integrity, sexual self-determination, or even the right to life.

[18] Fletcher, however, abstracts from the concrete victims and refers instead to a type of victim or a class of victims (1999: 55–57).

[19] For a recent approach to integrating the victim into a retributive conception of punishment, see: Katz 2023: 275–90. According to her, punishment rejects the devaluation of the victim inherent in the crime as well as the 'relation of subjection' established with the victim, thereby proving the moral value of the victim.

[20] Murphy's approach of taking the victim's need to get even with the offender as a starting point and containing it through a retributive framework (1990) is to be left out of consideration here.

[21] This is a basis from which one can also criticise Tadros' 'duty view of punishment', according to which punishment is justified by recourse to the duties and burdens that an unjustified attacker owes to the attacked person due to her right to self-defence (2011: 169–360). For, in the end, these duties are exclusively rectificatory: their content is such that the attacker withdraws from the legal sphere of the person she attacked. If the damage has occurred, then the attacker owes compensation. In my opinion, Tadros does not succeed in substantiating his claim that the aggressor has further duties beyond this rectification, though this would be necessary to justify punishment as distinct from civil damages (for further criticism of this approach, see Levanon 2012; Husak 2013; Stewart 2015).

Additionally, it could be asserted that the offender may lack the financial means to compensate for the harm caused, necessitating the existence of criminal law for this reason as well (see Lippke 2003: 130, Tadros 2011: 277). This would mean, however, that in cases where only material interests, those that can be replaced by money, are affected – such as theft, for example – and the perpetrator is financially capable, punishment should not be imposed, which does not seem very plausible (see Husak 2013: 20–22). Most importantly, if one were to connect the inequality created by the crime between the perpetrator and the victim to the damage suffered by the victim, particularly her violated rights, it becomes challenging to see how punishment could contribute to rectifying this inequality and restoring equality. For, in terms of these rights, punishment provides no restitution to the victim (see Nussbaum 2015: 41–42, 47–48). On the contrary, it may even result in depriving the offender of the means, such as money or labour, needed to compensate for the harm she caused.

Thus, the inequality brought about by the offender must be understood differently, and it is understood differently by Hampton and Fletcher (see, for similar approaches, Dubber 1994, 2004, Hörnle 2006). As mentioned, according to them (and as previously noted by Feinberg 1965), both crime and punishment possess an expressive dimension. In their view, the crime itself signifies that the offender regards herself as superior to the victim, effectively denying the victim's status as a free and equal legal person. This, in turn, calls upon the entire political community to stand in solidarity with the victim. By punishing the offender, the community expresses that her claim of superiority is false, thus subjugating her as she previously subjugated her victim. Regardless of one's perspective on the plausibility of such victim-centred forms of retributivism (or expressivism), it becomes apparent that they too are concerned with a concept far more profound than the (particular) right violated by the crime, namely the attack on the victim's capacity for rights itself (see Hegel 1991: § 95) or, to borrow a phrasing from Hannah Arendt (1973: 296), *her very right to have rights*.[22] And there is a certain necessity for this. For

[22] One could, of course, argue that such an approach also fails to explain the genuine task of criminal law in distinction from civil law, since also the latter could be interpreted as confirming the validity of the law and the personal status of the injured party. After all, the condemnation to damages, too, expresses the fact that the state of affairs that triggered it was not legal. However, this is not what civil law is about (see the similar considerations of Katz 2023: 288–9). In principle, civil law is only concerned with remedying the effects of an event or state of affairs that is objectively incompatible with the legal order, or with giving the person affected by it the opportunity to prevent such an event in advance by granting legal remedies, but not with communicatively rejecting a questioning of the law and marking it as irrelevant. That civil law lacks this expressive dimension becomes clear from the fact that a claim for damages, at least under German civil law, does not necessarily require culpability, responsibility or even agency. The owner of a biting dog for example must compensate for the damage caused by it even if she had no chance of preventing it (e.g. because she was asleep or unconscious). The different tasks of civil law and criminal law also explain why civil law generally applies an objective standard of care to the question of whether conduct is tortious, i.e. why the sole criterion for liability is whether an average person in the place of the actor could have avoided the damage and not whether she was individually able to do so. In all these cases, there is no behaviour that could be interpreted as calling into question the 'right as right' or the personhood of the injured party, which is why there is no need for a response in the form of punishment.

even when placing the victim at the centre of the justification of punishment, one must still identify the *differentia specifica* that distinguishes criminal law from tort law and (related to this) justify why, in criminal law, it is not the victim herself but the political community, the state, that confronts the offender and administers punishment. If criminal law were essentially about the rights of the victim violated by the crime, neither aspect could be adequately explained. Those who argue otherwise cannot provide a satisfactory justification for the modern form of criminal law but would instead need to design an entirely new institution to replace it.[23]

5. Conclusion

My contribution aimed to show that the question as to the role the victim's individual rights violated by a criminal offence play in criminal law can be answered only by recourse to the preliminary question of why punishment should be imposed at all. Whether criminal law is essentially (also) about individual rights can only be ascertained once one has come to an account of the specific task of criminal law as distinguished from other parts of the legal order, and that also implies taking a position in the debate on the meaning and purpose of punishment. The subsequent investigation found that none of the theories of punishment examined associate punishment with the individual rights infringed by the offence. Regarding the preventive or consequentialist theories, this conclusion arises from the fact that the crime committed is not an essential element in the justification of punishment. According to these theories, punishment is imposed to prevent future crimes, so that individual rights are only relevant insofar as the rights of all members of society as potential victims of crime are concerned. But retributive theories are not concerned with the individual rights of the victim either. Prima facie, these theories seem more promising for establishing that the punishment of the offender is also related to the rights of the victim, as they are retrospective in that they establish a normatively significant connection between the crime committed (and the violation of individual rights that may be associated with it), that is, they justify punishment as a reaction or response to the crime committed. But even the retributive theories that include the crime victim in the justification of punishment do not claim that punishment responds essentially to the infringement of the victim's right connected with the crime, but rather to the inherent attack on her status as a free and equal legal person, that is, on her personhood. This is not coincidental because only this aspect of disregard for the personality of another extends beyond the legal sphere of the victim and affects the broader principles of equality and freedom within the general society, therefore, making it

[23] This becomes apparent in attempts to establish restitution or the like as the new central paradigm (see e.g. Christie 1977; Barnett 1977; Cavadino and Dignan 1997).

plausible why it should concern the general public to respond to this with punishment. If it were primarily about the violation of the individual right of another, this would not be intelligible, as the injured party already has the option of seeking compensation under civil law.

Just to clarify, this does not address whether the alleged victim of the crime should play an active (or a more active) role in the criminal proceedings. If we assume that the purpose of the punishment is, in part, to deal with the conflict between the offender and the victim inherent in the crime, then one can certainly justify granting the injured party procedural opportunities for active participation. However, according to those who argue in this direction, such a role in the trial is mainly intended to assist the presumptive victim to psychologically process the (allegedly) experienced event. It aims to prevent re-traumatisation and secondary victimisation – legitimate concerns which, however, have nothing to do with the violated individual right itself and its restitution, but with the much more profound experience of becoming a victim. Whether the criminal process is the right place to deal with this, or whether the victims would not be better served by welfare state support (in form of psychological care or monetary victim compensation), is of course another matter (see Kleinert 2008: 350–56).

11

On the Two Victim's Rights Underlying the State's Right to Criminal Sanctions and their Significance for Criminal Law

MARKUS ABRAHAM

1. Introduction

The standard view on criminal punishment is that the *right to punishment* does not belong to the injured person, but rather to the state.[1] This standard approach relies on a division of tasks between civil law and criminal law (see Dyson, Chapter 2 in this volume). Civil law's function is about compensation, whereas criminal law's function is about inflicting pain. In the famous words of Karl Binding[2] ([1922] 1965: 288, transl. M.A.): Civil law is about 'healing an existing wound', whereas criminal law 'is about striking a new one' (for critique see Pawlik 2010: 82).[3] Or as William Blackstone (1813: 5; see Ashworth 1986: 91) put it:

> Private wrongs, or civil injuries, are an infringement or privation of the civil rights which belong to individuals, considered merely as individuals: public wrongs, or crimes and misdemeanours, are a breach and a violation of the public rights and duties, due to the whole community, considered as a community, in its social aggregate capacity.

The distinction between civil and criminal law is not solely evident in the legal consequences, but also in the way the conflict is viewed. As a victim of a violation of your rights, you have the right to seek compensation according to civil law.

[1] I am grateful to Matthew Dyson, Philipp-Alexander Hirsch and Elias Moser for helpful comments on this chapter.

[2] Karl Binding (1841–1920) is one of the most influential (and contested) figures in criminal law theory in Germany. On Binding, see Kubiciel et al. (2020).

[3] Of course, civil law can do much more than that, e.g. determination of obligations, injunctions and so on. Binding refers explicitly to civil law damages versus criminal law punishment.

That's *your right*. The conflict is framed as dispute between two private parties viewed as a horizontal conflict. In contrast, criminal punishment is perceived as a matter of public concern, as evidenced by Blackstone's quote.[4] When an individual commits a crime, they not only face consequences with the victim, but also with the collective. Therefore, criminal punishment possesses a quality that transcends the intersubjective and horizontal dimension. It has a vertical dimension, it is public law, with the state assuming the role of prosecutor, adjudicator and executor. In essence, criminal punishment is a matter of state business.[5]

The presented distinction between civil and criminal law, which posits that civil law is concerned with a horizontal conflict between an injured party and an injurer, whereas criminal law is concerned with the vertical conflict between the state and an offender, appears to be a problematic dichotomy (also Abraham 2018: 230 et seq.; Hirsch 2021: 132 et seq. and Chapter 8 in this volume). In contrast to this conventional understanding, I argue that the state's right to criminal sanction is based on a private conflict *in the first place*. The state's assertion of competence to resolve the conflict, however, is an additional, an *accessory* competence. I argue that the victim is not merely a side figure or a mere beneficiary of criminal law. In contrast, the victim is – constructively viewed, that is from the perspective of legitimacy[6] – the main right holder.[7]

In the initial part of the chapter, I will demonstrate the plausibility of the thesis by reconstructing the state's competence to punish. I will illustrate that this competence is founded on two rights of the injured person. Section 1 will focus on the first of these rights, namely the victim's right to sanction. The other right, that is the victim's right to a solidary response against the legal community, will be the subject of Section 2. In order to support the aforementioned reconstruction, I will demonstrate in Section 3, that the proposed thesis is able to connect with concepts that have already been developed within legal thought.

The second part of the chapter then attempts to shed light on the implication of the thesis that the injured person is constructively the primary protagonist in the context of criminal sanctions and has not merely a secondary, accessorised role. Some consequences concern the general way, in which we conceive criminal law as well as implications for substantial and procedural law (Section 4). A significant

[4] Blackstone 1813: 5 on murder: 'Murder is an injury to the life of an individual; but the law of society considers principally the loss which the state sustains by being deprived of a member, and the pernicious example thereby set for other to do the like.'

[5] Even if there are interruptions of this contrast of horizontal/vertical (e.g. compensation orders adjudicated by criminal courts in the United Kingdom or compensation payments within victim-offender mediation in Germany), these interruptions nevertheless remain embedded in the framework of vertical conflict regulation.

[6] I use the characterisation 'constructive' to describe the level at which the claim to punishment can be legitimised. However, this does not necessarily imply consequences for the specific rights of victims within criminal proceedings.

[7] To the important objection as to how this relates to criminal norms that do not know a concrete victim, but protect general legal interests, see the convincing defence of a right's view by Hirsch 2021: 120 et seq.

consequence concerns the praxis of punishing altogether, the praxis of intentionally inflicting pain onto a person (Section 5).

2. Reconstruction I: Right to Sanction (vis-à-vis the Offender)

Let me first put the rabbit in the hat, in order to make the trick work. My argument is based on the plausibility of the idea that there are *first* conflicts and sanctions, which can be defined as rules, rule infringements, and reactions to rule infringements. *Only later* does the state emerge. Only with the state there is state punishment. There are two versions of the origin of state punishment, which I now briefly outline. The first version is an idealistic one, which can be described as a theoretical construction of the competence to punishment (i). The second version is a historical perspective, which makes it possible to understand how the competence to punishment originated from a process of centralisation of political power (ii).

The first narrative is one possible version of a social contract theory (i): John Locke for instance starts with an agent's natural right to punish in his *Second Treatise of Government*. From the natural equality of humans, which consists in being creatures of the same species and in having the same disposition to abilities, follows for Locke the requirement of equality of rights.

> A state also of equality, wherein all the power and jurisdiction is reciprocal, no one having more than another; there being nothing more evident than that creatures of the same species and rank, promiscuously born to all the same advantages of nature and the use of the same faculties, should also be equal one amongst another without subordination or subjection … (Locke [1689] 2002: Chap II Nr 4)

From the idea that all actors are equal and independent follows according to Locke 'rationally' the principle of *neminem laedere*: no one should harm another in terms of life, property, health and freedom ([1689] 2002: Chap II Nr 6). This prohibition to harm serves to achieve the central goal of natural law, which is to establish peace and ensure the preservation of humanity (Locke [1689] 2002: Chap II Nr 7).

In the absence of an authority in the state of nature that guarantees this ultimate goal of natural law, its implementation is placed in the hands of all. Every person is entitled to further the realisation of the goal (Locke [1689] 2002: Chap II Nr 7).[8] According to Locke, this results in the emergence of a natural criminal law. An individual who harms another individual without just cause demonstrates disrespect toward the prohibition of harm resulting from the

[8] This universal right to punishment is also assumed – presumably for the first time (1625) – by Grotius (De Jure Belli ac Pacis, liber II, chap. 20). I owe this hint to Joachim Renzikowski, see Renzikowski 2015: 216.

equality of rights. By doing so, she violates the principle of reason and general equality, thereby becoming a danger to humanity. The aforementioned universal right to preserve humanity thus gives rise to the right to punish the perpetrator (Locke [1689] 2002: Chap II Nr 8; Abraham 2018: 195; Hirsch 2021: 311). According to Locke, state criminal law is thus founded upon the competence of the individual to impose sanctions, a competence which any individual is authorised to exercise.

In the following paragraphs, I will attempt to transpose the picture drawn by Locke into a modern version of the social contract and linguistic interaction. In order to do this, it is first necessary to explain what it means – because this is the starting point of classical and also modern contract theories – to begin with individuals who have *natural rights* (see Stepanians 2005: 280, who speaks of *moral rights*). The term 'natural rights' may give rise to suspicion, and therefore some clarification may be required. Natural rights, as I use the term here, are not considered to be ontological entities that are ever existing (for clarification Stepanians 2005: 283). Rather natural rights are understood as normative statuses of obligation and authorisation that are assigned by the agents toward each other based on moral reasons. Moral reasons in turn are employed in a purely formal sense, not presupposing any specific set of values. The moral reasons that I refer to here simply stem from cooperation, such as the shared, same-directed pursuit of activities.

In this pre-law scenario, the agents are connected by the speech acts they perform (Bung 2016: 69 fn. 2 drawing on Hobbes [1651] 1997: 76). Indeed, the speech acts exchanged can be viewed as promises, namely promises, to regard what is asserted as relevant. Furthermore, the normative statuses ascribed by the agents towards each other form a proto-legal connection among individuals (Bung 2016: 69 et seq.). The extent to which this normative connection is asymmetrical or symmetrical is not a matter for discussion here. What is decisive is only the fact that the actors grant each other the aforementioned normative statuses of obligation and authorisation – i.e. grant each other natural rights (Bung/Abraham 2020: 101 et seq.). These 'rights' have not yet reached the status of proper legal rights – as long as they have not yet been stabilised and formally recognised, as long as there is no social contract in place.

However, it seems reasonable to suggest that such proto-rights towards each other are already implied, when we engage in social interaction. These proto-rights entail not only the liberty to defend oneself from an upcoming attack, but also the liberty to a sanctional reaction[9] – if an attack has been carried out. The concept of *state* punishment is only introduced once the social contract has been concluded and the state has been established. By entering into the social contract, the individuals transfer their proto-rights to punish to the state.

[9] On the connection between self-defence and punishment with a different reasoning Tadros 2011: 266 et seq. He argues that if the offender has not fulfilled the duty to tolerate the intentional infliction of pain before the offence is committed (self-defence), he must comply with the duty to tolerate after the offence has been committed (punishment). On Tadros' legitimatory idea of punishment Abraham 2018: 139 et seq.

The first narrative, that of the social contract, whether unfolded with Locke or in its modern version as a theory of contract and linguistic interaction, posits that state punishment originates with *the transfer* of the proto-right to sanction to the state.

The second narrative (ii), which is compatible and arrives at the same result, is a perspective of centralisation of political power. It is not my intention to draw normative conclusions from this perspective; rather I wish to use it to make plausible the role of the state as being a logically and timely subsequent actor in relation to the praxis of punishment. The narrative – highly simplified[10] – begins with conflicts between individuals. Each conflict is resolved by the parties involved or their clans. In order to dissuade the injured party from acts of revenge, deeds of atonement are negotiated. This is a horizontal solution to the conflict, a peace agreement between the parties to the conflict (Sarhan 2006: 55 et seq.; Abraham 2018: 237).

It is only in the late Middle Ages that political interests and fiscal interests led to the development of a system in which (pre-state) central power took control of the competence for the conflict (Sarhan 2006: 57).[11] This responsibility for conflicts is used as a tool of power: The ruler views the violation of the norm as an attack on their her or his authority. The reaction to the violation of norms, in the form of punishment, is therefore seen from the perspective of defending the ruler's sovereignty. By meting out punishment for the crime, the ruler is perpetuated as the crucial authority for permitting and stopping acts of violence. The interests of the victim, on the other hand, in being compensated and having punishment imposed, are pushed into the background. This is supported by historical developments: Whereas a private atonement contract used to be an *obstacle to proceedings* until then, it is now merely is a *reason for mitigation* (Sarhan 2006: 62 et seq.). The victim is sidelined in court, the victim's interests are neutralised. One can emphasise the positive elements of this neutralisation: the process of dealing with the crime is less emotionally charged, the decision does not lie with one of the parties or with a biased person, but with a neutral body, the reparation process is accompanied and monitored by public authorities. Alternatively, this process of neutralisation of the victim can be viewed critically as *expropriation of the conflict* (Christie 1977: 7 et seq.): the parties are deprived of control over the resolution of the conflict. The neutralisation may be thus used to make a case for an abolitionist or restorative justice position (Günther 2002: 212 et seq.; Lüderssen 1995: 50 et seq.).

What is decisive for the second narrative, the perspective of the centralisation of power, is that here, too, the development of the punitive reaction has its starting point in the intersubjective conflict. This means that the punitive reaction in its origin is viewed as a question of horizontal nature. It is only through the appropriation of the right to punish by the ruler and the relegation of the victim to the

[10] For deep analysis see Weigend 1989: 28 et seq.
[11] This analysis refers to the historical examples of Criminal Law in the Holy Roman Empire.

background that the conflict and its regulation acquire a predominantly vertical character (Sarhan 2006: 64 et seq.). A conflict is no longer seen as bilateral issue between the parties, but as an infringement of the sovereign. Crime is framed as an attack on the sovereignty of the state.

Both narratives, the perspective of social contract perspective (i) and the political power perspective (ii), illustrate the same development regarding the emergence of the state's right to punish: The competence to sanction has *just ended up* with the state – either through the transfer of the proto-rights to sanction to the state, that's the social contract narrative, or through the appropriation of the competence for the conflict, that's the political power perspective. In short, the conclusion is that the right to sanction has been entrusted to the state or it has been arrogated to the state.

3. Reconstruction II: Right to Effective Regulation (vis-à-vis Everyone)

The transfer of the proto-right to sanction or its appropriation was the first step in my reconstruction of the state's right to punishment. There is a second step, to which I will now turn, again conducted from the two perspectives presented in Section 1: the perspective of social contract theory (i) and the perspective of political power (ii).

Let us start with the perspective of political power (ii): if one uses the appropriation of a conflict as an instrument of power, then one cannot stop at declaring oneself competent for a conflict. You cannot just talk the talk, but you have to walk the walk: You have to regulate the conflict, bring peace, provide a solution that is binding for everyone. In other words, with the appropriation of the conflict there comes the necessity, from the point of view of maintaining power, to resolve it effectively – at least when more than short-term tactical gains are at stake. Otherwise, there would be a mere assertion of power, but in reality, a power vacuum. The thesis would be the following: claiming the competence to be the relevant authority in a conflict entails the necessity to use this authority to resolve the conflict. The 'duty' to regulate the conflict thus follows from the appropriation of a conflict – that is, it follows from the framing of crimes as an attack on state sovereignty. To put it more concretely: The Queen, who sees the murder of one of her subjects (also/primarily) as an attack on her own sovereignty, is obliged to respond to this attack. Only in this way can she restore the authority that has been attacked.[12]

[12] It is noteworthy, that this very idea is implicitly formulated in Hegel's Philosophy of Right: the offender, by his act, asserts a norm that deviates from the currently valid legal norm. This assertion must be contradicted, and this contradiction is delivered by punishment (Hegel [1821] 1986: 187 (§ 99); on that Günther 2014: 129 et seq.) On the reconstruction of crime as usurpation of state sovereignty see Thorburn, Chapter 14 in this volume.

The focus of the social contract perspective (i), to which I now turn, is on the question of legitimacy. How would social contract theory interpret the second step of the reconstruction? The transfer of the proto-right to punish is not an automatic part of the social contract. Rather, it is made *conditional*. The transfer of the proto-right to punish is agreed to by me as a member of the social contract, only if the social contract ensures that my natural rights are effectively protected by the other actors (or then: by the state). And this protection of rights is guaranteed by the promise that if my rights are violated, the other actors (or then: the state) will not simply accept this violation but will treat it as such. In this respect, the transfer of the proto-right to punishment is linked to the fact that the members of the social contract grant each other the right to demand the effective regulation of the conflict. This simply means that, in the event of a violation, a person has the right to demand that the other actors (or then: the state) recognise and deal with the violation as such. The exact content of this reaction – one could see it as an act of solidarity with the injured person in a very broad sense – is contingent. It could consist in not recognising the property situation created by the offender, for example by not considering a stolen book as the offender's property. It could also mean publicly condemning the offending act.

The victim, therefore, has the right to demand this solidary response – a right that was condition of the victim to give up and transfer her proto-right to sanction. This commitment to a solidary response is conceptually addressed *first* to all members of the legal community, bilaterally to each of them. Only in a second step do the members set up an institution charged with the task of issuing a generally binding condemnation. An institution that is professional, impartial and operates according to rules. This obligation to a solidary response constitutes the second right of the victim – in addition to the right of proto-reaction vis-à-vis the offender, see Section 1 – which underlies the state's right to punishment: the right, that is granted to the potential victim by all the members of the social contract, the right to demand the generally binding rejection of the offending act.

Let me summarise the results of my two-stage reconstruction of Sections 1 and 2 so far. The public claim, the claim of the state to punish, has been disentangled into two rights of the victim: first, the proto-right vis-à-vis the offender to sanction which has been transferred to the state and, second, the right vis-à-vis the legal community to a solidary response in view of the crime.[13]

[13] Perhaps a similarity becomes apparent here to Strawson's terms of *reactive attitude* and *vicarious reactive attitude* in reaction to a right's violation (Strawson 1962). That seems anything but wrong to me. After all, it is about the need for reaction on the part of the victim, on the one hand, and the attitude of solidarity of the other members of the legal community, on the other. However, it is important to emphasise, that the two perspectives of the victim and of the other members are here employed in the sense of *a right to*, they signify normative claims of the victim.

4. Support by Constitutional Court: Right to Investigation

The proposed reconstruction of the state's right to punish is compatible with the existing, current interpretation of the law.[14] This can be seen from the jurisprudence of the German Constitutional Court. For some years now, the court has been recognising – affirming the jurisdiction of the European Court of Human Rights[15] – a constitutional right of the victim to effective criminal prosecution.[16]

The rationale for such a right of the victim has been interpreted in the following way: The state has a duty to protect its citizens.[17] This duty implies that the state takes preventive measures to ensure that no serious crime is committed against one of its citizens. It also implies a duty to investigate whether such violations have occurred and to sanction them. If a citizen becomes the victim of a serious crime and the state fails to investigate the crime and to bring it to criminal justice, the Constitutional Court has ruled that the victim may demand effective prosecution. In other words, the victim can force the prosecuting authorities – through the state courts – to investigate adequately. The victim has the *right* to demand an effective investigation.[18]

What is most striking about this judicature, however, is the *reasoning* that leads to such a claim right to effective investigation. The effective prosecution of violent crimes is seen by the Constitutional Court – as well as by the European Court of Human Rights[19] and also the Inter-American Court of Human Rights[20] – as a specific application of the state's duty to protect. There is always a right to effective prosecution, so the Court states (para 10),

> where a person is not in a position to hinder significant criminal offences against his or her personal legal interests – life, physical integrity, sexual self-determination and freedom of the person – and where a failure to effectively prosecute such offences may lead

[14] Although the reconstruction above is meant to have normative weight on its own terms, I want to show that there are already commonalities with current doctrine of positive law – this is not a contradiction in terms, because the positive law in turn has and uses non-positive prerequisites.

[15] ECHR, Decision of 27 September 1995 – Nr 18984/91, *McCann and others v The United Kingdom*, Series A No 324, para 161.

[16] Constitutional Court, Decision of 26 June 2014 – 2 BvR 2699/10: para 8 et seq. in reception of the jurisprudence of the European Court of Human Rights, ibid: para 18; see further see Abraham 2018: 234 et seq.

[17] The basis of that duty is based by Constitutional Court's jurisprudence on art 2 I and art 1 II German Basic Law: The State is obligated to protection of life and physical integrity. Likewise, already the ECHR, Decision of 2 September 1998 – Nr 22495/93, *Yasa v Turkey*, para 98.

[18] Constitutional Court (n 16) para 10; already Holz 2007: 120 et seq. This does not mean that this claim right easily leads to renewed investigations. See recently Constitutional Court, Decision of 21 December 2022 – 2 BvR 378/20, para 50 et seq., where the court stated that state authorities and courts have sufficiently explained why further investigations are not promising.

[19] ECHR, Decision of 2 September 1998 – Nr. 22495/93, *Yasa v Turkey*, paras 98 and 100.

[20] IACHR, Decision of 29 July 1988, *Velásquez-Rodríguez v. Honduras*, paras 174 and 176 et seq.

to shaken the faith in the state's monopoly on the use of force and to a general climate of legal uncertainty and violence.

The Constitutional Court speaks of a loss of confidence in the monopoly of force and speaks of a threatening atmosphere of violence. This sounds like a direct allusion to the consideration of the social contract: The lack of punishment for serious crimes threatens to lead to a relapse into a climate of violence.[21] In order to prevent this relapse, the state must assume the responsibility that the citizens gave it by granting it the monopoly of force, namely, to prevent crimes and to punish them when they occur. For this is what the citizens trusted in the act of transferring the monopoly of force – and the state must be careful not to betray this trust.

One could also translate it more directly – in the sense of the consideration presented above (Sections 1 and 2): if the legal community is not prepared to take an interest in a case in which the commission of a crime is alleged, the construction of the victim's right, that underlies the state's right to punishment, *comes to the surface again*, the victim's proto-right *revives*. One could add an explanatory note *cum grano salis*: if the investigation is omitted, the injured party could understandably question the transfer of her proto-right to sanction and take measures of private revenge.

To address one objection: One could point out that the cited jurisdiction does not concern a right to *punishment*, but only a right to *effective investigation*. This is true, but the presented idea can still be reconciled with the thesis that the Constitutional Court ruling also concerns a *right to* punishment. For the right to effective prosecution includes a right to punishment, but only, one might say, in a conditional form: The victim's right to punishment is conditional on the prosecuting authorities concluding that a crime has indeed been committed. In other words: If I am the victim of an attempted murder, the right to prosecution implies the right to have punishment imposed[22] – precisely if the prosecution comes to the verifiable conclusion that this attempted murder has actually taken place. Admittedly, this answer of a 'conditional right' may not be precise in terms of legal theory. What we have, is rather a *de facto right* to punishment. So, I am not saying that the Constitutional Court explicitly recognises a right to punishment explicitly. What I am saying, however, is that the Court's reasoning is compatible with the victim's claim and that the Court makes use of it, namely that, in principle, there are victim's rights within the criminal justice system.

[21] The argument of relapse into violence is explicitly made by the German Constitutional Court. However, similar references can also be found, for example, in IACHR, Decision of 29 July 1988, *Velásquez-Rodríguez v. Honduras*, para 177: "Where the acts of private parties that violate the Convention are not seriously investigated, those parties are aided in a sense by the government, thereby making the State responsible on the international plane."

[22] Very explicit on the connection of investigation and punishment is the IACHR, Decision of 29th July 1988, *Velásquez-Rodríguez v. Honduras*, para 174: 'The State has a legal duty (…) to use the means at its disposal to carry out a serious investigation (…), to identify those responsible, to impose the appropriate punishment (…).'

5. Consequence I: Demystification! Hints for Substantive and Procedural Law?

What are the consequences of the aforementioned observations? I have argued that there is a connection between victim's rights and state punishment, a connection that finds support in current constitutional doctrine (Section 3). In more precise terms, the state's right to punish can be reconstructed as follows: there are two underlying rights of the victim. The first is the proto-right to sanction, which has been transferred to state authorities. This forms the legitimating core of the state's right to punish (Section 1). The second is the right to a solidary response in the face of the violation, a right, which is directed towards the other members of society (Section 2).

These two victim's rights form the basis of the state's right to punish. This very insight is also the first consequence: a demystification of the state's claim to punishment. The reconstruction demystifies the standard view of punishment, according to which the law knows two ways of responding to a crime: on the one hand, the civil claim of the victim, a horizontal conflict and a horizontal resolution of the conflict and, on the other hand, the state's claim to criminal punishment, a vertical conflict and a vertical resolution of the conflict.

The reconstruction challenges the prevailing view that criminal law is solely concerned with the offender and has nothing to do, or only marginally with the victim or with the victim or with the horizontal relationship between offender and victim. Rather, the specificity of the criminal law in comparison to civil law, the specificity that makes it a task of public institutions, is that through the response of the criminal law the victim violation is recognised by the community of citizens and the community is even obliged to adopt an attitude of solidarity (see similar[23] Hörnle 2006: 955; Abraham 2018: 243 et seq.).[24] This attitude of solidarity is transported and put into practice by the courts, which, not coincidentally, pronounce the sentence in the name of the people: By pronouncing a guilty verdict the legal community recognises the harm done to the victim and expresses that its unwillingness to accept the criminal act without reacting (Günther 2002: 218). The victim is told that he or she has indeed been wronged and that the harm is not due to fate or misfortune (Hörnle 2006: 955 and 93 in this volume: 'right to obtain a judgement'). Narratives of accusation by the perpetrator or third parties are thus debunked, as are self-accusations by the victim herself. In short, there is no second dimension of the violation, no vertical one that *replaces* the

[23] Even if Hörnle does not explicitly speak of a duty towards the victim, she comes pretty close: Hörnle states (2006: 955) that the verdict has the meaning for the victim, that condolences and solidarity are expressed and calls this an 'appropriate attitude'. At a later point she adds, that the verdict has to show solidarity with the victim (956).

[24] Without the obligation to adopt an attitude, but similar Günther 2002: 219: 'The public is informed, that the violation was wrong, not an accident, that it is not accepted and that neither the victim nor the public is responsible for the wrongful deed.' (transl. M.A.).

horizontal one (similar Hirsch 2021: 188 et seq. with footnote 198 and Chapter 8 in this volume). Rather, the injustice is considered by the legal community to be so serious that a collective response is required. The violation committed is, so to speak, a *violation affecting third parties* (Seelmann 1989: 675; Abraham 2018: 242 et seq.) This seems to be the core of the idea that the crime is an attack on society as a whole (see. Pawlik 2010: 83 and 88).

Can further conclusions be drawn apart from this demystification of the public right to punishment? If public punishment is based on the rights of the victim, does this not argue in favour of prioritising the victim's interests over their current legal status, both in substantive criminal law (i) and in criminal procedure (ii)?

In substantive criminal law (i), for example, it could be argued that this consideration favors a wider acknowledgment of the victim's consent as a justification: Consent is obviously already considered an important justification in criminal law, based on the principle of autonomy, *volenti non fit iniuria*. However, there are limits to consent that vary from one legal system to another. For example, in German criminal law, consent to bodily harm is invalid if the act in question is contrary to 'good morals' ('gute Sitten'). Because of this problematic reference to vague moral concepts, the majority interprets this clause narrowly. It is understood to mean that consent is only invalid if the conduct in question involves a real risk of death or serious irreversible and grave physical disability (Roxin/Greco 2020: § 13 para 41 et seq.). However, this interpretation is not uncontroversial. Moreover, there are tendencies to re-emphasise the limitation of consent – for example, recently in cases of arranged fights at hooligan meetings (see Engländer 2022: para 292). Could the emphasis on the victim thus argue for a broadening of the acknowledgment of consent? In addition, a victim-oriented understanding could play a role not only in the scope, but possibly also in the *preconditions* of consent: Consent presupposes that the person giving consent makes a free choice.[25] In this respect, the increased significance of the victim could suggest that his or her will should be taken even more seriously, for example, that consent is already invalid if it is obtained under reasonably significant psychological pressure.

Let us move from substantive criminal law to procedural criminal law (ii). The considerations set out above could motivate the view that the victim should be given an even stronger position in criminal proceedings. Already since the 1980s there has been as far as German criminal procedural law is concerned a clear shift towards victims (Barton 2012: 117 et seq.).[26] For example, the 'Nebenklage', the right to side with the prosecution having an independent legal status (with the right to speak and to inspect files), was expanded

[25] And does – that is the standard of German Criminal Law – not suffer from will deficiencies, like error or coercion (see Roxin/Greco 2020: § 13 para 97).

[26] In recent times, in Germany the 3. Opferrechtsreformgesetz of 21.12.2015 (Act to Strengthen Victim's Rights in Criminal Proceedings) has been introduced, which, inter alia, provides for 'psycho-social process support' for the victim (on the Act see Ferber 2016: 279 et seq.). With regard to most recent Acts, see Beulke/Swoboda 2022: Rn 303.

(Beulke/Swoboda 2022: para 889 et seq.). The position of the victim has also been strengthened by the fact that victim-offender mediation is also important in criminal proceedings too. Nevertheless, one could imagine an even stronger position of the victim in court proceedings, e.g. a more prominent role of victim impact statements – as it is the case in several Anglo-American jurisdictions – or easier access to legal aid, an increased likelihood of receiving compensation payments, and so on.

It is true that the considerations presented here could be used for such an extension of victim rights. However, I would like to emphasise the need for caution. Strengthening victim's rights usually goes hand in hand with limiting the rights of the accused (see Coleman Chapter 17 in this volume; see also on the rights of the accused see Duff, Chapter 15 in this volume). It is important to recognise that there is always the potential for the rights of the accused to be restricted too much. Indeed, the accused is in a particularly vulnerable position in criminal proceedings with regard to the realisation of his legal status.[27] Consequently, the benefits of neutralisation, as outlined previously, outweigh the potential for strengthening the legal status of the victim.

In addition, there is a conceptual reason for being cautious about strengthening the rights of the victim both in substantive law (i) and in criminal proceedings (ii). This does not mean that no other arguments can be found for such a programme elsewhere (see Moser 2020: 66 et seq.[28] and Hirsch 2021: 215 et seq. and 241 et seq.[29]). But the conceptual reason inclines me to doubt that the above illustration of the victim's rights for state punishment can be a support for a strengthened position of the victim in the process of state punishment. What is the conceptual reason? The reconstruction presented merely makes plausible the constructive role, that the rights of the victim play. That said, the victim's role is also nothing more than a *constructive one*. The right to sanction has been transferred to the state. Furthermore, the right to a solidary response has been transformed into the state's duty to protect and only comes to life as a right of the victim merely in the event of the state's failure to fulfill its duty to investigate (see Section 3). So, the creation of the state's right to punish, the process of *vertical transformation*, results in a status of *independence* and *alienation* of the state's right to punishment from the victim. Consequently, it is inadvisable to draw direct consequences[30] regarding the reshaping of institutes of substantive or procedural law from the *constructive* significance in the

[27] For example the (constitutional) right not to be punished, see Du Bois-Pedain 2014: 314 et seq.

[28] Moser searches for arguments from the theoretical basis of will theory.

[29] Hirsch argues from his understanding of crime as violation of victim's status. This violation is twofold: On the one hand, the normative authority of the victim is violated, which the person has by virtue of his or her right to consent to a violation. On the other hand, the normative authority of every legal subject of the legal community is violated (Hirsch 2021: 187 et seq.).

[30] But Hirsch 2021: 314 fn 448 sees for the strengthening of the victim's rights in criminal law a 'connection not of derivation but of justification'.

legitimation of the state's right to punishment (see also Hörnle 2017b: 41,[31] on this point also Coca-Vila, Hörnle, Hirsch, and Renzikowski, respectively Chapters 3, 5, 8 and 13 in this volume).[32]

6. Consequence II: *Pain of* Punishment Put Into Question

The issue of *vertical transformation*, that is to say, what happens when the right to punishment originally held by the victim is transferred to the state, shall be elaborated with a focus on the *content* of punishment. This is, because the content of punishment is the point at which the actual consequence of the reconstruction, in my opinion, becomes apparent.

With regard to the content of punishment, one could argue that the second source of the state's right to punishment, namely the victim's right to demand a solidary response from the members of the legal community (Section 2), requires that the other members of the legal community adopt a reactive attitude. A response must be made in a public manner. Apart from the public manner of the declaration of disapproval it is unclear, why a new category of reaction should be created that is distinct from the arsenal of civil law. In other words, the necessity of hard treatment such as imprisonment remains unclear.

The legitimacy of hard treatment has thus to be based on the other right, the transferred proto-right vis-à-vis the offender to sanction (Section 1). The content of the sanctional reaction depends on the question of how one interprets the proto-right to sanction *after* it has been transferred to the state, after its vertical transformation. This is a challenging question. My response is that upon transfer the state's right to punish does not remain identical to the unadulterated proto-right to react; rather, it undergoes a process of modification through the act of societisation. The victim's entitlement to respond, when transferred to the state, if one reduces it to its core, takes the shape of *mistrust towards the offender in being a law-abiding agent* (Abraham 2018: 212 et seq.). And this very *reaction of mistrust* is to be adopted by the other members of the legal community – since the criminal justice reaction consists precisely in this solidary response of the legal community towards the victim (see again Section 2). This is the idealised form of criminal sanction, which is based on the idea that we as a legal community withdraw trust from the convicted person – that is, trust in the convicted person acting as a reliable legal agent. The withdrawal of trust is enacted through the speech act of the conviction.

[31] The stronger recognition given to the communication with the victim does, according to Hörnle, not necessarily lead to a strengthening of victim's procedural rights. The state pronounces the judgement in the interest of the injured person.

[32] A concurring reason is, that the process of victim-neutralisation is also to be understood as an act of rationalisation.

Will this lead to a situation in which the ascription of guilt alone, the verbal declaration of disapproval, will become the sole sufficient reaction? This idea is welcomed by some as a point of convergence (Günther 2002: 219), and others regard it as a completely open question (Feinberg 1965: 421: 'The question is surely open.'). The ascription of guilt is sufficient for some cases and it is imperative to ask whether it could be applied to more cases in the future.[33] Nevertheless, it is reasonable to question the efficacy of a declarative response to serious crime, at least in the context of contemporary society. For critics of purely communicative theories of punishment[34] point out, not without reason, that in many cases a mere rebuke from the court and a simple verbal apology from the offender are insufficient (see Kleinig 1991: 417 et seq.). Even Antony Duff, who has himself developed a communicative theory of punishment (2001: 106 et seq.; see Abraham 2018: 158 et seq.), concludes that a verbal reaction in many cases is not enough. He notes in his conception of *punishment as repentance* that true repentance requires time and processing; therefore, it cannot occur in an immediate reaction to the sentence (Duff 2001: 108).

If the imposition of penalties must at least sometimes take more than the form of a verbal statement, what form should it take? To elucidate the conception of punishment as outlined here more explicitly, it can be posited that there is no longer a place for punishment to be understood as the intentional infliction of pain. After the speech act of the conviction has been delivered, the mistrust has been declared, the focus shifts to the offender's ability to reestablish their credibility as a reliable legal agent (Abraham 2018: 247 et seq.). Consequently, it falls to the convicted person to create conditions – by promises and deeds – to persuade the community of legal agents to reinstate trust in that person as a reliable legal agent. If one views this reaction as the core meaning of punishment, it also becomes evident that the focus of the activity of punishment is shifting (Abraham 2018: 268). The legal community is no longer the active agent seeking to inflict pain onto the offender in an adequate and just manner.[35] Rather, it is the offender who must act in order to regain the lost trust. This also makes it clear that the theory of punishment outlined here considers the pain of punishment to be a relic to be overcome and be eradicated (see Günther 2014: 135 et seq.). It is evident that the act of suffering on the part of the offender as it exists within the current system of prisons is an ineffective method of regaining trust.

With regard to the victim, it is important to consider the following: the process of regaining trust must not depend on the relationship between the concrete victim and offender. It is not about the unfiltered interests of the actual victim (see on the interests of the victim Kleinert, 2008: 37 et seq.). This is once again

[33] Günther 2014: 136 asks the rhetorical question: 'So why not think of the history of punishment as a development where hard treatment becomes more and more unnecessary for the conveyance of the message?'

[34] For general critique see Dolinko 2011: 417 et seq.

[35] See on the pain of imprisonment Golash 2005: 2 et seq.

due to the fact that – although *constructively* the legitimatory core – the claim to punitive response of the victim has been transferred from victim to state.[36] The community now exercises this right to punishment, it has taken it over. Consequently, it can therefore only be a matter of the offender being considered legally trustworthy again *from the point of view of the entire legal community*, which is represented by the courts, or potentially other instances (Abraham 2018: 245 et seq.). Nevertheless, the (concrete or standardised) victim plays an important role: actions directed towards the victim, such as apologies, the acceptance of reparations, and so forth, are conducive to the restoration of trust in the agent. The actions directed towards the victim represent paradigmatic acts of behaviour by an agent attempting to become legally trustworthy once more.[37]

7. Conclusion

The victim is the central figure in criminal law when discussing the legitimisation of state punishment from a *constructive* perspective. In order to demonstrate this, I have reconstructed the state's claim to punishment as an interplay of two claims of the victim: Firstly, that the victim has a proto-right to a punitive reaction, which has been transferred to the state (Section 1). And secondly, it is based on the right of the victim vis-à-vis the legal community, namely the right to demand a solidary response with regard to the violation of their interests suffered (Section 2). In essence, the public claim to punishment originates from the victim's right to punitive reaction towards the offender, taken together with the victim's right to a solidary response vis-à-vis the legal community. Furthermore, I have demonstrated that there is already a point of contact in legal theorising for the thesis presented here, namely in constitutional law doctrine on the so-called duty to protect, which the state bears towards its citizens (Section 3).

In light of this, I have sought to ascertain the potential implications of this thesis. One significant consequence is the deconstruction of the state's right to punish. With regard to the potential consequences for material and procedural criminal law, I have advocated for caution, given that the relevance ascribed to the victim is merely of a constructive nature (Section 4). Finally, I have discussed what I consider to be an important consequence of the thesis: a changed view with regard to the *content* of criminal sanction. Instead of inflicting pain, I have argued, it is about regaining trust. This is supported by the rights of the victim, which constructively underlie the state's claim to punishment (Section 5).

[36] Therefore, it is understandable that one ascribes a public law character to the criminal law norms of conduct (see Renzikowski 2015: 218 with reference to norm theory). But that does not contradict the possibility of victim's rights constructively playing the leading role.

[37] This goes beyond already installed victim-offender mediation (German Criminal Law, § 46a), which only leads to a reduction of the prison sentence, so that the victim-related response plays the role of being merely a partial substitution of the actual punishment.

PART IV

Criminal Law in a Rights-Based Legal Order

12

The Place of Criminal Law in a Rights-Based Legal Order

HAMISH STEWART*

1. Introduction

There are, broadly speaking, two ways to think about the purpose of legal order and therefore of the particular place of criminal law in a legal order. On the one hand, one might think that criminal law is, like any other set of legal doctrines and rules, an instrument that the state might or might not use to pursue objectives that are desirable apart from law. On the other hand, one might think that the state has a task to do that cannot be adequately defined apart from legal order, and that legal order is in that sense not instrumental to any other objective. That task would be to constitute a state of affairs in which each person, being a free person, can relate to every other free person in accordance with right – a rights-based legal order. One might then try to understand criminal law as inherent to that task, rather than as instrumental to something else.

I want to pursue the thought that even if the second understanding of the legal order is preferable to the first, even if the legal order is not instrumental to anything but constitutes something that is of moral importance apart from (or in addition to) anything else it does, criminal law is nevertheless best understood as instrumental to something independent of it, that something being the state's task of constituting a rightful condition. That is because, even if the legal order can be understood as constitutive, criminal law is not best understood that way. The targets of state punishment are reasonably well-specified forms of conduct that

* A very early version of this chapter was presented as a paper at a Workshop on Constitutional and Criminal Law held jointly by the Osgoode Hall Law School, York University, and the Faculty of Law, University of Toronto, in September 2018. I am very grateful to the organisers and participants, particularly Malcolm Thorburn, for their comments. A much-revised version was presented at a conference on Rights in Criminal Law, held at the University of Graz, Austria, in July 2022. I am very grateful to Philipp-Alexander Hirsch and Elias Moser for inviting me to participate in the Graz conference and for their comments on the paper. Finally, I thank Matt Dyson for the invitation to present the paper at the Criminal Law Discussion Group, Faculty of Law, Oxford University, in February 2023.

can, indeed must, be defined independently of the punishment. It is therefore preferable to understand criminalisation and criminal punishment as instruments for discouraging those acts and thereby as making a contribution of an instrumental nature to the legal order's non-instrumental task.

I begin by juxtaposing the views of two scholars – Lindsay Farmer and Malcolm Thorburn – who have analysed the function of criminal law in ways which appear at first to be very different, but which are, I think, fundamentally similar. Each of them argues that the criminal law is inherently institutional, that it has no existence apart from the state institutions that create it; each of them links this point about criminal punishment to an understanding of the legal order as constituting something that I will call a civil condition. Farmer is more concerned to describe this condition, Thorburn to endorse it; nevertheless, they share a broadly constitutive understanding of criminal law. Contrary to both of them, I will argue that their accounts are consistent with an understanding of criminal law as making a causal contribution to the maintenance of a civil condition. Even if private law and many parts of public law are understood as constituting a civil condition rather than as instrumentally promoting a value independent of the civil condition, criminal law is best understood as an instrument for the maintenance of the civil condition. In support of this claim, I will express serious doubts about Thorburn's account of the particular feature of human conduct that is inherently criminal, i.e. necessarily apt for punishment, in order for the civil condition to be properly constituted and will suggest that the most plausible alternative is not to continue searching for such a feature but to define the place of criminal law in a rights-based order in terms of its instrumental functions.

2. Two Accounts of the Function of Criminal Law

Let us suppose that the legal order as a whole is not orientated towards the achievement of some good that can be adequately defined independently of it, but that its purpose is rather to constitute a certain kind of ordering among free persons. My question is how criminal law – the practice of defining certain conduct as punishable and, at least sometimes, actually punishing people who engage in it – can be understood in such a legal order. Lindsay Farmer and Malcolm Thorburn have answered this question in ways that appear different but, I will suggest, are substantively quite similar. I will make use of but also depart from each of their answers in suggesting that criminal law is basically instrumental.

2.1. Lindsay Farmer: Securing Civil Order

In *Making the Modern Criminal Law*, Lindsay Farmer (2016) argues that we should understand the criminal law as an institution that has as its aim securing civil order.

His argument is 'anthropological' or historical, not conceptual (Farmer 2016: 27): it a claim about what criminal law does in existing legal systems, not a claim about what it must or should do in any conceivable legal system. The first two elements of this understanding – 'criminal law' and 'institution' – are relatively straightforward. Farmer's description of what 'criminal law' is relatively uncontentious: criminal law is a 'uniquely coercive' practice of 'defining prohibited actions' and punishing the breach of those prohibitions with hard treatment (Farmer 2016: 13). By calling the criminal law an 'institution', he means not just that the criminal law institutionalises norms and rules that might have their source elsewhere, but that there is also a sense in which those institutions 'constitute [the] legal norms' that they apply.[1]

The third element of Farmer's understanding – civil order – is a little more complex. Civil order 'is not merely order as such', nor should it be identified with 'social order', as order, in that sense, could come about in a variety of ways. Rather, it is 'a certain kind of institutional ordering in which the burden of guaranteeing social and normative order is taken on by centralized institutions …' (Farmer 2016: 41). It is therefore associated with the rise of the modern state and its claim to exclusive legal authority. Farmer illustrates his claim by discussing the historical development of several areas of substantive criminal law. His account of the emergence of 'sexual offences' is illustrative. As he shows, in the eighteenth century, there was no category of 'sexual offences' as such; the offences that are now categorised as 'sexual' were scattered across different categories of crime and were understood as protecting distinct interests. For example, although rape was an offence with an identifiable individual victim, its seriousness was 'measured in terms of its threat to property and family' rather than in terms of its effect on the complainant; prostitution offences were concerned with public order; sodomy was a crime against religion (Farmer 2016: 266–80). Even in the nineteenth century, 'crimes invoking, or committed by means of, sex … were not understood as sexual crimes' (Farmer 2016: 279). For that understanding, English law had to wait until the twentieth century, in particular for the Sexual Offences Act 1956, and the rapid development of the law in the years since then. Both the decriminalisation of homosexual conduct and the increasing criminalisation of various forms of unwanted sexual conduct can be understood as being related to new ways of thinking about sexuality in general, as 'giving expression to an idea of sexual autonomy that places sexual freedom and citizenship at the heart of the law' (Farmer 2016: 289). The reorientation of understanding of the harms in question around a gender-neutral ideal of sexual autonomy involves a positive attitude towards sexuality in general and therefore of the importance of consent: 'sexual autonomy [is understood as] a sphere of in which women and men have the right to pursue a range of sexual options, free from fear of unwanted sexual encounters'.[2]

[1] Farmer 2016: 22. Farmer draws on MacCormick (2007).

[2] Farmer 2016: 288. Farmer refers principally to English law, but the essentials of his account seem equally applicable to other common law jurisdictions such as the United States and Canada.

Some might take Farmer's account to be a narrative of progress, in two senses. It might be conceptual progress, in that we twenty-first-century humans have a better idea than those eighteenth-century Englishmen did of the idea around which sexual offences should be organised: they are supposed to define and to protect sexual autonomy, rather than a set of distinct and unconnected interests. And it might be political progress, in that the interest in sexual autonomy that the sexual offences are seen truly to protect is, on a proper understanding of the law's purposes, more worthy of protection than the interests protected by their predecessors, such as maintaining patriarchal power and punishing perceived immorality as such. Maybe Farmer would endorse this narrative (I would, more or less), but even if he would, that is not what he is interested in. In his view, sexual autonomy is not a natural fact about humanity that was only imperfectly recognised in the eighteenth century and is better protected today; rather, it does not exist apart from the institution of criminal law that protects it (Farmer 2016: 294). The law of sexual offences does not merely institutionalise a legal procedure for protecting an interest in sexual autonomy that is fully definable apart from the law; rather, the law of sexual contributes to the constitution of that interest.

Nor does it mean, in Farmer's view, that our understanding of the criminal law should be purely instrumental. Since Farmer speaks of securing civil order as 'a general and continuing aim of the criminal law' (Farmer 2016: 27) and, since he thinks criminal law has no essence,[3] one might expect him also to argue that criminal law is merely an instrument for achieving civil order. But his view is not quite that straightforward. Rather, he speaks of securing civil order as a 'purposive orientation' rather than as 'an aim in the instrumental sense' (Farmer 2016: 28), so that our contemporary understanding and practice of 'sexual autonomy' is, at least in part, constituted by our contemporary understanding of what a 'sexual offence' is (Farmer 2016: 292–4).

2.2. Malcolm Thorburn: Vindicating the State's Right to Rule

Thorburn offers a conceptual account of criminal law as public law, that is, of the 'role of criminal justice in the business of government'.[4] He develops this account by way of criticism of recent accounts of criminal law that he categorises as a form of legal moralism.[5] He argues both that legal moralism is indefensible as a justification for the practice of punishment by public officials and that legal moralism cannot account for what he takes to be central characteristics of criminal justice.[6]

[3] That is, he does not think there is any conduct which is inherently criminal, therefore the proper subject matter for criminalisation at all times and places: Farmer 2016: 63–117. He does think that criminal law is distinctive in its coerciveness, but that distinctive quality tells us nothing about what is being coerced.

[4] Thorburn 2017: 7.

[5] The specific targets are Hart (1968), Moore (1997), Duff (2007) and Gardner (2007a).

[6] Thorburn (2017) (the scope of criminalisation in existing legal systems); Thorburn 2011a: 32–36, (the nature of criminal law justifications); Thorburn 2011b: 103–5 (the role of *mens rea*).

Thorburn argues that legal moralism, even Antony Duff's 'rich and highly nuanced' version, cannot account for what Thorburn takes to be the striking lack of correlation between what is morally wrong and what is criminally punishable.[7] In his view, that is not surprising, because punishing someone for their moral wrongs is not a proper task for a public authority in the first place. '[C]riminal punishment has no parallel in ordinary life': as private individuals, we are perfectly entitled to criticise each other for our moral failings, but as a private individual, each of us lacks standing to deprive another of his or her liberty or property merely because one thinks another has done something wrong.

Thorburn's solution to the problem of punishment is to connect it with the central task of the liberal state: to create and maintain a system of equal freedom, to 'set[ ] out the necessary context within which we can be free and independent persons even as we live together with others' (Thorburn 2017: 7). To interact in this way, we need to be subject to a set of rules and principles that define permissible and impermissible uses of our powers. That is, our interactions need to be structured by the rights we have against each other and the duties we owe to each other. But it cannot be private individuals who make those rules and define those rights because, as private individuals, they lack the necessary authority over each other. So, we need an institution that can be understood as 'speak[ing] in the name of everyone's claim of freedom equally' (Thorburn 2011b: 98), that is, the state. The task of this state is not to promote any particular good, but to establish the framework within which everyone can interact on terms of equal freedom. When describing Thorburn's account, I will refer to the continuing existence of such a framework as a 'rightful condition'.[8] Only an institution with that kind of task – only the state in a rightful condition – could have the 'robust authority' over its subjects that would give it the standing to punish (Thorburn 2017: 22).

Moreover, Thorburn argues, the reason for punishing people in the rightful condition is not to enforce morality or to promote anything that is of independent value, but to uphold the state's authority. 'The role of punishment … is to reassert the continued authority of the legitimate authority in the face of an attempt by wrongdoers to usurp that role' (Thorburn 2017: 30). This reason for punishment explains not only the disconnect between criminal law and morality, but also the special role of intentional wrongdoing in criminal law. Since the purpose of criminal punishment is not to enforce morality but to enforce the state's authority, it is unsurprising that 'criminal law wrongdoing does not track moral wrongdoing even remotely closely' (Thorburn 2011a: 29). Criminal punishment is not only reserved for the state, it is also a necessary activity of the state, not just for instrumental reasons, but as a constituent part of the state's right to rule.

[7] Thorburn 2017: 13; the phrase 'rich and highly nuanced' is from Thorburn 2011b: 96.

[8] A 'rightful condition' is Kant's term (Kant [1797] 1996: 6:311, using the German Academy page numbering). Thorburn himself uses a number of phrases, including 'a liberal constitutional order' and the existence of a 'legitimate public authority'. Other participants in this Kantian approach to understanding the purpose of the legal order include Ripstein (2009), J Weinrib (2016) and E Weinrib (2022).

2.3. Affinities and Differences

I want now to point to certain affinities between Farmer's and Thorburn's accounts and to suggest that, in light of those affinities, criminal law may have a more instrumental character than either of them supposes. For both of them, there is an important sense in which the civil condition is constituted by law. For Farmer, as we have seen, there is a strong connection between the emergence of the maintenance of civil order as an aim of criminal law and the emergence of the modern state; moreover, there is a sense in which his conception of civil order is not something that exists separately from the legal order; it is rather (partly) constituted by law (Farmer 2016: 45). And, as we have seen, Thorburn also thinks that the rightful condition is (fully) constituted by law and that we should understand the criminal law in relation to that constitution.

But there is also a difference between their accounts. Thorburn's account of the rightful condition is offered as a way of understanding actually existing legal orders so that we can conceive of them as legitimate (or not). The state, he says, is not properly understood as a remedy for the actually existing inconveniences of the state of nature (though it may also be that); rather, the state is morally necessary because it has a role that no institution founded on the consent of individuals acting privately could have. Instrumentalist accounts cannot account for the robust public authority characteristic of the liberal state because they cannot explain how the state can acquire and exercise powers that individuals lack (Thorburn 2017: 29–30).

Farmer, on the other hand, is resolutely historicist in his account of the relationship between criminal law and the civil condition. He traces the ways in which changes in criminal law – in what is criminalised and in doctrines of responsibility – both correspond to and influence the development of the civil order. In Farmer's telling, civil order is not an abstract or conceptual ideal according to which the quality or justice of a legal order can be assessed; it is rather a normative construct the content of which varies from time to time and place to place (Farmer 2016: 57, 300–1). Nevertheless, Farmer links the idea of civil order (notwithstanding its changeable content) to what Charles Taylor calls the 'modern social imaginary', that is, 'an ideal … of modern law where self-governing individuals are guided by general rules and interact in civil society and the market'.[9]

And so, I suggest, there is a sense in which Farmer and Thorburn are talking about much the same thing, though approaching it from different directions. Farmer's civil order, considered in light of the modern social imaginary, is a version of the rightful condition that Thorburn works with; Thorburn's rightful condition is a version of Farmer's modern social imaginary. I will use the phrase 'civil condition' to refer to both.[10] Moreover, although both Farmer and Thorburn

[9] Farmer 2016: 6; see also Taylor 2007: Ch. 4.

[10] This is the term used by Oakeshott (1975) (cited by both Farmer and Thorburn); also by Kant [1797] 1996: 6:313, apparently as a synonym for the 'rightful condition', in contrast with the state of nature ([1797] 1996: 6:306, 6:313).

are reluctant to characterise the role of criminal law in the civil condition as instrumental to the maintenance of the civil condition, I will suggest that is exactly what it is. The rights (Thorburn) or the incidents of the social imaginary (Farmer) that constitute the civil condition necessarily precede the criminal law which, in its institutional operation, responds to wrongs that have been defined by other legal processes.

3. Criminal Law and the Civil Condition

In this section, I describe and criticise Thorburn's account of the particular quality of human conduct that makes it apt for punishment in a civil condition. I focus on Thorburn's account for two related (perhaps indistinguishable) reasons. First, I consider myself a member of the same tradition that he is working in – that is, like Thorburn, I think the task of the legal order is to constitute a rightful condition rather than to serve a value external to that condition; and I think that we must explain the function of criminal law in terms of its contribution to constituting a civil condition. Second, Thorburn's attempt to provide a purely constitutive account of that function is the best one available in the literature; if it does not succeed, others in the same tradition probably won't either.

3.1. A Purely Constitutive Role for Criminal Law?

Thorburn situates his account of criminal law in the tradition of those who understand the purpose of legal order as constituting a civil condition. Legal theorists working in this tradition tend to justify not just the legal order as a whole, but also specific bodies of law and even particular legal doctrines and rules non-instrumentally, i.e. in terms of their necessary contribution to the constitution of that condition rather than in terms of their instrumental contribution to promoting a good external to it.[11]

So, on this approach, as Thorburn puts it, 'Criminal punishment is best understood as a conceptually necessary part of the very idea of legal order' (Thorburn 2020a: 51). If criminal punishment is to be understood in this way, as an inherent and necessary function of the civil condition, then it should be possible to identify some feature of criminality that is inherent to it, such that any human conduct exhibiting that feature would be apt for punishment. It would then be necessary to identify a reason why the civil condition would be defective if it did not have the power to punish that behaviour. The dominant idea in this tradition is that conduct is punishable when it challenges the authority of the state in such a way

[11] See, e.g. Ripstein (2016) (torts); Benson (2019) (contracts); J Weinrib (2016) (public law); Stewart (2020b) (criminal procedure).

that the state's failure to punish it would, as Thorburn might say, also be a failure to vindicate the state's exclusive right to rule, that is, to authoritatively define the terms on which persons can rightfully interact (Thorburn 2020a). This basic idea appears in Kant ([1797] 1996: 6:362–3), in nineteenth-century German legal thought,[12] and, more recently, in Ripstein's restatement of Kant's legal philosophy (Ripstein 2009: 306–14). The difficulty with this view is to identify a feature of conduct that would, on the one hand, mark it as the kind of challenge to state authority that makes it apt for punishment and, on the other hand, distinguish it from conduct that, though otherwise legally wrongful, is not apt for punishment.[13] I doubt it is possible to do that. I cannot, of course, rule out the possibility that there might be such a feature, but I will argue that the one that Thorburn, among others, identifies does not do so.

That feature is intentional wrongdoing. The claim is that intentionally committing a wrong demonstrates a willingness to usurp the authority of the state, such that the conduct is not just a wrong to whatever private (e.g. bodily integrity) or public (e.g. tax collection) right may be involved, but is also, as Thorburn puts it, a 'wrong against the state's right to rule' (Thorburn 2020a: 49). Unintentional wrongdoings, in contrast, do not pose such a challenge to the state's right to rule. Whether or not there is another remedy for these wrongs (e.g. damages for battery or reassessment of tax liability), Thorburn argues that the intentionality of the wrongdoing is properly addressed by punishment that vindicates the authority of the state.[14]

Thorburn's argument, if successful, would explain the state's right to punish, the state's reasons for punishing, and the difference between punishable and non-punishable wrongdoing. But there are, I think, two difficulties with this argument. The first, and more serious, is that the concept of intention relevant to criminal law does not seem to be the same concept of intention that is required for this explanation of the role criminal punishment to work.[15] Although the details vary considerably from offence to offence and from jurisdiction to jurisdiction, proof of intention normally requires proof that the act was committed intentionally with knowledge of the circumstances that make it prohibited, and (if there are any consequential elements) either an intention to bring them about or actual knowledge that they would almost certainly come about. Proof of intention does not

[12] Specifically, in the work of Karl Binding, as discussed in Dubber 2018: Ch. 1.

[13] That condition, whatever it was, would provide only a necessary and not a sufficient condition for criminalising conduct (would make the conduct apt for punishment). It would not require punishment. That is to be expected, as any plausible account must take account of factors weighing against criminalisation.

[14] Thorburn 2020: 57. Happily, Thorburn does not insist that all such wrongs must be punished (Thorburn 2020: 60–61).

[15] A related difficulty is the extreme pressure that Thorburn's account puts on the distinction between true crimes, requiring proof of subjective fault, and regulatory offences, not requiring proof of subjective fault or, in some cases proof of any fault at all. He recognises the importance of the distinction (Thorburn 2017: p 8), but in the four papers under discussion here, he does not spell out precisely how his account would distinguish punishment for regulatory offences from punishment for true crimes.

require proof of knowledge that the act was in the circumstances (and with its consequences, if any) wrongful in any way, much less wrongful as defined by the state or by the criminal law. Put another way, proof of the accused's intention to substitute his rules for the state's is not normally required, so the description of intention as manifesting a willingness to usurp the authority of the state applies to very few offences. Theft is one: a conviction for theft normally requires proof of the accused's knowledge that the property taken did not belong to him, so there is a sense in which proof of theft does involve proving that the thief manifested a willingness to displace the rules that govern property relations.[16] But beyond theft, it is difficult to identify an offence that has this quality. It might seem that assault is one such offence: since the basic form of assault requires proof that the accused knew the complainant was not consenting, an accused whose defence was that he thought it was all right to touch another without consent might well be said to have manifested an intention to set his own rules in his physical interactions with others. However where the complainant's lack of consent is not an element of assault (put another way, where the law refuses to recognise the complaint's consent as a defence), the intention required to have manifested a willingness to set one's own rules would have to be awareness of the rule eliminating the element of non-consent in such cases. But that is not required: the only requirement of intention is that the accused be aware of the factual circumstances that bring the case within the relevant legal category. The same is true of other commonly prosecuted offences such as drug possession. Proof of that offence does require proof of knowledge of the substance, but there is nothing in a person's knowing what they are in possession of that manifests any willingness to usurp the state's authority. If the prosecution were also required to prove that the accused was aware of the prohibition in question, that would be another matter, but, of course, that is not normally required.[17] Ignorance or mistake of law is not an excuse and some of the common rationales for that rule do not fit very well with Thorburn's account. The pragmatic argument that it would be too difficult for the prosecution to prove knowledge of the law in every case cannot assist because that knowledge is the very thing that makes the conduct punishable by making it a manifestation of the offender's willingness to set their own rules. The argument from overlap – that everyone is deemed to know the law because of the significant overlap between what is morally wrong and what is legally wrong is not available to Thorburn precisely because of his insistence on the loose connection between what is morally wrong and what is legally wrong, let alone criminally prohibited (Thorburn 2020a: 13). The argument from notoriety – that prohibitions on offences such as theft, assault, impaired driving, and drug possession are so well-known that we can assume most people

[16] That is why the common law recognises a defence of 'colour of right', a mistaken belief that the accused does have a property right, as an exception to the usual rule that mistake of law is not a defence.

[17] With respect to drug offences in particular, see *Molis v The Queen* (1980), refusing to admit evidence of the accused's due diligence in attempting to ascertain that it was lawful to produce the substance in question.

are probably aware of them – is better as far as it goes, but it doesn't go far enough to show that the usual criminal law concept of intention is equivalent to defiance of state authority. In a legal and social environment where the list of prohibited substances does not explicitly include the substance the accused possessed,[18] can be quickly amended by executive action,[19] can differ from one jurisdiction to another,[20] or can be made unpunishable in one part of a nation while remaining punishable in the others,[21] it's not plausible to say that proof of knowledge of the substance possessed proves a willingness to set one's own rules.

Moreover, on Thorburn's account, the purest form of crime, the most blatant manner of defying the state's authority, would be to commit an act precisely because one believes it to be a crime, whether it is or not. But, as a matter of criminal law doctrine, this belief makes no difference. If the accused commits an act just because he thinks it is a crime and it is, in fact, a crime, that belief makes no difference to his liability. If the accused commits an act just because he thinks it is a crime, and it is, in fact, not a crime, that belief does not make him guilty of a crime in any jurisdiction of which I am aware. There is no liability for committing an imaginary crime (e.g. wearing a purple shirt on a Wednesday); yet, on Thorburn's account, such conduct would seem to be the purest form of criminality.

Thorburn might respond to this suggestion as follows: imposing liability for an imaginary crime would be the perverse mirror image of not imposing liability for real crimes, as in either case the accused, rather than the state, gets to be the judge of which norms apply to him. That is a good explanation of why, in general, legislatures do not impose liability for such conduct; but it does not explain what would be objectionable about a legislature's doing so, because the conduct in question would then indeed be a very deliberate and explicit violation of that state's authority.

The second difficulty with Thorburn's account of intentional wrong-doing as the mark of criminality is that even if it does show that intentional wrong-doing is apt for punishment, it does not tell us much about which kinds of intentional wrong-doing should be treated as crimes. As noted, theft is an offence that does

[18] *Perka v The Queen* (1984). The statute in question referred only to *cannabis sativa*; the accused, charged with importing marijuana, argued that they were not guilty because the prosecution had provided no evidence that their cargo consisted of *cannabis sativa*, the variety specifically mentioned in the statute, rather than *cannabis indica* or *cannabis ruderalis*. The Court rejected this 'botanical defence', holding that, at the time the statute was enacted, all varieties of the plant in the genus *cannabis* were considered sub-species of the species *cannabis sativa*, so that even if *cannabis indica* or *cannabis ruderalis* should now be considered distinct species within that genus (a matter for botanists), Parliament intended to refer to all of them. The Court's reasoning is a good example of purposive interpretation, but it is little comfort to the (probably hypothetical) accused who knew enough about both botany and the law to conclude that he was not committing an offence when he imported *cannabis indica* or *cannabis ruderalis*, and therefore was not trying to set his own rules but to stay just within the rules set by the legislature.

[19] *Molis v The Queen* (1980).

[20] *R v DeSousa* (2012).

[21] See British Columbia Ministry of Mental Health and Addictions, "B.C. receives exemption to decriminalize some illegal drugs for personal use", available at: web.archive.org/web/20220531202203/https://news.gov.bc.ca/releases/2022MMHA0029-000850.

appear to illustrate Thorburn's argument. But so would an intentional breach of contract, which, as far as disobeying the rules goes, has all the same features as theft. Yet such conduct is not characteristically criminalised in modern systems of penal law. This difficulty is less serious than the first, because Thorburn does not claim that all instances of intentional wrong doing must be punished, that there would be something defective about the legal order if the state did not criminalise or punish all of it (Thorburn 2020a: 60–1). So, if the first objection can be overcome, if Thorburn has provided us with a necessary but not sufficient condition for punishment, he has left open the reasons that might move the legal order to define conduct that is as apt for punishment as crime.

Perhaps intentional wrong doing is not the mark or essence of criminality. Perhaps that mark or essence is something else, such as a rights-violating choice (Brudner 2008: Ch. 2)[22] or attacking the central values of the community (Marshall and Duff 1998).[23] Perhaps; but I doubt it. Defining the appropriate scope of criminalisation with respect to any such feature will inevitably be under-inclusive or over-inclusive (or both): that is, it will implausibly limit or unacceptably expand the scope of criminalisation, or in some cases do both.[24] And if the remedy for over-inclusiveness is that the state should exercise some choice about what conduct to criminalise, from among all the available candidates, then it would seem that the common feature in question is not inherent after all: it is, at best, a necessary and not a sufficient condition for criminalisation. It seems plausible, as Farmer argues, that there is no conduct that is essentially criminal, that the behaviour the legal order regards as necessarily punishable to maintain its authority is, for contingent reasons, so variable that it is impossible to identify any common feature across space and time.

3.2. Rights and the Instrumentalism of Criminal Law

The best way to understand criminal law is as an instrument for the protection of a rights-based legal order. This claim may seem obvious, even banal, but it does have a number of important implications. First (and here I align with Thorburn), it implies that criminal law has a distinctively legal function: its purpose is not to enforce a system of morality that is external to legal order or to give people their moral just deserts or to promote some external good, but to protect the legal order. Second (and here I align in part with Farmer), because criminal law has no substantive essence, the most plausible way to understand a legislative choice to define certain conduct as criminal is as an attempt to discourage the incidence of that conduct.

[22] Brudner 2008: Ch. 2.

[23] Marshall and Duff (1998); see also Duff 2007: 51–56; 2018: Ch. 7.

[24] Over-criminalisation is not only a bad thing: it is also a very serious wrong to the idea of a rightful condition. Stewart (2018).

My claim is not that there is no conduct that is inherently wrongful from the point of view of a rights-based legal order. I accept that claim; indeed, it's essential to my argument. In a civil condition, as Thorburn says, people's interactions with each other are structured by right; conduct inconsistent with right is inherently wrongful; and the legal order must provide remedies for those wrongs. The claim is rather that there is no conduct that is inherently punishable – or, even if there is such conduct, punishing all of it would itself be inconsistent with a civil conviction – so that there is no conduct that the legal order is required to punish. Even if we do understand law in general non-instrumentally, as constituting a civil condition for the moral reasons that Thorburn and others identify, criminal law nevertheless has an essentially instrumental role to play. The claim is not that criminal law should be understood as making a causal contribution to some state of affairs that could be adequately characterised independently of the law; rather it is that the main function of the criminal law should be understood as causally contributing to the maintenance of the civil condition.

In order to constitute a rightful condition, people must have private rights: property rights, contractual rights (broadly conceived), and some status rights. Ripstein has argued – largely successfully, in my view – that private law is, in general, not instrumental to the achievement of any good or state of affairs that could be defined independently of it, but is rather a way – the way – of institutionalising a central moral and legal idea: that no private person is in charge of another.[25] Accordingly, in Ripstein's picture, private law is relational. My property rights are always rights against others' interference with my property; your contractual rights and obligations are always rights and obligations involving your acts and the acts of others; status relationships give rise to rights and duties as between various persons. To these rights correspond a host of human activities that must therefore be defined as wrongs: wrongful interference with another's person, taking another's property, failing to carry out one's contractual obligations, or interfering in a parent's decisions concerning their child (or, on the other hand, a parent's abusing the child). And if there was no remedy for such wrongs, the legal order would not constitute a rightful condition because it would in no way protect those rights.

In order to constitute a rightful condition, there must also be public institutions that operate so as to carry out the various legitimate functions of the state. These institutions will typically have rules that will restrict the conduct of the citizen in various ways, possibly including requirements that the citizens do certain things that no private individual could make them do. To take only two examples, the state must provide roadways and other means of communication between persons, and the state must raise revenue to fund its various activities; accordingly, the citizens are required to comply with the rules of the road, and the citizens may be required to pay taxes. Failure to do those things is also wrong – not a private

[25] Ripstein (2016). See also E Weinrib (1995) for a different way of working out a similar set of ideas.

wrong, not a wrong to anyone in particular, but a wrong to the legal order. The state needs to have ways of responding to those wrongs. In the context of roadways, those responses might include criminal punishment, but they might also include regulatory sanctions (assuming those can be distinguished from criminal punishments) and purely administrative measures such as licence suspensions. In the tax context, those responses might include criminal punishment for tax evasion, but non-punitive compliance procedures such as requiring source deductions of anticipated tax owing, auditing tax returns, or reassessing tax liability are likely to be far more significant.

So, in a rightful condition, there are private wrongs and there are public wrongs. At least some of these wrongs are constitutive of a rightful condition in the sense that, at some point, a legal order that does not recognise them cannot count as a rightful condition. But there is no constitutive reason why any of these wrongs need to be defined as crimes, that is, as prohibitions coupled with punishment for violating them, rather than as wrongs that could be remedied in some other way. On the contrary, it is possible to define conduct as wrongful independently of the decision to criminalisation that conduct. Indeed, that definitional strategy is unavoidable, because criminal offences are normally structured by a definition of the conduct that is prohibited, plus a penalty for committing that conduct.[26]

Criminalisation, then, is a decision to take some conduct that is definable independently of the criminal law (though not independently of the legal order), to prohibit that conduct, and to make the violation of the prohibition punishable.[27] It counts in favour of criminalisation that the conduct in question is damaging to the civil condition: typically violations of private rights and violations of the rules of the rightful condition. It counts in its favour that criminalising such conduct would reduce the incidence of that conduct, by either of two main causal routes: some people will avoid the prohibited conduct merely because it was prohibited, while others will be deterred by the prospect of punishment. It counts against criminalisation that compliance could be achieved by other policy instruments. It also counts against criminalisation if, as a matter of fact, the incidence of the conduct

[26] For basic rule-of-law reasons, it is highly desirable that they should be so defined.

[27] For an earlier argument somewhat along these lines, see Stewart (2010). Philipp-Alexander Hirsch has drawn my attention to affinities between my argument here and the views of other participants in the Graz conference. In his contribution to this volume, Ivó Coca-Vila advocates for a 'rights-of-others' principle of criminalisation, according to which a violation of the right of another person's private right or a public right that can be understood in terms of private right is a *pro tanto* reason, but also the only acceptable reason, for criminalising conduct. I see the affinity, but I am not persuaded by Coca-Vila that 'all acts of criminalisation [must be] passed through the individualist filter of rights infringements', as I suspect that that formulation will either be too restrictive or not as restrictive as Coca-Vila would like it to be. The approach proposed in Joachim Renzikowski's contribution (Chapter 13 in this volume) appears to be closer to mine, in that he takes criminal sanctions to be linked to what he refers to as 'the pre-criminal primary orders of civil and public law' and thence to violations of private or public subjective right, rather than to something inherently criminal. I am, however, hesitant to make a rights violation as such a necessary condition for criminality, as on the approach I propose, it is the inconsistency of the conduct with a rightful condition, whether or not it is appropriately characterised as a violation of right, that makes it at least a potential candidate for criminalisation.

would not be affected, or even increased, by prohibiting it. Criminalisation is thus instrumental to the maintenance of the civil condition.

Consider an example. In common law systems, there are (at least) two responses to one person's (the defendant's) intentional interference with another person's (the plaintiff's or complainant's) bodily integrity. The first is a tort, a private wrong, which I will refer to as battery. Battery is a private cause of action which, if proved, entitles the plaintiff to an award of damages against the defendant as compensation for the wrong. The second is a crime, a public wrong, which I will refer to as assault.[28] A criminal prosecution is carried by a public prosecutor;[29] if the offence is proved, the defendant is subject to punishment (typically, imprisonment, other restrictions on liberty, or a fine), but there is characteristically no remedy for the complainant. The tort of battery and the crime of assault have some common features: Both require proof of an actual or apprehended touching; neither requires proof of harm.[30] There are a number of standard differences between the tort of battery and the crime of assault. In the tort of battery, the plaintiff must prove the touching; to avoid liability, the defendant must then prove a justifying (or excusing) fact such as the plaintiff's consent or self-defence. The burden of proof is on the party asserting the relevant fact and the quantum of proof is on a balance of probabilities. In the crime of assault, the prosecution must prove all the elements of the wrong – the touching, the lack of consent, the relevant mental state of the defendant, and the absence of any defences that realistically arise on the evidence – and the quantum of proof is beyond a reasonable doubt. Moreover, as suggested by the list of elements, the relevant 'intention' differs depending on whether the defendant is alleged to have committed the tort of battery or the crime of assault. In battery, the only relevant intention is the defendant's intention to touch the plaintiff (an unintentional touching is not a battery); while the plaintiff's consent to the touching is a defence, the defendant's state of mind in respect of that consent is irrelevant.[31] But for the crime of assault, the prosecution must not only prove intentional touching (unintentional touching is not an offence[32]) but also a culpable state of mind in relation to the complainant's lack of consent.[33]

[28] At common law, battery (as tort or crime) involved an actual touching, whereas assault (as tort or crime) involved an apprehended touching. In our times, the precise terminology varies from jurisdiction to jurisdiction; my choice of the word 'battery' for the tort and 'assault' for the crime is for convenience only.

[29] In some common law jurisdictions private prosecutions remain a theoretical possibility, but in such cases the private prosecutor must be understood as exercising a delegated public power.

[30] This is another detail that may vary from jurisdiction to jurisdiction. In Canada, the weight of authority holds that the slightest unwanted touching constitutes the actus reus of assault, although it is sometimes suggested (erroneously, in my view) that the defence of *de minimis non curat lex* might be available.

[31] Ripstein 2016: 43–47; *Mann v Balaban* (1970); *Non-Marine Underwriters, Lloyd's of London v Scalera* (2000).

[32] Recklessness may be sufficient *mens rea* in some jurisdictions.

[33] This element is rarely an issue in non-sexual cases; in contrast, in jurisdictions where unwanted touching of a sexual nature is a branch of the law of assault (sexual assault or sexual battery), it is often the central factual issue in any given case and is also a contentious policy issue at the level of offence definition.

One intuitive way of understanding the tort of battery and the crime of assault is that they are both devices for the protection of a specific aspect of personal autonomy – bodily integrity – that, in some sense, exists independently of the law. On this understanding, every person has an interest in the protection of their own body but also an interest in physical interactions with other persons; the tort and the crime are different ways of encouraging everyone to behave in ways that in some sense promotes or maximises some combination of those interests for everyone. Depending on how you characterise those relevant interests, you may give different answers to difficult doctrinal questions such as whether and in what context the law should recognise consent to the intentional infliction of serious bodily harm or consent given in advance to an application of force that will occur when the plaintiff or defendant is unconscious, – and even what 'consent' means in the first place. But from this perspective, there is a way in which the choice of tort or crime is merely instrumental. If it turned out that one could adequately protect the interest in bodily integrity entirely through a suitably defined crime of assault, there would be no need for a tort of battery (and vice versa).

But those who understand the legal order as a way of constituting a civil condition reject this intuitive picture. In their view, a civil condition is a way of ordering the relations of a plurality of free and purposive persons, so the tort of battery is best understood not as protecting an interest that exists independently of the rightful condition, but as part of the system of legal rules that constitutes rightful relations among persons. The tort of battery – unauthorised touching of another person – and the interest that the tort protects – bodily integrity – are mutually defining. Together they define the private law conditions under which two persons' bodily interactions are rightful or wrongful, as the case may be.[34] A legal order that did not recognise this tort would be defective as a legal order. This account of the tort of battery is persuasive to me and I am going to accept it for the purposes of this chapter. My claim is that, even on this non-instrumental understanding of the tort, the criminal offence of assault is best understood instrumentally, as a way of protecting the interest in bodily integrity. This interest is not entirely independent of, but at least in part created by, the legal order. However, it is not created by criminal law; thus, when the law defines an offence of assault, it is best understood as a way of protecting an interest that is independent of the criminal law itself.

Crimes against the state are similar in that the wrongs in question are definable independently of the state's response to them. Consider, for example, tax evasion. There could be no crime of tax evasion if a system of taxation did not exist, but once there is such a system, there is no special difficulty in defining the wrong of not complying with it: failure to comply with the system of taxation is just not paying what you owe. And there are many ways of encouraging people to pay what the owe. Typically, in the modern world, employers are required to assist taxpayers in this task by deducting estimated tax from employees' income and remitting it

[34] Ripstein 2016: 68–73. Thus, the picture of the law as constituting, at least in part, the very interest it seems to protect is not exclusive to a historicist approach such as Farmer's.

directly to the state. The revenue authority typically has power to investigate and reassess taxpayers, even to penalise taxpayers who have not paid everything they owe in a timely manner. Prosecuting people for tax evasion is an additional tool that may serve not only to gather the tax in question but also to deter the wrong of tax evasion. But there is nothing about the idea of a civil condition that requires the state to prosecute tax evaders or even to have an offence of tax evasion. In the civil condition, people can be required to pay tax, and the tax authorities do need to have procedures in place for collecting taxes from people who are not inclined to pay the taxes that they owe. However, there is no reason why those procedures must include the power to prosecute for tax evasion as long as a satisfactory tax system can be maintained.

Finally, there is conduct that is wrong not because it is independently a private wrong or independently a breach of one's obligations to the state, but only because the criminal law says so. But there is – again in contrast with private law – no difficulty conceptualising the conduct separately from the remedy for it. All driving offences are like this (exceeding the speed limit, driving without a licence, impaired driving, etc.) as are drug offences (manufacturing or possessing prohibited substances). The state must, of course, have a justification for criminalising such conduct that is consistent with its role in creating and maintaining a rightful condition; in the case of drugs, a purely paternalistic justification would probably not suffice, but if there is a way in which the consumption of certain substances systematically undermines people's freedom, a justification might be available.[35] If so, the decision to criminalise it is best understood as an instrument (though certainly not the only one) for discouraging it.

4. Conclusion

If all law is instrumental to some other value, it is natural to think that criminal law is also instrumental to that other value. If, however, legal order is best understood as constituting a system of right that is of moral importance in itself, it is tempting to try to find a constitutive role for criminal law, and thus a non-instrumental explanation for it, within that system of right. In this chapter, I have argued that, even if the second understanding of legal order is preferable, that temptation should be resisted. The place of criminal law in the legal order is not constitutive but instrumental to maintaining the system of right.

[35] For some thoughts along these lines, see Stewart (2011) and Stewart (2020a).

13

Rights and Duties and their Relevance in Criminal Law

JOACHIM RENZIKOWSKI*

1. Introduction

According to a widely held view, individual rights play no role in criminal law because crimes are not understood as violations of rights, but as harms or violations of 'Rechtsgüter' (legal interests). Regardless of this, criminal law does not seem to be concerned with the violation of individual rights, but with public wrongdoing that requires a public response – namely by the law enforcement authorities. In this chapter, I would like to put these criminal law certainties to the test and examine the relevance and role of rights in criminal law. My thesis is that while crimes are rightly understood as public wrongs, individual rights are necessarily the point of reference for legitimate criminalisation. In other words, criminal law and punishment can only be applied where the legal rights of the individual or the legal community are affected. To develop this argument, in the first part of this chapter I will establish what I mean by 'rights' (see section 2.). I will then explain how criminal law relates to these rights (see section 3.).

2. What is a Right? The Logic of Duties and Rights

To lay the conceptual grounds for understanding crimes as violations of rights, I will start by outlining and justifying a complex concept of right (later on called 'strong right') as it might be found in the historical development of the concept of right, which has its origins in the Latin *dominium*.[1] The special role of property is no coincidence, for it is the example *par excellence* for explaining rights.

* I am very grateful to Philipp-Alexander Hirsch and Elias Moser for their criticism and support to finish my chapter.

[1] For details see Brett 1997, and Tierney 1997.

I will also refer to property on various occasions in order to illustrate my concept in more detail. However, instead of drawing on the genealogy of this concept, I would like to analyse the most important deontic notions accompanying a 'strong right', namely the right-holder's liberty from duties (section 2.1) and the right-addressee's duties of non-interference (section 2.2). In the remainder, I'll compare my concept of a 'strong right' with Wesley Newcomb Hohfeld's influential account of legal relation, in order to highlight the similarities, but also important differences (section 2.3).

2.1. What is a Right? Liberty from Duties

Rights are often understood as permission to do or not to do something. But this way of speaking is imprecise. To show this, let me start with presenting the classical[2] concept of the deontological square.[3] A certain action can be 'forbidden'; it can be 'obligatory'; it can be 'not forbidden'; it can be 'not obligatory'. 'Forbidden' is adversarial to 'not forbidden', just as 'obligatory' is adversarial to 'not obligatory'. 'Forbidden' and 'obligatory', however, are contrary and incompatible. It follows from an obligation that the act in question is not forbidden, and from a prohibition that the act in question is not obligatory. Anything else would be a contradiction of norms. 'Not forbidden' and 'not obligatory', on the other hand, are compatible, i.e. an action can be both at the same time.

Figure 13.1 Deontic Square

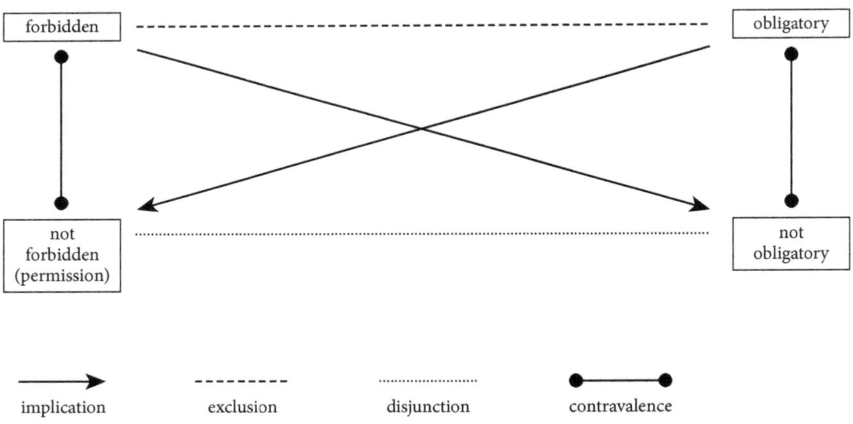

[2] For the historical development of the basic notions of the deontological square, see Armgardt 2017: 53 et seq., 59 et seq.; these notions can for example also be found in Bentham (1798) 1970: 96 et seq.; see also Hart 1971: 62; Raz 1980: 55 et seq.; modern deontic logic now deals with completely different problems.

[3] For the following see Joerden 2012: 202 et seq.

One can extend the deontological square to a deontological hexagon, in order to fully map all logical relationships of the basic concepts and their negations.[4] Two further exclusions exist, namely between 'forbidden' or 'obligatory' and 'indifferent'. If an action is neither 'forbidden' nor 'obligatory', then it is (normatively) 'indifferent' or 'absolutely permitted', that means, one can do what she or he likes. The opposite of 'indifferent' is when the performance or omission of the action is prescribed. If an action is either 'obligatory' or 'forbidden', then it is 'duty-bound' or normatively determined. This means that someone cannot do what he or she wants, but is subject to an obligation. Two further exclusions can also be recognised. A normatively determined action is incompatible with its classification as 'not forbidden' or 'not obligatory'.

Figure 13.2 Deontic Hexagon

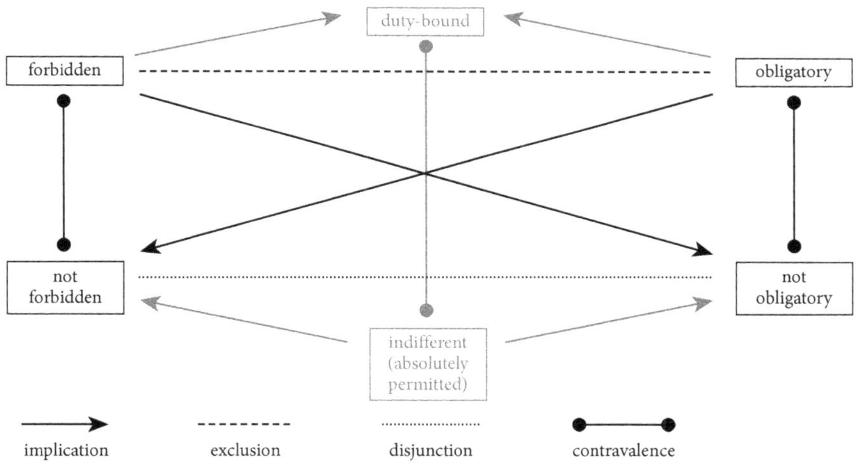

It is not uncommon to use the term 'permission' for an act which is not forbidden (see von Wright 1951: 3; Hart 1971: 62). However, a 'not forbidden' act can be 'obligatory', just as a 'not obligatory' act can be 'forbidden'. An example of the former is the so-called emergency assistance. Child C is in danger of drowning in the lake. His father F could save him if he rowed to him in O's boat. To do so, however, he would have to destroy the chain and the lock with which the boat is fastened to the shore. According to German law, the father is basically obliged to do everything necessary to save his son. Since C's life is worth considerably more than the material value of the chain and lock, the damage to O's property is not

[4] As far as I know, Achenwall 1767: § 26, seems to be the first to have worked out this complete set of notions. The following scheme was probably first developed by Kalinowski 1972: 106 et seq., 119; see also Jackson 1985: 90 et seq.

prohibited in this example.[5] It is required in order to fulfil F's duty to rescue. The reason for the unlawfulness of the damage to property is not F's own right here, but C's right to life, which outweighs O's right to property.[6] If, on the other hand, the example is formed in such a way that F would have to endanger O's life to save C, this act would be prohibited. Saving C in this way would not be commanded. So, a 'not obligatory act' is 'forbidden'. The case in which his not obligatory act is forbidden is, if you will, the ordinary case of the legal system.[7]

The word 'permission' is therefore misleading in defining the notion of 'right', because in these cases the norm addressee cannot freely decide whether to perform or refrain from performing the act. Rather, he or she is bound by an obligation or a prohibition. Only if an action is neither 'obligatory' nor 'forbidden' one does really have the freedom to choose what to do (likewise Joerden 2012: 203 et seq.). And only here I would like to speak of a *strong right*.[8] It might help to illustrate this by drawing on the definition of property rights in the German Civil Code, Sec. 903 sentence 1: 'The owner of a thing may (...) deal with the thing *as he pleases* and exclude others from any influence.'[9] Or to make the same point in terms of freedom of action: I can read the newspaper in the morning, drink coffee or tea as I please or eat whatever I want for breakfast. The law does not impose any rules on me in this respect. Nevertheless, it would be wrong to speak of a legal vacuum here.[10] The liberty what an agent may do or not do is essential for a right. So, 'indifference' or 'strong right' and 'duty-bound' are adversarial to each other. Since 'not forbidden' and 'not obligatory' together make up the 'strong right', right and 'duty-bound' are in the relation of contravalence, i.e. the opposite of a right is a duty. In other words: Where my right ends, my duty begins – and *vice versa*.

2.2. What is a Right? Protected Freedom from Interference

But liberty from duties as outlined so far is only a necessary condition of having a 'strong right'. Another one is freedom from interference, as is – once again – vividly demonstrated by property rights. Again, I repeat the definition of property rights in the German Civil Code: 'The owner of a thing may (...) deal with the thing as

[5] The example of necessity presupposes a gradable scale of rights, which will not be further substantiated here.

[6] In this example, it is not a question of an original right of the norm addressee. Rather, he is asserting the right of another on his behalf.

[7] Here, too, F's dispensation from the duty to rescue C does not arise from his own right, but from O's right to life.

[8] This is the same that Wright 1968: 22 later called 'free choice permission'; see also Hart 1982: 166 et seq.: 'bilateral character of liberty rights'. This term is also used by Kalinowski 1972: 113: 'permission bilatérale'.

[9] Italics added. 'Der Eigentümer einer Sache kann ... mit der Sache *nach Belieben verfahren* und andere von jeder Einwirkung ausschließen.

[10] Such as Williams 1956: 1130: liberties as an 'extra-legal phenomenon'.

he pleases and *exclude others from any influence*.'[11] Accordingly, ownership is characterised as the right to dispose of a certain object and to exclude unauthorised persons. This double power characterises every right, regardless of the object to which the right relates, such as my body, my data, or even the free development of my personality. This is the legal meaning of private autonomy: the unity between the legal position granted and the realisation of individual preferences. The function of use and the function of exclusion are different descriptions of one and the same legal relationship, once viewed from the perspective of the entitled, once from the perspective of the non-entitled. This shows that rights have the structure of a relation between at least two persons, the entitled party and the obligated party.[12] The right as a power to use the object of the right as one sees fit thus corresponds to the duty of the unauthorised person not to interfere.

Immanuel Kant explains this connection between right and duty in his 'Introduction to the Doctrine of Right' based on the freedom of the individual as a legally protected freedom. This freedom as 'independence from being constrained by another's choice' is 'the only original right belonging to every man by virtue of his humanity'.[13] Consequently, the 'universal principle of right' is

> Any action is *right* if it can coexist with everyone's freedom in accordance with a universal law, or if on its maxim the freedom of choice of each can coexist with everyone's freedom in accordance with a universal law.[14]

Conversely, it follows that an action that cannot coexist with another person's freedom of choice is wrongful. Wrongful actions, however, are forbidden and it is a conceptual implication of rights that their holder may prevent such wrongful acts:

> [I]f a certain use of freedom is itself a hindrance to freedom in accordance with universal laws (i.e., wrong), coercion that is opposed to this (as a *hindering of a hindrance to freedom)* is consistent with freedom in accordance with universal laws, that is, it is right. Hence there is connected with right by the principle of contradiction an authorization to coerce someone who infringes upon it.[15]

[11] Italics added. 'Der Eigentümer einer Sache kann … mit der Sache nach Belieben verfahren und *andere von jeder Einwirkung ausschließen*.'

[12] For details see Haas 2002: 56 et seq.

[13] Kant (1797) 1907: 237: 'Freiheit (Unabhängigkeit von eines anderen nöthigender Willkür), sofern sie mit jeder andern Freiheit nach einem allgemeinen Gesetz zusammen bestehen kann, ist dieses einzige, ursprüngliche, jedem Menschen kraft seiner Menschheit zustehende Recht.' See also Hart 1955; Ripstein 2006: 231.

[14] Kant (1797) 1907: 230: 'Eine jede Handlung ist recht, die oder nach deren Maxime die Freiheit der Willkür eines jeden mit jedermanns Freiheit nach einem allgemeinen Gesetze zusammen bestehen kann.'

[15] Kant (1797) 1907: 231: 'Folglich, wenn ein gewisser Gebrauch der Freiheit selbst ein Hinderniß der Freiheit nach allgemeinen Gesetzen (d. i. unrecht) ist, so ist der Zwang, der diesem entgegengesetzt wird, als Verhinderung eines Hindernisses der Freiheit mit der Freiheit nach allgemeinen Gesetzen zusammenstimmend, d. i. recht: mithin ist dem Rechte zugleich eine Befugniß, den, der ihm Abbruch thut, zu zwingen, nach dem Satze des Widerspruchs verknüpft.' For details see Ripstein 2008: 232 et seq.

Jeremy Bentham argues similarly:

> It is by imposing obligations, or by abstaining from imposing them, that rights are established or granted. (…) but it is not possible to create rights which are not founded upon obligations. (…) How can I possess the *right* of going into all streets of a city? It is … because everybody is bound by an obligation not to hinder me (Bentham 1843b: 181; see also Hart 1982: 173).

Thus, a right without legal protection through a legally enforceable duty cannot even be conceived.

As much as Kant and Bentham agree (and I agree) that rights and duties are two sides of the same coin, indeed that rights are inconceivable without duties to 'protect' them, they differ on which side is primary. According to Bentham's imperative theory, rights are merely reflections of corresponding duties. Legal norms granting rights are dependent norms without a regulatory meaning of their own, because they do not prescribe anything. Rather, based on the command of the authorities, the question is whether the beneficiary of a legal obligation is also entitled to a corresponding claim.[16] Strictly speaking, citizens are obliged to obey the law only vis-à-vis the state, which issues the imperatives and thereby grants them their rights. Accordingly, rights are therefore not reasons for duties, but duties can possibly lead to rights. Thus Bentham (1843c, 217 et seq.) writes:

> Obligation … is the product of a law. … A law, when entire, is a command; but a command supposes eventual punishment; without eventual punishment, or the apprehension of it, obedience would be an effect without a cause. …
>
> Obligation has place, when the desire on the part of the superior, the obliger, being signified to the obligee, he understands that in the event of his failing to comply with such desire, evil will befal him ….
>
> *Right* – Otherwise than from the idea of obligation, no clear idea can be attached to the word *right*.
>
> … The … efficient cause of right is, presence of correspondent obligation: This obligation is the obligation imposed on other persons at large, to abstain from disturbing you ….

In this view, it is the state alone that decides at its own discretion to whom it will distribute which rights.

This model of the imperative theory, however, is hardly compatible with a liberal state, which tends to run along Kantian lines. The assumption of human rights, for example, presupposes that they are not being awarded by the state, but are granted to everyone by virtue of everyone's humanity. Accordingly, these fundamental rights are not created by the state, but found. That implies that duties must be justified with regard to those rights, because every duty limits someone's

[16] See Bentham 1843b: 159: 'The law prohibits me from killing you – it imposes upon me the obligation not to kill you – it grants you the right not to be killed by me (…) – it requires of me the negative service of abstaining from killing you.'

freedom. Positive law also picks up on that, e.g. Article 2(1) of the German constitution (*Grundgesetz*), according to which duties result from 'the rights of others':[17] 'the right to the free development of his or her personality, insofar as he or she does not violate the rights of others'.[18]

However, regardless of whether the duty grounds the right (see Bentham 1843b: 181; Kelsen 1960: 132 et seq.) or the right the duty (see Raz 1986: 167, 183), no strong right can exist without legal protection through the obligation of others. Or in Bentham's words: Naked rights 'are not worth a straw' (Bentham [1798] 1970: 136 fn.). Only the restriction of freedom of the one through the imposition of obligations makes the legally guaranteed freedom of the other possible.[19] Hobbes' right of 'every man … to every thing, even to one another's body' (Hobbes [1651] 1997: 64) is therefore in fact not a *right*, but only denotes the factual capacity that every person has in the state of nature, i.e. in the state of lawlessness. If, however, we take the concept of 'strong right' that I have outlined as a starting point, then (irrespective of the justificatory primacy of right or duty) my right ends, where your right begins – and *vice versa*.

2.3. Hohfeld on Rights

The concept of a complex or 'strong' right outlined so far, however, may be unfamiliar to those who follow Wesley Newcomb Hohfeld's analysis of legal relations. Hohfeld (1913/17: 30) identifies eight fundamental legal relations: 'Jural opposites' are right and no-right, privilege and duty, power and disability as well as immunity and liability. 'Jural correlatives' are right and duty, privilege and no-right, power and liability as well as immunity and disability.

The first four relations describe the perspective of the entitled or non-entitled person. The next four relations denote the interpersonal relationship between persons. The other four relations describe different aspects of the connection between rights and duties. Using the example of property as the paradigm for the right: the owner has a claim against the non-owner not to be disturbed in the use of his property. Hohfeld (1913/17: 32) speaks of the right as 'claim', in reference to compliance with the correlative duty. So, your duty corresponds to my right. The owner can dispose of his property as he wishes without being subject to

[17] The question whether intrinsic duties could be possible without any entitled party (Raz 1986: 210–13) must not be discussed here. Raz himself cites the duty of benevolence as an example. If A owes B benevolence, it does not follow that B is entitled to it. But other examples such as kindness or charity show that these are moral and not legal duties.

[18] 'Jeder hat das Recht auf die freie Entfaltung seiner Persönlichkeit, soweit er nicht die Rechte anderer verletzt …'.

[19] See Bentham 1843a: 503: 'But as against the coercion applicable by individual to individual, no liberty can be given to one man but in proportion as it is taken from another.' Of course, this does not mean that every right must correspond exactly to a particular duty. Rights can give rise to a bundle of different duties, see also Raz 1984: 199 et seq.

any obligations. Hohfeld (1913/17: 36, 41) calls this liberty 'privilege'. Besides, the owner can authorise others to use his property or transfer it. Hohfeld (1913/17: 44 et seq.) refers to such a legal ability as 'power': 'the person (or persons) whose volitional control is paramount may be said to have the (legal) power to effect the particular change of legal relations that is involved in the problem.' The concept of a complex right (or 'strong right') developed above contains all these elements: right with correlative duties, privilege with correlative no-right, power as legal ability.

But that is not Hohfeld's view. On the contrary, he repeatedly and urgently warns against an improper confusion of right and privilege (Hohfeld 1913/17: 34 et seq.).[20] He also does not consider it necessary to link a privilege with a duty of others not to prevent the holder of the right from exercising his privilege:

> It is equally clear, as already indicated, that such a privilege or liberty to deal with others at will might very conceivably exist without any peculiar concomitant rights against 'third parties' as regards certain kinds of interference. Whether there should be such concomitant rights (or claims) is ultimately a question of justice and policy; and it should be considered, as such, on its merits. The only correlative logically implied by the privileges or liberties in question are the 'no-rights' of 'third parties'. It would therefore be a non sequitur to conclude from the mere existence of such liberties that 'third parties' are under a duty not to interfere etc. (Hohfeld 1913/17: 36 et seq.)

If, for example, X has the privilege of eating a shrimp salad he has paid for, this in no way implies a prohibition for others of preventing X from doing so (Hohfeld 1913/17: 34 et seq.). The strange consequence of this view is that two privileges are opposed to each other. 'X may eat the shrimp salad' and 'A may prevent him from eating the shrimp salad'. For X, the purely factual possibility of performing the act would remain in contrast to the purely factual possibility of A's obstruction. The state authorities would not be allowed to intervene against this hindrance, because then A would have no privilege. Ultimately, the 'law of the strongest' would prevail, but naked violence is not a legal point of view.[21]

But not only Hohfeld's stand on duties not to hinder the exercise of a right differes from my complex account of a right. The same holds for the second element of a 'strong right', namely the power to exclude unauthorised persons.

[20] He gives the example that X, as the owner of the land, enters into a contract with Y, which includes the obligation that X must walk over his own land (for example, to check its state). Now property is a classic example of a privilege and X in this sense has the privilege of walking on his own land. But by contract he is at the same time obliged to do so (Hohfeld 1913/17: 32 et seq.). It is easy to see that in Hohfeld's example duty and privilege are no longer jural opposites because they are not mutually exclusive (Moritz 1960: 30 et seq.). The problem is that Hohfeld obviously uses the term privilege with a double meaning (Moritz 1960: 56).

[21] Possibly Hohfeld understands this example differently, as the following quote shows: 'But it is equally clear, that if A had succeeded in holding so fast to the dish that X couldn't eat the contents, no right of X would have been violated' (Hohfeld 1913/17: 35). Seen in this light, the problem is not the link between a privilege and a correlative duty, but the clarification of the content of the privilege or right. So, X has no exclusive right to help himself to the shrimp salad to the exclusion of all others but can only eat it while there is still some left – according to the principle of priority.

Hohfeld asserts a connection between X‘s claim that Y does not enter his or her property and X‘s privilege to enter his or her property (Hohfeld 1913/17: 32). However, such a connection does not follow from his account. It only follows from X‘s permission to enter his land that Y may not prevent him or her from doing so. But it is not always the case that when Y enters X‘s property, he thereby prevents X from exercising his right. There is therefore no direct connection between his or her right to enter and the obligation of others to accept this exclusion. If, on the other hand, we take the concept of a ‘strong right’ that I have outlined as a basis, then having a right implies the exclusion of others.

I’ll leave it at that. My aim here was simply to clarify the extent to which the concept of ‘strong rights’ that I have outlined differs from the narrow definition of the term ‘right’ in terms of a claim right that dominates the current debate. Admittedly, Hohfeld’s detailed analysis reveals further elements of a concept of a complex right beyond the two elements that I put special emphasis on: the liberty to dispose and the power to exclude, e.g. as mentioned in section § 903 of the German Civil Code. However, I do not agree with him insofar as he limits the term ‘right’ to ‘claims’ only.[22] To me the more complex concept of a ‘strong right’ – as composed of various Hohfeldian molecules (see Honoré) – seems preferable for describing legal relations in a liberal state.

3. Duties and Rights in Criminal Law

What relevance does the above analysis of a complex right have for criminal law? My short answer is that ‘strong rights’, as I have tried to define them, are the reference point for legitimate criminalisation. I’ll argue for this thesis from a norm-theoretical perspective. My starting point is the norm-theoretical distinction between (primary) norms of conduct and (secondary) norms of punishment (or more generally: legal consequence). Norms of conduct impose duties directed at citizens, such as ‘Thou shalt not kill!’ or ‘Thou shalt render assistance in emergencies!’ The norms of punishment are the criminal law are addressed to law enforcement authorities and prescribe what punishment should be imposed for the violation of a norm of conduct, for example ‘Whoever kills another person shall be punished by imprisonment for not less than five years!’

The author of this distinction is Jeremy Bentham (Bentham [1798] 1970: 133 et seq.), whereas in Germany it is mostly associated with the name of Karl Binding (1872: 28 et seq.). Bentham, like Binding, presented this norm theory in the context of criminal law, but it can be applied to civil law as well. Civil law is about compensation for unlawful harm, and so a legal consequence could, for example, read: ‘Whoever injures another person shall pay compensation!’

[22] In contrast, Hirsch 2021: 38 et seq., who considers the restriction of rights to claims to be sufficient to explain their significance for criminal wrongdoing.

Following this norm-theoretical distinction punishment as a sanction for unlawful conduct logically presupposes a system of norms (and duties derived from them) from which the unlawfulness of the conduct in question results. Criminal law does not implement these norms itself but presupposes them. Therefore, criminal law is accessory to the duties that are already established by other areas of law, i.e. private and public law (see also Stewart, Chapter 12 in this volume).

However, these duties do not stand alone, but follow a pre-existing distribution of rights. For example, norms prohibiting damage to property presuppose a system of property rights. Consequently, if there is no system of rights and if neither a private person nor the state (embodying/representing the public) is entitled to demand an omission or an action (e.g. not to damage property), the authority to safeguard those rights by norms of conduct and – subsequently – to enforce them by means of threat of punishment is inconceivable. The same applies to civil law. An obligation to compensate for damage can only be established if a situation has arisen that contradicts the allocation of rights. The secondary legal consequences of civil law, such as compensation for harm or unjust enrichment, presuppose this standard.

This already illustrates the importance of rights in criminal law: Rights are the point of reference for legitimate criminal legislation – mediated by the norms that safeguard them. Punishment as a sanction for unlawful conduct logically presupposes a system of norms from which the unlawfulness of the conduct in question results. However, what constitutes lawful or unlawful conduct is ultimately defined by individual rights. Therefore, individual rights – 'strong rights' as I outlined them in the first part of this chapter – define and limit the scope of norms of conduct that can be backed up by criminal sanctions. This, of course, raises several questions. First, one might ask why the concept of a 'strong right' should be used as a point of reference for criminalisation (section 3.1). Secondly, the question arises as to whether this reference of criminal law to (individual) rights does not automatically lead to a privatisation of criminal law (section 3.2).

3.1. Rights as the Reference Point for Legitimate Criminalisation?

Rights are not usually the point of reference for criminalisation. Instead, in the German debate, the term 'Rechtsgut' is commonly used to legitimise criminal laws or norms of conduct backed up by criminal sanctions. According to this view, criminal law serves to protect legal interests. So, each norm backed up by criminal sanctions necessarily protects one or more legal interests – of individuals or the general public;[23] otherwise it is not legitimate. Insofar as the term 'Rechtsgut' is

[23] For a compilation of the differing provisions on legal interests, see Roxin/Greco 2020: § 2 N. 3. The wording 'Rechtsgut' as 'legally protected interest' goes back to Liszt 1883: 19.

not limited to indicating the purpose pursued by the law, it is used to formulate limits for state criminal law in a liberal society. In this respect, it coincides with the harm principle used in the Anglo-American debate since John Stuart Mill (1859: 22): 'That the only purpose for which power can be rightfully exercised over any member of a civilised community, against his will, is to prevent harm to others.'[24]

Irrespective of this intention, which I share, the use of the term 'legal interest' seems inappropriate, because referring to harm to legal interests or 'Rechtsgüter' does not yet indicate for what reason an individual interest should be worthy of protection by means of criminalisations. Consequently, it is at the state legislator's discretion which individual interests deserve this special protection. However, a selective choice among various factual interests is always subject to the suspicion of state paternalism. The law, however, does not have the task of optimising any individual interests, but of guaranteeing the freedom of each individual to pursue his or her needs. However, the realm of freedom thus delineated is the individual right as I have outlined in the beginning. Rights are the means of pursuing one's own interests but they are not identical with them. The traditional orientation of the harm principle or the 'Rechtsgutslehre' towards interests does not distinguish between the legal position granted and the motivation for its exercise and is thus based on a not sufficiently complex understanding of the tasks of criminal law within a liberal state. Once again, it is not simply a matter of securing a certain set of goods, but of securing freedom[25] – even if it relates to goods and requires certain goods for its realisation.[26]

Furthermore, the taking harm to legal interests or 'Rechtsgüter' as the reference point for criminalisation inevitably leads to a materialistic account of criminal wrongdoing. Ripstein (2006: 218–9) therefore accuses the harm principle of materialism. Due to the principle *casum sentit dominus*, however, the occurrence of harm does not yet establish the responsibility of another for it (see Haas 2002: 69; see also Ripstein 2006: 228–9). The emphasis on rights, on the other hand, opens up the possibility of recognising that the legal positions that are protected by the rules of conduct that are punishable by criminal law represent triangular relations between two legal subjects and a certain object of reference, on the basis of which one legal subject has the legal power to exclude the other legal subjects from its

[24] An impressive example for this discussion is Joel Feinberg's four-volume work 'The Moral Limits of the Criminal Law' (1984).

[25] Or 'souvereignty' Ripstein 2006: 231.

[26] At this point, the Anglo-American discussion between the 'theory of will' (see for example Hart 1982: 183), the 'theory of status' (for example Kamm 2002: 485–6) – to which my concept seems closer – and the 'theory of interest' (see Raz 1984: 195; 1988: 166) need not be dealt with in detail. An interest theory of law also takes a position on the power of the right holder to dispose of his legal interest. One can also ask whether these approaches to legal theory can be combined, for example Sreenivasan 2005 and Wenar 2005. The traditional doctrine of 'Rechtsgut' in Germany, against which my comment is primarily directed, is far removed from the subtleties of these discussions.

legal sphere by virtue of its will. From the perspective of the offender, a crime is thus always the disregard of the power of exclusion of the foreign right.[27]

This rights-based approach is not limited to crimes committed against individuals, but can also be extended to victimless crimes. In victimless crimes it is the general public whose public rights are violated – regardless of how such rights can be justified.[28] Here, the collective of the members of society legally constituted in the state is the owner of the right. The state authorities are called upon to exercise it, and they have the derived power of disposition with regard to the use of the object and the exclusion of unauthorised persons. They exercise it on behalf of the legally constituted community (see Renzikowski 2007: 569 et seq.). Thus, for example, the legal right subject to environmental offences can be reconstructed as the right of the general public to determine the state of natural resources and their management. Anyone who commits an environmental offence extends his or her own legal sphere in disregard of the right of the general public; they violate its exclusionary function. It is a misunderstanding that duties must be owed to a particular person in order to speak of a corresponding right (so Lyons 1969: 175). This is because, as we have just shown, there are also duties towards the general public that correspond to a right of the general public (see Steiner 1994: 66–7).

However, although there are good reasons to take rights (rather than interests or 'Rechtsgüter') as the point of reference for criminalisation, it does not follow that rights must always be protected by norms of conduct backed up by criminal sanctions. Obviously, norms of conduct do not cover the entire area of the distribution of rights, as can be seen, for example, in the rules of road traffic. The surest way to avoid the several thousand road deaths each year would be a widespread ban on automobile traffic – or at least general speed restrictions. If one wanted to completely exclude impairments of rights, one would have to prohibit all hazards. It is obvious that this would also mean that social life would have to come to a standstill to a large extent. However, in the interest of maximising freedom of action for all, the legislator weighs the potential dangers to the legal rights of those affected against the benefits of general social practice. In order to achieve a balance of interests in a concrete case of harm, the law uses strict liability, which is not linked to the culpable violation of a norm of conduct. That does not mean that the right is given up, but it is not protected by norms of *conduct*. This becomes particularly clear in the case of the vehicle owner's strict liability. The situation is

[27] Haas 2002: 56 et seq.; as well as Ripstein 2006: 227, 233 ff; This right of exclusion is also disregarded if the holder of the right is legally unable to dispose of the object of his right. One example is sexual offences against children. The right to exclude guarantees protection against external determination, which is always the case if the right holder has not given valid consent. In other – highly controversial – cases, such as the prohibition of killing on demand, it is debateable whether the killing taboo does conceal a public concern.

[28] One could, for example, attribute the subjective authorisation of the state to the fact that certain conditions (functioning administration of justice, safe road traffic, etc.) must be in place so that individuals can exercise their individual rights. Since everyone is (non-exclusively) entitled to this, the state is needed as a 'representative', see for example Raz 1986: 207–9.

similar in technical security law and in the area of industrial development, where strict liability systems are of high importance.

One might object that this takes us back to a Benthamite imperative theory, if norms of conduct are imposed by the sovereign and if – as a corollary – the legal community sets the rules of conduct according to its ideas of an optimal all-round distribution of freedom.[29] Admittedly, this is true to the extent that the state itself establishes the order of public life; the norms of conduct are norms of public law (see Haas 2002: 76 et seq.). However, it does not follow from this that the imperative theory must also be adopted insofar as, according to its classical variant, legal norms are justified solely from the perspective of the sovereign ruler. In a liberal constitutional state, however, law is justified from the perspective of the citizens. The imperative theory accurately describes the legal protection of citizens through norms of conduct 'from the top'. In addition to the setting of norms 'from the top', the justification of norms comes 'from the bottom', from the individual and its innate human as well as civil rights. The accessorial nature of criminal law, outlined in the beginning, means nothing else. It presupposes a distributive system of rights so that is only legitimate insofar it is necessary and conducive to the protection of those rights.[30] Thus, the object of protection of norms of conduct backed up by criminal sanctions is the right itself!

3.2. Criminal Offences as Public Wrongs

Criminal offences thus have a dual nature: horizontally as a violation of the right or a duty resulting directly from it and at the same time vertically as a violation of a public law norm of conduct. This dual nature of criminal wrongdoing explains why criminal offences are, on the one hand, limited to the violation of a right, whilst still retaining, on the other hand, a public dimension that justifies a public reaction to an otherwise seemingly private conflict.[31] To make this distinction clearer, I would like to speak of a public claim to legal obedience with regard to the public norm of conduct. In my view, therefore, there is a distinction to be made between the public right to the observance of the rule of conduct and the

[29] According to Bentham (1789) 1970: chap I, legislation must be guided by the imperative of maximising utility, but what is best for the common good is decided by the ruler. Therefore, Bentham (1843a: 501) calls the idea of inalienable rights as a limit to state power 'nonsense upon stilts'.

[30] Taking the example of property: its distribution is not effected by criminal law itself, but is presupposed by it. Civil law, not criminal law, regulates how property is acquired and disposed of. What constitutes a third-party property is a preliminary question under civil law.

[31] For example, if someone steals someone else's property, the owner can sue for the return of the stolen property. He can demand compensation for lost use and damages if the item can no longer be returned or is damaged. If, on the other hand, the thief is found guilty and sentenced to a penalty, the stolen owner often does not benefit from this. Instead, there is a risk that the convicted person will no longer be able to pay compensation due to the sentence. So why is the offender subjected to a state sanction, i.e. punishment, instead of leaving the resolution of the conflict to the discretion of the injured party by means of civil law?

individual right protected by the rule of conduct. It is only when the state's norms of conduct as such are violated by criminal wrongdoing that a public reaction is required, one that affirms the validity of the legal order in the face of the criminal's maxim, which is to be declared irrelevant (Ripstein 2008: 243–4). It is precisely for this reason that a criminal act, even if it violates a private right, is not just a private matter (see Haas 2002: 80; see also Lichtenthäler and Thorburn, Chapters 10 and 14 in this volume). Therefore, the victim has no influence on the prosecution. Thus, he or she cannot prevent the punishment of the offender by forgiving him or her, nor is he or she entitled to a certain amount of punishment.[32] It is therefore the general public whose right to compliance with the norm is disregarded if the offender violates the norm. The entitlement of the citizen favoured by the norm of conduct is therefore only an indirect one. Thus, the violation of the right is the *cause*, and the violation of the public law norm of conduct that serves to protect it is the *reason* for the punishment.

This also explains the fundamental restraint of the state in the procedural assertion of a norm violation. Rights are primarily realised through the private legal order. However, private autonomy by no means confers on the citizen the power to set norms of conduct; rather it opens up a framework for him or her within the *ius cogens* created by the state legal order. However, the recognition of rights is also accompanied by the fact that it is first and foremost incumbent on the citizen as the person harmed by the violation of a norm of conduct to assert his or her harm in court. The state does not impose its legal protection, but only offers citizens a legal protection procedure, which the injured parties can make use of according to their own interests. In this respect, the private law order seeks to ensure the optimal distribution of spheres of freedom in the interest of the individual. The state itself is primarily responsible for safeguarding the allocation of rights under public law (see Thorburn, Chapter 14 in this volume).

In consequence, the general public is not only the author of the norms of conduct, but it is also the public's entitlement to legal obedience that is violated when the offender violates a punishable prohibition. Admittedly, the norms of conduct as such (as well as the accessory norms of punishment) aim to protect individual rights. Nonetheless, the entitlement of the citizen benefited by the norm of conduct is only an indirect one. At this point, I disagree with Hirsch (Chapter 8 in this volume; 2021: 106 et seq.). In his view, the author of a norm and the beneficiary need not be identical. Since the citizen favoured by the norm of conduct by virtue of consenting to a criminalised behaviour deontically controls the duty to comply with that norm, he or she has a claim to the fulfilment of that very duty.[33] Criminal offences are therefore not committed against the general public, but against the citizen concerned. However, it is doubtful whether this conclusion

[32] This is why Lyons 1969: 177 believes that penal obligations do not correspond to rights. This, of course, is throwing the baby out with the bathwater.

[33] So, Hirsch also does need the power to dispose as an element of a concept of a right at this point.

can be drawn from the effect of consent. First of all, consent is nothing other than the manifestation of the power of disposition within the framework of the right. The holder of the right disposes of the object of his right by not excluding another person, but by allowing him to exert a certain influence. This eliminates the corresponding duty of behaviour on the part of the other person. Due to the accessoriness of criminal law, this disposition also has an effect on the public law norm of conduct, which derives its legitimacy precisely from the right. The task of state law is not only to protect rights from interference by others, but also to guarantee freedom through law. The deontic control of the consenting right holder is therefore only an indirect one, and it is not necessary to make him the beneficiary of the norm of conduct.[34]

4. Conclusion

As I have argued, rights and duties are mutually dependent. Only duties establish the legally guaranteed freedom of the other – his or her right. Without protective duties, there is no right. Conversely, in a liberal legal system, rights are the only legitimate reasons for the imposition of duties. So, every obligation describes a legal relationship between at least two legal subjects: the entitled and the obligated. Duty and right are two sides of the same coin; the duty of one is the freedom of the other and *vice versa* (see Gewirth 1986: 329 et seq.). Those legal relations are the reference point for public norms of conduct that the legistlator sets up and backs up with criminal sanctions to safeguard them. The analysis of rights and duties has consequences for understanding of criminal law as a violation of rights: It is the general public whose right to compliance with the norm is disregarded if the offender violates the norm. The entitlement of the citizen favoured by the norm of conduct (because it protects its individual rights) is therefore only an indirect one. Thus, the violation of the right is the *cause* and the violation of the public law norm of conduct that serves to protect it is the *reason*.

[34] A touchstone for Hirsch's concept is the punishability of an impossible attempt. If the offender intentionally shoots his victim without realising that he or she had died of a stroke shortly before, no right of any victim whatsoever has been violated, simply because there is no longer a holder of this right. Similarly, no rights holder can demand compliance with the duty. After all, nothing can happen. From the perspective of rights, an impossible attempt does not exist at all – even though, from the perpetrator's perspective, the intention is to disregard another person's right. But an imaginary or possible victim is not a real victim. The attempt thus only touches the level of public-law norms of conduct or in other words: the claim of the general public to legal obedience and not the right of an unknown right-holder. One could therefore dispute the punishability of the unsuitable attempt, but that is not Hirsch's opinion.

14

One Right to Rule them All

MALCOLM THORBURN*

1. Introduction

How could we ever justify the state's punishment of criminal offenders? Part of the story, of course, will have to come to terms with the enormous suffering that criminal punishment and associated criminal justice institutions cause to so many people. But before we even get to the question of *how much* suffering the state should be entitled to impose by way of punishment, we need, first, to answer the basic structural question: what gives the state the right to impose *any* amount of punishment on criminal offenders?

It will not do simply to point out that many of the things we recognise as crimes are morally awful acts. Even if we concede this point, as we should, this still tells us nothing about why the state should punish those who carry them out. It also will not do to point out that the state has good prudential reasons (indeed, we all have good prudential reasons) to deter people from committing many of these acts. Bernard Williams rightly refers to the control of criminal violence as the first political question (2005: 3), but that still does not explain how the state, and only the state (Thorburn 2008: 1070–1130) is *entitled* to impose punishments on criminal offenders. It is one thing to say that I have good reason to deter criminal wrongdoing (that is a reason for me), but it is quite another to say that I can justify doing so to those I punish (that would be a reason both for me and for the punished person) (Duff 2010b: 360). In short, although we all know that many crimes are morally awful and we all know that the world would be a better place if we could somehow deter them, neither of these arguments addresses the question at hand. What we are looking for is a *relational* justification – an account that explains how

* Thanks to audiences at the 'Markelloquium' seminar at Fordham Law School, New York; to the Public Law Workshop at the University of Ottawa; to the Legal Theory Workshop at Western University; and to the Faculty Workshop at the University of Toronto Faculty of Law. I owe special thanks to Alan Brudner, Vincent Chiao, Antony Duff, Larissa Katz, Arthur Ripstein, Hamish Stewart, and Clara Thorburn for extensive discussion of this chapter's themes. Responsibility for all the chapter's faults, of course, remains with the author.

the state has standing over criminal offenders that entitles it to punish them for their criminal wrongdoing.[1]

In this chapter, I argue that the key to answering this fundamentally relational question is a fundamentally relational idea. The state is entitled to punish criminal offenders because this is part and parcel of a larger right that a legitimate state holds against all its subjects: the exclusive right to rule over them. I set out the argument for this claim and some of its implications in several stages. In section 2, I sketch out a fairly familiar social contract argument for the morally crucial role of the state. According to this account, it is not just that the world would be a better place if the state set down laws for us all and used coercion where necessary to ensure compliance with them. Rather, the state is legally – and, under the right conditions, morally[2] – *entitled* to do so. Indeed, it is absolutely central to the very idea of the state and its ability to solve the moral problem of unilaterality that it, and it alone, should be entitled to do so.

In section 3, I consider the place of the state's exclusive right to rule in the structure of the criminal trial. The talk of wrongdoing in the criminal trial (and not merely of conduct that warrants a deterrent sanction) makes good sense, (contra Chiao 2019: 44–5) but the wrong that is of concern to us here is against the state's exclusive right to rule (rather than to the rights of any particular victim).[3] This focus on the state's right to rule explains many familiar features of the criminal trial: why we are concerned with violations of (the state's) positive law, rather than undesirable conduct as such; why it is state prosecutors who bring the case against the accused; and why we talk meaningfully of criminal *wrongdoing* even when the offender has not wronged any individual rights-holder. The right to rule account also explains the significance of the criminal trial beyond its role in justifying the infliction of punishment. When states try, convict, and punish criminal wrongdoing, they are not merely resisting a rights violation with coercive force (as they might do to an act of war by non-subjects); they are bringing the offender under the authority of their laws and institutions, reasserting their exclusive authority over him and passing judgment on him not only as a wrongdoer, but also as a subject.

In section 4, I consider the nature and limits of the state's exclusive right to rule and its implications for policing, prosecution, and punishment today. The state's right to rule is not one that it can exercise in just any way it might wish. Rather, it is entitled to rule only insofar as it actually solves the moral problem of unilateralism. Of course, this means that the laws of legitimate states are subject to

[1] Philipp-Alexander Hirsch provides a very different relational account of criminal wrongdoing, focused on the potential victim's power of consent and thereby to render permissible otherwise wrongful conduct. See Chapter 8 in this volume.

[2] That is, from the point of view of any working legal system, the state has the legal right to make and enforce its laws. When that state is also a legitimate authority, it is also morally entitled to use coercive force to enforce its laws. See further discussion of this point in section 4 below.

[3] But see Philipp-Alexander Hirsch's chapter in this volume, in which he argues that criminal wrongs concern the rights of individual victims.

familiar rule of law constraints of generality, publicity and the like. It also means, however, that states should aim to vindicate their exclusive right to rule through means that interfere as little as possible with the independence of their subjects. Whatever wrong the offender has committed, he remains a moral person and a legal subject. States must always ask whether they can justify harsh punitive treatment of the offender in light of all the alternatives they have at their disposal to accomplish the same end. There are usually better options.

2. Unilateralism and the Rule of Law

When we ask how the state is entitled to punish criminal wrongdoers, our answer must begin by pointing out the state's morally crucial role more generally. That is, one must consider the problem of governance (Green 2007: 165). According to a familiar social contract story (Rousseau 2019: 36; Kant [1797] 1996; Rawls 1993; Ripstein 2009), the state is a morally necessary institution because it and it alone allows us to escape from the otherwise intractable moral problem of unilateralism. This problem arises in any situation where we do not have a state and its institutions to make and enforce laws for all of us. Without a state, we can only live under terms that one party imposes unilaterally on the other. This is both morally problematic and structurally unavoidable. It is problematic because it means that whatever terms structure our relations with others, they are ones that one party imposes upon the other unilaterally. Whatever the substantive merits of those terms, the very fact that they are imposed unilaterally makes the situation morally problematic, for it is a situation of pure domination. The problem is also structurally unavoidable: even if the tables are turned from time to time and the party normally dictating the terms is subjected to terms dictated by the other party, the norms that govern our interactions are still imposed unilaterally by one party on the other. Indeed, the problem is even present in cases where the parties agree on the terms of their interaction. Under this condition, the parties are simply living under a structurally unstable overlap of unilateral opinions; it is still open to one of the parties to impose different terms should he so choose (Herzog 1989). In this sense, the relationship is – and structurally must always be – akin to a sort of slavery: one party is subject to the other's whims, whether they are kind, cruel, or otherwise.

The state can provide a solution to this deep moral problem of unilateralism only if it has certain basic features. First, it must plausibly claim to speak in the name of all of us, and not merely to be the tool of some to be used against others. Otherwise, it simply exacerbates the same problem of unilateralism: one group uses a powerful tool to impose its will over another, weaker group. As Rousseau puts the point, '[a] man, even if he had enslaved half the world, still remains nothing but a private individual; his interest, separate from that of the others, still remains nothing but a private interest' (Rousseau 2019: 50). This constraint gives rise to a number of familiar features of public offices and public law more generally: states and their officials cannot pursue the private purposes of any particular person or group; (Thorburn 2020b: 248–66) and they must only act for public reasons that all subjects can share (Rawls 1993: 212 et seq.). It means also that public law must be of general application: it will not do to have one set of laws for one group and another set of laws for others. If the law draws distinctions among us, it must do so in ways that are consistent with its public purposes (Fuller 1964: 81).

In addition to these general features of public power, there is another incident of the state's role as the necessary solution to the moral problem of unilateralism that is more specifically related to the criminal law. In order to solve the problem of unilateralism, the state must not only set out public laws and institutions to guide its subjects, it must also ensure that those laws – and *only* those laws – *actually govern the relations* among its subjects. It is no solution to the problem of unilateralism for a putative state merely to articulate a set of norms and then hope that everyone will conduct themselves accordingly (Aristotle 1985).[4] The state's promise is that it will put in place a set of norms that will actually structure our relations with one another on terms that are fundamentally ours together, and that it will resist all attempts to displace these laws and impose terms in their stead. And this requires coercive enforcement of some kind.

When states suppress criminal wrongdoing, they do so not simply because many crimes are independently harmful and morally wrongful acts. They do so because the very survival of the rule of law project requires it. David Garland neatly connects the ideas of sovereignty and law enforcement in the following terms:

> [I]n the conditions of contested and unstable authority that characterized early-modern Europe, victorious sovereign lords held out the promise of *pax et justitia* to their subjects as their forces fought to pacify their newly won territory and impose the King's peace. The guarantee of "law and order" … originally meant the suppression of alternative powers and competing sources of justice as well as the control of crime and disorderly conduct … (Garland 2001: 29)

Garland's point – that the state's crime control efforts are directly about ensuring its own right to rule and only indirectly about suppressing particular wrongs – is an important one, but we should reformulate it in one crucial respect. Whereas he distinguishes between 'the suppression of alternative powers and competing sources of justice' with 'the control of crime and disorderly conduct', we should elide that distinction. The direct significance of crime and disorderly conduct to the state's rule of law project *just is* the fact that it concerns alternative powers and competing sources of norms.

[4] Indeed, the distinction between wish (merely taking up something as valuable and worth pursuing) and decision, which involves taking up means in pursuit of that end, goes back at least as far as Aristotle's *Nicomachean Ethics*, Book III, chapter iii, 1111b2–28 (1985): 'we wish for the end […] but we decide to do that which promotes the end'.

Coercive enforcement is a basic feature not only of state authority but of any incident of the relationship of what I call 'robust authority' more generally (Thorburn 2017: 7–32). For present purposes, we are concerned with the relationship between the state and its subjects, but the need for coercive enforcement applies to other relationships with this same structural feature. If parents are in charge of certain questions for their children (say, what time they should go to bed, what they should eat, their access to screens, *etc.*), then an essential part of the relationship of robust authority is the parent's power to realise her decisions for her child. The very idea of one party being in charge of deciding certain questions for another is that she should be empowered in some way to make her decision *stick*. This point is often misunderstood and treated as though it justified *any* use of coercion to enforce the authority's decision over her charge, but that would be a serious misunderstanding. The moral basis for any position of authority does not lies in an absolute right of one person to impose his will on another through coercion; indeed, it is almost precisely the opposite. The justification of such a position of authority is to allow for decisions to be made in the interests of someone (the child, or the people taken as a collection of individuals) who is unable to make those decisions for himself (Fox-Decent and Criddle 2016). The point is that the decisions and the use of coercion to enforce them must be consistent with the best interests of the subject. Those who are in a position of robust authority have good reason to use force to make their decisions stick, but those reasons only go as far as the best interests of the party in whose name they are being made.

3. Rights, Wrongdoing, and the Criminal Trial

So far, we have been focused on the justification of the state's right to use coercion to ensure that its laws – and not the norms set by any private party – govern the interaction of its subjects. It will require some more work (which I pursue in Section 4 below) to connect this more directly to the state's right to punish. Before we continue to punishment, however, it is important first to pause and appreciate the centrality of the state's right to rule in the function and structure of the criminal trial. Those of a moralist disposition often take the criminal trial to be an opportunity for the state to prove that the accused engaged in conduct that is morally wrongful and without moral justification or excuse and thus, to show that moral condemnation (and perhaps retributive punishment) are appropriate. This way of thinking is deeply problematic for many reasons: we are brought to trial for a breach of the positive law, not for moral wrongdoing as such; the structure of justification and excuse defences have deep and well-theorised differences from their moral counterparts (Thorburn 2008; Thorburn 2011a); what is more, the move from proof of moral wrongdoing to coercive punishment (Moore 1997: 88) seems to be a spectacular *non sequitur* (von Hirsch and Ashworth 2005: 22).

Those with a more instrumentalist outlook often take the trial to be a testing ground for the preconditions of punishment. If the accused did, in fact, engage in conduct that we have reason to deter, then the state has good reason to carry out a deterrent sanction. But here, too, it is not obvious how the fact that the state has reasons of its own to want to deter the offender should generate relational reasons that the offender should accept for his punishment.

We can make better sense of the criminal trial if we think of it, like a civil action, as concerned with the adjudication of a rights dispute between two parties. In a civil action, the plaintiff might want the court to grant her a remedy such as a damage award or an injunction. But a remedy is not all we might want from a court, nor all that we get. Sometimes, we go to court simply to obtain declaratory relief: an authoritative statement of the nature of our legal relationship to the other party. What is more, even when the court grants a further remedy of damages or injunction, the order is always set out as a consequence of the rightful relations between them. Plaintiffs are awarded damages *because* they had certain rights that the defendant wrongfully interfered with. A civil judgment, then, sometimes includes a command of what *will* happen (the damage award, the injunction); but it is always an authoritative statement about how plaintiff and defendant relate to one another, *as a matter of legal rights*.

The same is true when state prosecutors bring a criminal case against an accused person. Of course, prosecutors are often motivated to go to court because they want the court to bring about a certain result: to authorise the punishment of the accused, which they hope will have a salutary effect. But states often have more efficient ways to deter conduct they don't like than criminal punishment. As with civil courts, criminal courts are only sometimes in the business of issuing orders, but they are always in the business of making authoritative statements of legal rights. Whether or not a criminal court issues a sentence, they always render an *authoritative verdict concerning criminal wrongdoing*. A criminal conviction, then, is not just a precondition to the application of punishment, it is a fundamental change in the accused's legal status: his presumption of innocence is officially dislodged, and he is publicly branded a criminal, bearing a criminal record that can last a lifetime. The criminal conviction establishes that the accused did, in fact, wrong the state in the relevant way.

The criminal trial, like the civil action, is not just a diagnostic tribunal seeking to determine whether the preconditions of a remedy have been met. It is, at its core, the adjudication of a claim about rights and alleged wrongdoing. It is important to notice, however, just what sort of relationship between the accused and the prosecution is presumed in a criminal trial. Although the state alleges that the accused has wronged it in its right to rule in some way, that wrong is of a kind that can only be committed *by one of its subjects*. Of course, states can also be wronged in their right to rule by parties who are outside their legal system altogether. This is the case, most obviously, in the case of war-making. When one country invades the territory of another and imposes its laws in the invaded country's territory, it has deeply wronged the invaded state in its right to rule.

But a foreign invasion is no ordinary crime, and the appropriate response is no ordinary criminal conviction and punishment (Thorburn 2019: 395). A wrong by one of the state's own subjects is a wrong that only a subject can commit because it is a wrong *against the relationship of legitimate sovereign and subject* that exists between them. A wrong by a foreign country is still a wrong – it still usurps the invaded state's exclusive right to rule over its territory – but it does so from the position of stranger to the relationship of sovereign and subject. As such, the invaded country's appropriate response is simply one of self-defence, maintaining is authority over its jurisdiction in the face of an attempted usurpation by the invader. Since it is not in any position of authority with respect to the foreign invader, however, the invaded country is in no position to assert its authority over the aggressor through criminal trial or punishment (Liss 2019: 727).

At this point, we are left with more questions than answers about the practical implications of this view of criminal law. What considerations should guide legislators as they draft a list of crimes and defences for the jurisdiction? When should prosecutors pursue a case against a particular accused? What factors should judges consider when deciding on the appropriate sentence for a particular offender? And how should sentencing levels generally be affected (if at all) by broader considerations such as crime rates and other mechanisms for addressing criminal conduct? These and other questions will require a good deal of fine-grained jurisdiction – and context-specific policy analysis, but they can and should be guided by certain principles that arise from the foregoing analysis of the nature of criminal wrongdoing and its place within a larger account of the state's exclusive right to rule.

4. Many Ways to Make Law Bind

In order for the state to solve the moral problem of unilateralism, it must not only make laws in the name of all, but it must also see to it that those laws actually govern our relations with one another – it will require resort to coercive enforcement where necessary. In earlier times, the state had precious few tools to eliminate the private projection of unilateral power and to ensure that its laws were supreme. There were local officials, most notably the county sheriff, the village constable, and justices of the peace, whose job it was to keep the King's peace, to enforce various regulations and to bring some criminal suspects before the courts (Braddick 2000: 27 et seq.).[5] But the modern regulatory state as we know it did not exist. As John Gardner chillingly reminds us, the state's usual way of asserting its dominance over rivals was, first, through violent

[5] Similar developments were taking place in France and elsewhere at the same time (Collins 1997: 603). It was also in the late sixteenth century that Jean Bodin wrote the most important early modern treatment of the sovereign state, his *Les Six Livres de la République* (1576).

displays of punishment and then through solemn rituals of state grandeur in the trial:

> At one time it was the ritual of the punishment itself which made the greatest contribution. The pillory, the stocks, the carting, the public execution and various other modes of punishment involving public display allowed the State to … exhibit … the offender in all his shame humiliation, in all his remorse and regret, while the proceedings remained under some measure of official control … But of course a new penal age dawned in the nineteenth century which put the offender out of reach and out of sight in the prison, where measured punishment and control of retaliation could be more successfully combined … From then on, the burden of providing ritual and majesty … was to a large extent shifted off the shoulders of the punishment system … and onto the shoulders of the trial system instead. The courts themselves now had to offer … the kind of public vindication which would once have been provided by the act of punishment, and the ritual and majesty of the courtroom had to substitute for the ritual and the recantation at the gallows (Gardner 2007c: 235–6.)

We now live in yet another, different, era. Not only do we have very few public trials[6] (Department of Justice 2021) and even fewer public punishments, but the state now has innumerable other tools at its disposal to educate, to discipline, to deter, to incentivise, and otherwise to lead its subjects to comply with its demands. In a modern regulatory state, we might try to reduce the incidence of murder through more surveillance and policing (Stuntz 2011; Lewis and Usmani 2022), with better street lighting (Shearing and Stenning 1984), with regulations on the manufacture and sale of handguns or other tools of killing (Moyer 2017). As David Garland has shown in great depth, the welfare state is a powerful tool for inducing compliance with the law's demands – and when we pare back the judicious use of welfare programs, these problems of compliance quickly become problems of criminal justice to be dealt with through prosecution and punishment (Garland 1985; Garland 2001).

The powers of the regulatory state go beyond just those measures that might target criminal wrongdoing directly. The regulatory state has the ability to address criminogenic factors in society at several steps of remove, as well. Public education, public health, job training, welfare support for families, and much more can all have important effects on crime levels (Needelman 2022). This is important to keep in mind for two different reasons. First, many of these measures not only reduce crime levels, but they also promote socially valuable ends in themselves, such as child development, economic development, public health, the proper functioning of the public sphere, and so on. That means that these measures can

[6] The rise of plea bargaining has meant that the vast majority of criminal convictions in the United States, Canada and an increasingly large number of other countries, come about without a contested trial. Department of Justice Canada (2021), 'Victim Participation in the Plea Negotiation process in Canada', 13 December. Available online: www.justice.gc.ca/eng/rp-pr/cj-jp/victim/rr02_5/p0.html: 'In Canada, it appears that about 90% of criminal cases are resolved through the acceptance of guilty pleas. […] At least 90% of criminal cases in the United States are decided on the basis of guilty pleas, most of which are the outcome of a plea bargain.'

usually be justified even without reference to their effects on crime levels – they are just good policy more broadly. Second, though, these measures can be justified much more easily than criminal punishment because they apply broadly to all those who will benefit from them. Whereas criminal punishment is the intentional infliction of undesirable consequences on individuals in virtue of their criminal conduct, these programs are of general application, targeting individuals only insofar as this is part of the program's general scheme.

It is hard to overstate the importance of the many non-criminal, non-punitive alternatives the modern regulatory state has at its disposal to guide its subjects to comply with the law's demands. It often seems, though, that it is only those who are highly critical of the regulatory state who recognise just how powerful it can be. There is a long tradition of writers who have described the essence of this regulatory relationship in quite overwrought, hyperbolical terms. Michel Foucault, citing the work of Guillaume de la Perrière, writes that regulation involves treating subjects like mere things (Foucault 2007: 96); Lord Hewart shook the British legal system by describing the then-new regulatory state there as a 'new despotism' (Hewart 1929); Alexis de Tocqueville warned of 'an immense and tutelary power, which takes upon itself alone to secure [the] gratifications [of the people's wishes], and to watch over their fate …' (de Tocqueville 1981: 385); and Markus Dubber, in his extensive work on the police power, argues that regulation (which he calls 'police'), 'doesn't deal with persons, but with resources and threats. An object of police governance is either a resource for the welfare of the community or a threat to that welfare. … Threats aren't at fault, nor are they guilty, properly speaking. That's also why they are eliminated, or abated, rather than punished' (Dubber 2005b: 180, 188).

Notwithstanding all this quite hyperbolical criticism of the regulatory state, however, it remains an essential state tool of social discipline. And this is a crucial fact that we will need to keep in mind when we consider the appropriateness of various punitive responses. For although the state must ensure that its laws actually govern relations among its subjects rather than allowing one party to impose terms unilaterally on another, it is now clear that there are many ways in which the state can pursue that end.

States can do many things that might incline their subjects to adhere to the law's demands but so far, we have only considered regulatory tools that have clear, forward-looking public purposes. There are good reasons to structure markets and public spaces in ways that reduce the likelihood of violence, to provide education and job training to subjects in ways that reduce the incentive to engage in crime, to empower police officers to engage in public order maintenance, and so on. But in all these cases, the use of coercion is justified in a wholly forward-looking way. When we require bar owners to abide by liquor licensing regulations, or when we impose a quarantine in times of pandemic, the use of coercion is justified insofar as it is directly necessary as a means to achieving an important public purpose. We quarantine people only insofar as this actually helps to promote public health. We impose liquor licensing requirements only on bar owners. After a person is no longer sick, there is no good reason to continue to use coercion to impose a quarantine on her, and after someone no longer runs a bar there is no good reason to continue to use coercion to impose liquor licensing regulations on her. If the coercion is not going to promote the policy end, then it loses all justification.

Criminal punishment is quite another matter. We most certainly cannot be sure that every act of criminal punishment will promote some important public purpose. Indeed, there is good reason to believe that a good deal of the criminal punishment we impose nowadays has a criminogenic effect on many criminal offenders (Damm and Gorinas 2020: 149). What is more, it is also clear that this is not just a failure in the pursuit of policy. Although enlightened jurisdictions usually try to do what they can to help offenders to avoid criminal wrongdoing in the future, this is not the point of criminal punishment. Although we might not be sent to prison *for* punishment, we are sent to prison *as* punishment. That is, the justifying point of criminal punishment vis-à-vis the individual offender just is the fact that it is coercive and undesirable. Its educative or other beneficial effects are desirable but not conceptually necessary. Seen up close, it might seem that punishment really is the imposition of harsh treatment for no public purpose at all.

We can begin to see a basis of justifying the state's punishment of criminal offenders, however, when we see the crucial role that the *threat* of sanction plays in the state's ability to solve the moral problem of unilateralism. The point here is that, in order to solve this moral problem, the state must actually impose shared terms of interaction on everyone in the jurisdiction and displace the unilateral terms each of us might like to impose instead. The state's ex ante coercive powers go some way to accomplishing this: I might want to go to enclosed spaces carrying a deadly disease, but state officials are entitled to use coercion to confine me in quarantine. But without the threat of punishment for criminal wrongdoing, the state would be without any coercive mechanism for addressing those who were able to avoid ex ante state coercion and imposed their unilateral terms on others. The crucial moment to pay attention to here is the moment of prohibition: if the state only says 'do not do X' but fails to prescribe any possible punishment for disobedience, it has not even tried to solve the problem of unilateralism in any real way. It has explicitly signalled that those who are clever enough to avoid the state's ex ante coercive powers are entitled to do so. For a law genuinely to do its work of controlling the terms of our interaction and displacing unilateralism everywhere and at all times in the jurisdiction, the law's commands must be accompanied with the threat of sanction for their violation. As Immanuel Kant puts the point, 'All lawgiving can therefore be distinguished with respect to the incentive … That lawgiving which … is juridical … has an incentive … which must be drawn from pathological determining grounds of choice, inclinations, and aversions, and among these, from aversions; for it is a lawgiving, which constrains, not an allurement, which invites' (Kant [1797] 1996: 20)

We can see, now, how different the justification of criminal punishment is from the justification of other forms of state coercion. In cases of forward-looking coercion, the justification is ready to hand: is it a legitimate, effective, and proportionate means in pursuit of a legitimate public purpose? If it is, then that is the end of the matter. Individuals will need to accept this sort of coercion as members of a well-governed polity. In cases of backward-looking punishment, however, that form of justification is not available to us. It is rare that the imposition of criminal punishment, in itself, will pursue a public purpose. When we impose a fine, a prison sentence, or other punitive measures, it is more likely than not that more harm than good will come of it. The central justifying reason for the imposition of criminal punishment is to make good on the state's promise to solve the problem of unilateralism by making genuinely binding laws for the whole jurisdiction. But that form of justification requires an additional stage of reasoning that is not present elsewhere. Before there is any justification for the imposition of punishment, we need to be certain that the person we are about to punish actually is someone who undermined the state's rule of law project by imposing his terms unilaterally on his fellow subjects. It requires proof of criminal wrongdoing.

It is at this point that we move from a discussion of the state's right to rule as an organising idea for making sense of state legitimacy and the structure of public law, to the state's right to rule as a justiciable right the violation of which leads to a judicial remedy. The justifying ground for the use of coercion as punishment (rather than in the promotion of a regulatory scheme of some kind) turns crucially on proof that the subject actually disobeyed the state's law and imposed his own unilateral terms of his fellows. This is because the use of coercion as punishment, as opposed to the use of coercion in the direct pursuit of some public purpose, calls for punishment only as a remedy for a failure to do as the law requires. The very point of punishment is not the furtherance of any specific public purpose; its very point – the reason why punishment is threatened as part of the law giving itself – *just is* to make law bind. The crucial justifying condition of imposing punishment, then, must be proof that the accused did, in fact, violate the law's demands and thereby wrong the state in its right to rule.

Because criminal punishment follows from a finding of wrongdoing of the most serious sort – a wrong against the rule of law itself, as manifest in the state's exclusive right to rule – it might seem that criminal punishments should reflect the gravity of this wrong in their severity. There is certainly a long line of scholarship and practice that reflects that way of thinking. The ritual of criminal trial and punishment described above by John Gardner, the horrific torture and execution of the regicide Damiens recounted by Michel Foucault (1975), and what seem like blood-thirsty demands for draconian punishments from Enlightenment thinkers such as Jean-Jacques Rousseau[7]

[7] 'when the guilty man is put to death, it is less as a Citizen than as an enemy' (Rousseau 2019: 66–67).

and Immanuel Kant[8] all seem to suggest that the seriousness of criminal wrongdoing must be marked by wildly severe criminal punishments in every case.

But we must not be misled by these horrific descriptions of, and demands for, punishment from centuries past. The point here is not that the serious threat to the rule of law posed by criminal wrongdoing must always be marked by draconian punishments. The deeper truth behind these calls for extreme punishments is that, one way or another, *criminal wrongdoing must not become banal*. If the rule of law is to survive, then the state must retain its exclusive right to rule. If criminal wrongdoing becomes widespread – if it becomes a banal fact of life that the law that governs our lives is made at the whim of private individuals rather by the state in the name of all – then the rule of law is no more. The stakes in criminal law are, indeed, high. But it is an enormous leap from the recognition of the incompatibility of criminal wrongdoing with the rule of law to the need for draconian punishment of each criminal wrongdoer.

The point of criminal punishment, fundamentally, is a regulatory one. At the end of the day, criminal punishment is indeed just one state tool among many to secure the state's stable authority to make the law around here. So, we must reflect on what measures a state should take if it is genuinely concerned with preserving its exclusive right to rule. As it turns out, the arguments in favour of prevention rather than punishment championed by Cesare Beccaria (1995: 29),[9] David Garland (1985), and Vincent Chiao (2019) and many other promoters of the regulatory approach are not at odds with the right-to-rule account of criminal law I set out here. Indeed, the right-to-rule account provides the strongest arguments in favour of prevention over punishment. For the fundamental concern of the right-to-rule account of criminal wrongdoing is the preservation of the state's exclusive right to make the law in the jurisdiction. With each incidence of criminal wrongdoing, the state's right to rule is weakened. Even if every criminal wrongdoer were found out and punished, the injury done to the rule of law – the way in which each crime undermines the people's claim to be their own rulers – would remain. Punishment, on the right-to-rule account, is a very poor second-best to prevention.

The only way properly to ensure the state's right to rule is for the state to rule effectively. The more often that the state's right to rule itself is a question that must be litigated and vindicated, the weaker the state's claim becomes. The seriousness of criminal wrongdoing and the deep threat it poses to the rule of law itself is the strongest argument in favour of preventative measures. It is not just that preventative measures are often cheaper, more effective, and more humane; the crucial

[8] 'if a civil society were to be dissolved by consent of all … the last murderer remaining in prison would first have to be executed' (Kant [1797] 1996: 106).

[9] 'Among the measures effective in forestalling the dangerous amassing of popular emotions are street-lighting at public expense, the posting of guard in various districts of the city, sober and moral sermons delivered in the silence and sacred peace of churches protected by public authorities …' (Beccaria 1995: 29).

point is that they actually accomplish the end that is of concern to the right-to-rule account: rather than trying to react in some way to a wrong against the state's right to rule, prevention ensures the reality of that right itself. It is for this reason that the same Jean-Jacques Rousseau who called for draconian punishment was also well aware of what a reliance of punishment really means: 'frequent resort to corporal punishment is always a sign of weakness and laziness on the part of the Government' (Rousseau 2019: 67).

5. Conclusion

In America today – and, to a lesser extent in Canada, England and many other twenty-first century developed countries – the criminal law has taken a shape that is almost unrecognisable as the successor to the paradigm that has been our focus so far. The number of offences on the books has ballooned; the structure of offences has changed dramatically, often doing without any subjective fault element (or, in some cases, any fault element at all); the traditional procedural protections associated with the criminal process have fallen away in many instances; and the number of people convicted of criminal offences (and, in America, incarcerated) has skyrocketed (Ashworth 2013: 30). What can a theoretical account of the point of criminal trials based on the idea of legal wrongdoing against the state's exclusive right to rule possibly have to say about all this?

There are two important points on which this account speaks loudly and clearly. First, criminal trials and punishments of individual wrongdoers only make sense in a context of isolated incidents of criminality. In such a context, an isolated individual is singled out as having violated the people's laws and undermined the people's right to rule. A public and authoritative declaration of wrongdoing followed by a deterrent sanction, in such a context, is a plausible response because it is a way of singling out the weakness and the isolation of the offender, and the futility of his efforts to rival the state in making and enforcing laws. But in the context of mass criminality – where a substantial portion of the community has a criminal record, often for quite serious violent crime – the special meaning of a criminal conviction and punishment is almost entirely lost. In that context, criminal punishment is reduced to just another (especially cruel and ineffective) tool of the administrative state.

Second, the right-to-rule account is focused squarely on the vindication of the people's right to rule themselves, rather than being subject to the private wills of criminal wrongdoers. And that means that the concern at the heart of the criminal trial – recognising the serious wrongdoing against the state's right to rule – calls out for government not simply to impose penalties on those who undermine the rule of law in this way but to do more to prevent wrongdoing in the first place. Criminal wrongdoing is not just a matter of individual moral wrongdoing and individual victims. As Tommie Shelby and others have documented (Shelby 2016), widespread criminality (particularly when it involves violent crime, as it so often does) (Pfaff 2017) creates whole areas where the rule of law promise that we shall all live under the same shared laws rings entirely hollow. The tendency of many governments today to rely on criminal punishment rather than policing (Lewis and Usmani 2022) (not to mention job training, income support, health care, etc.) shows not only a lack of concern for the welfare of those caught up in the criminal justice dragnet; it shows a lack of concern for the rule of law itself.

PART V

Individual Rights in Criminal Procedure

15

The Procedural Rights (and Responsibilities) of the Guilty

ANTONY DUFF*

1. Introduction

Article 6 of the European Convention on Human Rights declares the 'Right to a fair trial', and defines various specific rights that give more determinate content to the idea of a fair trial; Article 6(3) specifies the 'minimum rights' that accused persons must enjoy:

(a) to be informed promptly, in a language which he understands and in detail, of the nature and cause of the accusation against him;
(b) to have adequate time and facilities for the preparation of his defence;
(c) to defend himself in person or through legal assistance of his own choosing or, if he has not sufficient means to pay for legal assistance, to be given it free when the interests of justice so require;
(d) to examine or have examined witnesses against him and to obtain the attendance and examination of witnesses on his behalf under the same conditions as witnesses against him; and
(e) to have the free assistance of an interpreter if he cannot understand or speak the language used in court.[1]

These rights are to be enjoyed by all defendants, whether innocent or guilty, but my concern here is with the grounds on which the guilty should enjoy them, and with the kind of wrong suffered by a guilty person who is denied these rights.

I begin (Section 2) by criticising a familiar instrumental view of criminal trials, as a process that aims simply to establish the truth about whether this person committed this offence. On this view, the denial of these rights wrongs innocent

* Thanks for helpful comments and suggestions are due to the editors of this volume; to Anne Ruth Mackor, Ferry de Jong, and Merle Kooijman; and to participants in seminars of the Scottish Criminal Law Discussion Group and at Utrecht University.

[1] We could equally begin with the 'due process' rights derived from the Fourteenth Amendment to the US Constitution.

defendants regardless of whether they are convicted, but does not wrong guilty defendants. If we abandon a purely instrumentalist account, in favour of one that either sets non-instrumental side-constraints on the trial, or adds an independent aim to do with, for instance, the respect that is due to all defendants, we can see how any defendant, innocent or guilty, is wronged if denied these procedural rights. But a guilty defendant who is denied such rights is still not wronged by being convicted: the court still reaches a just, correct verdict, even if it does so by improper means, or by means that frustrate another of the trial's aims. I then (Section 3) offer an alternative conception of criminal trials, as a process that calls an accused person to answer a charge of wrongdoing. On this view, a guilty person who is convicted by a trial that denies his procedural rights is wronged by the conviction itself; we cannot now say that the court reached a just verdict. On this account, procedural rights such as those enumerated in the ECHR enable defendants to play the active role in their trial that they are called on to play. They thus also, I will argue (Section 4), enable defendants to discharge their civic responsibilities: for in a just system of law in a decent society, those accused of crimes not only have a right to take part in their trial. They have a civic responsibility to do so – to answer to their fellows for their alleged wrongdoing. Fair trial rights thus belong to all defendants, innocent or guilty, on just the same basis; if they are denied, both the trial and its verdict are unjust.

Before proceeding, I should note three caveats. First, though my account of criminal trials is set in 'adversarial' terms, I hope that it can also apply, with minor modifications, to 'inquisitorial' systems (and the ECHR 'minimum rights' apply to both adversarial and inquisitorial systems).

Second, this is a normative account of what criminal trials ought to be – not a description of trials as they operate in our existing systems. If it is not to be a philosopher's mere fantasy, it must be related to existing practices: it must be a persuasive 'rational reconstruction' of those practices, in terms of values that can be discerned in them (see MacCormick 1990). But the fact that it is not accurate as a description of those practices as they now operate does not undermine it. It rather shows how defective our existing practices are in the light of the values they should serve.

Third, it is an account of what criminal trials ought to be in a reasonably just system of law in a reasonably just society; a different account is needed of the rights and responsibilities of defendants in unjust societies with unjust laws. This might seem to make the account even less relevant to our present practices. But it is important to develop such idealising accounts of what criminal law and trials should be in the kind of society that we should aspire to build – both as a distant goal towards which we can aspire, and as a model against which we can criticise our current institutions and practices.[2]

[2] The account is idealising, but not wholly idealised. It envisages a society much better than our own, but not a utopia of perfect beings who would have no need of criminal law.

2. Instrumentalism and the Procedural Rights of the Guilty

Some of those who appear in criminal courts as defendants are factually innocent: they did not commit the crime(s) with which they are charged. In a decently efficient system there will be relatively few such defendants because only those against whom there is strong evidence will be prosecuted; but there will be some. Some of these innocent defendants will be convicted: there will be few in a system that recognises the importance of avoiding the unjust conviction of innocent persons; but in any human, therefore fallible, system there will be some. Innocents who are convicted are wronged, even if the trial was impeccably fair and respected all their procedural rights, and no one is to blame for their conviction: the court, and the polity in whose name it acts, wrongs them, albeit unintentionally and non-culpably. If their conviction was due to violations of their procedural rights, for instance if they were not given adequate time to prepare a defence, they are doubly wronged, by their conviction and by this denial of rights. They are also wronged if they are denied their procedural rights, even if they are acquitted: they do not suffer the injustice of being convicted, but they still suffer that procedural injustice.

What precisely is that injustice, if it is inflicted despite their acquittal? A tempting answer is that they are wronged because the procedural violations exposed them to an unjustified risk of being mistakenly convicted: I wrong you if I expose you to an unjustified risk of harm, even if that harm does not ensue (Oberdiek 2017). A viable criminal process cannot be guaranteed *never* to convict an innocent person: the only way to ensure that would be to convict no one. But if we take seriously the right not to be convicted if innocent, and recognise that it is much more important to avoid convicting the innocent than it is to convict the guilty, we can so design our criminal process that we minimise, as far as is reasonably possible, the risk that an innocent will be convicted. The presumption of innocence, which places the burden of proof on the prosecution, and the weight of that burden (to prove guilt 'beyond reasonable doubt'), serve that aim; so do the rights specified in Article 6(3), which enhance an innocent accused's ability to rebut the charges that she faces.[3]

This account of the wrong reflects an instrumental view of the criminal trial. Its function is to identify those who are eligible for punishment because they have committed a crime; it must, accordingly, aim to establish as far as is practicable whether this person committed this crime, although its procedures should weight the scales in favour of the accused. Or, we can say, given the importance of protecting the innocent against conviction, it should aim to establish whether it can be *known* ('beyond reasonable doubt'), that this person committed this crime.

[3] For different versions of this kind of view, see Dworkin 1985: ch 3; Alexander 1998; Wellman 2017: ch 5.

This implies that a trial that acquits a guilty person has not failed to achieve its aim, if the acquittal results from the lack of proof of guilt: it is regrettable that a guilty person escapes justice, but the trial succeeds in its aim of convicting those, and only those, whose guilt is proved and thus known. A 'Not guilty' verdict does not declare the defendant innocent: it declares that she has not been proved guilty, and that the presumption of innocence has therefore not been defeated.

So we have an explanation of why the innocent should enjoy the 'fair trial' rights, and why they are wronged if they are denied those rights even if they are ultimately acquitted. But what of defendants who are in fact guilty? They are not wronged if they are convicted after a fair trial: for being guilty, they have no right not to be convicted. Suppose, however, that one is convicted after a trial at which he was denied his fair trial rights: perhaps he was denied the assistance of counsel or was not given time to prepare a defence. Is he wronged? It seems not. For on the instrumentalist view, the wrong consists in exposing the accused to an unjustified risk of being mistakenly convicted: but if the accused is guilty, his conviction cannot be mistaken. No matter what procedures are or are not followed at his trial, he can face no risk of being mistakenly convicted and the denial of his procedural rights does not expose him to such a risk. Those who deny him his procedural rights, or the court that allows such a denial, do wrong, because they fail to follow procedural rules that are designed to protect the innocent and thus, *for all they know*, expose an innocent to an unjustified risk of conviction.[4] His conviction should also be overturned on appeal as 'unsafe' (unless perhaps the appeal court can be sure that he would have been convicted even had all his procedural rights been respected), because the court should uphold the system of rules that protect the innocent against mistaken conviction. But *he* is not wronged. Rather, if his conviction is overturned on appeal, he is the lucky beneficiary of a process that is designed to protect not him, but the innocent; his legal right to have his conviction overturned does not reflect a genuine moral or political right – it is parasitic on the genuine rights of the innocent.[5]

Some are undisturbed by this implication of an instrumentalist account (e.g. Wellman 2017: 96–98): the guilty have no right not to be convicted, since conviction would be an accurate verdict; so they have no right to procedures that protect them against conviction or help them to avoid it.[6] Others, however, are disturbed by this, and think that even the guilty are wronged if denied their legal procedural rights (e.g. Dworkin 1985: 103): but wherein lies the wrong? One suggestion is that fairness is not simply a matter of taking adequate steps

[4] More precisely, for all they are formally allowed to know they are exposing an innocent to this risk: they must formally presume the accused to be innocent until his guilt is proved in court, whatever they might informally believe or even know about his guilt.

[5] Compare Amar 1996: 1133: 'The Constitution seeks to protect the innocent. The guilty … receive procedural protection only as an incidental and unavoidable by-product of protecting the innocent.'

[6] See Nozick 1974: 107: 'An unreliable punisher violates no right of the guilty person; but still he may not punish him.'

to guard against inaccurate verdicts – that we owe more than this to defendants, whether innocent or guilty. To say, for instance, that the trial 'seeks to determine whether or not a person has committed a particular criminal offence and to do so fairly' (Campbell, Ashworth and Redmayne 2019: 24) implies that there is more to fairness than attempts to ensure accuracy. That 'more' might then be expressed in terms of dignity: we owe it to defendants to treat them with the respect, the dignity, that we owe to all human beings. One implication of this is that a court should not determine the defendant's fate without giving her the chance to be heard ('*audi alteram partem*'); the Article 6(3) rights serve to enable defendants to exercise that right to be heard (see e.g. Tribe 2000: 666; Allan 2001: 77–87; Crummey 2020). We need not engage with the details of this kind of view, or with the precise meanings of such notions as 'dignity' and 'respect', here; we need only notice two ways in which such a conception of fairness could be incorporated into a primarily instrumental conception of the criminal trial as aimed at determining truth, and their implications for the rights of the guilty.

We could say, first, that although the justifying aim of the trial is to reach an accurate verdict (an aim that is achieved by convicting the guilty, even if their procedural rights are violated), our pursuit of that aim is subject to non-instrumental side-constraints, which rule out certain means even if they are effective in achieving the aim.[7] A plausible side-constraint is that the trial procedures must not violate the defendant's dignity, or deny her a fair chance to be heard in a process which can have such drastic effects on her life; but procedures that violate the rights enumerated in ECHR Article 6(3) do precisely that, and are therefore ruled out whether or not they contribute to the aim of accurate fact-finding.[8] Or we could instead argue that such respect for defendants' rights is 'not merely a side-constraint on the pursuit of accuracy', but 'a concomitant aim of criminal process' alongside the goal of accuracy (Campbell, Ashworth and Redmayne 2019: 46). One reason for making this a 'concomitant aim' rather than a side-constraint might be that this will give it more obvious importance ('not *merely* a side-constraint'). It is not clear that this is necessary, since side-constraints can be important; indeed, they can set strict constraints on our pursuit of our consequential ends. Another, better reason might be that this makes clear that the law and the court must not just allow, but enable and assist, defendants to be heard. Side-constraints, as their name suggests, are typically negative in content: they preclude certain kinds of means, such as measures that positively silence the accused; but it is not clear that they would require more active measures to assist

[7] Compare a familiar account of punishment (Hart 1968: ch 1): its justifying aim is the effective prevention or deterrence of crime; but a non-instrumental side-constraint of justice is that we must not pursue that aim by punishing known innocents, even if their punishment would enhance the law's deterrent or preventive efficacy.

[8] It is worth noting that this kind of account of the right to be heard applies to a wide range of procedures that have significant impacts on people's lives – the right is not peculiar to, it has no particular significance in, the criminal trial. I'll argue in what follows that the right to be heard in one's criminal trial does have a special significance, connected to the aim of a criminal trial.

her. By contrast, if we make such respect for the right to be heard a positive aim, it will be more obvious that it should not merely forbid interference with, or the placing of barriers in the way of, being heard, but also require the kinds of positive assistance that Art. 6(3) specifies.

However, whether the right to be heard generates ('merely') a side-constraint on the trial, or a positive 'concomitant aim', this kind of account still separates the aim of determining whether the defendant committed the crime charged (accuracy) from the demand that his right to be heard be respected: a trial that denies a defendant his Article 6 rights might still (perhaps by luck) reach an accurate verdict, and thus successfully achieve, even if not *the* aim of the trial, at least one of its essential aims; which implies that whilst the defendant can properly complain of procedural injustice, and say that he has been wronged by that injustice, he cannot complain that the verdict is unjust, or that it wrongs him. For the verdict still expresses an accurate judgment on his guilt, which is at least a crucial part of what it is meant to do: he *is* guilty and cannot be wronged by an accurate judgment that he is – even if he is wronged by the procedure that led to that judgment.

I have no knock-down argument against this kind of view, which has obvious attractions. It recognises, unlike a purely instrumentalist account, that both innocent and guilty defendants are wronged if they are denied their fair trial rights: but it also insists, as does an instrumentalist, that a trial that convicts an actually guilty person gets *something* right, even if its procedures are badly flawed. Surely we can say, if the defendant's guilt is later independently established, 'But at least he was guilty, so the right verdict was reached'; surely we can recognise that, although he suffers an injustice, it is a far less serious injustice than that suffered by an innocent who is convicted at a trial that denies her procedural rights. However, I think that this kind of view still fails to do justice to the defendant's status as a participant in the trial, and to the character of the trial as a process that should seek to engage with, rather than just pass judgment on, the defendant. Were I convicted after a trial at which I was denied a fair hearing, I would still want to protest the verdict even if I knew myself to be guilty: I would still want to deny that the verdict was one that I ought to accept, since – I would claim – it would not have been justified, in particular justified to me, by the process that led to it. The kind of qualified instrumentalist view sketched above still separates the verdict from the trial process that leads to it, as an outcome whose truth and justice can be independently judged; but it is that separation that I would deny.

To explain this objection, I offer a different view of criminal trials that rejects this separation of verdict from procedure: the conviction of a defendant who is denied his procedural rights is intrinsically unwarranted, regardless of whether he is guilty. We cannot, on this view, say that the trial achieved the, or a, right end, albeit by improper means: for the 'means' are not separable from the 'end'. I will develop this account in two stages. First (in Section 3), I will explain why the criminal trial, as a process of determining and ascribing responsibility, must enable the accused to answer the charge that he faces. Second (in Section 4) I will explain why in a decent society, defendants have a civic duty to answer the charges that they face, so that the kinds of right specified in ECHR Article 6(3) are rights that enable defendants to discharge that duty: the right to be heard at one's trial brings with it a correlative duty to speak – to answer for oneself to one's fellow citizens.

3. The Criminal Trial as a Calling to Account[9]

We should see the criminal trial, I suggest, not simply as an inquiry about an accused person that aims to establish whether she committed an offence, but as a process in which she is to be an active participant: a process that calls her to answer to a charge of criminal wrongdoing, and to answer for that wrongdoing if it is proved against her. In an adversarial trial, the accused is first called to make a formal answer to the charge by pleading 'Guilty' or 'Not guilty'; though she is not forced to enter a plea, or punished for refusing to do so, it is expected of her. It is then, of course, for the prosecution to prove that she committed the offence, not for her to prove that she did not – though if the prosecution adduces strong evidence that she committed it, she might have to rebut that evidence if she is to avoid conviction; but if it is proved (or she admits) that she committed the offence, she is called to answer for that offence (she is held responsible for it). She can still avoid conviction, by offering a defence – an answer that exculpates her by showing that her commission of the offence was justified or excusable. But it is now up to her to answer, either by admitting her guilt or by offering a defence; and if she fails to offer an exculpatory answer that suffices at least to create a reasonable doubt about her guilt, she will be convicted – held formally and culpably liable for the offence.

(I do not suggest that this is the only plausible non-instrumentalist conception of the trial, or the only conception that provides a firmer grounding for fair trial rights as rights that belong on the same basis to both innocent and guilty defendants, and that shows the guilty to be wronged by their conviction if they were denied those rights. For one obvious instance, some theorists portray the trial as a process of holding to account, but argue that it is the state, rather than the defendant, that is called to account:[10] on such a view, all defendants have the same claim to fair trial rights, since such rights help them to call the state to account. Now criminal trials should indeed hold the state to account for its attempt to

[9] See Duff et al 2007; Duff 2018a: ch 5. It is important to bear in mind the points noted at the end of Section 1 about the normative, idealising character of this account.

[10] See e.g. Ho 2010, 2016; Owusu-Bempah 2018. Owusu-Bempah argues that defendants should therefore not be obligated to play any active role in the trial process; as will become clear in Section 4, although defendants in a just system of law have, in my view, a civic duty to take part in their trial, this should not be made a legal duty.

secure the conviction and punishment of the defendant – for this use of the coercive power of the criminal law; but this is an implication of, rather than an alternative to, the account I sketch here. That is, the manifest form of the trial is a process in which the defendant is called to account – formally called to answer to the charge. But calling to account, which is a form of holding responsible, must be reciprocal: if we call you to account, to answer, to us, we must be ready to answer to you (Duff 2018b): that is why a trial that calls a defendant to account must be a process in which the state is also held to account.)

This conception of the criminal trial is grounded in a conception of the role of the criminal law in a democratic republic of free and equal citizens. The law of such a polity is a 'common' law: it belongs to the citizens, who make it and subject themselves to it.[11] The substantive criminal law defines a set of 'public' wrongs: these are wrongs that violate the polity's self-defining values; they therefore concern the whole polity and require a formal, public response. The criminal trial, and the punishments to which it leads, constitute that response. That response should take the form of a calling to account (to answer) because citizens must treat each other, and the law must treat them, as responsible agents – members of the polity who can, and should, answer for their own conduct. The response is required, because a polity that takes its self-defining values seriously will take violations of those values seriously: it will care about wrongs that flout those values, as 'public' wrongs, which require a response. The response must do justice to the victims of such wrongs, recognising that they have been not merely harmed, but wronged; it must also do justice to the perpetrators of such wrongs, recognising their status as responsible members of the political community. We do such justice by calling the perpetrators to public account. They must answer for what they did, not just to their victims, but to their fellow citizens collectively, for violating the values that structure their civic life as a political community. If offenders were, or were properly seen as, enemies or outsiders,[12] we would not owe it to them to respond to their wrongdoing by calling them to account: we would need to find ways of dealing with their crimes and preventing their repetition – ways that were not cruel or inhumane; but we would not need to address them as responsible agents. However, on a more inclusively communitarian view of political community, we should recognise and treat them as responsible fellow members of the polity;[13] one implication of this is that we should hold them responsible, call them to answer, for their wrongdoing. The point here is not just that *if* we are to respond to their crimes, or subject them to coercive treatment because of those crimes, we should do so by a process that calls them to answer and gives them a chance to answer. It is the stronger point that we *should* respond to their crimes in

[11] A 'common' law not as distinct from statute law (much of it will be in statutory form), but as opposed to law that is imposed on subjects by a sovereign: see Postema 1986: chs 1–2; Cotterrell 1995: ch 11.

[12] Compare Jakobs' notorious conception of *Feindstrafrecht*, on which see Ohana 2014.

[13] For such a view see Duff 2018a: chs 3, 5 (and ch 3.3 on those who are guests rather than members).

this way: we owe this to them as well as to their victims and to the polity as a whole. In thus calling them to account we treat them not merely as subjects to whom the law is applied, but as agents – agents, indeed, of the law itself.

This is not to assert a 'legality principle' according to which *every* crime *must* be prosecuted if there is evidence sufficient to prove the offender's guilt (see e.g. Perrodet 2002). Just as, whilst there is good reason to criminalise any public wrong, there are also often better reasons to respond in other ways to a public wrong (see Duff 2018a: ch. 7), so there is always good reason to prosecute any provable commission of a public wrong, but there might sometimes be better reasons to deal with the case in a different way: hence the importance of the 'public interest' test by which English prosecutors must decide whether to prosecute.[14]

Two related points should be noted here. One concerns the very idea of responsible agency: to be a responsible agent is to be an agent who can answer for himself and his conduct; to deny me the opportunity to do so is to deny my standing as a responsible agent (Gardner 2007b). A criminal trial seeks to determine the accused's responsibility for an alleged crime: the indictment accuses him of being culpably responsible for the crime; the prosecution offers evidence that he is thus responsible; a conviction holds him culpably responsible. To hold a person responsible is to call him to answer: but if we are to call someone to answer, we must allow and enable him to answer (and be ready to listen to his answer). The other point concerns citizenship in a democratic polity. Democratic citizens will be active members of the polity, agents of its institutions, including the institutions of the criminal law; an important way to exercise that agency is to answer for one's alleged wrongdoing in a criminal court. These two points are connected because if the polity is in some sense a liberal polity, the recognition of, the respect for, and the exercise of, its members' responsible agency will be central to the values by which it defines itself.

In calling an accused person to answer, we assign her a specific role in the enterprise of the criminal law: she is called to contribute to the enterprise of holding wrongdoers to public account, by answering for her own alleged wrongdoing. But we must then enable her to play the role that she is called on to play. We – our officials and courts – must treat her with the respect due to a responsible agent who is to answer for her conduct; and we must give her a fair chance, and the resources, to answer. Hence the importance of the right to 'effective participation', which the European Court of Human Rights (2022) emphasises in applying Article 6.[15] We can distinguish three dimensions to that right (only two of which are dealt with by Article 6(3)).

First, the accused must have the *capacity* to participate in his trial: he must be 'fit to be tried'. If, for instance, he has succumbed since the alleged offence

[14] See Crown Prosecution Service 2018: s 4: even when there is 'sufficient evidence to provide a realistic prospect of conviction', the prosecutor must 'consider whether a prosecution is required in the public interest'.

[15] See European Court of Human Rights 2022: paras 153–8, and the cases cited there.

to a mental disorder so severe that he cannot understand the trial or take part in it, he cannot now be tried – even if he was sane and responsible at the time of the offence, and even if his guilt could be conclusively proved without his participation (see Sprack and Engelhardt-Sprack 2019: para 17.36).[16] For if an accused lacks the capacities required for answering a criminal charge in a criminal court, we cannot properly call him to answer; his trial would be a travesty.[17]

Second, the accused must be given a fair *opportunity* to participate, to answer to the charge: she must be informed of the charge, in a language she can understand,[18] allowed time to prepare a defence, allowed to put her defence to the court and to examine witnesses. For if we are to call a person to answer, we must give her an opportunity to do so: it would be a travesty to call her to answer, but then proceed to judgment without giving her a chance to answer. We must also, of course, be ready to listen to her answer: the court must attend carefully to any defence, or mitigation, that she offers.

Third, the accused must be given the *resources* necessary to make use of that opportunity – to answer to the charge, and to defend himself if that is the form his answer takes. Hence, for instance, the rights to legal assistance, to an interpreter, to detailed information, to time to prepare a defence, to obtain the attendance of witnesses, specified in ECHR Article 6(3): information and time are crucial resources, and the law's assistance may be needed to secure the attendance of witnesses. The ancient joke that both the millionaire and the pauper have the right to stay in an expensive hotel (though only the millionaire has the resources to do so) applies here. If the right to effective participation is to be enjoyed by all citizens as equals under the law, it must be not just a negative right not to be actively hindered from participating, but a positive right to be enabled to participate, which involves providing essential resources for those who might otherwise lack them.

It is important to emphasise that on this account the right to effective participation matters not just because accused persons must have a chance to defend themselves and thus avoid conviction. It matters because they must be enabled to answer the charge as responsible citizens who are called to account by their fellows; and this matters even (perhaps especially) if their answer will be 'Guilty as charged'. For some defendants will want to plead guilty – and not merely as part of a coercive plea bargain that makes their actual guilt or innocence irrelevant; they will want to admit their wrongdoing. But such admissions of guilt, as formal confessions of wrongdoing, can have value only if they are based on an understanding of the charge and its implications.

[16] For a comparative survey, see Mackay and Brookbanks 2018.

[17] Which is not to say that there is nothing we can properly do about or with him in the light of his alleged crime. See, for instance, the provisions in English law for unfit defendants: Criminal Procedure (Insanity) Act 1964 ss 4A–5A.

[18] Which is to say not just that the charge must be put to her in her native language or a language in which she is reasonably fluent, but that it must be expressed through concepts that she can be expected to understand: the law must be normatively accessible to those whom it claims to bind.

If an accused lacks the necessary capacity to answer the charge, or is denied the opportunity or resources to answer, his trial and conviction are unjust – even if he is provably guilty. For to convict him would be to say that he has failed to answer the charge, failed to offer an answer that exculpates him; but if he was denied a fair opportunity to answer or the resources to make use of that opportunity, or he lacks the capacity to do so, he has not *failed* to answer. A polity that calls an accused to answer, through its criminal courts, must allow and enable him to answer; it owes him that as a responsible agent. The denial of fair trial rights therefore delegitimises his conviction, even if a conviction would be 'safe', in the sense of 'empirically reliable', without his participation. We cannot now say, as we could say on the instrumentalist views discussed in Section 2, that at least the court reached 'the right verdict' in convicting an actually guilty defendant through a process flawed by breaches of fair trial rights. For the aim of the trial is not simply to establish the truth about whether the accused committed the offence charged (were that the aim a right, i.e. true, verdict could indeed be reached by a process that denied the accused's fair trial rights). It is to call the accused person to answer the charge, so that what makes a verdict 'right' is that it expresses a justified judgment on whether the accused provided an exculpatory answer to that charge; thus whatever the truth of the charge, a verdict of 'Guilty', which is a judgment that he failed to offer such an answer, is unjustified if he was not allowed and enabled to answer.

A defendant might, of course, refuse to answer: she might refuse to take any part in her trial, perhaps to express her denial of the court's legitimate authority, or to protest against an unjust system of law. That cannot bar her trial or conviction, if the prosecution offers unrebutted evidence that suffices to prove her guilt. For she has been called to answer, has been given the opportunity and offered the resources to answer; she has failed to offer an exculpatory answer, and can be justly held culpably responsible.[19]

4. Duty-Enabling Rights

To talk, as I have talked and as the ECtHR talks, of a right of effective participation in one's trial might suggest that defendants should be able to participate or not, as they choose: if I have a right to Φ, or to be allowed and enabled to Φ, it is usually up to me whether I Φ or not; others may not hinder, and must perhaps assist, my Φ-ing, but should not force me to Φ. This is, in the end, true of defendants' fair trial rights as *legal* rights, but in a decent society with a just criminal law defendants have a *civic* duty to exercise their right of effective participation. The fair trial rights enumerated in Article 6(3) can therefore be seen as 'duty-enabling'

[19] As long as the court has the standing to try her – the right thus to call her to account: see Duff 2019.

rights: they make it possible for the rights-holders to do, and assist them in doing, what they have a duty to do.[20] The denial of those rights, the failure to satisfy them, is then even more troubling: if the polity demands that a defendant answer for his alleged wrongdoing, insisting that he has a duty to do so, but denies him the opportunity or resources to do so, it commits a particularly egregious wrong against him. I must now explain the basis of this duty to participate, and why it should not be a legal duty whose violation would be criminal.

The duty is grounded in the character of criminal law (in a decent democratic republic) as a common law that belongs to the citizens, and as a law in relation to which citizens should be not merely subjects, but agents. I owe it to my fellow citizens to assist in the shared enterprise of the criminal law. Central to that enterprise is the process through which alleged criminal wrongdoers are called to account – called to answer to the charge of wrongdoing, and to answer for the wrongdoing if it is proved or admitted; if I am formally accused of crime, I ought therefore to play my part in the process and appear in court to answer the charge. The accusation mut be justified: it must not be discriminatory or oppressive; it must be backed by evidence that constitutes a 'case to answer' since, given the burdens that a trial imposes on defendants, I should not be expected to answer ill-founded accusations. But if those conditions are satisfied, I have a civic duty – a duty owed to my fellow citizens in virtue of our shared membership of the polity – to participate in my trial.[21]

I have that civic duty even if I know that I am innocent of the charge. For the process of calling alleged wrongdoers to account will inevitably call some who are actually innocent to answer to a criminal charge, and I have a civic duty to assist that process; and I owe it to my fellow citizens to answer well-founded (even if mistaken) accusations of having committed a public wrong. If I know that I am guilty of the crime charged, I have a stronger duty: I ought to answer for my wrongdoing – I owe this to those I wronged, and to fellow members of the community whose values I violated; and the criminal trial is the forum in which I can formally answer for it as a criminal wrong (there are other fora in which I answer for it as a moral wrong). Further, if I know that I am guilty, I ought to plead 'Guilty': not because a plea of 'Not guilty' would necessarily be perjury (I am not on oath when I plead, and a not guilty plea could be read not as a denial of guilt but as a challenge to the prosecution to prove guilt), but because I ought to answer for my wrongdoing honestly, with an apologetic confession of guilt (Duff 2023).

If we have a civic duty to participate in our trial, we have reason to make it a legal duty, and to criminalise refusals to participate: a violation of a civic duty is a public wrong that concerns the whole polity; and we have reason to criminalise any public wrong (Duff 2018a: chs 6–7). However, reasons, even good reasons,

[20] On duty-enabling rights, see Wenar 2013. The right to participate is therefore a 'mandatory' right: Klepper 1996.

[21] I have such a duty only in a decent polity in which I am treated with the respect and concern due to a citizen, within a criminal process that treats me justly.

might not be conclusive; and we have very good reason not to turn this civic duty into a legal duty. More precisely, we might make it a legal requirement that defendants appear for trial, so that the court can challenge them to answer to the charge:[22] but that would not be a legal duty to participate, since presence in the court room does not amount to participation, and the reasons not to make participation a legal duty do not apply to a legal duty to appear. For, first, the law should respect the consciences of those who have principled objections to the trial process to which they have been summoned. Such objections cannot save them from being tried; but they should be allowed to express their objections by refusing to play an active part in the trial, since to play such a part, even to enter a plea, would be to recognise the authority of the court (by contrast, merely appearing in court need not express such a recognition). Second, a legal duty to take part in one's trial would give yet more power to the state's officials, a power that could all too easily be abused. An accused person already faces familiar kinds of pressure and risks of oppressive treatment; to impose a legal duty to participate would add to that pressure and those risks. Any duty to play an active part in one's trial should be a purely civic, rather than a legal, duty – a duty that we owe our fellow citizens, and that we can be criticised for failing to fulfil, but not a duty that should be given the force of law.

The argument that a civic duty to participate in one's trial should not, even in a just society, be made into a legal duty leads to a larger point – that the right to participate must bring with it a correlative right *not* to participate. Some of the procedural rights that ought to be recognised are precisely rights that have to do with non-participation, rather than with enabling and assisting participation.

A preliminary question is this. I have argued that a civic duty to participate in one's trial should not be made into a legal duty. We should at least have a legal right not to participate: we should not be subject to legal coercion to participate,[23] or be liable to adverse legal consequences if we refuse to do so.[24] But should we also recognise a civic right not to participate – a right to do wrong, we might say, by violating this civic duty?[25] That will depend on what kind of right this would be. If it consisted, for instance, in a right not to be subject to coercive social pressure to participate, and depending how we understand 'coercive', it might be plausible to assert such a right; but if it involved or implied a right not to be criticised for refusing to participate, that would be less plausible.

Whatever our answer to the question about a civic right not to participate, we should at least insist on a legal right not to participate, and the right of silence

[22] See e.g. the English Bail Act 1976, s 7, and the German Criminal Procedure Code (*Strafprozeßordnung*) §§ 230–6: defendants are legally required to appear for trial, and only exceptionally may trials proceed in their absence (see e.g. *Jones (Anthony)* [2003] 1 AC 1.

[23] Contrast the '*peine forte et dure*' to which those who refused to enter a plea were once liable to be subjected in England: see Mckenzie 2005.

[24] Consequences that could consist in conviction for an offence of non-participation; or in allowing or requiring courts to draw adverse inferences from a defendant's refusal to participate.

[25] On a right to do wrong, see Herstein 2012.

is an obvious implication of this. That right involves not just the absence of an enforceable legal duty to participate, but also (if it is to have a substantial rather than largely formal significance) a right not to have adverse inferences drawn from one's silence: it is violated, or seriously undermined, if although remaining silent is not subject to formal legal sanction, courts are entitled to treat it as evidence of guilt.[26] Such a right is important, as a defence against the kinds of oppressive pressure that a legal duty to speak would enable officials to exert, and because we should allow principled dissenters to express their dissent by refusing to take part in their trial. It is, we might say, an important part of what makes a trial 'fair', although it does not figure among the rights specified in ECHR Article 6 as integral to a 'fair trial'. We have (in a decently just society) a civic duty to participate, to answer; but the law must also leave us free to refuse to speak. However, the role of this right in a plausible normative theory of the criminal trial is quite different from the role of the rights to 'effective participation' in one's trial on which I have focused in this chapter. Those rights flow, I have argued, from the proper aim of the trial itself, as a process through which a polity calls alleged wrongdoers to answer for their alleged wrongdoing. By contrast, the right of silence is a right that constrains our pursuit of that aim – we can, through the law, call on the defendant to answer, but should not use the law to enforce that call. The right to effective participation, and the specific rights that give that right more determinate content, are central to a proper normative understanding of the criminal trial; but they do not exhaust the idea of a fair trial, or the procedural rights that defendants should enjoy.

5. Conclusion

This completes my sketch of an argument about the grounding of defendants' procedural rights and responsibilities in the criminal process, in particular the right to effective participation, and the more specific rights declared in ECHR Article 6(3) that spell out some of what is necessary for effective participation. An instrumental account of what grounds such rights, that they serve the aim of achieving accurate verdicts, is, I argued inadequate, and is still inadequate even if we add in non-instrumental side-constraints, or further aims, that have to do with defendants' dignity. A better account portrays the trial as a process that calls alleged criminal wrongdoers to formal public account: we can then see such procedural rights as necessary if defendants are to be able to answer the charges that they are called to answer, and so to discharge their civic duty to answer. My focus has been on these rights as rights enjoyed by guilty as well as innocent

[26] This right has in recent years been seriously eroded in English law (Quirk 2019): defendants cannot be legally compelled to give evidence; but courts are increasingly allowed to draw adverse inferences from a defendant's silence.

defendants, by defendants who know that they are guilty as much as by those who do not know this. My argument has been that the rights have the same grounding and significance for *all* defendants – whereas other accounts portray such rights as properly rights of the innocent, so that guilty defendants' enjoyment of them is somehow parasitic on the rights of the innocent. But I am not suggesting that these are peculiarly rights of the guilty:[27] they are rights that properly belong to all defendants, in virtue simply of their role as defendants. Any defendant who is denied those rights is wronged; any defendant, whether innocent or guilty, who is convicted through a trial that denies those rights is wronged by that conviction.

[27] Indeed, a defendant who intends to plead guilty has no need of some of the art 6(3) rights, as Mark Dsouza pointed out to me.

16

Justice Interests: Victims of Crime and Democratic Citizenship

ROBYN L HOLDER

1. Justice Interests: Victims of Crime and Democratic Citizenship

Criminal justice systems form part of the architecture of states. For contemporary constitutional democracies, criminal justice is dominated by the rule of law in which core principles include prior knowledge, predictability, and clarity of laws. The institutions comprising criminal justice – police, prosecutors, courts and judiciary – must be independent, and apply and interpret the law without fear or favour (Bingham 2010b). The criminal laws that the system administers have deep normative roots and are backed by state coercion. All citizens and public officials are deemed to be equal before the law. Yet criminal justice, concerned with allegations of wrongdoing, attracts radically different assessments. It is described both as a 'public good … with a necessary and virtuous role to play' (Loader and Walker 2007: 7) and an 'expanding infrastructure' of control (Garland 2001: 16). Both accounts acknowledge dynamic social, economic and political environments in which criminal justice is embedded, and both acknowledge abiding political and popular debate about the shape, tone and processes of criminal justice and its actors. Centre stage in these debates are persons victimised by violence and other crimes. When involved in criminal justice, the victim is largely subsumed within 'the public interest'.[1] This capacious concept permits maximum room for manoeuvre for criminal justice professionals. Critically, it permits the state to use individual victims as it sees fit.

This largely unfettered monopoly stands in contrast to the usual expectations that citizens might have of public institutions in a constitutional democracy. Expectations, for example, of inclusion in and information about decision-making that affects them, equal treatment by authorities, personal liberty and freedom to

[1] As Göhler (2019) writes, although civil and common law jurisdictions differ in important ways, these mostly share the dominance of the state's version of public interest.

choose, and respect for individual dignity. However, criminal justice institutions are experienced by victims as profoundly non-democratic (for a research overview, see Hoyle and Zedner 2007). Theirs is generally an experience of routine disrespect and discourtesy shown to them by justice professionals – public officials who 'have severe difficulties in coming to terms with victims' (Shklar 1990: 37). Stripped of their dignity by the commission of violence, victims are exhorted to step up and report their victimisation to authorities and, when doing so, to step back and let those authorities deal with it as they will. Victims see themselves rejected or valorised – characterised as vengeful and focused on their own ends, on the one hand, and as traumatised supplicants, on the other. They are said to enter the public space of criminal justice seeking only private goals, without any social and political status as members of the public. As 'victim', they lose their multiple identifications and, instead, become an instrument in the service of other ends, their rights as victim are more rhetorical than real.

In this chapter, I argue that the victim has an identity independent of state agents in criminal justice.[2] They have a direct interest in the processing by authorities of the criminal matter that affects them, and this interest is a democratic one. In developing this argument, I use three concepts that are central to democracy: citizen, citizenship and interests. I emphasise the victim as a 'citizen first' (Holder 2018a; 2023);[3] a term that encompasses legal status, membership of a political community, and a wide variety of social practices. As a citizen, their engagement with criminal justice is a practice of democratic citizenship. My re-focusing on the victim's status as citizen draws attention to two key questions: what victims' political relation to state authority are, and what 'interests' in criminal justice victims have that might be considered *democratic*. It is through this political lens that the chapter explores the 'citizen-victim' as both an anti-democratic and democratic actor.

Of course, criminal justice is generally regarded as outside the realm of 'the political'. The latter is what politicians do within and alongside parliaments. The Judiciary is distinguished from the Executive and Parliamentary branches as per the separation of powers principle (Bingham 2010b: 168). For criminal lawyers, the messiness of democracy is outside the reasoned and rule-bound criminal justice system. Nonetheless, the association of criminal justice with 'the political' has long been explored through the discriminatory effects of criminal justice on offenders.[4] On these accounts, criminal justice is part of the power structure of an oppressive state. Less seen is the oppressive intrusion of the state's criminal justice machinery on victims (Holder 2017a). To address this gap, I use a broad

[2] The alleged offender's distinct and individual interests are likewise independent of the state. These interests are protected by independent legal representation. Mostly, the victim in criminal justice has no such independent representation.

[3] The citizen-first perspective is an argument about the *human* victim. I use the term 'victim' broadly as a self-assessment construed in social interaction.

[4] The literature on discriminatory effects is too vast to offer a single citation. The discriminatory effects are examined from perspectives of race, gender, class, age and type of disability.

approach to 'the political' as reflecting both 'the conflictual dimension in social life' (Mouffe 2005: 4) and its manifestation in the varying engagements and relations between the practices and institutions of authority and ordinary people (Thumim 2006). I build on my earlier work on victims' 'justice interests' (Holder 2018a: 50) to consider the character[5] and tone of these interests and ask what democracy requires of citizen-victims engaged with criminal justice. I come to suggest that both democracy and justice in plural societies require from citizens the contestation and passion usually associated with anti-democratic or populist sentiment *in addition to* tolerance and reasoning. On this basis, citizens do not need to be good or ideal all the time; indeed, they are not. As democracy expects, citizens do not need to speak with the one voice nor agree with each other. But all citizens *do* require a criminal justice system that takes the rights, interests, and views of victim and offender seriously and demonstrably through their inclusion, participation, and representation. Citizen status creates a robust and rigorous platform that gives rise to legitimate expectations and upon which each of these participants may base rights claims (Zivi 2012). Through these concepts, I seek to democratize criminal justice.[6] The chapter concludes with some brief reflections on the implications of my argument. To simplify things, I focus on domestic common law jurisdictions.

To begin, I sketch the argument for seeing the victim as a citizen first and what justice interests look like from this perspective. I discuss how these interests are political in debate about victims and criminal justice as well as in political theory. For the latter, I draw on Judith Shklar's meditation on *The Faces of Injustice* as well as democracy and citizenship theorists Jane Mansbridge (2010; 2019) and Engin Isin (2008; 2009). I then draw from my own and others research to explore the idea that democratic citizenship has anti-democratic as well as democratic characteristics. The idea rests on the agonism of Chantal Mouffe (1992; 2005), a perspective well suited to the contestation of truth and moral disagreement intrinsic to criminal justice in pluralistic societies.

2. Victims as Citizens First

To address some of the problems that victims experience, many countries have implemented support and other initiatives for those with particular attributes such as their age, gender or capacity or in relation to types of victimisations such as sexual assault (for example, Hall 2007). These narrow eligibility to 'vulnerable' victims even though many others would benefit. While the identity and needs

[5] By character, I mean how persons are represented to be in social and political associations and contexts, and not character as personality trait.

[6] Even as I reference 'contemporary constitutional democracy', I am well aware of its faults and fault lines, as I am aware of the same for criminal justice systems. In this chapter, I am less interested in debate about democracy *per se* than I am in what people *do* within the democratic order.

focus has given rise to improved access to, and the experience of, criminal justice for certain victims, well-recognised problems persist (Holder 2023). In particular, the approach segments and fractures a diverse constituency and cements the ideal, good and deserving victim as recipient of governmental favours and institutional recognition. Definitional authority to determine who is 'special' remains with power-holders and respect for the universality of victims' human rights is undermined. Meanwhile, institutional arrangements are preserved and their functions and priorities remain undisturbed. And the ambiguity to the victim role is maintained.

My alternative – recognising people as citizens first before, during and after their experience of victimisation and of justice institutions (police, prosecutors and courts) – is to see them in a different political relationship to the state. The unstable and transitory nature of victimisation can obscure the multiple relations that individuals have with state authorities, whether for good or ill. Principally therefore, citizen status creates a kind of 'constitutional stability' to a relationship that the victim construct disallows (Holder 2018a: 108). The term facilitates a uniform identity in the victim constituency that is marked by multiple differences; along characteristics of sex, race, and age (for example) or type of victimisation – whether individual or mass atrocity or property or personal. A focus on citizen status provides a more emphatic boundary between state institutions and ordinary persons. As an example, accepting the victim as independent citizen frees the public prosecutor (representing the state) to unambiguously prosecute on behalf of the public at large (Bowden, Henning and Plater 2014). While the interests of the citizen-victim and the prosecutor may overlap, they are not the same. At its simplest, respect and recognition are then due not because a person is traumatised or vulnerable nor because they angrily stir media attention; these are due because the citizen is the source of political authority and legitimacy of the state (Beetham 2012). Respect, recognition, and the protection of citizens' rights is a duty of states.[7] Viewed in this way, victim and offender share a kind of constitutional and representational independence from the state.

Claiming citizen status as primary in the victim's relationship with criminal justice asks for more depth on who or what is the *citizen*. Traditionally, the citizen is said to be bounded through membership of a territory (Marshall [1950] 2013).[8] Within that territory, citizens act, in formal and informal ways, to articulate the norms, rules and institutions by which they agree to be bound (Duff 2010a). Citizens, write Philippe Schmitter and Terry Karl, 'are the most distinctive element of democracies' and their rights are 'indispensable to [democracy's] persistence' (1991: 81). Theorists then argue that citizen-status may be oppressive and exclusionary of out-groups, or that it is empowering if

[7] See Moyn 2019. Available at: www.abc.net.au/religion/reclaiming-the-language-of-duty-in-an-age-of-human-rights-samue/11412158 (last accessed 28.4.2024).

[8] This focus on the legal status of the citizen does raise significant debate about rights of and duties to persons as refugees and undocumented workers.

citizens embrace their diverse identifications (Isin 2009). Citizens are not confined to the public sphere but also act in private spaces (Walby 1994). Even as a formal status, therefore, the citizen is not as fixed as first appears.

What citizens *do* are social and political *practices*. These are enacted in multiple domains, formal and informal, and both horizontally in relation to others and vertically in relation to power structures. Here we are asked to notice the 'extent and quality … of one's participation' as members of a community (Kymlicka and Norman 1994: 353). This account suggests that the citizen can be active or passive in responding to 'already written scripts such as voting, taxpaying and enlisting' (Isin 2009: 381). Additionally, attention to what people do, individually or in groups, foregrounds 'acts of citizenship' that are constitutive of the very idea of a citizen (Isin and Nielson 2008: 2); that it facilitates recognition of and accommodation to others (Bosniak 2000) and enacts their 'political subjectivity' (Isin 2009: 383). The idea of 'citizenship-as-desirable-activity' is then both a reflection of one's status as citizen and the performance of it (Kymlicka and Norman 1994). While some have observed shifts in authorities' representation of the citizen – for example, as consumer (Williams 1999) or as responsible (Garland 2001) – the status of the citizen *does not require* them to be active, good, responsible or ideal.[9]

At the risk of over-simplifying, the representation of the rights and responsibilities of citizenship – its substance – underpin fierce political and academic debate about what citizens 'owe' themselves, each other and the state, as well as what the state owes and can expect from its citizens. Persons as the subject-victim may transform themselves through the articulation of an injustice into, as Engin Isin writes, 'citizens as claimants of rights'. However, this claim for rights and recognition from the status of citizen cannot be a zero sum because, as Isin emphasises, all citizens have rights (Isin 2009: 368, 376). Thus, the public space of criminal justice becomes a place where victim or accused both appear as rights-bearing citizens and a public space where state entities discharge their duties to respect and uphold those rights.

Nothing of this rather extended depiction of citizen-status creates a difference between victims and offenders. Citizens have moral, social and political identifications and attachments that are prior to the victim or offender attribution, and which continue beyond. Each has the formal status of citizen, and each undertakes a wide range of citizenship practices across different domains. Some acts of citizenship such as voting are heavily scripted in constitutional democracies. Some, such as reporting crime and violence to authorities is less so; indeed, are almost always subject to individual discretion (Zemans 1983). Therefore, the idea

[9] It is important to observe some changes in public policy and discourse about these 'requirements' of citizenship that have emerged in the last 20 years. One is the way that states have reformulated citizen obligations through a lens of security and public health threats to the nation-state and to population groups. Another is the spread of the 'sovereign citizen movement' that purports to reject any obligation to formal governance structures.

of citizenship-as-desirable-activity assumes some motivation or interest to push or pull the citizen. What this looks like for the citizen-victim will be explored in the next section.

3. Justice Interests of Citizen-Victims

Citizens are said to have general and common interests in the arrangements of institutions, rules, and the distribution of status, rights, and entitlements amongst and within the polity. They also have interests in the values, norms, criteria, and principles by which they and their social, civic, and political institutions work. Political and social theorists often assign interests to social, community or lobby groups (Hirst 2013) or argue that interests drive rational and self-seeking behaviour (Hindess 2002). For Jane Mansbridge and colleagues to have an interest is to have an 'enlightened preference. That is, what hypothetically one would conclude after ideal deliberation was one's own good or one's policy preference, including other-regarding and ideal-regarding commitments' (Mansbridge et al. 2010). It is a Rawlsian understanding that citizens have interests in how others are treated, as well as themselves. Taken together, interest-oriented action blends instrumental and ethical concerns that are always contingent and socially embedded (Spillman and Strand 2013). While this depiction of citizen interest may appear to emphasise the virtuous, it does provide a frame from which to ask if, when and how it is in the interests of the citizen-victim to report violence and crime to authorities and cooperate with them: how and why is it desirable for a democratic state that they do so?

Citizen-victims are motivated by a range of factors to report their victimisation to authorities (Holder 2017b). While reporting rates vary considerably, surveys consistently show clusters of motives around normative reasoning, a sense of civic duty, and desire to protect oneself and others (van Dijk, Van Kesteren and Smit 2007: 109). As a citizenship practice, calling another to account necessarily involves a number of actions undertaken by different citizens including reporting the crime and participating in the resolution of that report.[10] Taken together, these practices are demanding. The citizen-victim must allocate time and make decisions that may be uncomfortable for themselves and others. They must be available on demand by authorities. They must answer unwelcome questions and subject themselves to scrutiny. They must think deeply on the nature of justice they seek (Holder 2018b).

However, individuals taking action in these ways are commonly said to have 'justice needs' that arise from the acts or omissions of criminal justice authorities (Sebba 1996). To have a 'need' draws attention to the personal. It is a term imported

[10] By attending to the *process* of being called to account, Antony Duff reminds us that within formal and informal systems citizens interact – with each other *and* with the process. Wrongdoers are called to account 'to fellow citizens' (Duff 2010a: 10–11; and see Chapter 15 in this volume).

from mental health and social service literatures (ten Boom and Kuijpers 2012).[11] The 'needs' of crime victims have led some to frame victim engagements with criminal justice within a therapeutic argument (Wemmers 2008). Consequently, as Williams (1999) suggests, a 'need' can turn a victimised person into a consumer and a criminal court into a 'service'. Of course, satisfaction of victim needs may occur within criminal justice but a focus on need misses the point. People victimised by violence and crime do not turn to criminal justice with an objective of 'healing' their needs (or the consequences and impacts of the victimisation). Rather they turn to the criminal justice system with the objective of achieving justice (Holder 2018b). The public-facing citizen-victim mobilises the law through the criminal justice system to advance this objective (Zemans 1983); of course, not always, not always willingly, and generally not with any certainty that justice (in whatever form) will be achieved.

While some scholars have written on 'the interests of victims' (Doak 2005: 658), the term has been used without definition.[12] More recently, Kathleen Daly has described victims' justice interests as comprising five empirically derived elements identified as participation, voice, validation, vindication, and offender accountability-taking responsibility. She proposes that these elements be used to assess and compare responses to victims of sexual violence across conventional and innovative justice mechanisms (Daly 2017: 386). These elements are comprehensive but present justice interests as victim-focused when neither the concept of justice nor the purposes of criminal justice are only about the victim. Indeed, as I have shown elsewhere, victims themselves recognise this (Holder 2018a). Their goals for justice point in multiple directions: towards themselves as victim, to the offender and to their community of others. The extension I argue for is that, from a citizen-first perspective, *interests* in justice speak to both to this recognition of justice for all but also to the wider obligations and responsibilities of civic membership. That is, of responsibilities to others as well as to oneself along with engagement and participation in a civic institution.

4. The Political and Democratic Citizenship

If taking the path of reporting victimisation to authorities and participating in the investigation, prosecution, and adjudication of an alleged offender is a citizenship practice, is it also a democratic practice? A practice of democratic citizenship?

[11] The notion of a 'need' is also often inadequately defined. Usually it is framed as 'basic' or 'essential' and ranges from those that ensure 'essential functioning' to those which enable 'optimal functioning'. Defined in this manner, human needs are passive. They are not a full accounting of human action in context.

[12] I note others' difficulty with the question of victim interests. For example, the international human rights organisation, REDRESS, promotes the rights and interests of victims before the International Criminal Court. It provides no definition of 'interests' save for those elements in Articles 68 and 75 of the Rome Statute. See www.redress.org/wp-content/uploads/2017/12/2011_VRWG_ASP10.pdf (last accessed 23 January 2024).

On this point, we need to briefly re-visit earlier discussion on citizen interests as political, given oft-repeated assertions that (a) criminal justice is *not* political and (b) that victims' rights claims in criminal justice *are* political. On both accounts, 'the political' is deemed inimical by legal experts to the adjudication of wrongs and harms. Indeed, victims' claims are said to 'undermine the forms of solidarity and responsibility necessary for democratic institutions' (Simon 2007: 7). Both assertions end up as arguments for exclusion, whether of the individual victim as claimant or of demands made by different social groups and movements for attention to particular victims (e.g. of sexual violence, of police violence, or of transnational corporate fraud).

Political theorists step back from this version of the political. Citizens have interests in '[t]he rules and policies of any institutions [that] serve particular ends, embody particular values and meanings, and have identifiable consequences for the actions and situation of the persons within or related to those institutions' (Young 1990: 211). From this viewpoint, *all* aspects of institutions[13] in a society are political. Individual victims and offenders experience the impact of decisions made within criminal justice. Equally, the decisions affect society at large due to the system's societal role.

The question remains, however, if victims' justice interests, their citizen interests, are practices of *democratic* citizenship. Democratic citizenship is commonly addressed as a matter for education (Lockyer, Crick and Annette 2017). Here there are familiar engagements with an active citizen who is 'willing, able and equipped to have an influence in public life and with the critical capacities to weigh evidence before speaking and acting' (Crick Report 1998 cited in Lockyer et al. 2017: 1). Equally there is lament about an ill-informed public that is barely equipped for either citizenship or democracy (Sniderman 2017). Democratic citizenship engages two philosophic orientations: either that its function is to 'facilitate and maximise individual autonomy within the rules of justice' or that it 'serve the common good' (Lockyer et al. 2017: 3). These orientations bring us uncomfortably close to familiar problems regarding good or bad citizens and, equally, to deserving and undeserving victims. They also return us to depictions of citizenship itself. To break this regression, I turn to portrayals of the citizen-victim that characterise them as an anti-democratic actor or as a democratic actor. These terms avoid labelling citizen-victim as illiberal or liberal – markers which appear overly associated with ideological affiliation (Main 2022).

In identifying the anti-democratic and democratic character of citizen-victims, I draw upon Chantal Mouffe's recognition that a plural political community is necessarily agonistic and that this 'adversarialism' is 'a necessary condition' of democracy (2005: 4). That is, societies are constituted by an essential antagonism of ideas, identifications, and interests – at times manifest

[13] Here I refer mostly to public institutions. I do not say that private institutions are non-political.

in victimising or exploitative activities. As such, contemporary constitutional democracies are too heterogenous for a shared vision of a single common good, whether this vision is enacted – or contested – in electoral politics or inside a courtroom. But this plural political community nonetheless recognises a set of values that permits actions of the social agent and also contains them (Mouffe 1992: 79). However, what quickly becomes apparent within this framework is the way 'good' ascriptions can attach to the descriptions of democratic actions and actors and those that are 'bad' are called anti-democratic. I map a way through the bifurcation by focusing on what citizen-victim actions and inactions that may shape a broad culture of involvement – for good or ill.

5. The Victim as Anti-Democratic Actor

There are many ways in which persons as victims and their associated interest groups have been described as anti-democratic. In this section I select four such ways: victims challenge of justice professionals, the knowledge claims victims make, their vilification of offenders, and the failure of most victims to confront the injustice of their victimisation. Much of this is contained in writings about penal populism: 'the notion of politicians tapping into, and using for their own purposes, what they believe to be the public's generally punitive stance' (Bottoms 1995: 40). In these descriptions, 'the public' is then merged with the outraged victim – or at least, with 'victims' groups that are highly visible and demand more punishment' (Miller 2013: 287). The purported link of a mass public to a 'victims' movement', is then declared to be an anti-democratic challenge to the established legal and political order.

5.1. Victim Challenges to Justice Professionals

In their review of the conceptual literature on populism, Jane Mansbridge and Stephen Macedo identify a common conceptual core to be the 'moral battle [of the people] against the elites' (2019: 60). Elites occupy positions of power in economic, political, legal, or cultural arenas amongst others. In the account of the victim as anti-democratic, the elites are judges, courts and legal professionals who are insiders to the victim outsider. The technical expertise and ritual of the insider is incomprehensible and used to keep 'the people' on the outside. Victims are said to work from a position of low information and should stay out of the justice process. From this vantage point, the language of neglect and disrespect, of being 'unfairly marginalized and ignored' is said to motivate 'the people' against 'elites' (Mansbridge and Macedo 2019: 61).

Victims decry their treatment by justice professionals (for a research overview, see Hoyle and Zedner 2007). 'These people', it is said, belittle the harm that victims suffer. The experience of having one's concerns disregarded and being spoken down to adds to the humiliation of the initial victimisation (Verdun-Jones and Rossiter 2010). Deeply connected to these disappointments is a public perspective that authorities do not treat victims equally to offenders; that is, authorities are seen to respect the rights of offenders but not those of victims.[14] The outraged victim perceive an abrogation by elites of assumed shared values of equal and respectful treatment and fairness due to all.

5.2. Victims' Knowledge Claims

A 'frequent correlate' to challenge from below is 'the valorization of the authentic folk knowledge of the people combined with the devaluation of deliberation and expertise' (Mansbridge and Macedo 2019: 65). Folk wisdom is multi-faceted. It is 'common sense', or part of culture and custom, popular myth and social legend, or anecdote and stories. Victims may be (though are not always) claimed as part of 'we folk'. They are ordinary people 'seldom seen and rarely heard' (Thumim 2006: 266). This alignment may be more likely at certain moments. For example, a common sight on courthouse steps is a gathering of people exclaiming to waiting media that an acquittal or low sentence, 'is not justice'. Although the meaning or reasoning behind such statements are seldom pursued, at such moments listeners will connect with their own experience of being belittled by someone in authority.[15] Victims also argue that they have insights about an offender's conduct that none else know and that the court *should* hear to make 'a proper decision' (Holder 2018a: 196).

At such moments, victims of crime have a 'moral force' (Ettema and Glasser 1989 quoted in Wood 1999: 152). It is this moral force that charges the status of a victim's lived experience within legal and political contexts. On its own account, lived experience leads 'fact' (Edmond 2017). It becomes a 'truth'; a form of knowledge contesting the old and posed as incompatible with it. Taken up as a public narrative, stories of lived experience then argue against the status quo in a manner that outrages the forensic rationale of a criminal court (Bandes 1996). The emphasis on reason and objectivity that the legal elite insist upon further aggravates victims' insistence on the legitimacy and weight of lived experience. The emotional language of the anti-democratic citizen-victim challenges the value that legal professionals and bureaucrats place on expertise (Levin 2022). Those who adhere to the old knowledge – the legal and technocratic elite – are then presented as out of touch with the ordinary folk.

[14] A majority (70%) of Australians who responded to a national survey were confident that criminal courts have regard for the rights of the defendant. Under half said the same for the criminal courts regard for victims' rights (Indermaur and Roberts 2009).

[15] Thompson 2006: 129 discusses Aristotle's analysis of anger as, in part, arising from perceived insult.

5.3. Victim Vilification of Offenders

A further frequent correlate within populism is 'opposition to vilified vulnerable out-groups' (Mansbridge and Macedo 2019: 65). To argue against another's rights is deeply anti-democratic. Victims, individually and collectively, often vilify offenders to the latter's detriment. Researchers have observed victims voicing negative views about the offender and demanding that the person's rights be curtailed in a range of contexts such as sentencing in non-capital cases and capital cases (Szmania and Gracyalny 2006; Kleinstuber Zaykowski and McDonough 2020), and in parole decision-making (Friedman and Robinson 2014). Victims' negative accounts rest on anger that social rules have been broken without sound or reasonable cause or justification. They tell of a desire for the temporary or permanent expulsion of the wrong doer from society and into custody where they can do no further harm to others (Bergstrøm, Evjetun and Bendixen 2017). Victims want to get even with the offender (Merry 1990). These findings about victims and their views about offenders are anti-democratic in that they de-humanise the 'other' and deny tolerance for diversity and difference when democracy requires empathy and solidarity.

5.4. Victims Fail their Civic Responsibility

Less acknowledged as anti-democratic is the bad or passive citizen who will 'turn away from actual or potential victims' or themselves fail to act on their victimisation. Shklar writes that turning away 'is to fall below personal standards of citizenship' in 'our public roles and their political context' (1990: 40–1). Bad citizens may ignore a homeless person being set upon by thugs. Less obviously, the passive citizen may shrug at a work colleague who chortles about their tax avoidance or say 'that's the way things are' at the news of a prosecutor's decision not to proceed on an allegation of rape. The victim may turn away from injustice and so, too, may different societies. Impunity may then result whether for mass atrocity, police use of torture, transnational financial crime, domestic violence, or gay hate crime (Engle, Miller and Davis 2016; Taylor 2019; Passas 2016; United Nations 2014; Hartman 2023).

To ignore such wrongdoing is to redefine injustice as misfortune or bad luck; or to tolerate greed and the abuse of power. Shklar's stringent expectation of the demands of citizenship necessarily casts a harsh light on those majority of 'ordinary' crime victims who tolerate or disregard their own victimisation. Those who 'lump it' set aside their 'civic responsibility' (Duff and Marshall 2023: 2). Of course, there are a wide range of reasons why people victimised by crime do not report to authorities. The point here is that democracy as a social and political project is, in part, about the public interest (inclusive of victim and offender) in peace, order and security. Anti-democratic actors who tolerate injustice undermine this shared project.

6. The Victim as Democratic Actor

It is tempting to simply flip those anti-democratic elements attributed to the citizen-victim to demonstrate their concomitant democratic character. It is true that stepping from the anti-democratic victim as passive can lead directly to an interest, shared by democracy theorists, in the active citizen.[16] The active citizen participates in public affairs. If they don't, the state and its apparatus atrophies. Constitutional democracies emphasise both scripted pathways for the active citizen (jury duty for example) *and* the citizen's discretion, consent, and agreement (cooperation with authorities for example). Further, neo-liberal democracies twist active citizens into responsible ones (Williams 1999) while authoritarian governments oblige citizen action (Jiang 2021). Nonetheless, demands for accountability are central to the democratic character of active citizens (Schmitter and Karl 1991). In this section I use this insight to organise argument for victims as democratic actors; specifically, the relationship of accountability to victim participation in criminal justice, their rights claims, and their passion.

6.1. Accountability and Victim Participation

Active citizens are participatory citizens, whether individually or in groups (Cornwall and Gaverta 2001). They create space for action. They access the 'ensemble' of institutions that constitute democratic systems (Schmitter and Karl 1991: 76). Criminal courts are one such institution through which citizen-victims meet 'the demand that offenders be called to public account for their crimes' (Duff and Marshall 2023: 2). As political scientist, Frances Zemans has written

> The legal system, limited as it is to real cases or controversies involving directly injured or interested parties, provides a uniquely democratic … mechanism for individual citizens to invoke public authority on their own and for their benefit (Zemans 1983: 692).

Indeed, the criminal process is dependent (often but not always) on citizens to activate the law. Activating the law as an accountability mechanism gives rise to contestation of facts and truths, the nature and applicability of a relevant normative rule, and what should be done with an alleged breach. The formality of the process, commonly perceived as alienating to civilians, also creates a framework in which the victim can participate and speak (Laugerud and Langballe 2017). They speak to what happened and why in their particular case and, through the aggregation of cases, draw attention to the limits and possibilities of public policy. Assumed shared values, norms and rules require testing. Without victims, accountability for wrongs is thin and fragile and the law is lifeless.

[16] However, the term, active citizenship, may be specific to the English language and its variants carry different meanings in different country and cultural contexts (see Newman and Tonkens 2011).

6.2. Accountability and Victims' Rights Claims

Citizens are rights-bearing. Democratic citizens' claim their rights (Marshall [1950] 2013). Rights claims may be about the distribution of power and resources and/or about the specific human rights of individuals (Holder, Kirchengast and Cassell 2021). A rights claim creates a bridge for a private experience to become public. These are co-constitutive. Consciousness of their rights is one factor that influences a citizen-victim to mobilise the law (Zemans 1983: 697). Of course, the citizen-victim is generally accepted as having no actionable rights within criminal justice in common law jurisdictions. This leads them to point out that respect for the offender's rights and their legal representation amounts to unequal treatment from the state. The situation, they argue, damages the duty of states to treat citizens equally and to protect the rights of all. From the perspective of democracy theory, this is entirely logical claim so long as it does not derogate from another's rights.

A rights claim made by the citizen-victim is a call for accountability on two main grounds: that an offender has breached their rights and should be held to account and that justice institutions should also account for their duty to protect rights. On the first, the offender's behaviour 'calls into question … the respect and rights owed to persons' and criminal justice provides the opportunity for the offender, as a respected agent, to be brought to account by the victim (Dearing 2017: 5). On the second, justice agencies are duty-bound to uphold the law, to protect citizens and provide an avenue for redress. Multiple justice decision-makers exercise discretion and, in consequence, frequently set aside allegations of crime.[17] Victims challenge the basis for these decisions through mechanisms such as complaint processes and private prosecutions (Holder and Kirchengast 2021; Michel 2018). In these ways, activist citizens challenge orthodoxy and established power relations or, as we have seen, 'the elite'. Active and activist citizens transform themselves from acted upon to actors. Rights claims shift the citizen from a consumer of services to someone who demands acknowledgement, recognition, and a specific type of response(s) from state authority that only duty can oblige.[18] Activist citizens operate with high information and ask why 'the way things are' is right or reasonable and should remain. As such, rights claiming is, …

> … an opportunity for individuals and groups to form and share ways of seeing the world; to shed light on and reimagine ways of thinking, being, and doing; and to take an active role in the political life of a community (Zivi 2012: 115).

[17] Discretionary decision-making in monopoly institutions potentially constitute an abuse of power. The 1985 UN Declaration of Basic Principles of Justice for Victims of Crime and Abuse of Power is rarely engaged on this point.

[18] See Moyn 2019 (fn 7).

6.3. Victims Challenge Injustice with Passion

At the heart of any rights claim is the identification of injustice, unfairness, or wrong that is not shared equally. Contemporary constitutional democracies rely on citizens (if at times reluctantly) to identify and call out injustice. To reprise Jonathon Simon (2007), it is a form of responsibility necessary for democratic institutions. To call injustice into the public realm, of which criminal justice is a part, 'encompasses the making [*and re-making, R.H.*] of collective norms and choices that are binding on society and backed by state coercion' (Schmitter and Karl 1991: 77). To do so takes courage and 'a special kind of anger' (Shklar 1990: 83). To identify injustice is to identify 'feelings which moved people'.[19]

Feelings, or passion, drive social action, here the victim's engagement with criminal justice. The experience of injustice raise strong emotions that are 'indispensable to a fully democratic polity' (Hall 2005: 4). The victimisation itself may have generated fear, distress and anger, but underpinning the passion to act are also factors weighed up by victims: feeling blameless, attacked without provocation, and their evaluation of seriousness (Holder 2018a: 118). Reasoning with passion 'incorporates cognitive judgements about value' (Hall 2005: 8). Outrage is intolerant of impunity: of those who plunder, violate and maim, or of those in positions of power who abuse that power. Such abuse may arise from, for example, the prosecutor's plea agreement which maximises efficiency over justice where 'by training [*they are, R.H.*] unwilling to step outside the rules and routines of their offices and peers' (Shklar 1990: 6). Or where criminal justice professionals are without functional and accessible oversight or review processes and act from the logic of unconstrained power (Sarat and Clarke 2008). Either way, the perceived impunity of decision-makers generates outrage that demands accountability.

However, as Shklar points out, the sense of injustice and associated morally charged language on their own are insufficient. Both the experience of injustice and recognition of it by others influence the citizen-victims to act and to take the injustice forward into the public sphere. In these spaces, interpretation necessarily involves reflection and deliberation, again between self and others. Thus, the citizen-victim needs some confirmation that their wider social world shares their 'special anger' directed against *this* victimisation against *this* person within *this* context and by *this* offender. Here, writes Shklar, the victim enters 'society and its rules' – on justice as well as injustice (1990: 88). As such, a rights claim that injustice be addressed cannot trump completely the authoritative third-party decision-maker. Rather, it enters a space of political disputation where the emotional and moral accounting does not belong to the victim alone.

[19] Kenneth Minogue (1969) writes that 'to understand the [populist] movement is to discover the feelings which moved people' (quoted in Demertzis 2016).

7. Conclusion

Society and its rules tolerate a 'world of irremediable inequalities' (Shklar 1990: 84). Living in this world, citizens are neither simply good nor only bad; neither deserving nor undeserving but likely all these at different times. They clash against each other. No-one is intrinsically ideal. There is no clean separation of anti-democratic and democratic elements. The practices of the citizen-victim are likewise two-sides of this same coin. They challenge 'elite' decision-makers and their rules, yet will, by and large, play by those rules. Citizen-victims will tolerate injustice against themselves, and some will seek to rectify it. Their responses are context sensitive. Victims' preparedness to claim their rights and to respect those of others is a profound demonstration of citizenship; a preparedness, however, that is contingent. To act and seek to hold others to account is to listen to passion – outrage, anger, fear, and grief. Enacting democratic citizenship on these terms does not mean citizen-victims, indeed any citizen, are always right. As victims we can 'accuse wildly' (Shklar 1990: 4).

The criminal justice system provides a channel for the antagonisms that victimisation can generate. For the victim as well as the offender, criminal justice is a channel through which to present and contest their interests and claims. It may thereby amplify the 'the conflictual dimension in social life' (Mouffe 2005: 4). Yet criminal justice is, to use Seyla Benhabib's phrase, a place of 'legitimised contestation' (1996: 7) adjudicated by a judicial third party. Criminal justice comprises a political site, albeit a highly technical one, that provides a 'common symbolic space' comprising a 'shared set of rules' (Mouffe 2005: 52) in which self-interest is constrained (Mansbridge et al. 2010: 70). The victim and offender may adopt adversarial positions that are 'ultimately irreconcilable' but which can or should be nonetheless 'accepted as legitimate perspectives' (Mouffe 2005: 52). On this account, criminal justice is, like democracy itself, a method of (re)integration.[20] Moreover, criminal justice brings individual citizens into a site where they are exposed not only to others' views, but also to the lives of others. They may be exposed to reasoning that can deepen worldviews. As a set of public institutions made for the public, criminal justice may act to nurture the judgement of citizens.

Yet the operative word is *may*, in part because the citizen-victim's views and concerns, independent of the state's agents, continue to be trenchantly resisted by criminal justice professionals. From the standpoint of these practitioners and criminal law theorists, the exclusion of the citizen-victim is as it should be. Indeed, the anti-democratic as well as democratic character of victims only provide further justification for their stringently restricted role. These characteristics

[20] The idea stems from Joseph Schumpeter's famous definition of 'the democratic method' as an 'institutional arrangement for arriving at political decisions which realizes the common good by making the people itself decide issues through the election of individuals who are to assemble in order to carry out its will's (cited in Pettit 2017: 493).

urge great caution. From the standpoint of democracy theorists, however, these are the expected ingredients of citizenship and, consequently, are anticipated. Understanding the varying actions taken (and not taken) by citizen-victims as acts of democratic citizenship makes them legible, if not always welcome. The people's 'moral battle with elites' arises when the latter does not listen (Mansbridge and Macedo 2019: 70 et seq.). Grievances need careful responses. So too do grievances *about* criminal justice and its profoundly anti-democratic stance, for which I share Shklar's conclusion of *The Faces of Injustice*. She writes

> Whatever decisions [*on inclusion*, R.H.] we do make will, however, be unjust unless we take the victim's view into full account and give her voice its full weight. Anything less is not only unfair, it is also politically dangerous. Democratic citizens have the best chance of making the most tolerable decisions but certainly not always, given the extent, variety, and durability of human injustice (Shklar 1990: 126).

Criminal justice, so important to societies, must be made safe by and for democracy. All citizens have interests that it functions efficiently and effectively, and that it is fair and inclusive to all.

17

Rights in Conflict?

Exploring the Expansion of Victims' Rights in Light of the Presumption of Innocence

MICHELLE COLEMAN

1. Introduction

Taking a rights-based approach to criminal justice can help ensure that all participants within the process are treated with a greater degree of fairness and humanity. There can be a greater sense of justice for all involved and it might help strengthen our sense of restitution and retribution. In recent years there have been increasing calls for the recognition and incorporation of victims' rights in the criminal justice process.[1] These stem from the belief that victims are different from other witnesses, because they have a personal interest in the criminal justice process. However, new rights cannot be added to the existing criminal justice framework without consideration of existing rights. The defendant in a criminal trial has a number of rights because of their status as an accused person. The trial cannot happen without a defendant and, in fact, without the existence of an accused person there is no need for a criminal trial. Because the state makes criminal accusations and justifies punishment based on criminal convictions, the accused person must be protected from unjustified punishment at the hands of the state, arbitrary punishment, and other tyrannical practices.[2] Therefore, any victims' rights that are adopted must take care not to infringe upon or violate the rights of the accused.

Key among the defendant's rights is the right to be presumed innocent. Seen also as a legal principle, the presumption of innocence, at least as it applies to criminal procedure, is a required instruction to the factfinder that the defendant

[1] See for example Marsy's Law in the United States: 'About Marsy's Law' available at: www.marsyslaw.us (last accessed 12 August 2024); or arguments identifying weaknesses in the ability of victims to participate in international criminal law such as Safferling and Petrossian 2021.

[2] Some jurisdictions have private prosecution, where the prosecution is brought about by the victim or other interested party, rather than the state. This is not the focus of this chapter.

cannot be found guilty unless and until the standard of proof is met by the person who has that burden or onus. (Coleman 2021: 78–105) Going beyond procedure, the presumption of innocence also prevents accused people from being treated in the same manner as convicted people; furthering its role in preventing unjustified punishment. (Coleman 2021: 106–135) As the foundation for determining accountability and justifying punishment, the presumption of innocence is a right of the accused which is central to the mechanism of the criminal trial. Thus, it is essential that victims' rights are not expanded in a way that permits infringement on or violation of the presumption of innocence.

Taking a more human rights-based approach to criminal justice, however, could allow for greater victim participation within the criminal justice process. This chapter explores the possibility of expanding victims' rights without infringing on the presumption of innocence.[3] Section 2 will discuss a human rights-based approach to criminal law and criminal justice. It will argue that this already exists for the defendant and could theoretically exist for victims as their interests are affected in the process. Section 3 identifies the current and ongoing conflict between the defendant's right to the presumption of innocence and victims' rights within criminal justice. It argues that the presumption of innocence is fundamental to the structure of criminal justice as it is currently configured and, as a result, significant change to the structure would be required for victims' rights to be widely expanded. Moving on to rights to which victims may be entitled, Section 4 argues that there is a fundamental issue with the right to identification and acknowledgement because it is too tied to a criminal harm within criminal law. This section advocates for decoupling the definition of victim from the idea that the harm is caused by a criminal act to allow for greater identification and acknowledgment of victims and their rights. Section 5 considers victim participation in the criminal justice process. Section 5.1 focuses on the right to information; Section 5.2 introduces the right to active participation; and Section 5.3 identifies how victims' post-trial rights might be enhanced. Finally, Section 6 concludes the chapter. In order to have a much wider expansion of victims' rights, the criminal justice process as a whole needs to be reevaluated to allow for compatibility of rights between the various participants.

2. A Human Rights-Based Approach to Criminal Law and Justice

A human rights-based approach to criminal law and justice implies the normative requirement that individuals involved in the process have rights, have knowledge

[3] The chapter deals with this tension specifically from the perspective of adversarial criminal procedure and international criminal procedure. I think the arguments advanced in this chapter could also apply in inquisitorial systems.

of those rights, and have an ability to claim remedy when the rights are violated.[4] This allows for individuals to be better protected, to exercise agency over their actions, and allows for greater oversight and accountability over institutions that are entrusted with respecting and protecting those rights (United Nations 2023).

A rights-based approach is already applied to the accused, although whether those rights are sufficiently protected and respected in practice varies widely based on the jurisdiction and circumstances. Rights of the accused are enshrined in every general human rights treaty and in domestic constitutions and criminal codes (Coleman 2021: 23; Bassiouni 1993: 235–97). These rights include the right to presumed innocence, right to defend oneself, and the right to legal representation.

Engaging in a rights-based approach to criminal justice for accused persons is required because the accused is essential to the criminal justice process. Without an identified accused person, trials which ascribe accountability lose meaning. A complaint needs to be raised and proof must be provided, but this could come from either the state, the victim, or possibly another interested person. While other roles, such as accuser or judge are necessary, only the specific accused person is required to be involved in, or at least identified before, a criminal trial. Further, the accused's rights are at stake throughout the process. The trial process imposes itself upon the accused and its outcome of 'guilty' is what is used to justify punishment. It is through this justification that defence rights help ensure that the right person is held accountable and prevent government overreach and unjustified punishment.

Until recently, the accused has been the only individual with specific rights to be upheld within the criminal process. The accused, however, is not the only individual who may have rights involved in substantive criminal law. Violations of criminal law involve harm against either the state, an individual victim, or both. A rights-based approach to criminal law would see the harm experienced by a victim as a violation of or infringement on their own rights. By this view, victims have a normative interest in criminal law and procedure and should have rights which allow them to engage in the process of seeking redress for the harm they have suffered. Victims, however, have traditionally not benefited from specific rights during the criminal process. Rather, they have only been able to participate as regular witnesses during the trial phase and at times, have been permitted to give impact statements during the post-trial sentencing phase.

One way of applying a rights-based approach to criminal justice might be to formally acknowledge that substantive criminal law is not only a harm against the state. Rather, victims suffer from infringements and violations of their own rights when criminal wrongs are committed against them. If this is recognised,

[4] United Nations Sustainable Development Group, (2023) 'Human Rights-Based Approach'. Available at: https://unsdg.un.org/2030-agenda/universal-values/human-rights-based-approach (accessed: 17 December 2023); UAB Institute for Human Rights Blog, (10 December 2018) 'What is a Human Rights-Based Approach?'. Available at: https://sites.uab.edu/humanrights/2018/12/10/what-is-a-human-rights-based-approach/ (accessed 17 December 2023).

then victims' rights should be identified and protected. Within international criminal law and many domestic jurisdictions there are calls to expand, recognise, and protect victims' rights beyond the traditional role of witness. Examples include, the expansion of victims' participation at the International Criminal Court or activist movements lobbying for domestic legislation in the United States to provide victims with rights to participation and information. However, as will be seen in the next section, the identification of victims can be a problematic barrier to providing victims with rights, particularly when considered together with the rights of the accused.

3. The Presumption of Innocence and Victims' Rights

The accused person's right to the presumption of innocence is a primary concern with taking a wider view of victims. This is because of the presumption's structural and thematic underpinning throughout the criminal justice process. In current criminal justice systems, the presumption of innocence is essential in preventing arbitrary punishment and contributing to the rule of law. The function of this presumption is to protect individuals from being treated as if they are guilty of a crime without a conviction (Coleman 2021: 25; Ashworth 2006 246–7). It involves procedural and non-procedural aspects which means that it applies both inside and outside the courtroom. (Coleman 2021) Therefore, the presumption of innocence has wide-ranging application within the context of criminal law and procedure which can come into conflict with victims' rights of identification, participation, and restoration or reparations. This is because if victims have particular rights within the criminal justice process before the verdict, enactment of those rights could assume, state, or imply that the accused person is in fact guilty of the crime of which they are accused.

The procedural aspect of the presumption of innocence is a mandatory rebuttable presumption of law that requires the factfinder to approach the case assuming the accused person is innocent. (Coleman 2021: 96) This is because it acts as an instruction to the factfinder to not find the accused guilty unless the relevant standard of proof has been reached within the available evidence. Further, that evidence and standard must only be met by the person who has the burden to fulfil the standard of proof, typically the prosecutor. This means that a conviction can only be secured if the factfinder is satisfied that the standard of proof is met by the person who has the burden. If this is not the case, then liability cannot be found. Therefore, the procedural presumption of innocence is the mechanism that allows for criminal liability to be secured. This procedural aspect describes the only mechanism whereby individuals can be found guilty, that is, that the standard of proof must be met by the burden or onus bearer to overcome the presumption. Only by achieving this can a person be found guilty of a crime, publicly held accountable for that crime, and receive punishment. So, that part of the presumption of innocence must not come into conflict with other rights that may be held within the trial process.

Expanding victims' rights to include active participation in investigation or trial, is likely to come into conflict with the procedural aspect of the presumption of innocence because by permitting greater participation in investigation or prosecution, the victim could become a second burden or onus holder which would change the ability of the burden holder to meet their burden. By causing information and proof to come from more than one source, the standard of proof would no longer necessarily be met by the burden holder, but rather met by the burden holder and the victim. This, in turn, could cause issues with the way evidence is determined to be accurate or reliable, because victims as private individuals do not have the same responsibilities for obtaining evidence as public entities such as prosecutors. It would also cause issues for equality of arms as the accused would have to defend themselves against more than one opponent.

The non-procedural aspect is a right to be enjoyed by the accused both inside and outside the courtroom. (Coleman 2021: 106–35) This aspect requires that public authorities not treat any individual as if they are guilty of a crime unless they have been convicted. This includes not punishing individuals without a conviction first being entered against them, but also means that non-convicted people cannot be publicly portrayed or referred to as guilty, the media must not undermine a person's presumption of innocence, and non-convicted individuals must not receive the same treatment that is reserved for convicted people. One of the main reasons for this is preventing extrajudicial punishment, which, if allowed, would obviate the need for the justice system altogether. (Coleman 2021).

Expansion of victims' rights to identification and reparations or restoration can easily come into conflict with the non-procedural aspect of the presumption of innocence. As is discussed in far more detail below, referring to victims as victims within the criminal justice context implies that they are victims of crime, rather than mere sufferers of some harm. By connecting this criminal idea of the status of being a 'victim' implies that a crime took place and that the accused person is the person who committed that crime. The conflict that can occur with restoration or reparations is when a criminal conviction is required for those rights to become active. If a person is a victim, they should be normatively entitled to some restoration to correct the harm, however that cannot be provided before conviction as that would imply the guilt of the accused.

In addition to the role that the presumption of innocence plays within the current framework of criminal justice, the presumption of innocence must take precedence over victims' rights if there is a conflict between the two rights because of role the particular individuals play within criminal trials. A trial focused on liability rather than harm must have a named defendant, who is the holder of the right to the presumption of innocence. However, a trial does not require a victim. In some cases, the victim no longer exists or cannot be located and in others the crime is 'victimless' but nevertheless a trial can proceed. Further, in both inquisitorial and accusatorial systems there is no specific role for victims. At the International Criminal Court victims can play a much more active role as participants to the proceedings, however they are still not required. (ICC RPE, Rule 89) Therefore, victims are not essential to trials, unlike the accused.

Because the presumption of innocence has a role in protecting the accused both inside and outside the courtroom, an unexamined increase in victims' rights can cause accused people to be treated as if they are guilty either by the court itself or by public officials within the wider community. However, this does not mean that victims cannot have rights within criminal justice, only that their rights cannot be in conflict with the presumption of innocence. This presents a difficult, but perhaps not impossible, challenge if the definition of victim requires them to have been subjected to harm from a crime, then there is already a presumption of innocence issue. However, if victims are thought about more broadly and unmoored from criminal actions then we can start to think about what rights they might have that would not affect the defence's presumption.

Taking a human-rights-centric approach to criminal justice could mean expanding victims' rights so that they take precedence over the presumption of innocence but would require a reconceptualisation of the criminal justice system and processes. The purpose of criminal trials would have to be re-examined and adjusted to not be fundamentally about ascribing criminal responsibility but would have to include other goals such as assessment of harm and rehabilitation and restoration to the victims. One way that this might occur is if the criminal justice system more closely resembled restorative justice practices that involve the victim and the defendant in conversation with each other to come to a reconciliation (Braithwaite 1998). These types of processes, however, almost always requires the defendant to admit responsibility for the harm they caused and so is problematic for defendants who choose to exercise their right to the presumption of innocence. A restorative justice process would work more effectively if those who are guilty had responsibilities such as those suggested by Duff, Chapter15 in this volume.

4. The Right to Identification and Acknowledgment – Two Competing Notions of Victims

While the complainant in a criminal case is generally the state, victims of crime can be physically harmed and normatively wronged.[5] In substantive criminal law, a victim is often defined as an individual who has suffered some harm as a result of a criminal act.[6] Because the trial is the mechanism that determines whether a

[5] This chapter ignores the idea that private, or victim lead prosecution exists in some jurisdictions. Rather the paper is concerned with 'traditional' notions of the criminal trial, where the state is the prosecutor and has the burden or onus of proof which are far more prevalent across jurisdictions.

[6] UK Ministry of Justice 2020: 3.28 CFR § 94.102; International Criminal Court Rules of Procedure and Evidence Rule 85(a).

criminal act has occurred, this definition implies that a person cannot be identified as a victim until there has been a determination that a criminal act caused their harm and criminal liability has been ascribed. If that is the case, then this narrow definition of 'victim' further implies that victims cannot have specific rights within or during the criminal trial because they cannot properly be identified as a victim before the conclusion of a trial. Thus, all witnesses, including victims, should be treated the same because it has not been legally determined who, if anyone, is the victim.

This definition may sit well within criminal law and its purpose of ascribing liability; however, it does not comport with a common understanding of what the term 'victim' means or what happens in legal practice. A wider and more commonly understood definition of 'victim' includes individuals who suffer harm in general (Coleman 2020). This could include those who suffered as a result of criminal behaviour, accidents, harmful acts which are not criminal, and things which are a result of nature. Importantly, within this wider understanding, victims of crime are still victims, if they have suffered some harm, regardless of whether that crime is ever reported or investigated, or whether liability for that crime is determined. However, criminal law is not concerned with all things happening everywhere, rather it is concerned with determining individual liability for those who have not acted in accordance with criminal law.[7] To that end, criminal law is not particularly concerned with individuals as victims at all. Thus, 'victim' is defined in limited terms.

This terminology problem is highly related to victims' right to identification or acknowledgement. There is no reason why victims should not have a right to identification or acknowledgement of their status as victims. In fact, the expansive definition could be considered the normative definition as well and provides the means of identification. If someone who suffers some harm is a victim, then victims have a right to be identified and acknowledged by definition. The conflict occurs when the criminal justice system is involved, because of the requirement that the harm results from a criminal act.

One way of solving this terminology issue might be to have a word for those who claim or may have indeed suffered some harm, but criminal liability has not (yet) been ascribed. Perhaps the term 'victim' should be used for those who have suffered harm in general, whether from a criminal act or not, while there should be a different term for those victims who are involved in criminal proceedings. This allows for identification and acknowledgement of their harm, but it also allows for the idea that whether that harm was the result of a criminal act and whether criminal liability can be ascribed to that harm is yet to be determined.

Criminal law provides such duality for defendants. The presumption of innocence prevents a person who has not been convicted from being referred to as a guilty person or criminal within the court system until an actual conviction has

[7] Also known as the *nullem crimen sine lege* principle.

occurred. (Coleman 2021: 106–35) Rather, there is a plethora of terms such as suspect, accused, and defendant that denote the suspected but not (yet) confirmed status of legal guilt. For someone who is possibly a victim of a crime however, there is no term like 'suspect' or 'accused' to denote recognition that they may have suffered harm, but criminal liability has not (yet) been determined.

Instead, the person who is identified as the victim is referred to as a victim unless it is determined that they did not suffer harm as a result of a crime. This is seen, in practice, as a potential victim of a particular crime is identified during the investigation and will be referred to as a victim throughout the investigation and subsequent criminal proceedings, despite the fact that it has necessarily not yet been determined whether they have suffered harm as a result of a criminal act or who might be criminally liable for their harm, as that is determined by the outcome of the proceedings. Despite common use, using the term 'victim' in this way goes against the narrow definition commonly set out in criminal codes, as it has not yet been determined that a crime has occurred.

This discussion of who is identified as a victim might help to explain their traditional role in criminal law versus a more modern and rights-based understanding. Traditionally, in the common law system, victims were treated as mere witnesses to the criminal process (Doak 2008; Garkawe 1994; Christie 1977). They did not have specific rights, beyond those of any other witness, and they were generally ignored throughout the criminal process. This means that they did not know what investigation, if any, was occurring, they were not informed of court dates and they did not receive support. At times, victims were re-traumatised because of their treatment while testifying and throughout the trial process (Roberts and Zuckerman 2022: 21; Doak 2008: 52–64; Hoyle and Zender 2007: 473). However, thinking about victims in a more expansive way allows for identification of victims well before the verdict. In turn, this allows a group to be identified which allows for investigation into whether they may have rights and responsibilities before the end of trial and what those potential rights and duties might be. Further, it is recognition that the treatment of victims is improving and that there may be room for (more) victims' rights within criminal justice systems.

5. The Right to Participate in Criminal Proceedings – The Possibility of Human Rights Centric Procedure

Beyond recognition and acknowledgement, it may be possible for victims to have greater participation rights within the criminal justice process. Within the process as it stands, victims do not have to be informed of dates or the progress of their case, however, a right to information may be justified on a normative basis without infringement on the rights of the accused. Victims also typically do not have independent participation rights within the investigation or trial process. This is harder to justify within the existing structure of criminal trials. It, however, might be possible, despite the presumption of innocence and other defence rights if a victim centric or rights-orientated approach was taken.

5.1. Right to Information

The right to information and dates is a very important right within victims' rights advocacy. Victims also may want information about when court hearings will be held, whether and who might be charged with an offence, and whether those accused will be held in pretrial detention or released.[8] On the surface these seem to be reasonable and, at times necessary, pieces of information that the victims should receive. Further, this information is often publicly available although may be difficult for victims to find.

Victims have an interest in the criminal procedures that follow from the incident which caused them to be harmed or wronged. Normatively, this is because the criminal justice process and determination of criminal liability acts can act as some recognition that they were wronged. If victims have an interest in the criminal process that results from the harm they suffered, then they should have a right to information about that process.

Generally apprising victims of court dates should not violate or infringe upon either aspect of the presumption of innocence or other defence rights. Court dates are generally accessible and court hearings are observable by the public. Letting victims know when a court date is and keeping them updated if that date changes does not affect the burden or standard of proof of the procedural aspect of the presumption of innocence. Further, the non-procedural aspect is not affected because having someone observe the court hearing does not state or imply that the accused person is guilty, but rather demonstrates that the trial process is moving along. Victims have a personal interest in whether the alleged crime occurred and whether it was committed by the accused person and so some victims may want to follow the trial in person. Even if the victim is convinced that the person accused of the crime against them committed that crime, it does not violate the presumption of innocence to keep them up to date on when court hearings will take place or to allow them to observe the court proceedings should they choose to do so.

Updating the victim as to personal information about the defendant, however, is more likely to violate or at least infringe upon the presumption of innocence, depending on what is implied or even stated about the defendant. Notification of when the accused person is released from pretrial detention alone might not have implications for the presumption of innocence. It has nothing to do with whether the person is treated as if they are guilty, and notifying the victim of the defendant's changed detention status does not seem to affect that, however, commentary or advice that accompanies that information might imply that the accused is guilty.

[8] This is one of the biggest issues for Marsy's Law in the United States. See 'About Marsy's Law (n 1) above.

For example, telling the victim that the accused is released from jail and that they should take extra precautions implies that the accused person is likely to be a risk to the victim. The underlying assumption of this is that the accused is a person who is likely to engage with threatening behaviour toward the victim which is something that a law-abiding person would not do. Therefore, it implies that the person is guilty or at least not law abiding. Which goes against the right to be presumed innocent. Further, one could imagine that in situations with high profile crimes or wide media coverage, or possibly in smaller communities, the communication of this risk to the victims might cause more infringement on the presumption of innocence for the accused person. Finally, while providing information about the defendant's detention status might be acceptable, providing personal information, such as their address, would not be acceptable because in addition to the possible presumption of innocence issues other rights such as the right to privacy would be violated.

5.2. Right to Active Participation in Criminal Proceedings

Beyond notification, some victims could have a right to conference with the prosecutor and have notice of pretrial disposition. If this right is part of the right to information discussed above, then there are few problems with regard to the presumption of innocence. If, however, this is a conference in which the prosecutor could potentially take advice from or make decisions with the victims, then the right to conference would almost certainly violate the presumption of innocence as it is currently understood. This is because of the prosecutor's position to not only have the burden to meet the standard of proof, but also because the judgement involved in the charging decision and what cases should go to trial involves an evaluation of whether that standard of proof can be met.

From a practical point of view this would be difficult to enact because the prosecution has many more considerations than just the victims' interests. Further, prosecutors need to be able to work impartially, making charging decisions, pretrial disposition decisions and trial strategy decisions based on the facts of the case, the amount and quality of evidence available, the law and the public interest. All of this can lead to the prosecutor not being able to accommodate or even realistically consider the victims' wants or needs. Aside from the practical, however, several of these decisions implicate the procedural presumption of innocence. Anything having to do with the amount or quality of the evidence and how the case may be disposed goes to the burden and standard of proof. If a victims' conference may involve the procedural presumption of innocence, then that cannot be a victim's right. Within a human rights-based approach an expansion of victims' rights could include the right to conference with the prosecutor. Using this approach, it would already be acknowledged that the victim has suffered some harm regardless of whether it was the result of criminal activity and therefore has an active interest in how that harm is remedied or otherwise dealt with, including whether any criminal liability is ascribed to the events leading to the harm. Thus, the victim should be able to discuss with the prosecutor what evidence is available and the likelihood of conviction. This approach may also help the victims achieve further recognition of their harm and the ability to tell their version of events aside from acting as witnesses.

It is possible to imagine a criminal justice system where victims have independent participation rights, perhaps even as a party to the proceedings. There are examples of greater participation by victims in international criminal law and domestic law, however these examples have not risen to the level of a victim's right to participate in part because of the effects such participation would have on the presumption of innocence. This would almost certainly violate the presumption of innocence unless the criminal justice system was completely restructured because the burden and standard of proof must both be met by one person who is usually the prosecutor. If the victims participated in a trial, they would not be able to contribute to the standard of proof without violating the presumption of innocence, and so it would open questions as to how their role could be effective.

One place where a trial has been partially rethought in this regard is at the International Criminal Court, where victims can participate at trial. Their role is limited, however, in that they can seek permission to present evidence and question witnesses, but the court does not have to grant that permission (ICC RPE 89) Further, the evidence they present cannot unduly prejudice the accused or conflict with the burden and standard of proof. (Rome Statute, Article 68) In practice, this has meant that they have largely been able to present their own evidence about the context or background involved in the crimes rather than helping to prove the *actus reus* or *mens rea*. Even at the International Criminal Court, where victim participation is purposely included in the founding documents of the Court, victim participation, while occurring to some degree in all the cases to date, still leaves questions open about how effective that participation is (Safferling and Petrossian 2021). This has led to a number of questions about whether victims can meaningfully present their own evidence. Perhaps the biggest being that if the evidence presented by victims needs to be relevant, and comply with these requirements, it is doubtful that evidence other than background evidence could be presented, unless it helps the defence. (Coleman 2020). Domestic courts would need to be restructured to allow victims to actively participate in a meaningful way without violating the presumption of innocence. A domestic example comes from the United States where activists have been seeking to introduce legislation in states to provide victims with the rights both to information and participation in criminal procedure which would be protected in state and federal constitutions.[9]

A human rights-based approach taken to allow for a victims' right to active and meaningful participation in trial could be possible, but it would change the structure and function of the trial process. If the victims were driving the prosecution

[9] See (n 1) above.

of the accused, it would allow them to fully pursue their interest in the criminal outcome resulting from the harm they experienced. However, such a shift would ignore the state's interest in determining criminal liability and it would not provide the state with justification for enacting punishment against criminal wrongdoers. This would create a situation where criminal liability is more akin to private civil liability in that the damages or sentence sought would be more personal to the victim rather than be publicly orientated toward the state.

Ultimately, this might be a more effective way of dealing with the harm that results from criminal acts. There are questions about whether current modes of punishment that the state can provide, such as imprisonment, are effective in satisfying the interests of victims or the public. At least with a victim-oriented approach, the victims' interests would be taken into account and hopefully satisfied, even if the interests of the public or state is not.

5.3. Right to Participate in Post-Trial Proceedings Including Sentencing and Restitution Determinations

Victim participation in post-conviction processes will generally not violate or infringe upon the presumption of innocence because a conviction necessarily means that the presumption has been overcome for that particular crime. That is, that the standard of proof has been met by the burden holder. Some degree of post-trial participation has already been fairly widely adopted. Victims are often able to make a statement to the court before sentencing or restitution has been determined. These statements usually state how the victim has been harmed by the defendant and can be quite emotional, graphic and specific in nature. They are meant to let the victim have their say about the case and how it has affected them and allows the court to take into consideration some of the victims' concerns. Therefore, generally post-conviction participation by victims would not infringe upon the presumption of innocence. Even if it is reinstituted during the appeal process, the fact that the victims participated in post-conviction proceedings should not infringe upon the presumption of innocence, because the trial court must operate as if the presumption no longer applies, or it will not be possible to sentence the accused at all.

Where the case's outcome is not a conviction there are issues with a victim's right to reparations or restoration and the presumption of innocence. Where reparations, restitution or other forms of restoration are reliant on a conviction, victims who suffered harm are unable to repair that harm if the criminal trial results in anything other than conviction because the restitution or other forms of restoration are linked to the punishment of the accused. The presumption of innocence has not been overcome in a case that does not result in conviction thus, the accused person cannot be punished. Unfortunately, this leads to people who have suffered harm from receiving restoration or restitution to repair that harm. Thus, despite the fact that the person is suffering, it is implied that they will continue suffering that harm only because criminal liability cannot be determined. A rights-based approach to criminal justice would uncouple conviction from restoration allowing those who have suffered harm to have a right to restoration regardless of whether that harm was caused by a criminal act or criminal liability was ascribed to a particular person. (Doak 2008: 238–9) This could allow victims to start to benefit from services before a criminal investigation or trial are complete, it would ensure that they are restored regardless of whether liability is determined; this would generally help remedy the harm that they have endured. However, for this to happen, the restitution or restoration would have to be completely uncoupled from the idea of criminal liability and the defendant.

6. Conclusion

Within criminal justice as it is currently configured, victims have limited rights. This is, in part, because the presumption of innocence is so fundamental to the proof structure and liability determination in criminal trials. However, if a more human rights-based approach to criminal procedure were to be taken, where the victims were able to exercise more of their interest in remedying the harm they have suffered, victims could exercise many more rights. This, however, would require restructuring criminal justice, perhaps to a restorative justice practice, because the accused person would almost certainly need to accept some responsibility for the criminal harm.

A rights-based approach requires identification of right holders, rights that they can exercise, and remedy for when those rights are violated. Taking such an approach toward victims in criminal justice would acknowledge that both victims and the state suffer some harm when a criminal act occurs. This would allow for earlier identification of victims and acknowledgement of the harm that they have suffered. Victims could be identified as victims regardless of whether there was a criminal action that caused them harm. However, identifying victims within criminal justice almost necessarily requires simultaneous identification of the criminal act (and liability) that caused that harm which causes conflict with the defence's right to the presumption of innocence.

Once victims are properly identified, then they could have much greater rights to participation. These could include more rights to information and rights to active participation within the proceedings. However, for victims to be able to access a right to active participation, a reconfiguration of the criminal justice process would need to occur. The presumption of innocence prevents more than one entity from having the burden or onus of proof. The right to active participation would work best if there was a duty on the part of the guilty accused to confess guilt or at least accept some liability, however, this risks ignoring the state or public interest in addressing the criminal harm. This further shifts the focus away from sentencing toward private redress of the harm. In turn, this would cause criminal justice to more closely resemble civil remedies for harm. When it comes to restitution for the victim, uncoupling conviction and the need to restore would allow for earlier access to services and resources. This would allow for the harm to be properly acknowledged and corrected without need for conviction. An increase in victims' rights to participate in the criminal process fits within our notions of justice and punishment. It may help to satisfy our individual urge for retribution, increase the sense that restoration has occurred, and provide a sense of justice as the victim is able to exercise some control and agency over what has happened to them as opposed to occupying an entirely passive role. Victims' rights provide victims with greater control and autonomy over the harm that they have suffered; however, they cannot be considered in a vacuum. In its current form, the requirement of the current criminal justice system's structure requiring the presumption of innocence severely limits how victims may participate. To allow victims to participate fully in the system, the procedures and processes of the criminal justice system would need to be restructured, defendants who were found guilty would have to accept at least some responsibility for the harm they have caused, and whether and what the state's interest is in criminal harm would need to be reconsidered. Because criminal justice is focused on determining liability, rather than harm, victims' rights and concerns will always be second to the court's established mechanisms. If made more prominent, many victims' rights are likely to infringe upon the rights of the accused and may change the risk of wrongful conviction. To better include victims' rights in the criminal justice process and make them meaningful and effective in application there should be a reconsideration of criminal justice. This should start with uncoupling the status of victims from crime but also should consider what the goals of trial should be and how the state, defendant and victims can all play a meaningful role.

BIBLIOGRAPHY

Abraham, M (2018), *Sanktion, Norm, Vertrauen. Zur Bedeutung des Strafschmerzes in der Gegenwart*, Berlin: Duncker & Humblot.

Achenwall, G (1767), *Prolegomena Iuris Naturalis*, Göttingen: Bossiegel.

Alexander, L (1996), 'The Moral Magic of Consent (II)', *Legal Theory*, 2 (3): 165–74.

Alexander, L (1998), 'Are Procedural Rights Derivative Substantive Rights?', *Law and Philosophy*, 17(1): 19–42.

Alexander, L (2000), 'Insufficient Concern: A Unified Conception of Criminal Culpability', *California Law Review*, 88(3): 931–54.

Alexander, L and Ferzan, KK (2009). *Crime and Culpability: A Theory of Criminal Law*, New York: Cambridge University Press.

Allan, TRS (2001), *Constitutional Justice*, Oxford: Oxford University Press.

Altenhain, K (2002), *Das Anschlußdelikt*, Tübingen: Mohr Siebeck.

Amelung, K (1972), *Rechtsgüterschutz und Schutz der Gesellschaft*, Frankfurt aM: Athenäum.

Anderson, E (2017), *Private Government: How Employers Rule Our Lives (and Why We Don't Talk about It)*, New Jersey: Princeton University Press.

Antill, G (2022), 'Fitting the Model Penal Code into a Reasons-Responsiveness Conception of Subjective Culpability', *Yale Law Journal*, 131(4): 1346–84.

Arel, A (2005), 'Theories of Rights', in MP Golding and WA Edmundson (eds), *The Blackwell Guide to the Philosophy of Law and Legal Theory*, 191–206, Oxford: Blackwell.

Arendt, H (1973), *The Origins of Totalitarianism*, San Diego, CA: Harvest.

Arendt, H ([1968] 2006) 'What is Authority?' in H Arendt (ed), *Between Past and Future: Eight Exercises in Political Thought*, 91–140, New York: Penguin Books.

Aristotle (1985), *Nicomachean Ethics*, trans. T Irwin, Indianapolis: Hackett Publishing.

Armgardt, M (2017), 'Law and Logic in Leibniz's Legal Philosophy', in D Krimphove and GM Lentner (eds), *Law and Logic*, 53–65, Berlin: Duncker & Humblot.

Ashworth, A (1986), 'Punishment and Compensation: Victims, Offenders and the State', *Oxford Journal of Legal Studies* 6(1): 86–122.

Ashworth, A (1993), 'Some Doubts About Restorative Justice', *Criminal Law Forum* 4(2): 277–306.

Ashworth, A (2006), 'Four Threats to the Presumption of Innocence', *International Journal of Evidence and Proof*, 10(4): 241–79.

Ashworth, A (2013), 'Is the Criminal Law a Lost Cause?' in A. Ashworth (ed), *Positive Obligations in Criminal Law*, 1–29, Oxford: Oxford University Press.

Ashworth, A, von Hirsch, A, and Shearing, C (2005). 'Restorative Justice: A "Making Amends" Model', in A Ashworth and A von Hirsch (eds), *Proportionate Sentencing: Exploring the Principles*, 110–30, New York: Oxford University Press.

Baker, DJ (2016), *The Right Not to Be Criminalized: Demarcating Criminal Law's Authority*, Abingdon: Routledge.

Baldwin, P (2021), *Command and Persuade. Crime, Law, and the State Across History*, Cambridge, MA: MIT Press.

Bandes, S (1996), 'Empathy, Narrative, and Victim Impact Statements', *University of Chicago Law Review*, 63(2): 361–412.

Barnett, RE (1977), 'Restitution: A New Paradigm for Criminal Justice', *Ethics*, 87(4): 279–301.

Baron, M (2005), 'Justification and Excuse', *Ohio State Journal of Criminal Law*, 2(4): 387–406.

Barton, S (2012), 'Strafrechtspflege und Kriminalpolitik in der viktimären Gesellschaft. Effekte, Ambivalenzen und Paradoxien', in S Barton and R Kölbel (eds), *Ambivalenzen der Opferzuwendung des Strafrechts*, 111–37, Baden-Baden: Nomos.

Bassiouni, MC (1993), 'Human Rights in the Context of Criminal Justice: Identifying International Procedural Protections and Equivalent Protections in National Constitutions', *Duke Journal of Comparative and International Law*, 3(2): 235–97.

Bayles, M (1974), 'Criminal Paternalism', in JR Pennock and JW Chapman (eds), *The Limits of Law*, 174–88, New York: Lieber-Atherton.

Beccaria, C and R Bellamy (1995), *On Crimes and Punishments and Other Writings*, Cambridge: Cambridge University Press.

Beetham, D (2012), *Democracy: A Beginner's Guide*, London: Simon and Schuster.

Benhabib, S (1996), *Democracy and Difference: Contesting the Boundaries of the Political*, Princeton, NJ: Princeton University Press.

Benson, P (2019), *Justice in Transactions*, Cambridge, MA: Harvard University Press.

Bentham, J ([1789] 1970), *An Introduction to the Principles of Morals and Legislation*, ed. HLA Hart, London: Athlone Press.

Bentham, J ([1798] 1970), *Of Laws in General*, ed. HLA Hart, London: Athlone Press.

Bentham, J (1843a), 'Anarchical Fallacies', in J Bowring (ed), *The Works of Jeremy Bentham*, vol 2, 489–534, Edinburgh: W Tait.

Bentham, J (1843b), 'A General View of a Complete Code of Laws', in J Bowring (ed), *The Works of Jeremy Bentham*, vol 3, 154–210, Edinburgh: W Tait.

Bentham, J (1843c), 'Pannomial Fragments', in J Bowring (ed), *The Works of Jeremy Bentham*, vol 3, 211–30, Edinburgh: W Tait.

Berger, B (2014), 'Constitutional Principles', in MD Dubber and T Hörnle (eds), *The Oxford Handbook of Criminal Law*, 422–44, Oxford: Oxford University Press.

Bergelson, V (2009), *Victims' Rights and Victims' Wrongs: Comparative Liability in Criminal Law*, Stanford: Stanford University Press.

Bergelson, V (2014), 'The Meaning of Consent', *Ohio State Journal of Criminal Law*, 12(1): 171–80.

Bergstrøm, H, Evjetun, P, and Bendixen, M (2017), 'Punishment Justifications in Rape Cases: A Community Study', *Journal of Scandinavian Studies in Criminology and Crime* Prevention, 18(2): 123–40.

Berlin, I (1969), 'Two Concepts of Liberty', in I Berlin, *Four Essays on Liberty*, 118–172, London: Oxford University Press.

Berman, M (2021), 'Proportionality, Constraint, and Culpability', *Criminal Law and Philosophy*, 15(3): 373–391.

Bessler, JD (2023), 'The Philosophy of Punishment and the Arc of Penal Reform: From Ancient Lawgivers to the Renaissance and the Enlightenment, and through the Nineteenth Century', in MC Altman (ed), *The Palgrave Handbook on the Philosophy of Punishment*, 23–52, Cham: Palgrave Macmillan.

Bettinson, V and Bishop, S (2015), 'Is the Creation of a Discrete Offence of Coercive Control Necessary to Combat Domestic Violence?', *Northern Ireland Legal Quarterly*, 66(2): 179–97.

Beulke, W and Swoboda, S (2022), *Strafprozessrecht*, 16th edn, Heidelberg: CF Müller.

Binder, G (2016), *Criminal Law*, New York: Oxford University Press.

Binding, K (1872), *Die Normen und ihre Übertretung: eine Untersuchung über die rechtmäßige Handlung und die Arten des Delikts. Erster Band: Normen und Strafgesetze*, Leipzig: Wilhelm Engelmann.

Binding, K (1922), *Die Normen und ihre Übertretung, Band 1: Normen und Strafgesetze*, 4th edn, Leipzig: Wilhelm Engelmann.

Binding, K ([1922] 1965), *Die Normen und ihre Übertretung, Band 1: Normen und Strafgesetze*, 4th edn, Leipzig, Aalen: Scientia.

Bingham, L (2010a), 'The Uses of Tort', *Journal of European Tort Law*, 1(1): 3–15.

Bingham, T (2010b), *The Rule of Law*, London: Allen Lane.

Birks, P (1997), 'The Concept of a Civil Wrong', in D Owen (ed), *The Philosophical Foundations of Tort Law*, 34–35, Oxford: Clarendon Press.

Blackstone, W (1765–1769), *Commentaries on the Laws of England*, Oxford: Clarendon Press.

Blackstone, W (1813), *Commentaries on the Law of England in Four Books: With the Last Corrections of the Author*, vol 4, London: Apollo.

Bloom A (1987), *The Closing of the American Mind: How Higher Education Has Failed Democracy and Impoverished the Souls of Today's Students*, New York: Simon and Schuster.
Bodin, J (1576), *Les Six Livres de la République*, Paris: Du Puys.
Bogg, A (2017), 'Republican Non-Domination and Labour Law: New Normativity or Trojan Horse', *The International Journal of Comparative Labour Law and Industrial Relations*, 33(3): 391–417.
Bosniak, L (2000), 'Citizenship Denationalized', *Indiana Journal of Global Legal Studies*, 7(2): 476–509.
Bottke, W (2003), 'Das Straftaterfordernis der Rechtsgutsverletzung', in D. Dölling (ed), *Jus humanum: Grundlagen des Rechts und Strafrecht. Festschrift für Ernst-Joachim Lampe zum 70. Geburtstag*, 463–89, Berlin: Duncker & Humblot.
Bottoms, A (1995), 'The Philosophy and Politics of Punishment and Sentencing', in C Clarkson and R Morgan (eds), *The Politics of Sentencing Reform*, 17–50, London: Clarendon Press.
Bowden, P, Henning, T, and Plater, D (2014), 'Balancing Fairness to Victims, Society and Defendants in the Cross-Examination of Vulnerable Witnesses: An Impossible Triangulation? *Melbourne University Law Review*, 37(3): 539–84.
Braddick, MJ (2000), *State Formation in Early Modern England*, Cambridge: Cambridge University Press.
Brake, E (2023), 'Emotional Abuse and the Law', in D Sobel, P Vallentyne and S Wall (eds) *Oxford Studies in Political Philosophy*, vol 1, 34–64, Oxford: Oxford University Press.
Braithewaite, J and Pettit, P (1990), *Not Just Deserts: A Republican Theory of Criminal Justice*, Oxford: Calderon Press.
Braithwaite, J (1999), 'A Future Where Punishment is Marginalized: Realistic or Utopian?', *UCLA Law Review*, 46(6): 1727–50.
Brett, AS (1997), *Liberty, Right and Nature: Individual Rights in Later Scholastic Thought*, Cambridge: Cambridge University Press.
Bricola, F (1974), *Teoria generale del reato, Estratto dal "Novissimo digesto italiano"*, Turin: UTET.
Brink, DO and Nelkin, DK (2013), 'Fairness and the Architecture of Responsibility', in D. Schoemaker (ed), *Oxford Studies in Agency and Responsibility*, vol 1, 284–313. Oxford: Oxford University Press.
Bronsther, J (2021), 'The Corrective Justice Theory of Punishment', *Virginia Law Review*, 107(2): 227–79.
Brudner, A (2008), *Punishment and Freedom*, Oxford: Oxford University Press.
Brudner, A (1995), *The Unity of the Common Law: Studies in Hegelian Jurisprudence*, Berkley: University of California Press.
Bullock, E (2018), 'Valid Consent', in A Müller and P Schaber (eds) *The Routledge Handbook of the Ethics of Consent*, 86–95, New York: Routledge.
Bung, J (2016), 'Sprachperformanz als Grundlage des Gesellschaftsvertrags', in L Bülow, J Bung, Jochen, R Harnisch, and R Wernsmann (eds), *Performativität in Sprache und Recht*, 63–77, Berlin: de Gruyter.
Bung, J and Abraham, M (2020), 'Sprachphilosophie: Davidson und Brandom', in S Buckel, R Christensen, and A Fischer-Lescano, *Neue Theorie des Rechts*, 87–103, 3rd edn, Tübingen: Mohr Siebeck.
Burghardt, B (2018), *Zufall und Kontrolle*, Tübingen: Mohr Siebeck.
Bussani, M, Sebok, AJ, and Infantino, M (2022), 'Negligence (and Strict Liability)', in M Bussani, AJ Sebok and M Infantino (eds), *Common Law and Civil Law Perspectives on Tort Law*, 21–50, Oxford: Oxford University Press.
Calabresi, G (1965), 'The Decision for Accidents: An Approach to Nonfault Allocation of Costs', *Harvard Law Review*, 78(4): 713–45.
Campbell, T (2006), *Rights: A Critical Introduction*, London: Routledge.
Cane, P (2001), 'Distributive Justice in Tort Law', *New Zealand Law Review*, 401(4): 413.
Cane, P (2002), *Responsibility in Law and Morality*, Oxford: Hart Publishing.
Casey, J (1990), *Pagan Virtue: An Essay in Ethics*, Oxford: Oxford University Press.
Cassidy, RM (2021), 'Character, Credibility, and Rape Shield Rules', *Georgetown Journal of Law & Public Policy*, 19(1): 145–76.

Cavadino, M and Dignan, J (1997), 'Reparation, Retribution and Rights', *International Review of Victimology*, 4(4): 233–53.
Chamallas, M (2000), 'Vanished from the First Year: Lost Torts and Deep Structures in Tort Law', in J Balkan and S Levinson (eds) *Legal Cannons*, 104–29, New York: New York University Press.
Chan, W and Simester, AP (2005), 'Duress, Necessity: How Many Defences', *King's College Law Journal*, 16(1): 121–31.
Chiao, V (2016), 'Two Conceptions of the Criminal Law', in C Flanders and Z Hoskins (eds), *The New Philosophy of Criminal Law*, 19–36, London: Rowmann & Littlefield.
Chiao, V (2019), *Criminal Law in the Age of the Administrative State*, Oxford: Oxford University Press.
Christie, N (1977), 'Conflicts as Property', *The British Journal of Criminology*, 17(1): 1–15.
Chwang, E (2009), 'A Defense of Subsequent Consent', *Journal of Social Philosophy*, 40(1): 119–31.
Clark Miller, S (2022), 'Toward a Relational Theory of Harm: on the Ethical Implications of Childhood Psychological Abuse', *Journal of Global Ethics*, 18(1): 15–31.
Collins, JB (1997), 'State Building in Early Modern Europe: The Case of France', *Modern Asian Studies*, 31(3): 603–33.
Corbin, AL (1920/1921), 'Jural Relations and Their Classification', *Yale Law Journal*, 20(3): 226.
Cornwall, A and Gaverta, J (2001), 'Bridging the Gap: Citizenship, Participation and Accountability', *PLA Notes*, 40: 32–35.
Coleman, J (1988), 'The Structure of Tort Law', *Yale Law Journal*, 97(6): 1233–53.
Coleman, J (1992), *Risks and Wrongs*, Oxford: Oxford University Press.
Coleman, J (2001), *The Practice of Principle: In Defence of a Pragmatist Approach to Legal Theory*, Oxford: Oxford University Press.
Crawford, A and Goodey, J (2000), *Integrating a Victim Perspective within Criminal Justice. International Debates*, Abingdon: Routledge.
Currie, D (1986), 'Positive and Negative Constitutional Rights', *University of Chicago Law Review*, 53(3): 864–90.
Coca-Vila, I (2023), 'Demokratisierung des Strafrechts? Zur Rolle der Strafrechtswissenschaft in der demokratischen Gesetzgebung', in L Staffler, G Ege, O Jany, L Lichtenberger, A Payer, L Ranzoni, F Reinicke, T Schweiger and D Tsilikis (eds), *Strafrecht und Demokratie*, 79–107, Baden-Baden: Nomos.
Coca-Vila, I (2016), *La colisión de deberes en Derecho penal, Concepto y fundamentos de solución*, Barcelona: Atelier.
Coenen, DT (2017), 'Freedom of Speech and the Criminal Law', *Boston University Law Review*, 97(4): 1533–1606.
Coleman, M (2020), 'The Tension Between the Presumption of Innocence and Victims' Participation Rights at the International Criminal Court', *International Criminal Law Review* 20(2): 371–93.
Coleman, M (2021), *The Presumption of Innocence in International Human Rights and Criminal Law*, Abingdon: Routledge.
Cotterrell, R (1995), *Law's Community*, Oxford: Oxford University Press.
Cottingham, J (1979), 'Varieties of Retribution', *The Philosophical Quarterly*, 29(116): 238–46.
Coughlin, AM (1994), 'Excusing Women', *California Law Review*, 82(1): 1–94.
Crown Prosecution Service (2018), *Code for Crown Prosecutors*. Available at: www.cps.gov.uk/publication/code-crown-prosecutors.
Cruft, R (2005), 'Rights: Beyond Interest and Will Theory', *Law and Philosophy*, 23(4): 347–97.
Crummey, C (2020), 'Why Fair Procedures Always Make a Difference', *Modern Law Review*, 83(6): 1221–45.
Dagger, R (2011), 'Republicanism and the Foundations of Criminal Law', in A Duff and S Green (eds), *Philosophical Foundations of Criminal Law*, 44–66, Oxford: Oxford University Press.
Daly, K (2017), 'Sexual Violence and Victims' Justice Interests', in E Zinstagg and M Keenan (eds), *Restorative Responses to Sexual Violence*, 108–139, Abingdon: Routledge.
Dam, CV (2013), 'Strict Liability', in C van Dam (ed), *European Tort Law*, 297–306, Oxford: Oxford University Press.

Damm, AP and Gorinas, C (2020), 'Prison as a Criminal School: Peer Effects and Criminal Learning Behind Bars', *The Journal of Law and Economics*, 63(1): 149–80.
Dan-Cohen, M (2002). 'Defending Dignity', in M Dan-Cohen (ed), *Harmful Thoughts: Essays on Law, Self, and Morality*, 150–71, Princeton, NJ: Princeton University Press.
Dan-Cohen, M (2006/2007), 'Thinking Criminal Law', *Cardozo Law Review*, 28(6): 2419–426.
Dan-Cohen, M (2014), 'Dignity, Crime, and Punishment: A Kantian Perspective', in MD Dubber (ed), *Foundational Texts in Modern Criminal Law*, 101–18, Oxford: Oxford University Press.
Darwall, SL (2006), *The Second-Person Standpoint: Morality, Respect, and Accountability*, Cambridge, MA: Harvard University Press.
Darwall, SL (2013a), 'Authority and Second-Personal Reason for Acting', in SL Darwall (ed), *Morality, Authority and Law: Essays in Second-Personal Ethics I*, 135–50, Oxford: Oxford University Press.
Darwall, SL (2013b), 'Morality and Principle', in SL Darwall (ed), *Morality, Authority and Law: Essays in Second-Personal Ethics I*, 73–90, Oxford: Oxford University Press.
Darwall, SL (2013c), 'Bipolar Obligation', in SL Darwall (ed), *Morality, Authority and Law: Essays in Second-Personal Ethics I*, 20–39, Oxford: Oxford University Press.
Darwall, SL (2013d), 'Law and the Second-Person Standpoint', in SL Darwall (ed), *Morality, Authority and Law: Essays in Second-Personal Ethics I*, 168–78, Oxford: Oxford University Press.
Davidov, G (2017), 'Subordination vs Domination: Exploring the Differences', *The International Journal of Comparative Labour Law and Industrial Relations*, 33(3): 365–89.
Davidov, G and Langille, B (2011), *The Idea of Labor Law*, Oxford: Oxford University Press.
de Tocqueville, A (1981), *De la Démocratie en Amérique*, vol 1, Paris: Flammarion.
Deutsch, E (1976), *Haftungsrecht*, Cologne: Heymanns.
Dearing, A (2017), *Justice for Victims of Crime: Human Dignity as the Foundation of Criminal Justice in Europe*, Basel: Springer.
Demertzis, N (2006), 'Emotions and Populism', in S Clarke, P Hoggett and S Thompson (eds), *Emotion, Politics and Society*, 103–122, London: Palgrave Macmillan.
Devlin, P (1965), *The Enforcement of Morals*, New York: Oxford University Press.
Doak, J (2008), *Victims' Rights, Human Rights, and Criminal Justice: Reconceiving the Role of Third Parties*, London: Bloomsbury Publishing.
Doak, J (2005), 'Victims' Rights in Criminal Trials: Prospects for Participation', *Journal of Law and Society*, 32(2): 294–316.
Dolinko, D (2003), 'Restorative Justice and the Justification of Punishment', *Utah Law Review*, 2003(1): 319–42.
Dolinko, D (2011), 'Punishment', in J Deigh and D Dolinko (eds), *The Oxford Handbook of Philosophy of Criminal Law*, 403–40, Oxford: Oxford University Press.
Dripps, DA (1992), 'Beyond Rape: An Essay on the Difference between the Presence of Force and the Absence of Consent', *Columbia Law Review*, 92(7): 1780–1809.
Dsouza, M (2015), 'Criminal Culpability After the Act', *King's College Law Journal*, 26(3): 440–62.
Dsouza, M (2017), *Rationale-based Defences in Criminal Law*, Oxford: Hart Publishing.
Dsouza, M (2024), 'Justifications and Rights-Displacements' *Criminal Law and Philosophy*, 18: 519–535.
Duarte d'Almeida, L (2015), *Allowing for Exceptions: A Theory of Defences and Defeasibility in Law*, Oxford: Oxford University Press.
Dubber, MD (1994), 'Rediscovering Hegel's Theory of Crime and Punishment: Hegel's Political Philosophy', *Michigan Law Review*, 92(6): 1577–1621.
Dubber, MD (2004), 'A Political Theory of Criminal Law: Autonomy and the Legitimacy of State Punishment'. Available at: https://dx.doi.org/10.2139/ssrn.529522.
Dubber, MD (2005a), 'Theories of Crime and Punishment in German Criminal Law', *American Journal of Comparative Law*, 53(3): 679–707.
Dubber, MD (2005b), *The Police Power: Patriarchy and the Foundations of American Government*, New York: Columbia University Press.
Dubber, MD (2010), 'Criminal Law between Public and Private Law', in RA Duff, L Farmer, SE Marshall, M Renzo and V Tadros (eds), *The Boundaries of Criminal Law*, 191–213, Oxford: Oxford University Press.

Dubber, MD (2018), *The Dual Penal State: The Crisis of Criminal Law in Comparative-Historical Perspective*, Oxford: Oxford University Press.

du Bois-Pedain, A (2014), 'The Place of Criminal Law Theory in the Constitutional State', in AP Simester, A du Bois-Pedain and U Neumann (eds), *Liberal Criminal Theory. Essays for Andreas von Hirsch*, 305–25, Portland: Hart Publishing.

Duff, RA (1996), *Criminal Attempts*, Oxford: Clarendon Press.

Duff, RA (2001), *Punishment, Communication, and Community, Studies in Crime and Public Policy*, Oxford: Oxford University Press.

Duff, RA (2002), 'Rule-Violations and Wrongdoings' in S Shute and AP Simester (eds), *Criminal Law Theory: Doctrines of the General Part*, 47–74, Oxford: Oxford University Press.

Duff, RA (2003a), *Punishment, Communication, and Community*, Oxford: Oxford University Press.

Duff, RA (2003b), 'Restoration and Retribution', in A. von Hirsch, J.V. Roberts, A. Bottoms, K. Roach, M. Schiff (eds), *Restorative Justice and Criminal Justice: Competing or Reconcilable Paradigms?*, 43–60, Oxford: Hart Publishing.

Duff, RA (2007), *Answering for Crime*, Oxford: Hart Publishing.

Duff, RA (2009), *Answering for Crime*, Oxford: Hart Publishing.

Duff, RA (2010a), 'Towards a Theory of Criminal Law?', *Aristotelian Society Supplementary*, 84 (1): 1–28.

Duff, RA (2010b), 'Reply' in R Cruft, MH Kramer, and MR Reiff (eds), *Crime, Punishment, and Responsibility: The Jurisprudence of Antony Duff*, 360, Oxford: Oxford University Press.

Duff, RA (2011), 'Responsibility, Citizenship and Criminal Law', in RA Duff and SP Green (eds), *Philosophical Foundations of Criminal Law*, 125–148, Oxford: Oxford Univ. Press.

Duff, RA (2014a), 'Torts, Crimes and Vindication: Whose Wrong Is It?', in M Dyson (ed), *Unravelling Tort and Crime*, 146–73, Cambridge: Cambridge University Press.

Duff, RA (2014b), 'Towards a Modest Legal Moralism', *Criminal Law and Philosophy*, 8, 217–35.

Duff, RA (2018), *The Realm of Criminal Law*, Oxford: Oxford University Press.

Duff, RA (2018), 'Responsibility and Reciprocity', *Ethical Theory and Moral Practice*, 21: 775–87.

Duff, RA (2019), 'Moral and Criminal Responsibility: Answering and Refusing to Answer', *Oxford Studies in Agency and Responsibility*, 5: 165–90.

Duff, RA (2023), 'When Should We Plead Guilty?', in J Roberts and J Ryberg (eds), *Sentencing the Self-Convicted*, 15–33, Oxford: Hart Publishing.

Duff, RA Farmer, L, Marshall, SE, and Tadros, V (2007), *The Trial on Trial (3): Towards a Normative Theory of the Criminal Trial*, Oxford: Hart Publishing.

Duff RA, Farmer, L, Marshall, SE, Renzo, M, Tadros, V (eds) (2014), *Criminalization: The Political Morality of the Criminal Law*, Oxford: Oxford University Press.

Duff, RA and Green, S (2015), *Defining Crimes: Essays on The Special Part of the Criminal Law*, Oxford: Oxford University Press.

Duff, RA and Marshall, SE (2023), 'Reporting Crimes and Arresting Criminals: Citizens' Rights and Responsibilities Under Their Criminal Law', *Criminal Law and Philosophy*, 18: 557–77.

Duranti, M (2017), *The Conservative Human Rights Revolution*, Oxford: Oxford University Press.

Dworkin, G (1983), 'Paternalism', in R. Sartorius (ed), *Paternalism*, 19–34, Minneapolis: University of Minnesota Press.

Dworkin, G (1988), *The Theory and Practice of Autonomy*, Cambridge: Cambridge University Press.

Dworkin, G (2011), 'The Limits of the Criminal Law', in J Deigh and D Dolinko (eds), *The Oxford Handbook of Philosophy of Criminal Law*, 3–16, Oxford: Oxford University Press.

Dworkin, R (1966), 'Lord Devlin and the Enforcement of Morals', *The Yale Law Journal*, 75(6): 986–1005.

Dworkin, R (1985), *A Matter of Principle*, Cambridge, MA: Harvard University Press.

Dyson, M (2014), 'Ligations Divide and Conquer: Using Legal Domains in Comparative Legal Studies', in G Helleringer and K Purnhagen (eds), *Towards a European Legal Culture*, 131–54, Oxford: CH Beck, Hart, Nomos.

Dyson, M (ed) (2015), *Comparing Tort and Crime: Learning from Across and Within Legal Systems*, Cambridge: Cambridge University Press.

Dyson, M (2021), 'Age Before Beauty; Pearls Before Swine: When the Criminal Law's Content Gives Way', in M Engelhart, H Kudlich, and B Vogel (eds), *Digitalisierung, Globalisierung und Risikoprävention: Festschrift für Ulrich Sieber zum 70. Geburtstag*, 15–25, Berlin: Duncker & Humblot.

Edmond, G (2017), 'Judging Facts: Managing Expert Knowledges in Legal Decision-Making', in G Edmond (ed), *Expertise in Regulation and Law*, 136–65, Abingdon: Routledge.

Edmundson, WA (2012), *An Introduction to Rights*, 2nd edn, Cambridge University Press.

Edwards, JR and Simester, AP (2014), 'Prevention with a Moral Voice', in AP Simester, A du Bois-Pedain, and U Neumann (eds), *Liberal Criminal Theory: Essays for Andreas von Hirsch*, 43–66, Portland: Hart Publishing.

Ellis, A (1994), 'Rights and the Criminal Law', *Analysis*, 54(2), 79–83.

Emerson, RW (2015), 'Self-Reliance' in RA Bosco and J Yerson (eds), *Ralph Waldo Emerson: The Major Prose*, 127–51, Cambridge, MA: Harvard University Press.

Engländer, A (2015), 'Revitalisierung der materiellen Rechtsgutslehre durch das Verfassungsrecht?', *Zeitschrift für die gesamte Strafrechtswissenschaft*, 127(3): 616–34.

Engländer, A (2022), *Strafrecht Besonderer Teil 1. Straftaten gegen Persönlichkeits-und Gemeinschaftswerte*, 46th edn, Heidelberg: CF Müller.

Engle, K, Miller, Z and Davis, D (2016), *Anti-Impunity and the Human Rights Agenda*, Cambridge: Cambridge University Press.

Enneccerus, L and Nipperdey, HC (1959), *Allgemeiner Teil des Bürgerlichen Rechts*, 15th edn, Tübingen: Mohr Siebeck.

Eser, A (1976), 'Justification and Excuse', *American Journal of Comparative Law*, 24(4): 621–37.

Farmer, L (2011), 'Disgust, Respect, and the Criminalization of Offence', in R Cruft, M Kramer, and M Reiff (eds) *Crime, Punishment, and Responsibility: The Jurisprudence of Antony Duff*, 273–91, Oxford: Oxford University Press.

Farmer, L (2016), *Making the Modern Criminal Law*, Oxford: Oxford University Press.

Farmer, L (2017), *Making the Modern Criminal Law: Criminalization and Civil Order*, Oxford: Oxford University Press.

Farrell, DM (1985), 'The Justification of General Deterrence', *The Philosophical Review*, 94(3): 367–94.

Fassin, D (2018), *The Will to Punish*, ed. C Kutz, New York: Oxford University Press.

Feinberg, J (1965), 'The Expressive Function of Punishment', *The Monist*, 49(3): 397–423.

Feinberg, J (1966), 'Duties, Rights, and Claims', *American Philosophical Quarterly*, 3(2): 137–44.

Feinberg, J (1980), '*The Nature and Value of Rights', Rights, Justice and the Bounds of Liberty: Essays in Social Philosophy*, Princeton Series of Collected Essays, 143–58, Princeton, NJ: Princeton University Press.

Feinberg, J (1984), *The Moral Limits of the Criminal Law, Volume 1: Harm to Others*, Oxford: Oxford University Press.

Feinberg, J (1985), *The Moral Limits of the Criminal Law, Volume 2: Offense to Others*, Oxford: Oxford University Press.

Feinberg, J (1986a), *The Moral Limits of the Criminal Law, Volume 3: Harm to Self*, Oxford: Oxford University Press.

Feinberg, J (1986b), 'Voluntary Euthanasia and the Inalienable Right to Life', *Philosophy & Public Affairs*, 7 (2): 93–123.

Feinberg, J (1988), *The Moral Limits of the Criminal Law, Volume 4: Harmless Wrongdoing*, Oxford: Oxford University Press.

Ferber, S. (2016), 'Stärkung der Opfferrechte im Strafverfahren: Das 3. Opferrechtsreformgesetz', *Neue Juristische Wochenschrift*, 69(5): 279–82.

Feuerbach, JPA (1799), *Revision der Grundsätze und Grundbegriffe des positiven peinlichen Rechts*, Erfurt: Henningsche Buchhandlung.

Feuerbach, JPA (1801), *Lehrbuch des gemeinen in Deutschland geltenden Peinlichen Rechts*, Gießen: Georg Friedrich Heyer.

Finnis, J (2011), *Natural Law and Natural Rights*, 2nd edn, Oxford: Oxford University Press.

Fletcher, GP (1974), 'The Individualization of Excusing Conditions', *Southern California Law Review*, 47(4): 1269–309.

Fletcher, GP (1975), 'The Right Deed for the Wrong Reason: A Reply to Mr. Robinson', *UCLA Law Review*, 23(2): 293–321.

Fletcher, GP (1978), *Rethinking Criminal Law*, Boston: Little Brown and Co.

Fletcher, GP (1999), 'The Place of Victims in the Theory of Retribution', *Buffalo Criminal Law Review*, 3(1): 51–63.

Fletcher, GP (2010), 'Punishment and Responsibility', in D Patterson (ed), *A Companion to Philosophy of Law and Legal Theory*, 504–20, Chichester: Wiley Blackwell.

Flume, JW (2021), 'Strict Liability in Austrian and German Law: On the Concept of Strict Liability in the Age of Technological Advancement', *Journal of European Tort Law*, 12(3): 205–20.

Foucault, M (1975), *Surveiller et Punir*, Paris: Gallimard.

Foucault, M, Sennelart M, and Burchell, G (2007), *Security, Territory, Population: Lectures at the Collège de France 1977–78*, New York: Picador.

Fox-Decent, E and Criddle, E (2016), *Fiduciaries of Humanity: How International Law Constitutes Authority*, Oxford: Oxford University Press.

Fredman, S (2008), *Human Rights Transformed: Positive Rights and Positive Duties*, Oxford: Oxford University Press.

Friedman, DR and Robinson, JM (2014), 'Rebutting the Presumption: An Empirical Analysis of Parole Deferrals Under Marsy's Law', *Stanford Law Review*, 66(1): 173–216.

Frisch, W (2015), 'Strafe, Straftat und Straftatsystem im Wandel', *Goltdammer's Archiv für Strafrecht*, 162(2): 65–85.

Frisch, W (2019), 'Straftheorie, Verbrechensbegriff und Straftatsystem im Umbruch', *Goltdammer's Archiv für Strafrecht*, 166(3): 185–204.

Frydrych, D (2017), 'The Theories of Rights Debate', *The American Journal of Jurisprudence*, 62(2): 197–207.

Fuller, LL (1964), *The Morality of Law*, New Haven, CT: Yale University Press.

Gädeke, D (2020), 'Does a Mugger Dominate? Episodic Power and the Structural Dimension of Domination', *The Journal of Political Philosophy*, 28(2): 199–221.

Gallas W (1965), 'Gründe und Grenzen der Strafbarkeit. Gedanken zum Begriff des Verbrechens', in *Heidelberger Jahrbücher*, vol 9, 1–16, Berlin: Springer.

Gärditz, K (2010), 'Strafbegründung und Demokratieprinzip', *Der Staat*, 49(3): 331–67.

Gärditz, K (2015), *Staat und Strafrechtspflege*, Paderborn: Schöningh.

Gärditz, K (2016), 'Demokratizität des Strafrechts und Ultima Ratio-Grundsatz', *Juristenzeitung*, 71(13): 641–50.

Gardner, J and Shute, S (2000), 'The Wrongness of Rape', in J Gardner (ed), *Oxford Essays in Jurisprudence*, vol 4, 193–218, Oxford: Oxford University Press.

Gardner, J (2007a), *Offences and Defences*, Oxford: Oxford University Press.

Gardner, J (2007b), 'The Mark of Responsibility', in J. Gardner (ed), *Offences and Defences*, 177–200, Oxford: Oxford University Press.

Gardner, J (2007c), 'Crime: in Proportion and in Perspective', in *Offences and Defences*, 235–36. Oxford: Oxford University Press.

Gardner, J (2014), 'What is Tort Law For? Part 2: The Place of Distributive Justice' in J Oberdiek (ed) *Philosophical Foundations of the Law of Torts*, 334–53, Oxford: Oxford University Press.

Garkawe, S (1994), 'The Role of the Victim During Criminal Court Proceedings', *UNSW Law Journal*, 17(2): 595–616.

Garland, D (1985), *Punishment and Welfare: A History of Penal Strategies*, Aldershot: Ashgate Publishing.

Garland, D (2001), *The Culture of Control: Crime and Social Order in Contemporary Society*, Chicago: University of Chicago Press.

Garland, D (2018), 'The Rule of Law, Representational Struggles, and the Will to Punish', in C Kutz (ed), *The Will to Punish*, 154–68, New York: Oxford University Press.

Garvey, S (2003), 'Restorative Justice, Punishment, and Atonement', *Utah Law Review*, 2003(1): 303–18.

Gewirth, A (1986), 'Why Rights are Indispensable', *Mind*, 95(379), 329–44.

Göhler, J (2019), 'Victim Rights in Civil Law Jurisdictions', in DK Brown, JI Turner, and B Weisser (eds), *The Oxford Handbook of Criminal Process*, 267–88, Oxford: Oxford University Press.
Golash, D (2005), *The Case Against Punishment. Retribution, Crime Prevention, and the Law*, New York: New York University Press.
Goldberg, JCP (2015), 'Inexcusable Wrongs', *California Law Review*, 103(3): 467–512.
Goldberg, JCP and Zipursky, BC (2006), 'Seeing Tort Law from the Internal Point of View: Holmes and Hart on Legal Duties', *Fordham Law Review*, 75(3): 1563.
Goldberg, JCP and Zipursky, BC (2012), 'Rights and Responsibility', in Nolan, D and Robertson, A (eds), *The Law of Torts*, 251–74, Oxford: Hart Publishing.
Goldberg, JCP and Zipursky, BC (2020), *Recognizing Wrongs*, Cambridge, MA: Harvard University Press.
Gray, A (2021), *The Evolution from Strict Liability to Fault in the Law of Torts*, Oxford: Hart Publishing.
Green, L (2007), 'The Duty to Govern', *Legal Theory*, 13(3/4): 165–85.
Green, S (2007), *Lying, Cheating, and Stealing: A Moral Theory of White-Collar Crime*, Oxford: Oxford University Press.
Green, S (2017), 'Tax Evasion as Crime', in M Bhandari (ed), *Philosophical Foundations of Tax Law*, 57–78, Oxford: Oxford University Press.
Green, S (2020), *Criminalizing Sex: A Unified Liberal Theory*, New York: Oxford University Press.
Greenawalt, K (1984), 'The Perplexing Borders of Justification and Excuse', *Columbia Law Review*, 84(8): 1897–927.
Greenawalt, K (1986), 'Distinguishing Justifications from Excuses', *Law and Contemporary Problems*, 49(3): 89–108.
Greenberg, J (1984), 'The Victim in Historical Perspective: Some Aspects of the English Experience', *Journal of Social Issues*, 40(1): 77–102.
Gregg, M and Seigworth, G (2010), *The Affect Theory Reader*, Durham NC: Duke University Press.
Griffin, J (1986), *Well-Being: Its Meaning, Measurement and Moral Importance*, Oxford: Clarendon Press.
Griffin, J (2008), *On Human Rights*, Oxford: Oxford University Press.
Grosse-Wilde, T (2018), 'Die Vielheit der Normen(-theorien) im englischsprachigen und deutschsprachigen Rechtsdiskurs', in A Schneider and M Wagner (eds), *Normentheorie und Strafrecht*, 215–43, Baden-Baden: Nomos.
Grotius, H (1680), *De jure belli ac pacis libri tres*, Den Haag: Arnold Leers.
Grünewald, A (2010), *Das vorsätzliche Tötungsdelikt*, Tübingen: Mohr Siebeck.
Günther, K (2000), 'De la vulneración de un derecho a la infracción de un deber. ¿Un 'cambio de paradigma' en el Derecho penal?', in Instituto de Ciencias Criminales de Frankfurt (ed), *La insostenible situación del Derecho Penal*, 489–505, Granada: Comares.
Günther, K (2002), 'Die symbolisch-expressive Bedeutung der Strafe: Eine neue Straftheorie jenseits von Vergeltung und Prävention', in C Prittwitz and K Lüderssen (eds), *Festschrift für Klaus Lüderssen zum 70. Geburtstag*, 205–19, Baden-Baden: Nomos.
Günther, K (2014), 'Criminal Law, Crime and Punishment as Communication', in AP Simester, A, du Bois-Pedain, and U Neumann (eds), *Liberal Criminal Theory: Essays for Andreas von Hirsch*, 123–39, Oxford: Hart Publishing.
Günther, K (2016), '(Bedrohte) individuelle Freiheiten im aufgeklärten Strafrecht: Welche Freiheiten?', *Kritische Justiz*, 49(4): 520–34.
Gur-Arye, M (2003), 'Legitimating Official Brutality: Can the War against Terror Justify Torture?'. Available at: https://dx.doi.org/10.2139/ssrn.391580.
Gur-Arye, M (2011), 'Justifying the Distinction Between Justifications and Power (Justifications vs. Power)', *Criminal Law and Philosophy*, 5(3): 293–313.
Haas, V (2002), *Kausalität und Rechtsverletzung. Ein Beitrag zu den Grundlagen strafrechtlicher Erfolgshaftung am Beispiel des Abbruchs rettender Kausalverläufe*, Berlin: Duncker & Humblot.
Hall, C (2005), *The Trouble with Passion: Political Theory Beyond the Reign of Reason*, London: Routledge.

Hall, M (2007), 'The Use and Abuse of Special Measures: Giving Victims the Choice?', *Journal of Scandinavian Studies in Criminology and Crime Prevention*, 8(1): 33–53.
Halperin, J-L (2010), 'French Doctrinal Writing' in N Jansen (ed), *The Development and Making of Legal Doctrine*, 73–95, Cambridge: Cambridge University Press.
Hampton, J (1988), 'The Retributive Idea', in JG Murphy and J Hampton (eds), *Forgiveness and Mercy*, 111–61, Cambridge: Cambridge University Press.
Harcourt, BE (1999), 'The Collapse of the Harm Principle', *Journal of Criminal Law and Criminology*, 90(1): 109–94.
Harel, A (2015), 'The Duty to Criminalize', *Law and Philosophy*, 34(1): 1–22.
Hart, HLA (1948), 'The Ascription of Responsibility and Rights', in S Brewer (ed), *Precedents, Statutes and Analysis of Legal Concepts*, 171–94, London: Routledge.
Hart, HLA (1955), 'Are There Any Natural Rights?', *The Philosophical Review*, 64: 175–91.
Hart, HLA (1961), *The Concept of Law*, Oxford: Clarendon Press.
Hart, HLA (1963), *Law, Liberty and Morality*, Oxford: Oxford University Press.
Hart, HLA (1964), *The Morality of the Criminal Law: Two Lectures*, Jerusalem: Magnes Press.
Hart, HLA (1968), *Punishment and Responsibility*, Oxford: Oxford University Press.
Hart, HLA (1971), 'Bentham's Of Law in General', *Rechtstheorie*, 2 (1–2): 5–66.
Hart, HLA (1973), 'Bentham on Legal Rights' in AWB Simpson (ed), *Oxford Essays in Jurisprudence (Second Series)*, 171–201, Oxford: Oxford University Press.
Hart, HLA (1982), 'Legal Rights', in HLA Hart (ed) *Essays on Bentham: Studies in Jurisprudence and Social Philosophy*, 162–93. New York: Clarendon Press.
Hartman, C (2023), 'Don't Say Gay: How Laws are Tools for Hate, Discrimination, and Violence', *Electronic Theses, Projects, and Dissertations*. Available at: https://scholarworks.lib.csusb.edu/etd/1572.
Hasan, R (2021), 'Republicanism and Structural Domination', *Pacific Philosophical Quarterly*, 102(2): 292–319.
Hassemer, W (1973), *Theorie und Soziologie des Verbrechens. Ansätze zu einer praxisorientierten Rechtsgutslehre*, Frankfurt aM: Suhrkamp.
Hassemer, W (1990), *Einführung in die Grundlagen des Strafrechts*, Munich: Beck.
Hassemer, W and Neumann, U (2017), 'Vorbemerkungen zu § 1' in U Kindhäuser, U Neumann, and H-U Paeffgen (eds), *Strafgesetzbuch*, 5th edn, Baden-Baden: Nomos.
Hegel, GWF ([1821] 1986), *Grundlinien der Philosophie des Rechts*, eds E Moldenhauer and K Michel, vol 7, Frankfurt aM: Suhrkamp.
Hegel, GWF ([1821] 1991), *Elements of the Philosophy of Right*, ed. AW Wood, trans HB Nisbet, Cambridge: Cambridge University Press.
Hellwege, P and Wittig, P (2015), 'Delictual Liability and Criminal Accountability in German Law', in M Dyson (ed), *Comparing Tort and Crime*, 123–72, Cambridge: Cambridge University Press.
Herstein, O (2012), 'Defending the Right to Do Wrong', *Law and Philosophy*, 31(3): 343–65.
Herzog, D (1989), *Happy Slaves: A Critique of Consent Theory*, Chicago: University of Chicago Press.
Hewart, G (1929), *The New Despotism*, London: Benn.
Hilgendorf, E (2020), 'System-und Begriffsbildung im Strafrecht', in E Hilgendorf, H Kudlich, and B Valerius (eds), *Handbuch des Strafrechts. Band 2: Strafrecht Allgemeiner Teil I*, 3–37, Heidelberg: CF Müller.
Hillenkamp, T (1981), *Vorsatztat und Opferverhalten*, Göttingen: Schwartz.
Hindess, B (2002), 'Neo-liberal Citizenship', *Citizenship Studies*, 6(2): 127–43.
Hirsch, P-A (2017), *Freiheit und Staatlichkeit bei Kant: Die Autonomietheoretische Begründung von Recht und Staat und das Widerstandsproblem*, Berlin: De Gruyter.
Hirsch, P-A (2020), 'Verletzung in eigenen Rechten: Zur strafrechtsdogmatischen Stellung des Verletzten', in M Abraham, JC Bublitz, J Geneuss, P Krell and, K Wegner (eds), *Verletzte im Strafrecht*, 31–52, Baden-Baden: Nomos.
Hirsch, P-A (2021), *Das Verbrechen als Rechtsverletzung. Subjektive Rechte im Strafrecht*, Duncker & Humblot: Berlin.

Hirst, P (2013), *Associative Democracy: New Forms of Economic and Social Governance*, New Jersey: John Wiley & Sons.
Ho, HL (2010), 'Liberalism and the Criminal Trial', *The Sydney Law Review*, 32(2): 269–87.
Ho, HL (2016), 'The Criminal Trial, the Rule of Law and the Exclusion of Unlawfully Obtained Evidence', *Criminal Law and Philosophy*, 10: 109–31.
Hobbes, T ([1651] 1997), *Leviathan*, ed. RE Flathman and D Johnston, London: WW Norton.
Hohfeld, WN (1913/1917), 'Fundamental Legal Conceptions as Applied to Judicial Reasoning', *The Yale Law Journal*, 26(8): 710–70.
Holder, RL (2017a), 'Seeing the State: Human Rights Violations of Victims of Crime and Abuse of Power', in L Weber, E Fishwick, and M Marmo (eds), *The Routledge Handbook of Criminology and Human Rights*, 419–28, Abingdon: Routledge.
Holder, RL (2017b), 'Victims, Legal Consciousness, and Legal Mobilisation', in A Deckert and R Sarre (eds), *The Palgrave Handbook of Australian and New Zealand Criminology, Crime and Justice*, 649–64, London: Palgrave Macmillan.
Holder, RL (2018a), *Just Interests: Victims, Citizens and The Potential for Justice*, Cheltenham: Edward Elgar.
Holder, RL (2018b), 'Untangling the Meanings of Justice: A Longitudinal Mixed Methods Study', *Journal of Mixed Methods Research*, 12(2): 204–20.
Holder, RL (2023), 'Beyond Vulnerability: Reconceiving Victims as Citizens', in G Varona Martínez (ed), *Victimology and Violence: Connecting with Victims*, 35–54, Cizur Menor: Aranzadi Publishing.
Holder, RL and Kirchengast, T (2021), 'Victims' Rights Commissioners: Public Interest Entities in a Regulatory Regime', *International Journal of Comparative and Applied Criminal Justice*, 45(1): 67–87.
Holder, RL Kirchengast, T, and Cassell, P (2021), 'Transforming Crime Victims' Rights: From Myth to Reality', *International Journal of Comparative and Applied Criminal Justice*, 45(1): 1–13.
Holz, W (2007), *Justizgewähranspruch des Verbrechensopfers*, Berlin: Duncker & Humblot.
Honoré, T (1961), 'Ownership', in AG Guest (ed), *Oxford Essays in Jurisprudence*, 107–47, Oxford: Oxford University Press.
Honoré, T (1995), 'The Morality of Tort Law: Questions and Answers' in D Owen (ed), *Philosophical Foundations of Tort Law*, 73–96, Oxford: Clarendon Press.
Honoré, T (1998), 'Responsibility and Luck: the Moral Basis of Strict Liability', *Law Quarterly Review*, 104(3): 530–53.
Hörnle, T (2005), *Grob Anstößiges Verhalten: Strafrechtlicher Schutz von Moral, Gefühlen und Tabus*, Frankfurt aM: Vittorio Klostermann.
Hörnle, T (2006), 'Die Rolle des Opfers in der Straftheorie und im materiellen Strafrecht', in *Juristenzeitung*, 61(19): 950–58.
Hörnle, T (2014), 'Theories of Criminalization', in MD Dubber and T Hörnle (eds), *The Oxford Handbook of Criminal Law*, 679–701, Oxford: Oxford University Press.
Hörnle, T (2014), 'Rights of Others' in Criminalisation Theory', in AP Simester, A du Bois-Pedain, and U Neumann (eds), *Liberal Criminal Theory Essays for Andreas von Hirsch*, 169–86, Oxford: Hart Publishing.
Hörnle, T (2016), 'Theories of Criminalization: Comments on AP Simester/Andreas von Hirsch: Crimes, Harms and Wrongs. On the Principles of Criminalisation', *Criminal Law and Philosophy*, 10: 301–14.
Hörnle, T (2017), 'Menschenrechte als universale Rechte?', in K. Seelmann (ed), *Menschenrechte: Begründung - Universalisierbarkeit - Genese*, 23–40, Berlin: Walter de Gruyter.
Hörnle, T (2017), *Straftheorien*, 2nd edn, Tübingen: Mohr Siebeck.
Hörnle, T (2018), 'Rape as Non-Consensual Sex', in A Müller and P Schaber (eds) *The Routledge Handbook of the Ethics of Consent*, 235–46, New York: Routledge.
Hörnle, T (2019a), 'One Master Principle of Criminalization: Or Several Principles?', *Law, Ethics and Philosophy*, 7: 208–20.

Hörnle, T (2019b), 'The Role of Victims' Rights in Punishment Theory', in A Bois-Pedain and AE Bottoms (eds), *Penal Censure: Engagements Within and Beyond Desert Theory*, 207–26, Oxford: Hart Publishing.
Hörnle, T (2021), 'Criminal Law in Multicultural Societies', in K Ghanayim and Y Shany (eds), *The Quest for Core Values in the Application of Legal Norms*, 85–101, Cham: Springer.
Horder, J (2018), *Criminal Misconduct in Office: Law and Politics*, Oxford: Oxford University Press.
Horder, J (2021), 'Criminal Law and Republican Liberty: Philip Pettit's Account', *Criminal Law and Philosophy* 16(1): 193–213.
Horder, J and Ashworth, A (2022), *Ashworth's Principles of Criminal Law*, 10th edn, Oxford: Oxford University Press.
Hoskins, Z and Duff, A (2022), 'Legal Punishment', in EN Zalta (ed), *The Stanford Encyclopedia of Philosophy* (Summer 2022 Edition).
Hoyle, C and Zedner, L (2007), 'Victims, Victimization, and Criminal Justice', in M Maguire, R Morgan, and R Reiner (eds), *The Oxford Handbook of Criminology*, 4th edn, 461–95, Oxford: Oxford University Press.
Hruschka, J (1977), 'Extrasystematische Rechtfertigungsgründe', in H-H Jescheck (ed), *Festschrift Für Eduard Dreher: Zum 70. Geburtstag Am 29. April 1977*, 189–210, Berlin: De Gruyter.
Hurd, H (1996), 'The Moral Magic of Consent', *Legal Theory*, 2(2), 121–46.
Hurd, H (2004), Blaming the Victim: A Response to the Proposal that Criminal Law Recognize a General Defense of Contributory Responsibility, *Buffalo Criminal Law Review*, 8(2): 503–22.
Husak, DN (1989), 'Justifications and the Criminal Liability of Accessories', *Journal of Criminal Law and Criminology*, 80(2): 491–520.
Husak, DN (1999), 'Conflicts of Justifications', *Law and Philosophy*, 18(1): 41–68.
Husak, DN (2005), 'Applying Ultima Ratio: A Skeptical Assessment', *Ohio State Journal of Criminal Law*, 2(2): 535–45.
Husak, DN (2005a), 'On the Supposed Priority of Justification to Excuse' *Law & Philosophy*, 24(6): 557–94.
Husak, DN (2005b), 'Criminal Law Theory', in MP Golding and WA Edmundson (eds), *The Blackwell Guide to the Philosophy of Law and Legal Theory*, 107–21, Oxford: Blackwell.
Husak, DN (2008), *Overcriminalization: The Limits of the Criminal Law*, Oxford: Oxford University Press.
Husak, DN (2010), 'Paternalism and Consent', in FG Miller, A Wertheimer (eds), *The Ethics of Consent*, 107–30, New York: Oxford University Press.
Husak, DN (2013), 'Retributivism in Extremis', in *Law and Philosophy*, 32(1): 3–31.
Husak, DN (2016), *Ignorance of the Law: A Philosophical Inquiry*. Oxford: Oxford University Press.
Husak, DN (2023), 'Six Questions About Overcriminalization', *Annual Review of Criminology*, 6: 265–84.
Indermaur, D and Roberts, L (2009), 'Confidence in the Criminal Justice System', in *Trends and Issues in Crime and Criminal Justice*, vol 387, Canberra: Australian Institute of Criminology.
Isin, EF (2009), 'Citizenship in Flux: The Figure of the Activist Citizen', *Subjectivity*, 27: 367–88.
Isin, EF and Nielson, GM (2008), 'Introduction: Acts of Citizenship', in EF Isin and GM Nielson (eds), *Acts of Citizenship*, 1–12, London: Zed Books.
Jackson, BS (1985), *Semiotics and Legal Theory*, London: Routledge & Kegan Paul.
Jakobs, G ([2000] 2017), 'Strafrechtliche Zurechnung und die Bedingungen der Normgeltung', in M Pawlik (ed), *Günter Jakobs. Strafrechtswissenschaftliche Beiträge*, 163–79, Tübingen: Mohr Siebeck.
James, A (2007), 'Legal and Other Governance in Second-Person Perspective', *Loyola of Los Angeles Law Review*, 40(3): 911–38.
Jareborg, N (2005), 'Criminalization as Last Resort (Ultima Ratio)', *Ohio State Journal of Criminal Law* 2(2): 521–34.
Jiang, J (2021), 'The Eyes and Ears of the Authoritarian Regime: Mass Reporting in China', *Journal of Contemporary Asia*, 51(5): 828–47.
Joerden, JC (2012), 'Deontological Square, Hexagon, and Decagon: A Deontic Framework for Supererogation', *Logica Universalis*, 6, 201–16.

Johnston, D (2010), 'A History of Consent in Western Thought', in FG Miller and A Wertheimer (eds), *The Ethics of Consent*, 107–30, Oxford-New York: Oxford University Press.
Jones, P (1994), *Rights, Issues in Political Theory*, London: Macmillan.
Jones, W ([1828] 2007), *An Essay on the Law of Bailments*, ed. DN Ibbetson, Cardiff: Welsh Legal History Society.
Jung, H (2000), 'Zur Renaissance des Opfers: Ein Lehrstück kriminalpolitischer Zeitgeschichte', *Zeitschrift für Rechtspolitik*, 33(4): 159–63.
Kalinowski, G (1972), *La logique des normes*, Paris: Presses Universitaires de France.
Kamm, F (2002), 'Rights', in J Coleman and S Shapiro (eds), *The Oxford Handbook of Jurisprudence and Philosophy of Law*, 476–513, Oxford: Oxford University Press.
Kamm, F (2007), *Intricate Ethics: Rights, Responsibilities, and Permissible Harm*, Oxford: Oxford University Press.
Kant, I ([1785] 2016), 'Grundlegung zur Metaphysik der Sitten', in W Weischedel (ed), *Immanuel Kant Werkausgabe*, vol 7, 11–102, Frankfurt aM: Suhrkamp.
Kant, I ([1797] 1907), 'Metaphysik der Sitten', in Königlich Preußische Akademie der Wissenschaften (ed), *Kants Gesammelte Schriften*, vol. 6, 203–493, Berlin: Georg Reimer.
Kant, I ([1797] 1996), The Metaphysics of Morals, in MJ Gregor (ed) *The Cambridge Edition of the Works of Immanuel Kant: Practical Philosophy*, 353–605, Cambridge: Cambridge University Press.
Kardas, P (2019), *Zarządzanie konfliktem: Dlaczego w prawie karnym potrzebne jest umorzenie kompensacyjne*, Kraków: Krakowski Instytut Prawa Karnego Fundacja.
Katz, L (2023), 'How Victims Matter: Rethinking the Significance of the Victim in Criminal Theory', *University of Toronto Law Journal*, 73(3): 263–92.
Kearns, TA (1975), 'Rights, Benefits and Normative Systems', *Archiv für Rechts- und Sozialphilosophie* 61(4): 465–84.
Keedy, E (1949), 'History of the Pennsylvania Statute Creating Degrees of Murder', *University of Pennsylvania Law Review*, 97(6): 759–77.
Kelsen, H (1960), *Reine Rechtslehre*, 2nd edn, Vienna: Franz Deuticke.
Kelman, M (1981), 'Interpretive Construction in the Substantive Criminal Law', *Stanford Law Review*, 33(4): 591–673.
Khaitan, T and Steel, S (2022), 'Theorizing Areas of Law: A Taxonomy of Special Jurisprudence', *Legal Theory*, 28(4): 325–51.
Khaitan, T and Steel, S (2023), 'Areas of Law: Three Questions in Special Jurisprudence', *Oxford Journal of Legal Studies*, 42(1): 76–79.
Kindhäuser, U (2021), 'Zur "Drittwirkung" strafrechtlicher Verhaltensnormen', in U Kindhäuser (ed), *Analytische Strafrechtswissenschaft*, 481–98, Baden-Baden: Nomos.
Kirchengast, T (2006), *The Victim in Criminal Law and Justice*, New York: Palgrave Macmillan.
Kleinert, T (2008), *Persönliche Betroffenheit und Mitwirkung. Eine Untersuchung zur Stellung des Deliktsopfers im Strafrechtssystem*, Berlin: Duncker & Humblot.
Klepper, H (1996), 'Mandatory Rights and Compulsory Education', *Law and Philosophy*, 15(2): 149–58.
Kleinert, T (2008), *Persönliche Betroffenheit und Mitwirkung. Eine Untersuchung zur Stellung des Deliktsopfers im Strafrechtssystem*, Berlin: Duncker & Humblot.
Kleinig, J (1991), 'Punishment and Moral Seriousness', *Israel Law Review* 25(3–4): 401–21.
Kleinig, J (2008), *Ethics and Criminal Justice*, Cambridge: Cambridge University Press.
Kleinig, J (2010), 'The Nature of Consent', in FG Miller and A Wertheimer (eds) *The Ethics of Consent: Theory and Practice*, 3–24, Oxford: Oxford University Press.
Kleinig, J (2017), 'Paternalism and Human Dignity', *Criminal Law and Philosophy*, 11: 19–36.
Kleinig, J (2023), 'Punishment and Forgiveness', in MC Altman (ed), *The Palgrave Handbook on the Philosophy of Punishment*, 595–612, Cham: Palgrave Macmillan.
Kleinstuber, R, Zaykowski, H, and McDonough, C (2020), 'Ideal Victims' in Capital Penalty Hearings: An Assessment of Victim Impact Evidence and Sentencing Outcomes', *Journal of Crime and Justice*, 43(1): 93–109.
Kloepfer, M (2011), *Verfassungsrecht*, vol 1, Munich: CH Beck.

Koch, F (2018), 'Consent as Normative Power', in A Müller and P Schaber (eds), *The Routledge Handbook of the Ethics of Consent*, 32–42, New York: Routledge.

Kocourek, A (1920), 'The Hohfeld System of Fundamental Legal Concepts', *Illinois Law Review*, 15 (1): 24.

Kramer, MH, Simmonds, N, and Steiner, H (eds) (1998), *A Debate Over Rights*, Oxford: Oxford University Press.

Kramer, MH and Steiner, H (2007), 'Theories of Rights: Is There a Third Way', *Oxford Journal of Legal Studies*, 27(2): 281.

Królikowski, M (2005), *Sprawiedliwość karania w społeczeństwach liberalnych: Zasada proporcjonalności*, Warsaw: CH Beck.

Królikowski, M (2014), 'Wokół problematyki tzw. umorzenia restytucyjnego', in A Błachnio-Parzych, J Jakubowska-Hara, and H Kuczyńska (eds), *Problemy wymiaru sprawiedliwości karnej: Księga jubileuszowa Profesora Jana Skupińskiego*, 69–84, Warsaw: Wolters Kluwer Polska.

Kubiciel, M (2018), 'Kriminalpolitik und Strafrechtswissenschaft', *Juristenzeitung*, 73(4): 171–79.

Kubiciel, M, Löhnig, M, Pawlik, M, Stuckenberg, C-F, and Wohlers, W (eds) (2020), *Eine gewaltige Erscheinung des positiven Rechts. Karl Bindings Normen und Strafrechtstheorie*, Tübingen: Mohr Siebeck.

Kymlicka, W and Norman, W (1994), 'Return of the Citizen: A Survey of Recent Work on Citizenship Theory', *Ethics*, 104(2): 352–81.

Lacey, N (1995), 'Contingency and Criminalization.', in I Loveland (ed), *The Frontiers of Criminality*, 1–27, London: Sweet and Maxwell.

Lacey, N (2009), 'Historicising Criminalisation: Conceptual and Empirical Issues', *The Modern Law Review* 72(6): 936–60.

Lacey N, Wells, C, and Quick, O (2012), *Reconstructing Criminal Law*, Cambridge: Cambridge University Press.

Lagodny, O (2011), 'Basic Rights and Substantive Criminal Law: The Incest Case', *University of Toronto Law Journal*, 61(4): 761–81.

Lamond, G (2007), 'What Is a Crime?', *Oxford Journal of Legal Studies*, 27(4): 609–32.

Laugerud, S and Langballe, A (2017), 'Turning the Witness Stand into a Speaker's Platform: Victim Participation in the Norwegian Legal System as Exemplified by the Trial Against Anders Behring Breivik', *Law & Society Review*, 51(2): 227–51.

Lauterwein, CC (2010), *The Limits of Criminal Law: A Comparative Analysis of Approaches to Legal Theorizing*, Surrey: Ashgate.

Lazarus, L (2013), 'Positive Obligations and Criminal Justice: Duties to Protect or Coerce?', in L Zedner and LV Roberts (eds), *Principles and Values in Criminal Law and Criminal Justice: Essays in Honour of Andrew Ashworth*, 135–56, Oxford: Oxford University Press.

Lee, Y (2009), 'The Defense of Necessity and Powers of the Government', *Criminal Law and Philosophy*, 3(2): 133–45.

Lee, A (2015), 'Public Wrongs and the Criminal Law', *Criminal Law and Philosophy*, 9(1): 155–70.

Lerouge, L (2010), 'Moral Harassment in the Workplace: French Law and European Perspectives', *Comparative Labor Law & Policy Journal*, 32(1): 109–52.

Levanon, L (2012), 'Punishment, Duty, and Self Defense: A Comment on Victor Tadros' The Ends of Harm', *Jerusalem Review of Legal Studies*, 5(1): 75–88.

Levin, B (2022), 'Criminal Justice Expertise', *Fordham Law Review*, 90(6): 2777–837.

Lewis, C and Usmani, A (2022), 'The Injustice of Under-Policing in America', *American Journal of Law and Equality*, 2: 85–106.

Lippke, RL (2002), 'Criminal Offenders and Right Forfeiture', *Journal of Social Philosophy*, 31(1): 78–89.

Lippke, RL (2003), 'Victim-centered Retributivism', *Pacific Philosophical Quarterly*, 84(2): 127–45.

Liss, R (2019), 'Crimes Against the Sovereign Order: Rethinking International Criminal Justice', *American Journal of International Law*, 113(4): 727–71.

Liszt, F (1883), 'Der Zweckgedanke im Strafrecht', *Zeitschrift für die gesamte Strafrechtswissenschaft*, 3: 1–47.

Loader, I and Walker, N (2007), *Civilizing Security*, Cambridge: Cambridge University Press.
Locke, J ([1689] 2002), *The Second Treatise of Government and A Letter Concerning Toleration*, Mineola, NY: Dover.
Lockyer, A, Crick, B, and Annette, J (2017), *Education for Democratic Citizenship: Issues of Theory and Practice*, Abingdon: Routledge.
Loughnan, A (2019), *Self, Others, and the State: Relations of Criminal Responsibility*, Cambridge: Cambridge University Press.
Lovett, F (2022), 'Republicanism', in EN Zalta (ed), *The Stanford Encyclopedia of Philosophy* (Summer 2022 Edition).
Lüderssen, K (1995), 'Die Krise des öffentlichen Strafanspruchs', in K. Lüderssen (ed), *Abschaffen des Strafens?*, 22–73, Frankfurt aM: Suhrkamp.
Luxon, N (2013), *Crisis of Authority: Politics, Trust, and Truth-Telling in Freud and Foucault*, Cambridge: Cambridge University Press.
Lyons, D (1969), 'Rights, Claimants, and Beneficiaries', *American Philosophical Quarterly*, 6(3), 173–85.
Lyons, D (1970), The Correlativity of Rights and Duties, *Noûs*, 4(1): 45–55.
Lyons, D (1985), *The Ethics and the Rule of Law*, Cambridge: Cambridge University Press.
MacCormick, N (1976), 'Children's Rights: A Test-Case for Theories of Rights', *Archiv für Rechts- und Sozialphilosophie*, 62(3): 305–18.
MacCormick, N (1977), 'Rights in Legislation', in PMS Hacker and J Raz (eds) *Law, Morality, and Society: Essays in Honour of HLA Hart*, 189–209, Oxford: Clarendon Press.
MacCormick, N (1990), 'Reconstruction after Deconstruction: A Response to CLS', *Oxford Journal of Legal Studies*, 10(4): 539–58.
MacCormick, N (2007), *Institutions of Law*, Oxford: Oxford University Press.
Mackay, R and Brrokbanks, W (eds) (2018), *Fitness to Plead: International and Comparative Perspectives*, Oxford: Oxford University Press.
Maine, H (1861), *Ancient Law: Its Connection with the Early History of Society, and Its Relation to Modern Ideas*, New York: Charles Scribner.
Marshall SE and Duff RA (1998), 'Criminalization and Sharing Wrongs', *Canadian Journal of Law & Jurisprudence*, 11(1): 7–22.
McCammon, C (2018), 'Domination', in EN Zalta (ed), *The Stanford Encyclopedia of Philosophy* (Fall 2018 Edition).
McConnell, TC (2000), *Inalienable Rights: The Limits of Consent in Medicine and the Law*, Oxford: Oxford University Press.
McKenzie, A (2005), '"This Death Some Strong and Stout Hearted Man Doth Choose": The Practice of Peine Fort et Dure in Seventeenth- and Eighteenth-Century England', *Law & History Review*, 23 (2): 279–313.
Maihold, H (2005), *Strafe für fremde Schuld? Dis Systematisierung des Strafbegriffs in der spanischen Spätscholastik und Naturrechtslehre*, Cologne: Böhlau.
Main, TJ (2022), *The Rise of Illiberalism*, Washington, DC: Brookings Institution Press.
Majewski, J (2015), 'Umorzenie postępowania karnego w trybie art. 59a k.k. a działania obrońcy', in P. Wiliński (ed), *Obrońca i pełnomocnik w procesie karnym po 1 lipca 2015 r: Przewodnik po zmianach*, 170–81, Warsaw: Wolters Kluwer Polska.
Malby, S (2019), *Criminal Theory and International Human Rights Law*, Abingdon: Routledge.
Mañalich, JP (2009), *Nötigung und Verantwortung. Rechtstheoretische Untersuchungen zum präskriptiven und askriptiven Nötigungsbegriff im Strafrecht*, Baden-Baden: Nomos.
Mañalich, JP (2021), 'The Closure of Systems of Penal Sanction Norms as Systems of Constitutive Rules', *Revus: Journal for Constitutional Theory & Philosophy of Law*, 44: 57–83.
Mansbridge, J, Bohman, J, Chambers, S, Estlund, D, Føllesdal, A, Fung, A, Lafont, C, Manin, B, and Martí, J (2010), 'The Place of Self-Interest and the Role of Power in Deliberative Democracy', *Journal of Political Philosophy*, 18(1): 64–100.
Mansbridge, J and Macedo, S (2019), 'Populism and Democratic Theory', *Annual Review of Law and Social Science*, 15: 59–77.

Marshall, TH ([1950] 2013), 'Citizenship and Social Class', in S Lazar (ed), *The Anthropology of Citizenship: A Reader*, 52–59, New Jersey: Wiley Blackwell.

Marshall, SE and Duff, RA (1998), 'Criminalization and Sharing Wrongs', *Canadian Journal of Law and Jurisprudence* 11(1): 7–22.

Melissaris, E (2014), 'Theories of Crime and Punishment', in M Dubber and T Hörnle (eds), *The Oxford Handbook of Criminal Law*, 355–78, Oxford: Oxford University Press.

Mendlow, G (2021), 'The Moral Ambiguity of Public Prosecution', *The Yale Law Journal* 130 (5): 1146–1187.

Michel, V (2018), *Prosecutorial Accountability and Victims' Rights in Latin America*, Cambridge: Cambridge University Press.

Mill, JS (1859), *On Liberty*, London: John W Parker & Son.

Miller, FG and Wertheimer, A (2010), 'Preface to a Theory of Consent Transactions: Beyond Valid Consent', in FG Miller and A Wertheimer (eds) *The Ethics of Consent*, 79–106, Oxford: Oxford University Press.

Moore, MS (1997), *Placing Blame: A Theory of the Criminal Law*, Oxford: Oxford University Press.

Moore, MS (1999), 'Victims and Retribution: A Reply to Professor Fletcher', *Buffalo Criminal Law Review*, 3(1): 65–89.

Moore, MS (2014), 'Liberty's Constraints on What Should Be Made Criminal', in RA Duff, L Farmer, SE Marshall, M Renzo, and V Tadros (eds), *Criminalization: The Political Morality of the Criminal Law*, 182–212, Oxford: Oxford University Press.

Moritz, M (1960), *Über Hohfelds System der juridischen Grundbegriffe*, Lund: Berlingska Boktryckeriet.

Morris, H (1968), 'Persons and Punishment', *The Monist*, 52(4): 475–501.

Moser, E (2019), 'Rights in Criminal Law in the Light of a Will Theory', *Criminal Justice Ethics*, 38(3): 176–97.

Moser, E (2020), 'The Will Theory of Rights and Criminal Law: A Normative Account on Rules and Restrictions that Protect Individual Entitlements', *Archiv für Rechts- und Sozialphilosophie*, 106(1): 55–74.

Mouffe, C (1992), 'Democratic Citizenship and the Political Community', in C Mouffe (ed), *Dimensions of Radical Democracy: Pluralism, Citizenship, Community*, 225–39, London: Verso.

Mouffe, C (2005), *On the Political*, London: Routledge.

Newman, J and Tonkens, E (eds) (2011), *Participation, Responsibility and Choice: Summoning the Active Citizen in Western European Welfare States*, Amsterdam: Amsterdam University Press.

Moyer, MW (2017), 'Four Laws That Could Stem the Rising Threat of Mass Shootings', *Scientific American*, 10 November. Available at: www.scientificamerican.com/article/4-laws-that-could-stem-the-rising-threat-of-mass-shootings/.

Munzer, SR (1990), *A Theory of Property*, New York: Cambridge University Press.

Murphy, JG (1973), 'Marxism and Retribution', *Philosophy & Public Affairs*, 2(3): 217–43.

Murphy, JG (1990), 'Getting Even: The Role of the Victim', *Social Philosophy & Policy*, 7(2): 209–25.

Namie, G and Namie, R (2009), *The Bully at Work: What You Can Do to Stop the Hurt and Reclaim your Dignity on the Job*, 2nd edn, Naperville, IL: Sourcebooks.

Naucke, W (1985), *Die Wechselwirkung zwischen Strafziel und Verbrechensbegriff*, Stuttgart: Franz Steiner.

Naucke, W (1993), 'Schwerpunktverlagerungen im Strafrecht', *Kritische Vierteljahresschrift für Gesetzgebung und Rechtswissenschaft*, 76(2): 135–58.

Naucke, W (2015), *Negatives Strafrecht*, Münster: LIT.

Needelman, J (2022), 'Midnight Basketball Returns, and Brings Community with It', *New York Times*, 3 October. Available at: www.nytimes.com/2022/10/03/sports/midnight-basketball-oakland-community.html.

Nietzsche, F (2006), *Thus Spoke Zarathustra*, ed. A Del Caro and R Pippin, trans A Del Caro, Cambridge: Cambridge University Press.

Nolan, D (2019), 'Assumption of Responsibility: Four Questions', *Current Legal Problems*, 72 (1): 123–158.

Nolan, D and Robertson, A (2012), 'Rights and Private Law' in D Nolan and A. Robertson (eds), *Rights and Private Law*, 1–33, Oxford: Hart Publishing.

Nozick, R (1974), *Anarchy, State, and Utopia*, New York: Basic Books.

Nuotio, K (2010), 'Theories of Criminalization and the Limits of Criminal Law: A Legal Cultural Approach', in RA Duff, L Farmer, SE Marshall, M Renzo, and V Tadros (eds), *The Boundaries of the Criminal Law*, 238–61, Oxford: Oxford University Press.

Nussbaum, M (2015), Transitional Anger, *Journal of the American Philosophical Association*, 1(1): 41–56.

Oakeshott, M (1975), *On Human Conduct*, Oxford: Clarendon Press.

Oberdiek, J (2004), 'Lost in Moral Space: On the Infringing/Violating Distinction and its Place in the Theory of Rights', *Law and Philosophy*, 23(4): 325–46.

Oberdiek, J (2017), *Imposing Risk: A Normative Framework*, Oxford: Oxford University Press.

Ohana, D (2014), 'Günther Jakobs's Feindstrafrecht: A Dispassionate Account', in MD Dubber (ed), *Foundational Texts in Modern Criminal Law*, 353–71, Oxford: Oxford University Press.

Oliphant, K (2017), 'Rationalising Tort Law for the Twenty-First Century', in K Barker, K Fairweather, and R Grantham (eds), *Private Law in the 21st Century*, 19, 47–66, Oxford: Hart Publishing.

O'Shea, T (2019), 'Are Workers Dominated?', *Journal of Ethics & Social Philosophy*, 16(1): 1–24.

Owusu-Bempah, A (2018), *Defendant Participation in the Criminal Process*, Abingdon: Routledge.

Passas, N (2016), *Transnational Financial Crime*, London: Routledge.

Pawlik, M (2004), *Person, Subjekt, Bürger: Zur Legitimation von Strafe*, Berlin: Duncker & Humblot.

Pawlik, M (2010), 'Staatlicher Strafanspruch und Strafzwecke', in E. Schumann (ed), *Das strafende Gesetz im sozialen Rechtsstaat. 15. Symposion der Kommission "Die Funktion des Gesetzes in Geschichte und Gegenwart"*, 59–93, Berlin: de Gruyter.

Pawlik, M (2012), *Das Unrecht des Bürgers: Grundlinien der allgemeinen Verbrechenslehre*, Tübingen: Mohr Siebeck.

Pawlik, M (2017), *Normbestätigung und Identitätsbalance*, Baden-Baden: Nomos.

Pawlik, M (2020), 'Norm Confirmation and Identity Balance: On the Legitimacy of Punishing', *Critical Analysis of Law*, 7(1): 1–50.

Perrodet, A (2002), 'The Public Prosecutor', in M Delmas-Marty and JR Spencer (eds), *European Criminal Procedures*, 415–58, Cambridge: Cambridge University Press.

Perry, S (1992), 'The Moral Foundation of Tort Law', *Iowa Law Review*, 77(2): 449–514.

Peršak, N (2007), *Criminalising Harmful Conduct: The Harm Principle, its Limits and Continental Counterparts*, New York: Springer.

Pettit, P (1997), *Republicanism: A Theory of Freedom and Government*, Oxford: Oxford University Press.

Pettit, P (2014), 'Criminalization in Republican Theory', in RA Duff, L Farmer, SE Marshall, M Renzo, and V Tadros (eds), *Criminalization: The Political Morality of the Criminal Law*, Oxford: Oxford University Press.

Pettit, P (2017), 'Democracy Before, In, and After Schumpeter', *Critical Review*, 29(4): 497–504.

Pfaff, J (2017), *Locked In: The True Causes of Mass Incarceration and How to Achieve Real Reform*, New York: Basic Books.

Pinckaers, S (2001), *Morality: The Catholic View*, South Bend: St. Augustine Press.

Pinckaers, S (2005), *The Pinckaers Reader: Renewing Thomistic Moral Theology*, Washington: Catholic University of America Press.

Poama, A (2018), 'Corrective Justice as A Principle of Criminal Law: A Prolegomenon', *Criminal Law and Philosophy*, 12(4): 605–23.

Pollard, D (2002/2003), 'Banning Child Corporal Punishment', *Tulane Law Review*, 77(3): 575–658.

Posner, R (1973), *Economic Analysis of Law*, New York: Little, Brown & Co.

Posner, R (1995), 'Wealth Maximization and Tort Law: A Philosophical Inquiry', in D Owen (ed), *Philosophical Foundations of Tort Law*, 99–112, Oxford: Clarendon Press.

Postema, G (1986), *Bentham and the Common Law Tradition*, Oxford: Oxford University Press.

Quirk, H (2019), 'The Case for Restoring the Right of Silence', in JJ Child and RA Duff (eds), *Criminal Law Reform Now*, 253–69, Oxford: Hart Publishing.

Radin, M (2006), 'Boilerplate Today: The Rise of Modularity and the Waning of Consent', in O Ben-Shahar (ed), *Boilerplate: The Foundation of Market Contracts*, 189–99, Cambridge: Cambridge University Press.
Rawls, J (1955), 'Two Concept of Laws', *The Philosophical Review*, 64(1): 3–32.
Rawls, J (1993), *Political Liberalism*, New York: Columbia University Press.
Rawls, J ([1971] 1999), *A Theory of Justice*, 2nd edn, Cambridge, MA: Harvard University Press.
Raynor, P and Robinson, G (2005), *Rehabilitation, Crime and Justice*, Basingstoke: Palgrave Macmillan.
Raz, J (1970), *The Concept of a Legal System*, Oxford: Clarendon Press.
Raz, J (1980), *The Concept of a Legal System*, 2nd edn, Oxford: Clarendon Press.
Raz, J (1984), 'On the Nature of Rights', *Mind*, 93(370): 194–214.
Raz, J (1986), *The Morality of Freedom*, Oxford: Clarendon Press.
Renzikowski, J (2007), 'Pflichten und Rechte: Rechtsverhältnis und Zurechnung', *Goltdammer's Archiv für Strafrecht*, 154(10): 561–78.
Renzikowski, J (2012), 'Strafrecht und Strafbegründung bei Rousseau', *Jahrbuch für Recht und Ethik*, 20: 155–68.
Renzikowski, J (2015), 'Dimensionen der Straftat: Täter – Opfer – Gesellschaft', in W Kohte and N Absenger (eds), *Menschenrechte und Solidarität im internationalen Diskurs. Festschrift für Armin Höland*, 210–22, Baden-Baden: Nomos.
Renzikowski, J (2020), 'Einleitung: Das strafrechtliche Programm', in H Matt and J Renzikowski (eds), *Strafgesetzbuch: Kommentar*, 2nd edn, 1–9, Munich: Vahlen.
Renzikowski, J (2021), 'Kant on Punishment and Criminal Law: Nine Theses', *ULP Law Review*, 15(1): 4–16.
Ripstein, A (2006), 'Beyond the Harm Principle', *Philosophy & Public Affairs* 34(3): 215–45.
Ripstein, A (2008), 'Hindering a Hindrance to Freedom', *Annual Review of Law and Ethics* 16: 227–50.
Ripstein, A (2009), *Force and Freedom: Kant's Legal and Political Philosophy*, Cambridge, MA: Harvard University Press.
Ripstein, A (2016), *Private Wrongs*, Cambridge, MA: Harvard University Press.
Roberts, JV and Erez, E (2004), 'Communication in Sentencing: Exploring the Expressive Function of Victim Impact Statements', *International Review of Victimology*, 10(3): 223–44.
Roberts, JV and Manikis, M (2011), *Victim Personal Statements: A Review of Empirical Research. Report for the Commissioner for Victims and Witnesses in England and Wales*, London: Office of the Commissioner for Victims and Witnesses of England and Wales.
Roberts, P and Zuckerman, A (2022), *Criminal Evidence*, 2nd edn, Oxford: Oxford University Press.
Robinson, PH (1975), 'A Theory of Justification: Societal Harm as a Prerequisite for Criminal Liability', *UCLA Law Review*, 23(2): 266–92.
Robinson, PH (1990), 'Rules of Conduct and Principles of Adjudication', *University of Chicago Law Review*, 57(3): 729–71.
Robinson, PH (1996), 'Competing Theories of Justification: Deeds versus Reasons' in AP Simester and ATH Smith (eds), *Harm and Culpability*, 45–70, Oxford: Clarendon Press.
Robinson, PH (1997), 'The Bomb Thief and the Theory of Justification Defenses', *Criminal Law Forum*, 8(3): 387–409.
Robinson, PH (2013), *Intuitions of Justice and the Utility of Desert*, Oxford: Oxford University Press.
Robinson, PH and Dubber, M (2007), 'The American Model Penal Code: A Brief Overview', *New Criminal Law Review*, 10(3): 319–41.
Robinson, PH and Grall, J (1983), 'Element Analysis in Defining Criminal Liability: The Model Penal Code and Beyond', *Stanford Law Review*, 35(4): 681–762.
Rosenberg A (forthcoming 2024), 'Law and the Material Turn', in L Bilsky (ed), *Society and Culture*.
Rostalski, F (2019), *Der Tatbegriff im Strafrecht*, Tübingen: Mohr Siebeck.
Rousseau, J-J (2019), *The Social Contract and Other Later Political Writings*, trans V Gourevitch, Cambridge: Cambridge University Press.
Roxin, C (1997), *Strafrecht: Allgemeiner Teil I*, 3rd edn, Munich: Beck.

Roxin, C and Greco, L (2020), *Strafrecht Allgemeiner Teil. Volume I: Grundlagen. Der Aufbau der Verbrechenslehre*, 5th edn, Munich: CH Beck.
Safferling, C and Petrossian, G (2021), *Victims Before the International Criminal Court: Definition, Participation, Reparation*, Cham: Springer.
Sakowicz, A (2013), 'Opinia prawna na temat projektu ustawy o zmianie ustawy – Kodeks postępowania karnego, ustawy – Kodeks karny i niektórych innych ustaw', in A Sakowicz (ed), *Przed pierwszym czytaniem. Projekt ustawy o zmianie ustawy – Kodeks postępowania karnego, ustawy – Kodeks karny i niektórych innych ustaw*, 45–62, Warsaw: Wydawnictwo Sejmowe.
Salzberger, M (forthcoming 2024), 'Domestic Violence and Abuse: Expanding Our Conceptual Repertoire', *Journal of Applied Philosophy*. Available at: https://doi.org/10.1111/japp.12722.
Sandel, M (2001), *Democracy's Discontent: America in Search of a Public Philosophy*, Cambridge, MA: Harvard University Press.
Sarat, A and Clarke C (2008), 'Beyond Discretion: Prosecution, the Logic of Sovereignty, and the Limits of Law', *Law & Social Inquiry*, 33(2): 387–416.
Sarhan, A (2006), *Wiedergutmachung zugunsten des Opfers im Lichte strafrechtlicher Trennungsdogmatik. Plädoyer für eine opferorientierte Neuausrichtung des Strafgrundes*, Berlin: Berliner Wissenschafts-Verlag.
Scanlon, T (1996), 'The Status of Well-Being', *The Tanner Lectures on Human Values*, 16: 91–143.
Schiefer, D and van der Noll, J (2017), 'The Essentials of Social Cohesion: A Literature Review', *Social Indicators Research*, 132: 579–603.
Schildt, B (1997), '"Die Tat tötet den Mann": Die Überwindung eines Prinzips', *Zeitschrift der Savigny-Stiftung für Rechtsgeschichte: Germanistische Abteilung*, 114(1): 380–97.
Schmitter, PC and Karl, TL (1991), 'What Democracy is … and is Not', *Journal of Democracy*, 2(3): 75–88.
Schneebaum, G (2015), 'What is Wrong with Sex in Authority Relations? A Study in Law and Social Theory', *The Journal of Criminal Law & Criminology*, 105(2): 345–86.
Schneebaum, G (2021a), 'Conceptualizing Workplace Bullying as Abuse of Office', *South Carolina Law Review*, 73(65): 65–99.
Schneebaum, G (2021b), 'What is Wrong with Intimate Partner Abuse', *Cardozo International & Comparative Law Review*, 5(1): 41–80.
Schulhofer, S (1998), *Unwanted Sex: The Culture of Intimidation and the Failure of Law*, Cambridge, MA: Harvard University Press.
Schünemann, B (1982), 'Einige vorläufige Bemerkungen zur Bedeutung des viktimologischen Ansatzes in der Strafrechtsdogmatik', in HJ Schneider (ed), *Das Verbrechensopfer in der Strafrechtspflege*, 407–21, Berlin: de Gruyter.
Schünemann, B (1984), 'Einführung in das strafrechtliche Systemdenken', in B Schünemann (ed) *Grundfragen des modernen Strafrechtssystems*, 1–68, Berlin: de Gruyter.
Sebba, L (1996), *Third Parties: Victims and the Criminal Justice System*, Columbus, OH: The Ohio State University Press.
Seelmann, K (1989), 'Paradoxien der Opferorientierung im Strafrecht', *Juristenzeitung* 44(14): 670–76.
Sendor, BB (1990), 'Mistakes of Fact: A Study in the Structure of Criminal Conduct', *Wake Forest Law Review*, 25(4): 707–82.
Sepioło, I (2013), 'Pojednanie pokrzywdzonego ze sprawcą jako podstawa do umorzenia postępowania w świetle projektu Komisji Kodyfikacyjnej Prawa Karnego', *Ekonomiczny i Socjologiczny*, 2(75): 113–22.
Shapiro, I (2012), 'On Non-Domination', *The University of Toronto Law Journal*, 62(3): 293–335.
Shapiro, I (2016), *Politics against Domination*, Cambridge, MA: Belknap Press.
Shearing, C and Stenning, P (1984), 'From the Panopticon to Disney World: The Development of Discipline' in AN Doob and EL Greenspan (eds), *Perspectives in Criminal Law: Essays in Honour of John LLJ Edwards*, 335–49, Toronto: Canada Law Book.

Shelby, T (2016), *Dark Ghettos: Injustice, Dissent, and Reform*, Cambridge, MA: Harvard University Press.
Sher, G (1987), *Desert*, Princeton, NJ: Princeton University Press.
Shklar, J (1990), *The Faces of Injustice*, New Haven, CT: Yale University Press.
Silva Sánchez, JM (2008a), *La expansión del Derecho penal. Aspectos de la Política criminal en las sociedades postindustriales*, 2nd edn, Madrid: Civitas.
Silva Sánchez, JM (2008b), 'Doctrines Regarding the Fight Against Impunity and the Victim's Right for the Perpetrator to be Punished', *Pace Law Review*, 28(4): 865–84.
Silva Sánchez, JM (2018), *Malum passionis: Mitigar el dolor del Derecho penal*, Barcelona: Atelier.
Silva Sánchez, JM (2023), 'Tadel als public policy? Der strafrechtliche Vorwurf und die Arten von Straftaten', in B Brunhöber, C Burchard, K Günther, M Jahn, M Jasch, JM Silva Sánchez, and T Singelnstein (eds), *Festschrift für Cornelius Prittwitz zum 70. Geburtstag*, 193–205, Baden-Baden: Nomos.
Simester, AP (ed) (2005), *Appraising Strict Liability*, Oxford: Oxford University Press.
Simester, AP (2021), *Fundamentals of Criminal Law: Responsibility, Culpability, and Wrongdoing*, Oxford: Oxford University Press.
Simester, AP and von Hirsch, A (2011), *Crimes, Harms, and Wrongs*, Oxford: Hart Publishing.
Simmonds, NA (1998), 'Rights at the Cutting Edge', in MH Kramer, NA Simmonds, and H Steiner (eds), *A Debate Over Rights: Philosophical Enquiries*, 113–232, New York: Oxford University Press.
Simon, J (2007), *Governing through Crime: How the War on Crime Transformed American Democracy and Created a Culture of Fear*, Oxford: Oxford University Press.
Simons, K (2006), 'A Restatement (Third) of Intentional Torts?', *Arizona Law Review* 48(4): 1061–102.
Singer, JW (1982), 'The Legal Rights Debate in Analytical Jurisprudence from Bentham to Hohfeld', *Wisconsin Law Review*, 1982: 975–1049.
Skinner, Q (1998), *Liberty before Liberalism*, Cambridge: Cambridge University Press.
Sniderman, P (2017), *The Democratic Faith: Essays on Democratic Citizenship*, New Haven, CT: Yale University Press.
Spena, A (2010), 'Harmless Rapes? A False Problem for the Harm Principle', *Diritto & Questioni Pubbliche* 10: 497–524.
Spillman, L and Strand, M (2013), 'Interest-oriented Action', *Annual Review of Sociology*, 39: 85–104.
Sprack, J and Engelhardt-Sprack, M (eds) (2019), *A Practical Approach to Criminal Procedure*, 16th edn, Oxford: Oxford University Press.
Sreenivasan, G (2005), 'A Hybrid Theory of Claim-Rights', *Oxford Journal of Legal Studies*, 25(2): 57–274.
Stächelin, G (1998), *Strafgesetzgebung im Verfassungsstaat*, Berlin: Duncker & Humblot.
Stark, F (2013), 'Necessity and Nicklinson', *Criminal Law Review*, 12: 949–65.
Steiner, H (1994), *An Essay on Rights*, Oxford: Blackwell.
Steiner, H (2013), Directed Duties and Inalienable Rights, *Ethics*, 123(2): 230–44.
Stephen, JF (1873), *Liberty, Equality, Fraternity*, New York: Holt & Williams.
Stepanians, M (2005), 'Menschenrechte als moralische Rechte und als juridische Rechte', in K Girardet and U Nortmann (eds), *Menschenrechte und europäische Identität: Die antiken Grundlagen*, 271–89, Stuttgart: Franz Steiner.
Stewart, H (2003), 'The Role of Reasonableness in Self-Defence', *Canadian Journal of Law and Jurisprudence*, 16(2): 317–36.
Stewart, H (2010), 'The Limits of the Harm Principle', *Criminal Law and Philosophy*, 4(1): 17–35.
Stewart, H (2011), 'The Limits of Consent and the Law of Assault', *Canadian Journal of Law and Jurisprudence*, 24(1): 205–23.
Stewart, H (2012), 'The Definition of a Right', *Jurisprudence: An International Journal of Legal and Political Thought*, 3(2): 319–39.
Stewart, H (2015), 'Criminal Punishment as Private Morality: Victor Tadros' The Ends of Harm', *Criminal Law and Philosophy*, 9(1): 21–36.
Stewart, H (2018), 'The Wrong of Mass Punishment', *Criminal Law and Philosophy*, 12(1): 45–57.

Stewart, H (2020a), 'The Place of Instrumental Reasoning in Law', *Jurisprudence* 11(1): 28–47.
Stewart, H (2020b), 'Procedural Rights and Factual Accuracy', *Legal Theory* 26(2): 156–79.
Stevens, R (2007), *Torts and Rights*, Oxford: Oxford University Press.
Stevens, R (2014), 'Private Rights and Public Wrongs', in M Dyson (ed), *Unravelling Tort and Crime*, 111–45, Cambridge: Cambridge Univ. Press.
Strawson, PF (1962), 'Freedom and Resentment', *Proceedings of the British Academy*, 48, 187–211.
Stuckenberg, CF (2013), 'The Constitutional Deficiencies of the German "Rechtsgutslehre"', *Oñati Socio-Legal Series*, 3(1): 31–41.
Stuntz, B (2011), *The Collapse of American Criminal Justice*, Cambridge, MA: Harvard University Press.
Sullivan, GR (2014), 'Wrongs and Responsibility for Wrongs in Crime and Tort', in M Dyson (ed), *Unravelling Tort and Crime*, 82–110, Cambridge: Cambridge University Press.
Sumner, LW (1987), *The Moral Foundation of Rights*, Oxford: Clarendon Press.
Sumner, LW (2013), 'Rights', in H LaFollette and I Parsson (eds), *The Blackwell Guide to Ethical Theory*, 354–73, Oxford: Wiley Blackwell.
Szmania, SJ and Gracyalny, ML (2006), 'Addressing the Court, the Offender, and the Community: A Communication Analysis of Victim Impact Statements in a Non-Capital Sentencing Hearing', *International Review of Victimology*, 13(3): 231–49.
Tadros, V (2005), 'The Distinctiveness of Domestic Abuse: A Freedom Based Account', *Louisiana Law Review*, 65(3): 989–1014.
Tadros, V (2007), *Criminal Responsibility*, Oxford: Oxford University Press.
Tadros, V (2011), *The Ends of Harm: The Moral Foundations of Criminal Law*, Oxford: Oxford University Press.
Tadros, V (2016), *Wrongs and Crimes*, Oxford: Oxford University Press.
Taylor, C (1992), *The Ethics of Authenticity*, Cambridge, MA: Harvard University Press.
Taylor, C (2007), *A Secular Age*, Cambridge, MA: Harvard University Press.
Taylor, F (2020), *The Torture Machine: Racism and Police Violence in Chicago*, Chicago: Haymarket Books.
Ten, CL (1987), *Crime, Guilt, and Punishment: A Philosophical Introduction*, Oxford: Clarendon Press.
Ten Boom, A and Kuijpers, KF (2012), 'Victims' Needs as Basic Human Needs', *International Review of Victimology*, 18(2): 155–79.
Thompson, M (2006), 'What Is It to Wrong Someone? A Puzzle about Justice', in RJ Wallace (ed), *Reason and Value: Themes from the Moral Philosophy of Joseph Raz*, 333–84, Oxford: Clarendon Press.
Thomson, JJ (1986), *Rights, Restitution, and Risk: Essays in Moral Theory*, Cambridge, MA: Harvard University Press.
Thomson, JJ (1990), *The Realm of Rights*, Cambridge, MA: Harvard University Press.
Thompson, S (2006), 'Anger and the Struggle for Justice', in S Clarke, P Hoggett and S Thompson (eds), *Emotion, Politics and Society*, 123–44, London: Palgrave Macmillan.
Thompson, MJ (2013), 'Reconstructing Republican Freedom: A Critique of the Neo-republican Concept of Freedom as Non-Domination', *Philosophy & Social Criticism*, 39(3): 277–98.
Thorburn, M (2008), 'Justifications, Powers, and Authority', *Yale Law Journal*, 117(6): 1070–130.
Thorburn, M (2011a), 'Criminal Law as Public Law', in RA Duff and S Green (eds), *Philosophical Foundations of Criminal Law*, 21–43, Oxford: Oxford University Press.
Thorburn, M (2011b), 'Constitutionalism and the Limits of the Criminal Law', in RA Duff, L Farmer, S Marshall, M Renzo, and V Tadros (eds), *The Structures of the Criminal Law*, 85–105, Oxford: Oxford University Press.
Thorburn, M (2017), 'Punishment and Public Authority', in A du Bois-Pedain, M Ulväng, and P Asp (eds), *Criminal Law and the Authority of the State*, 7–32, Portland: Hart Publishing.
Thorburn, M (2019), 'Soldiers as Public Officials: A Moral Justification for Combatant Immunity', *Ratio Juris*, 32(4): 395–414.

Thorburn, M (2020a), 'Criminal Punishment and the Right to Rule', *University of Toronto Law Journal* 70(1): 44–63.

Thorburn, M (2020b), 'Policing and Public Office', *University of Toronto Law Journal*, 70(2): 248–66.

Thumim, N (2006), 'Mediated Self-Representations: "Ordinary People" in "Communities"', in S Herbrechter (ed), *Returning (to) Communities: Theory, Culture, and Political Practice of the Communal*, 255–74, Leiden: Brill Publishing.

Tierney, B (1997), *The Idea of Natural Rights: Studies on Natural Rights, Natural Law and Church Law, 1150– 1625*, Atlanta: Scholars Press.

Tribe, L (2000), *American Constitutional Law*, 3rd edn, New York: Foundation Press.

Turner, B (2016), 'We Are All Denizens Now: On the Erosion of Citizenship', *Citizenship Studies* 20(6/7): 679–92.

United Nations (2014), *Handbook on Effective Prosecution Responses to Violence Against Women and Girls*, New York: United Nations Publications.

Vandervordt, L (1990), Consent and the Criminal Law. *Osgoode Hall Law Journal*, 28(2): 485–500.

Vandieken, J (2019), 'Bipolar Obligations, Recognition Respect, and Second-Personal Morality', *The Journal of Ethics*, 23(3): 291–315.

van Dijk, J, van Kesteren, J, and Smit, P (2007), *Criminal Victimisation in International Perspective*, The Hague, NL: WODC.

van Duffel, S (2017), 'Adequacy Constraints for a Theory of Rights', in M McBride (ed) *New Essays on the Nature of Rights*, 187–201, Oxford: Hart Publishing.

Verdun-Jones, S and Rossiter, K (2010), 'The Psychological Impact of Victimization: Mental Health Outcomes and Psychological, Legal, and Restorative Interventions', in S Shoham, P Knepper, and M Kett (eds), *International Handbook of Victimology*, 661–37, London: Routledge.

Viney, G (2019), *Introduction à la responsabilité*, 4th edn, Paris: LGDJ.

Volkmann, U (2021), 'Allgemeine Grundrechtslehren', in M. Herdegen(ed), *Handbuch des Verfassungsrechts. Darstellung in transnationaler Perspektive*, 1051–1099, München: C.H. Beck.

von der Pfordten, D (2005), 'Normativer Individualismus und das Recht', *Juristenzeitung* 60(22): 1069–80.

von der Pfordten, D (2010), *Normative Ethik*, Berlin: de Gruyter.

von der Pfordten, D (2012), 'Five Elements of Normative Ethics: A General Theory of Normative Individualism', *Ethical Theory and Moral Practice*, 15(4): 449–71.

von der Pfordten, D and Kähler, L (2014), *Normativer Individualismus in Ethik, Politik und Recht*, Tübingen: Mohr Siebeck.

von Hirsch, A and Ashworth, A (2005), *Proportionate Sentence: Exploring the Principles*, Oxford: Oxford University Press.

von Hirsch, A (2008a), 'Harm und Offence: Schädigungsprinzip und Belästigungsprinzip als Kriterien für die Kriminalisierung von Verhalten', in T Hörnle, H Putzke, H Bernhard, R Merkel, J Scheinfeld, H Schlehofer, and J Seier (eds), *Strafrecht zwischen System und Telos Festschrift für Rolf Dietrich Herzberg zum siebzigsten Geburtstag*, 915–30, Tübingen: Mohr Siebeck.

von Hirsch, A (2008b), 'Direct Paternalism: Criminalizing Self-Injurious Conduct', *Criminal Justice Ethics*, 27(1): 25–33.

von Jhering, R (1865), *Geist des römischen Rechts auf den verschiedenen Stufen seiner Entwicklung*, vol 3, Leipzig: Breitkopf und Härtel.

von Wright, GH (1951), 'Deontic Logic', *Mind*, 60(237), 1–15.

von Wright, GH (1968), *An Essay in Deontic Logic and the General Theory of Action*, Amsterdam: North Holland Publishing.

von Savigny, FC (1841), *System des heutigen römischen Rechts*, vol 4. Berlin: Veit.

Vormbaum, T (2011), 'Fragmentarisches Strafrecht in Geschichte und Dogmatik', *Zeitschrift für die gesamte Strafrechtswissenschaft*, 123(4): 660–90.

Vormbaum, T and Bohlander, M (2014), *A Modern History of German Criminal Law*, Heidelberg: Springer.

Waldron, J (1981), 'A Right to Do Wrong', *Ethics*, 92(1): 21–39.

Waldron, J (ed) (1984), *Theories of Rights*, Oxford: Oxford University Press.
Waldron, J (1988), *The Right to Private Property*, Oxford: Clarendon Press.
Waldron, J (1989), Rights in Conflict, *Ethics*, 99(3): 503–19.
Waldron, J (2000), 'The Role of Rights in Practical Reasoning: "Rights" versus "Needs"', *The Journal of Ethics*, 4(1/2): 115–35.
Walen, A (2021), 'Retributive Justice', in EN Zalta (ed), *The Stanford Encyclopedia of Philosophy* (Summer 2021 Edition).
Walgrave, L (2023), 'Restorative Justice, Punishment and the Law', in MC Altman (ed), *The Palgrave Handbook on the Philosophy of Punishment*, 23–52, Cham: Palgrave Macmillan.
Wallace, RJ (2019), *The Moral Nexus*, Princeton, NJ: Princeton University Press.
Walby, S (1994), 'Is Citizenship Gendered?', *Sociology*, 28(2): 379–95.
Weeks, E (1879), *The Doctrine of Damnum Absque Injuria Considered in its Relation to the Law of Torts*, San Francisco, CA: Sumner Whitney & Co.
Weigend, T (1989), *Deliktsopfer und Strafverfahren*, Berlin: Duncker & Humblot.
Weinrib, E (1995), *The Idea of Private Law*, Cambridge, MA: Harvard University Press.
Weinrib, E (2001), 'Correlativity, Personality, and the Emerging Consensus on Corrective Justice', *Theoretical Inquiries in Law*, 2(1): 1–53.
Weinrib, E (2002), 'Corrective Justice in a Nutshell', *University of Toronto Law Journal* 52(4): 349–56.
Weinrib, E (2016), *Dimensions of Dignity*, Cambridge: Cambridge University Press.
Weinrib, E (2022), *Reciprocal Freedom*, Oxford: Oxford University Press.
Weir, T (2006), *An Introduction to Tort Law*, 2nd edn, Oxford: Clarendon Press.
Weissinger, J (2019), *Content and Competence: A Descriptive Approach to the Concept of Rights*, Tübingen: Mohr Siebeck.
Wellman, C (1985), *A Theory of Rights: Persons under Laws, Institutions, and Morals*, Totowa: Rowman & Allanheld.
Wellman, C (1995), *Real Rights*, New York: Oxford University Press.
Wellman, C (2017), *Rights Forfeiture and Punishment*, Oxford: Oxford University Press.
Wemmers, J (2008), 'Victim Participation and Therapeutic Jurisprudence', *Victims and Offenders*, 3(2/3): 165–91.
Wenar, L (2005), 'The Nature of Rights', *Philosophy & Public Affairs*, 33(3): 223–52.
Wenar, L (2013), 'The Nature of Claim-Rights', *Ethics*, 123(2): 202–29.
Wenar, L (2021), 'Rights', in EN Zalta (ed), *The Stanford Encyclopedia of Philosophy* (Spring 2021 edition).
Wertheimer, A (2003), *Consent to Sexual Relations*, Cambridge: Cambridge University Press.
Westen, P (2004), *The Logic of Consent: The Diversity and Deceptiveness of Consent as a Defense to a Criminal Conduct*, Aldershot: Ashgate.
Westen, P (2006), 'An Attitudinal Theory of Excuse', *Law and Philosophy*, 25(3): 289–375.
Whiteley, D (1998), 'The Victim and the Justification of Punishment', *Criminal Justice Ethics* 17(2): 42–54.
Wildt, A (1992), 'Recht und Selbstachtung, im Anschluss an die Anerkennungslehren von Fichte und Hegel', in M Kahlo, EA Wolff, and R Zaczyk (eds), *Fichtes Lehre vom Rechtsverhältnis: Die Deduktion der §§ 1-4 der "Grundlage Des Naturrechts" und Ihre Stellung in der Rechtsphilosophie*, 127–72, Frankfurt aM: Klostermann.
Williams, B (1999), 'The Victim's Charter: Citizens as Consumers of Criminal Justice Services', *The Howard Journal*, 38(4): 384–96.
Williams, B (2005), 'In the Beginning was the Deed' in B Williams (ed), *In the Beginning was the Deed: Realism and Moralism in Political Argument*, vol 3, 18–28, New Jersey: Princeton University Press.
Williams, G (1956), 'The Concept of Legal Liberty', *Columbia Law Review*, 56(8): 1129–50.
Williams, G (1957), *The Anctity of Life and the Criminal Law*, New York: Alfred A Knopf.
Witmer-Rich, J (2011), 'It's Good to be Autonomous: Prospective Consent, Retrospective Consent, and the Foundation of Consent in the Criminal Law', *Criminal Law and Philosophy*, 5: 77–398.

Wohlers, W (2000), *Deliktstypen des Präventionsstrafrechts: Zur Dogmatik "moderner" Gefährdungsdelikte*, Berlin: Duncker & Humblot.
Wolff, EA (1987), 'Die Abgrenzung von Kriminalunrecht zu anderen Unrechtsformen', in W Hassemer (ed), *Strafrechtspolitik. Bedingungen der Strafrechtsreform*, 137–224, Frankfurt aM: Peter Lang.
Wood, J (1999), 'Refined Raw: The Symbolic Violence of Victims' Rights Reforms', *College Literature*, 26(1): 150–69.
Wrage, N (2009), *Grenzen der staatlichen Strafgewalt*, Frankfurt aM: Peter Lang.
Wrong, DH (1995), *Power: Its Forms, Bases, and Uses*, New York: Routledge.
Wróbel, W (2012), 'Znaczenie zgody następczej oraz rezygnacji przez dysponenta dóbr prawnych z ochrony prawnokarnej w perspektywie zasady ultima ratio prawa karnego', in P Kardas, T Sroka, and W Wróbel (eds), *Państwo prawa i prawo karne. Księga Jubileuszowa profesora Andrzeja Zolla*, 751–64, Warsaw: Wolters Kluwer Polska.
Yaffe, G (2007), 'Reasonableness in the Law and Second-Personal Address', *Loyola of Los Angeles Law Review*, 40(3): 939–76.
Yaffe, G (2018), *The Age of Culpability*. Oxford: Oxford University Press.
Young, IM (1990), *Justice and the Politics of Difference*, Princeton, NJ: Princeton University Press.
Zimmerman, M (2002), 'Taking Luck Seriously', *Journal of Philosophy*, 99(11): 553–76.
Zedner, L (1994), 'Reparation and Retribution: Are They Reconcilable?' *The Modern Law Review*, 57(2): 228–50.
Zedner, L (2007), 'Preventive Justice or Pre-Punishment? The Case of Control Orders', *Current Legal Problems*, 60(1): 174–203.
Zemans, FK (1983), 'Legal Mobilization: The Neglected Role of The Law in The Political System', *American Political Science Review*, 77(3): 690–703.
Zivi, K (2012), *Making Rights Claims: A Practice of Democratic Citizenship*, Oxford: Oxford University Press.
Zylberman, A (2021), 'Relational Primitivism', *Philosophy and Phenomenological Research*, 102(2): 401–22.

SUBJECT INDEX

INDEX OF PERSONS

www.ingramcontent.com/pod-product-compliance
Ingram Content Group UK Ltd.
Pitfield, Milton Keynes, MK11 3LW, UK
UKHW020219041026
15470UKWH00012B/559